100 YEARS

BY RICHARD M. LANGWORTH
AND THE AUTO EDITORS OF CONSUMER GUIDE®

Louis Weber, CEO
Publications International, Ltd.
7373 North Cicero Avenue
Lincolnwood, Illinois 60712

Permission is never granted for commercial purposes.

ISBN-13: 978-1-4127-1512-6
ISBN-10: 1-4127-1512-1

Manufactured in China.

8 7 6 5 4 3 2 1

Library of Congress Control Number: 2007936268

Credits

Photography: The editors would like to thank the following people and organizations for supplying the photography that made this book possible.
Roger Barnes; Scott Baxter; Ken Beebe; Les Bidrawn; Scott Brandt; Chan Bush; Gary Cameron; John Conde; Gary Cook; Mitch Frumkin; Nina Fuller; Bob Garris; Thomas Glatch; Ed Goldberg; Mark Gordon; Gary Greene; Sam Griffith; Jerry Heasley; John Heilig; Don Heiny; Fergos Hernandez; Ron Hussey; S. Scott Hutchinson; David Jensen; Jeff Johnson; Bud Juneau; Bill Kanz; Harry Kapsalis; Milton Kieft; Nick Komic; Walt Kuhn; Dan Lyons; Vince Manocchi; Doug Mitchel; Steve Momot; Ron Moorhead; Mike Mueller; David Newhardt; Robert Nicholson; Neil Nissing; Morton Oppenheimer; Nina Padgett; Stephen Parezo; Jay Peck; Frank Peiler; Blake Ramick; Chris Ranck; Jeff Rose; E. T. Satory Collection; William Schinz; Tom Shaw; Mark Sincavage; Gary Smith; Dominic Sondy; Mike Spenner; Richard Spiegelman; Steve Statham; Stiemonts Studio; Cassie Stone; Tom Storm; David Temple; Bob Tenney Photographers; Phil Toy; Paul Tuttle; Dan Vecchio; Roger Wade; W. C. Waymack; Lee White; White Eagle Studio; Hub Wilson; Nicky Wright

Front Cover: Scott Baxter; GM Media Archives; Vince Manocchi; Doug Mitchel; Ron Moorhead; Gary Woolery
Back Cover: Gary Smith; GM Media Archives

Owners: Special thanks to the owners of the cars featured in this book for their cooperation.

Richard Abbate; Chuck and Laurie Abbott; Walter and Darlene Abela; Bill Acconcia; Dewayne Adams; Robert and Diane Adams; David Aiken; Erik Akins; John Albert; James Alexander; Daniel Allen; James Allen; Mark Alter; Fernando Alvare; Bill Anderson; Jim Anderson; John Andreason; Norman Andrews; Les Bieri and John Angwert; Barbara Ann; Mark Apel; Gordon Apker; Robert Matteoli and Charlene Arora; Ross Arterberry; Roy Asbahr; Jim and Mary Ashworth; Art Astor; Dennis Babcock; Edward Baker; Howard Baker; Donald Baldwin; Edward Ballenger II; Barry and Barbara Bales; Michael Bancroft; Glenn Bappe; Sam Bardic; Ben Barlage; C. C. Barnette; Alan Baumer; H. Fred Bausch; Denis Beauregard; Everett Belcher; Steve Bergin; Bert Bergstrom; Bill and Kathy Berkes; John and Mary Berkowicz; Tom Berthelsen; Michael Berzenye; Tom Bigelow; Rob Bilott; Brad Bishop; Melvin and Keith Blackford; The Blackhawk Collection; John Blackowski; Jim Blanchard; Frank Bobek; Bill Bodnarchuk; Jim Bombard; Hiram Bond; Bill Borland; David Bornemann; Jim Bowersox; James and Patricia Boyk; John Boyle; Julie Braatz; Roger Bridges; Bob Briggs; Frederick Brown; Robert Brueggemann; Nicola Bulgari; William Burgun; Bryan Burns; Virginia Burns; Winton and Kitty Burns; Paul Buscemi; Robert Bymers; Jim Cahill; Mike Callahan; Gary Cameron; Clay and Judy Campbell; Gary Campbell; Laurence Camuso; Jerry Capizzi; Charles Capps; Dean Cardella; Joe Carfagna; Monty Carpenter; Cars of Yesterday; James Carson; John Carson; Palmer Carson; Penny Casteele; June Cecil; David Chance; Bob and Brad Chandler; Burke Chaplin; Chevs N' Vettes; Chicago Car Exchange; David Chilson; Ed Cholakian; Dick Choler; Robert and Karen Christanell; Wayne Christian; Jerry Cinotti; John Clark; Roger Clark; Lew Clark; Gordon and Dorothy Clemmer; Marilyn Cliff; Dave Cobble II; Jerry Coffee; H. Curtis Cole; James Collins; Patrick and Kay Collins; Dr. Steven Colsen; Dave Comstock; Steve and Andrea Cook; Paul Cox; Lloyd Crabtree; Crawford Collection/Western Reserve Historical Society; Tom Crooks; Tom Cummings; Ed Cunneen; James Cunningham; Rick Cybul; Dr. John Joseph D'Attilio; Bill Dan/Custom Automotive; John Danell; Dan Darling; Edward and Joanne Dauer; Jim Davidson; Don and Linda Davis; Beau Day; Charles and Cathy Deaubl; Gene DeBlasio Jr.; Wallie and Mary Deck; Clarence DeClue; Paul DeGeorge; Gerard Depersio; Thomas Derro; Edward Devries; John Diefenbach; Tony and Robyn DiTrois; Greg Don; Patrick and Barbara Dugan; Tim Dunlop; Bud Dutton; Tim and Penny Dye; Ted and Dan Eagleson; Barney Eaton; Roger Eberenz; Les Edwards; Roland Eggerbrecht; Neil Ehresman; Glenn Eisenhamer; Howard Engerman; Fred Engers; Douglas English; Ernie's Wrecker Service; Don Essen; Margaret Evans; Tony and Betty Fabiano; Rex and Justin Fager; Fairway Chevrolet; Joseph Falore; Robert and Gene Fattore; Eugene Fattore Jr.; Forrest Feldt; Jose and Marina Felix; Gordon Fenner; David Ferguson; Jerry Ferguson; Jim Ferrero; Dennis Fink; Jeanne Finster; Phil Fischer; Bob Flack; John and MaryJean Flory; Jack Frank; Fraser Dante Limited; Anthony Freels; Tom and Christine French; Brooke Friedman; Marvin Friedman; Shawn Friedman; Howard Funck; Anthony Fusco; Ed and Donna Gabaldon; John Galanoak; Frank Gallagher; Bob Garcia; Mr. and Mrs. Raymond Garcia; George Gass; Gateway Classic Cars; Kenneth Geiger; Margaret Gelb; Joe Gergits; Robert Gernhofer; Jack Gersh; Murray and Al Gibb; Fred Gildner; Ken Gimelli; Gary Girt; Gary Glazier; Frank Goderre; Edward Goehring; Elmer Goehring; Golden Classics; Garth and Milli Goode; Eric Goodman; William Goodsene; Jerry Goodwin; Larry Gordon; Bill Grathic; Jack Gratziania; B. Benjamin Graves; Jim Greene; Michael Greene; Lee Greer; Danny and Monica Griffith; Gary Grillo; Grossinger Autoplex; Ed Gunther; Dave Gushwa; Greg Gustafson; Bernie Hackett; Harry and Donna Hadley; Whitney Haist; Mike Hall; Robert Hall; Tom Hall; Robert Hallada; William Hamann; JoAnn Hammel; Jerry Hammer; Robert Hannay; Don and Carol Hansen; David Hardgrove; Bill and Anna Harper; Rex Harris; Kelly Hartman; Jon Havens; Gregg and Nancy Hawley; George and Joyce Hawver; William T. Hayes and Sons; Jack Heacock; Bob Heffman; Dennis Helferich; Paul Helton; Jim Hemann; Chuck Henderson; Scott Henderson; Lloyd Heniger; Carl Herren; Richard Hibbard; Dave Higby; Garth Higgins; Mark and Jan Hilbert; Larry Hills; Dan Hoeck; Larry Hoekelberg; Bill Hoff; Dave Holls; Thomas Hollfelder; Jim Hollis; Chet Hook; Mac Horst; Marc Houser; Bob Howard; Owen Hoyt; David Hucke; Les Huckins; Bill and Lea Huetteman Jr.; Jack and Marie Hughes; Jeff Hughes; Bill and Margaret Hunter; Justin Hurn; Henry Isaksen; Joe James; Roger James; James and Ione Jander; E. J. and Rachell Jaymeson; Steve Jenear; Blaine Jenkins; Lewis Jenkins; Donald Jensen; Anthony Johnson; Erving and Katherine Johnson; Jay and Beth Johnson; Ron Johnson; Albert Jones; Bill Jones; John and Barbara Jones; Bud Juneau; Richard Kalina; Michael Kaminsky; Charles Karr; Roger Kash; Ken Kaufmann; Dennis Kay; Dave and Cindy Keetch; Jerry Keller; Austin Kelley; Ken Kettell; James Killian; Roger Kinder; Gary Kistinger; Larry Klein; George Kling; Barry Klinkel; Larry Knebel; Henry Koenig; Larry Koetting; Don Kreider; John Krempansky; Everett Kroeze; Herb Kromback; Mike Kuhn; Phil Kuhn; David and Anne Kurtz; Steven Kutsen; Edward Kuziel; Eli Lader; Jim Lahti; Ron and Lee Ann Laird; Donald Lambert; Larry Lange; Terry and Kathleen Lange; Chris Lapp; Wayne and Pat Lasley; Norbert Laubagh; Warren and Sylvia Lauridsen; Matt Lazich; Jim Lee; Kit Lee; Levy Venture Management; Basil Lewis; Fred Lewis; Mark Lob; James and Patricia Locher; Vince and Sandy LoPiccolo; Bob Lorenz; Terry Lucas; Ken Lund; Ron Lynch; The WM Lyon Collection; Dan and Joyce Lyons; Joseph and Suzanne Lysy; Bob Mack; Jack Macmillan; Bob Macy; Jack Macy; Jim Maher; Bill and Rita Malik; Donald and Janet Mallinson; Larry and Jan Malone; George Maniates; Philip Manoanici; Earl Manthey; Neil and Amber Maranaga; James and Sandy Marcellus; Anthony Marciniak; Larry Marin; James Marino; Billie Markos; Larry Martin; Neil Martin/Goldenrod Garage; Bob Masi; Bob Mason; Paul and Peg Mather; Cliff Mathos; Richard Matzer; Bill and Sue Mawbey; Bob Mayer; Larry Mays; Brian McArthur; Jade McCall; Roy and Bonnie McClain; Tim McClellan; Richard Beggs and Maureen McCullough; Mike and Nancy McCutcheon; Kenneth McDaniel; Garry McGee; Jim McGrew; Dick McKean; Dr. Milt McMillen; Paul Brieske and Milt McMillen; Charles McMullin; Kenneth McWhorter; Keith Meiswinkel; Tom Meleo; Ray Menefee; Chris Messano; Robert Messinger; John Messmore; Ed Mevrer; Alan Meyer; Paul and Mary Meyer; Don Micheletti; Larry Mikelsen; Ed Milas; Tom Milfort; Harold Miller; Jim Miller; Larry and Karen Miller; Dick Miller; Paul Miller; Rod Miller; Gary Mills; Greg Minor; Brian Minton; Jack Minton; Chuck Misetich; Ralph Moceo; Warren Moody; Alexanderia Moore; Bob Moore; Charlie Moore; Michael Morocco; Ron Mroz; Jim Mueller; John and Pat Mueller; Robert Muench; Dale Mueth; Manuel Munoz; Erville Murphy; John Murray; Dennis Murry; M. Randall Mytar; Linda Naeger; Yoshio and Eric Nakayama; National Automobile Museum; Tenny Natkin; Andre Ned; Dick Nelson; Don Nelson; Marshall Nelson; Harry Nicks; Northern Illinois Classic Auto Brokers; Louis and Inez Noss; Tim O'Brien; Jim and Linda O'Dell; Donald Oates; Dan Obele; Ed Oberhaus; Donald Oehlert; Gary and Lois Offstein; D. R. Ogsberger; Ben and Alice Oliver; Karl Oliver; Glenn Olsen; John Olsen; Ted Onufryk; Ray Ostrander; Otis Chandler Vintage Museum; Jack and Lee Oulundsen; Nicolas Pagani; Bob Painter; Carmine Palazzo; Chester Pallach; James Pardo; Dan Parrilli; B. Wayne Parsons; Steven Passek; Robert Paterson; Jim Patterson; Andre Pearson; Charlie Peck; John Pegg; Gene Peliter; John Petras; Joe Petrik; Edwin and Vivian Pettitt; Herman Pfauter; Dennis Phipps; Joseph Piccione; Scott Pickle; Vance Piper; R. C. "Buzz" Pitzen; Richard and Janice Plastino; David and Terry Plunkett; Melissa Polk; John Poochigian; Stuart Popp; Michael Porto; Merle Preinflak; Paul Price; Ralph Proscia; ProTeam Corvette; Dick Pyle; Gerald Quam; Ed Raden; Terry Rady; Todd Ragatz; Ted and Jo Raines; Ramshead Auto Collection; Bruno Ranch; M. G. Pinky Randall; Joshua Rasmussen; Arthur Rathbun; Les Raye; Dennis Reboletti; Myron Reichert; Chris Reuther; Gilbert Reyes; Steve Rhodes; Luanne and Rodney Rinne; Dave Ritchie; Rick Roberts; Hank Roeters; Tom Rohrich; Jim and Chris Ross; Larry Rowen; Glyn-Jan Rowley; Fran Roxas; RPM Lenders; James Ruby; Lydia and Byron Ruetten; Andy and Merlene Rueve; John Rutenberg; Bill Rutledge; Rod Ryan; Carl Sable; Anthony Sanders; Robert Sandkraut; Robert Sax; Al Schaeffer; Bob Schaffhauser; Steve Schappaugh; Tom Schay; Rick and Joanne Scheffer; Patricia Schelli; Paul Schinnerer; W. Grant Schmidt; Howard Schoen; William and Joseph Schoenbeck; Bob Schoenthaler; Ed and Judy Schoenthaler; Douglas Schone; Curtis Schuetz; Dave Schultz; Jerry Schumate; William Schwanbeck; Sam Scoles; John Scopelite; Ralph Segars; Robert Seiple; Owen Sessions; Donald Sharp; Leonard Shaw; Rick Shick; James Shiels; Raymond Silva Jr.; Chris Simko; R. C. and Virginia Simmons; Dave and June Simon; Larry Simon; Mary and Marshall Simpkin; Paul Singer; Dick Sitnick; Gary Skinner; John Skwirblies; Sloan Museum; Thomas Smiley; Fred Smith; Steve Smith; William Smith; David Snodgrass; Ray Sommers; Sheryl Sommers; Carol Spangenberg; Samuel Spedale; Ken Spencer; Roy Spencer; Ted Spicuzza; Frank Spittle; St. Louis Museum; Ed Stackman; Richard Stanley; Dean Stansfield; Ralph Stegall; Rick and Mary Steiner; William Stever; Charles Stinnett; David Stipp; Kimberly Strauss; John Strewe; Suburban Motors; Robert Supallo; Andrew Surmeier; Jim and Stacey Swarbrick; Larry and Loretta Swedberg; Steve Sydell; Fred and Jan Syrdal; Frank Tallarico; Leonard Teagle; Keith Thomas; Kent and Esther Thompson; Rich Thompson; Mick Thrasher; Earl Timko; Ed Tolhurst; Kris Trexler; Phil Trifaro; June Trombley; Phil Trost; Barry Troup; Dean and Deborah Tuggle; R. Wayne Turner; Sam Turner; Bill Ulrich; David Ulrich; Erik Unthank; Dennis Urban; Jim and Chery Utrecht; Bruce Valley; Jim Van Conlon; Howard and Yvonne Van Dereb; Charles Vance; Matthew Verzi; Howard Von Pressentin; Neal and Linda Voorhees; Dug and Sonja Waggoner; Christine and Robert Waldcock; Gary Walker; Murphy and Darla Walker; Ron Walker; Wendi Walker; Jim Wallace; David Walters; Heath Washburn; Peter Watson; Larry Webb; Bob Weber; Tom Weed; Glen Weeks; Ed Weichbrodt; Anthony and Eloise Wells; Dennis Wells; Leo Welter; Jack West; Tom West; Bobby Wiggins; John Williams; Leroy and Judy Williams; Gene Wilson; Larry Wilson; Rosanne Winney; Blake Withrow; Clarence Wittman Jr.; Kyle Wood; Bill Woodman; Henry Woodrow; Morgan Woodward; Garry Woolery; Al Worms Jr.; Daniel Wright; Richard Yech; Dave Yordi; Brad Young; Marty Young; Rich and Joan Young; William Young; Robert Zaitlin; Bill Zappen; Richard Zeiger, MD; Larry Zidek; Hedy Zikratch

Special thanks to General Motors Corporation and GM Media Archives

TABLE OF CONTENTS

FOREWORD

It is no secret that the first years of the 21st century have been challenging for General Motors and the entire automobile industry. But challenges also mean opportunities. That is why we at GM face the future with confidence and excitement. We look ahead with a new can-do spirit, even as we pause to look back at the proud 100-year heritage on which we are building our future.

Having been with General Motors for 35 years, I know that this company has never been more focused on developing dynamic, innovative, and creative vehicles for the marketplace, which is quite a statement when you consider all that GM has accomplished in the past 100 years.

Take vehicle design. General Motors established the industry's first centralized "Styling Section" under the legendary Harley Earl. Earl not only realized the importance of design to the company's success, he pioneered new techniques such as the use of modeling clay, which allowed our designers the freedom to explore far more creative shapes. Harley Earl's designs set the trends and influenced automobile design for decades.

Mr. Earl's five successors contributed their own fresh thinking to maintain GM's standing as the industry's design leader by far. Symbolizing that are the many GM models widely regarded as classics: the Cadillac Eldorados; the 1963 Buick Riviera; the forward-thinking 1966 Oldsmobile Toronado; more recently, the Art & Science Cadillacs with their dramatic presence; and most every Corvette ever built.

In engineering, too, GM has consistently set the pace for quality and innovation. Consider Hydra-Matic, the industry's first fully automatic transmission, or wonderful engines like the smooth, quiet Buick straight-eights, the Cadillac V-8 and V-16, and Chevrolet's potent "small block" V-8. These and many other GM powerplants were outstanding for their simplicity and longevity, and that tradition continues today. Among GM's many new technical advances are the OnStar in-vehicle communication system, a wide range of hybrid applications, not to mention advanced fuel cells, the Chevrolet Volt's E-Flex system, and the seamless integration of every element of today's General Motors cars and trucks—to name just a few.

Great products are born of great leaders, and GM has had more gifted executives than most any other company. In the 1920s and 1930s, president and CEO Alfred P. Sloan literally changed the face of the American corporation with his ideas on organization and marketing. I am proud to work for a company that has the bold, decisive leadership that we have today from

Rick Wagoner and Bob Lutz. Today's leaders have a laser-like focus on delivering outstanding cars and trucks to our customers.

Of course, success in any business depends on responding to your customers' needs, wants, and desires. A fascinating aspect of the GM story is the many ways the company has communicated with the public over the years. Memorable examples include the "Parade of Progress" shows, the fabulous 1950s "Motoramas," and World's Fair exhibits, which in a way have been replaced by the Internet today.

In the digital age, GM employs the latest technologies to promote public dialogue on issues such as vehicle safety, energy independence, environmental sustainability, community development, quality of life, and many more. GM also demonstrates its high sense of corporate duty by supporting a wide range of social, educational, and community projects through the GM Foundation.

As this book illustrates, General Motors' century of success stems from visionary leaders with the courage and determination to keep advancing the state of the automotive art. That, too, will continue as we move into our second century. In fact, GM is now leveraging its worldwide resources—284,000 people in 200 counties—to literally reinvent the automobile for a changing world. There's really no choice. Tomorrow's cars and trucks must shift from petroleum-based fuels to cleaner, renewable energy sources. Making that "green" vision a reality is a huge undertaking, but GM is already well on the road with breakthroughs like the Chevrolet Volt concept and its E-Flex propulsion system, a plug-in electric vehicle that can use bio-diesel, petroleum, ethanol, or a hydrogen fuel cell to extend its range. It promises to be a game-changer with enormous benefits for people all over the world.

I hope you enjoy this account of a great American company as told through its products, people, and significant achievements. It's a proud and distinguished record, yet we at GM truly believe that our best days lie ahead. Here's to the future!

Edward Welburn
Vice President of Design,
GM North America

Harley Earl and
the 1938 Y-Job

CHAPTER ONE

Before GM

"The whole was greater than the sum of its parts"
—Aristotle

General Motors was born in 1908, but its ancestry dates from the mid-19th century through the careers of David Dunbar Buick, Henry Martyn Leland, and Ransom Eli Olds. William C. Durant used the auto companies they built as the nucleus for his GM, starting with Buick Motor Company, then Olds Motor Works and, in early 1909, Leland's Cadillac Motor Car Company. Only later would names like Chevrolet, Pontiac, and GMC be added.

Buick, Leland, and Olds had quite different personalities, but also certain similarities in background. All were inventor-tinkerers with a fascination for things mechanical and how to make them. And all had achieved a measure of commercial success by the late 1880s, when Gottlieb Daimler and Karl Benz captured the world's imagination by building the first practical motorwagens. Others followed the Germans' lead, in America as well as in Europe, driven by the dream of untold riches by perfecting a self-propelled vehicle to replace the ubiquitous, ever-reliable horse.

Yet like many people in the 1890s, neither Buick, Leland, nor Olds took "horseless carriages" seriously at first. That was understandable. What few automobiles existed were spindly, cantankerous, smoky, smelly, and not infrequently dangerous—hardly a promising substitute for Old Dobbin. And being so rare, they were expensive—playthings for the rich. And where could you go? These fragile contraptions demanded smooth roads, but those existed mainly in major cities. So the idea that enough ordinary people might buy automobiles to make building them a profitable enterprise seemed dubious, especially when many mechanical goods were still made slowly, by hand, from individually crafted parts.

But the motorcar idea was unstoppable. Thus, by the early 1900s, Buick, Leland, and Olds were drawn to a nascent American auto industry that, for various reasons, coalesced mainly around

Detroit, Michigan. Each man made important contributions.

Ransom Olds was the first of them to build a car. The son of a machinery repairman with a thriving trade in Lansing, Michigan, "Ranny" had learned about machinery and tools from boyhood. In 1885, at the age of 21, he took over his dad's company which by then was building steam engines. In 1887, young Olds devised a small, simple three-wheel steam car. A second steam car with four wheels followed in 1892. In 1894 he turned his attention to gasoline-fueled internal-combustion engines.

Olds cobbled up his first gas-powered car in summer 1896. Another simple runabout, it was, like so many early cars, basically a buckboard without the horse. A five-hp water-cooled one-cylinder engine sat beneath a passenger seat to turn the rear axle via a simple chain and a two-speed planetary transmission. Though not an "Oldsmobile" (that name wasn't used until 1900 and not registered until 1902) this car ran well enough to encourage Olds to start limited production.

Olds, with financial help from lumber magnate Edward W. Sparrow and copper tycoon Samuel L. Smith, formed the Olds Motor Vehicle Company in August 1897, with Smith as president and Olds as general manager. The firm built and sold four cars in three months, not bad for the time and circumstances.

In 1899, reorganized as Olds Motor Works, the company built a new factory, the first specifically designed for producing cars. The plant rose not in Lansing, however, but in Detroit, because that was home for president Sam and his son Fred, who was OMW's secretary-treasurer. Ransom was general manager. The new company built very few cars in its earliest years, but they developed several prototypes—both gas and electric powered.

In 1900, Olds asked the firm of Leland & Faulconer to cure the noisy transmission he was using. Henry Leland, a stern, idealistic engineer-craftsman, determined that the gears didn't mesh properly. Within a few weeks, he showed Olds a completely redesigned unit with gears ground to a fine finish. Moreover, the cogs were completely interchangeable from one transmission to the next, which was almost unheard of at the time. Impressed by that and the near-silent operation, Olds ordered 300 of these new gearboxes on the spot.

He barely got to use them. On March 9, 1901, a fire destroyed the Olds Motor Works' Detroit factory with an estimated $72,000 loss. Among the few things to survive was a prototype single-cylinder two-seat runabout with a distinctive curved dashboard. Olds staked the company's future on this little car. Evidence suggests that Olds had already decided to concentrate on the curved dash—the fire just made the decision final. Wanting to keep Oldsmobile in Lansing, the local chamber of commerce gave Olds a 52-acre site for a new factory absolutely free. Until that was ready, Olds built cars in an open shed in Detroit, contracting with Leland & Faulconer for transmissions, brothers John and Horace Dodge for engines, and the C.R. Wilson Carriage Company for bodies. Olds would build cars in both locations until it phased out its Detroit plant in 1905. Despite the makeshift conditions, Olds Motor Works turned out 425 cars in 1901 to record its first profit. The car itself, variously advertised as "Oldsmobile" and "curved-dash runabout," used a water-cooled "one-lung" engine of 95.4 cid. As before, this mounted beneath the seat to drive the rear wheels by chain and two-speed planetary transmission. The radiator sat under the floorboard of a simple body on a rectangular-channel steel frame. Tubular steel axles were linked on each side by a long truss-shaped leaf spring that was flattened in the middle for attaching to the body, another common element of very early cars. With a petite 60-inch wheelbase and 56-inch axle width, the curved-dash weighed scarcely 700 lbs but would prove both strong and speedy.

The same could not be said for the first experimental Buick. David Buick, a native Scot who had lived in Detroit since age two, had made a small fortune by patenting an enameling process for cast iron (creating the first white bathtub), then by designing and selling plumbing fixtures through the Sherwood-Buick company. But when he tired of that business, he decided to make a small marine engine, setting up Buick Auto-Vim and Power Company to produce it. Not many were made, but one of these engines powered Buick's experimental car of 1901.

Buick, along with engineer Walter Marr and machinist Eugene C. Richard, developed a new engine featuring overhead valves. Unfortunately for all concerned, Buick Auto-Vim and Power Company was in financial trouble and reorganized as Buick Manufacturing Company in 1902. Desperate, David Buick turned to tycoon Benjamin Briscoe, who agreed to assume his $2000 in debts and pay $650 to finish another prototype car.

Buick was still sputtering. Ben Briscoe was fed up by the lack of progress toward serious production. Accordingly, he decided to unload Buick and put the proceeds toward a more promising motorcar venture with Jonathan Dixon Maxwell. Buick thus passed to James H. Whiting, head of the Flint Wagon Works, who was keen to enter the auto business. The deal looked a sucker-bet, as Whiting put down a princely $10,000 "deposit" and cleared David Buick's $3500 debt to Briscoe. But Whiting was no fool, and he was determined that Buick be profitable. By early 1904, he had moved the company to Flint and pumped in $75,000 through a stock sale, mainly to himself and several Flint grandees.

Meantime, Whiting pushed development—and thorough testing—of a new car, even while erecting a plant to build it. What many consider to be the first production Buick was built in 1904. Marr took the car (shown on the opening pages) on a 230-mile round trip between Flint and Detroit. Designated Model B, the production Buick used a 159-cid twin with horizontally opposed cylinders, overhead valves, and 16.2 hp, plus the usual two-speed transmission and rear-wheel chain drive. Exactly 37 Model Bs were built and sold in 1904, but that didn't begin to cover their costs. After blowing through a $37,500 reserve fund, Buick found itself $25,000 in the red. Now Whiting, like Briscoe before him, looked to unload Buick.

Enter William Crapo Durant, chief executive at Flint's Durant-Dort Carriage Company. Oddly, in view of things to come, Durant was skeptical about prospects for the automobile business. But after a ride in the car—and hearing a strong pitch from Whiting and J. Dallas Dort—"Wild Willie" decided he really would rather have a Buick. Somehow, this fast introduction convinced him that the auto business could bring the fame, fortune and power he craved.

The deal was done November 4, 1904. Typical of Durant, no money changed hands. Instead, he floated a stock issue that boosted Buick's capitalization to a cool half-million dollars. By year's end, Durant had purchased a 220-acre factory site in Flint, arranging for interim production in Jackson, Michigan, at a vacant plant of a Durant-Dort subsidiary. With the takeover, David Buick became company secretary, ceding the president's chair to Durant man Charles M. Bregole. Buick left his namesake company four years later, never to return. He died, penniless, in 1929 after several failed business ventures, including a brief stint running long-forgotten Lorrane Motors in Grand Rapids.

The genesis of Cadillac is a similarly tumultous tale. In 1902, the financial backers of Detroit's floundering Henry Ford Company were restless because Henry preferred spending his time on racing cars, not designing them for sale. Henry Leland was brought in as a consultant, but he and Ford clashed and Ford walked out in a huff. (He started Ford Motor Company the next year.) The upshot was that backers turned once more to Henry Leland, only this time they wanted him to liquidate the company.

Instead, Leland saw an opportunity. His firm, Leland & Faulconer, had recently reengineered the single-cylinder Olds engine, making it not only smoother than the original but three times more powerful. Leland hoped Olds Motor Works would buy the improved engine, but Olds exec Fred Smith rejected it as too costly.

Leland realized that he could not only rescue the Henry Ford Company, but in doing so find a customer for his improved engine. As a result, that outfit was reborn on August 27, 1902 as the Cadillac Automobile Company, named for the Frenchman who had "founded" Detroit (as Fort Pontchartrain) two hundred years earlier.

With a healthy $300,000 in funding, Cadillac immediately got cracking on a new car with no links to Henry Ford. Leland and his son Wilfred supervised the project, but most of the work was done by L&F engineers Ernest E. Sweet and Frank Johnson, assisted by Alanson P. Brush, a talented young draftsman. They worked very fast. Prototype testing was underway in September. The next month, the car was presented in Detroit as the Cadillac Model A with a $750 suggested price. An appearance at the January 1903 New York Auto Show netted 1000 orders, which helped to finance a new plant, located conveniently across the street from the Leland & Faulconer shops.

In the meantime, L&F built 1895 Cadillacs through March 1904. These included a new Model B, announced at the end of 1903. This was basically the Model A with a false "hood front" (the engine remained beneath the seat) and an available four-passenger rear-entry "tonneau" body as well as the usual two-seat runabout. Cadillac was off to the races.

Cadillac spent much of 1904 recovering from a fire that destroyed its factory on April 13th—an eerie echo of the Olds Motors Works blaze. Though the company had to refund deposits on 1500 orders, it hung on by selling 500 cars and 2000 engines that were stockpiled over at L&F. Despite all this, a total of 2457 Cadillacs were built this calendar year.

The 1904 news at Olds Motor Works involved policies and politics, not products. Even though Oldsmobile was best selling car in America, Fred Smith was unhappy with Ransom's methods, and began exerting greater operational authority. Tensions continued, as Fred and brother Angus chastised Ransom for being slow to come up with a new and more profitable car, preferably a higher-priced two-cylinder or four-cylinder model. Ransom Olds was now totally at odds with Fred Smith over what should come next. Olds saw little reason to change course, whereas Smith wanted larger, costlier cars, believing that's where the real money was. With the board of directors in his pocket, Smith prevailed in a January policy vote that prompted Ransom to resign. Olds set up the REO Motor Car Company later that year.

Buick and Cadillac did much better business in 1905. Buick volume jumped to 750 units, even though its "new" Model C differed little from the Model B it replaced. Meantime, another stock sale hiked Buick's capitalization by a million bucks to $1.5 million total. This was, of course, engineered by Durant, who needed big money to build the vast manufacturing complex he envisioned.

Cadillac output climbed to 3942 units in 1905 on the strength of a much broader lineup, though only one of the offerings was truly new. At the bottom was the Model E runabout, basically an updated Model B with the same 98-cid one-cylinder engine sitting mid-chassis, plus the superior rack-and-pinion steering Leland ordained. The only "improvements" were a wheelbase shortened two inches to 74 and rated horsepower of 8.5 versus the prior 9.7-10.3. One rung above was the mechanically similar Model F with a 76-inch wheelbase that available with four-passenger seating.

The genuine 1905 Cadillac breakthrough was the four-cylinder Model D. An open four-place tourer on a 100-inch wheelbase, it was notable for having its engine mounted between the front wheels, a three-speed transmission, and a sturdy steel driveshaft instead of an ordinary chain. The engine itself was equally state-of-the-art, an L-head design with a large 301-cid displacement and an impressive 30 hp. Price was no less impressive at $2800, a lot of money at the time. Still, Cadillac was not yet the pure luxury brand it would be as part of General Motors.

At Olds, Fred Smith began a determined push upmarket. The curved-dash was revised and joined by a "touring runabout" and

"light tonneau" also powered by a one-cylinder engine. The new models looked more modern and had wheel, rather than tiller, steering. The touring runabout was priced $100 higher ($750) than the curved dash. The big news for 1905 was Olds's first twin, the $1250 Model F, with a 196-cid T-head engine rated at 16 hp.

Going a step further was the 1906 Model S, the first Olds with four cylinders and the engine up front. The engine itself, a new L-head design, delivered 26-28 hp from 270 cid. A three-speed sliding-gear transmission took the drive through a cone clutch and open propeller shaft. Built on a 106-inch wheelbase and weighing 2200 lbs, the Model S offered lively acceleration, a 40-45 mph top speed, and good fuel economy. Touring, runabout, and nifty roadster versions were offered at around $2250, making this one of America's first medium-priced "fours." Olds also added the Model L with a new front-mounted two-cylinder engine: 196-cid unit with 20-24 hp sitting in an S chassis trimmed to a 102-inch wheelbase. Though priced at $1250 like the Model F it replaced, the L was a flop. So was this year's one-lung Olds, the Model B runabout, available with curved or straight dashboard. The Model S vindicated Smith by drawing some 1300 sales versus 400 combined for the smaller models, but overall volume was less than the previous year. And worse was coming.

Cadillac's 1906 line consisted of mildly updated single-cylinder models, the M and K, and a new Model H, a short-chassis version of the previous D. But there was also a new line-topper, the Model L. Riding a 110-inch wheelbase and powered by Cadillac's largest engine to date, a 393-cid L-head four with 40 hp, the Model L is significant as the first high-priced Cadillac, tagged a lofty $3750-$5000 depending on body style. Worrisomely, though, Cadillac output for the year dipped to 3559 units.

Buick carried its two-cylinder Model C into 1906 and added an improved version, the Model F. The latter won hillclimb races in New Jersey and on an out-of-the-way Colorado mountain called Pike's Peak, publicity that helped boost production this year to 1400 units. Of these, about 200 were Buick's first four-cylinder car, the Model D. Usually regarded as a 1907 model, it was another medium-priced job, a $2500 five-passenger touring on a 102-inch wheelbase. The engine was a 235-cid T-head unit that sent a rated 30 hp through a three-speed sliding-gear transmission with multiplate clutch and shaft drive.

Two more Buicks joined the four-cylinder D and two-cylinder in 1907: a new D-based roadster, the Model S, and the Model H touring, basically a Model D with the old two-speed gearbox and a friendlier $1750 price. Buick production more than tripled to 4641 units, second only to Ford in the American industry.

Buick's 1907 performance was the exception in a year when a financial "panic" rattled Wall Street and depressed car sales. Cadillac's unit volume, for example, plunged to 2347, and those were mainly single-cylinder cars. The grand Model L was gone, and the carryover Model H drew very few orders. A major sales disappointment was a new midrange Cadillac, the four-cylinder Model G. Offered as a $2000 runabout or $3600 touring, it featured a lightweight 226-cid L-head engine with 26-27 horsepower, plus equally modern running gear, yet managed only 422 sales. However, Cadillac sales would rebound nicely the next year.

Olds Motor Works fared even worse in 1907. It now offered just four-cylinder cars, the Model A touring and Model H roadster. Both were mechanically like the previous Model S, but cost $500 more ($2750 for either). But sales withered again, this time to 1200 units, which forced Fred Smith to start borrowing cash and pray that a re-expanded lineup would turn things around.

Oldsmobile was shaky, Cadillac was growing, and Buick was strong. These were the foundation stones on which Durant would erect General Motors. From these small companies in a fledgling industry would grow one of the largest corporations in the world. The whole was greater than the sum of its parts.

1. Ransom Olds is at the controls of his first gas-engined car. The car was demonstrated for a Lansing, MI newspaper on August 11, 1896, just two months after Henry Ford tested his first car. Top speed was 18 mph. **2.** The curved dash that gave the model its name was similar to that of a horse-drawn sleigh. Olds liked to photograph its curved-dashed runabout in difficult situations. This light snow in the winter of 1901 is nothing compared to the axle-deep mud in other photos. The curved-dash Oldsmobile was light and flexible, yet strong, making it well suited to the poorly maintained dirt roads of the time. An Oldsmobile was the third car to cross the continent. The trip took 80 days, but proved that Olds were rugged and dependable. The tiller steering (seen in the driver's lap) was a lever to steer the front wheels. The steering wheel was necessary as cars became heavier and faster, but for early horseless carriages the tiller was simple and effective.

1

2

WILLIAM CRAPO DURANT 1861–1947

His enemies made fun of his family name (his grandfather, Henry H. Crapo, was a governor of Michigan), but Billy Durant's business career was anything but "crapo." Yet he died nearly penniless, obscure in GM official histories, sustained by a small pension supplied by Alfred Sloan, whose name remained synonymous with GM's successes.

He was, as William Pelfrey notes in his excellent book, *Billy, Alfred, and General Motors*, "the Warren Buffet of his day, at one time leading an investment syndicate with more than $4 billion in paper assets."

Born of an alcoholic father who abandoned his family, Billy was raised by his divorced mother and dropped out of high school at the age of 16. He grew up in Flint, a Michigan backwater that began as a fur trading post. In his youth he seemed unable to hold a job, but he was a dreamer of dreams with silver tongue. At his best, Billy Durant could talk the birds out of the trees.

Durant got into the carriage business in 1886, intrigued by a horse-drawn "road cart" demonstrated by his friend Dallas Dort. He talked a bank manager into loaning him $2000, visited the manufacturers in Coldwater, Michigan, bought the company, and moved it to Flint. Here, like Tom Sawyer's picket fence, the enterprise soon had friends begging to participate. Dallas Dort put in $1000 to become Billy's partner. The renamed Durant-Dort Carriage Company sold 4,000 vehicles in the first year of production, and made $18,000. Ten years later, Durant-Dort was building 75,000 a year with a gross revenue of $5 million.

Billy was not originally an admirer of gas-powered vehicles. Undoubtedly he shared the view of another buggy maker, "Wheelbarrow Johnny" Studebaker, who described cars as "clumsy, dangerous, noisy brutes [which] stink to high heaven, break down at the worst possible moment, and are a public

nuisance." When in 1902 his daughter Margery told him she'd actually ridden one he replied, "How could you be so foolish as to risk your life on one of those things!" But like Studebaker, Durant soon changed his mind.

One of Billy's protégés was Alexander Brownell Cullen Hardy ("ABC" to his friends), a prescient

1. Although Henry Ford put America on wheels, Ransom Olds helped get things rolling. Olds had mass production with a moving assembly line several years before Ford. Before the Model T was selling millions, the curved-dash Olds was the best selling car in America, even though sales were only in the thousands. The curved-dash Olds cost a reasonable $650 for all seven years of production. The 1902 model shown has the optional top ($50 in leather; $25 in rubber) and back seat ($25). Also optional were fenders, headlights, and wood artillery wheels in place of the bicycle-style wires. The one cylinder engine developed four hp and top speed was 25 mph.

1

production manager. After a trip to Europe, where he observed the proliferation of self-powered vehicles, he advised his boss to "get out of the carriage business before the automobile ruins you." In frustration, Hardy left and founded the Flint Motor Company in 1901. Later he rejoined the empire, and was a General Motors vice president through 1925.

Shortly after Hardy's return from Europe Durant took a two-year sabbatical in New York, where he dabbled in the stock market and met key financiers, including J. P. Morgan. Exposure to the automobiles now plying Manhattan streets probably made an impression. In 1904 Billy was back in Flint. Test drives of an early Buick convinced him to take charge of the floundering car company founded by David Dunbar Buick.

Buick was one of those brilliant inventors with good ideas—in this case the valve-in-head engine—but lacking business ability. Buick's principals approached Durant to become their general manager, and then president. Four years later, a prosperous Buick was the first

company in the new General Motors.

In 1910, the bankers wrested GM from Billy's hands and he immediately started over again with Little, and then Chevrolet. Eventually he leveraged Chevy into GM, by buying enough GM stock to give him and his ally, Pierre DuPont, control of the company again. Four years later, it was DuPont's turn to hoist Billy out, and again Durant had to start over.

Durant Motors, founded in 1921, had the same aims as GM: a car for every price class, from the low priced Star, which competed with the against Model T, to the luxurious Locomobile, the top of the line. By then, however, the competition was formidable, and Durant's makes never seriously rivaled those of GM or Chrysler—another famous Durant protégé who built his own lasting empire.

When the stock market crashed on "Black Tuesday" in 1929, Durant joined with the Rockefellers in buying large blocks of stock in an attempt to reassure public confidence. But the Rockefellers could afford the financial perils far better than the overextended

Durant. The ensuing Depression put paid to Billy's final empire in 1933. His last business venture, ironically and sadly, was a Flint bowling alley, which he managed until his death at 85.

Billy Durant's memorial is at the Flint Cultural Center, now unkempt and neglected, like so many reminders of vanished glory.

1. Oldsmobile was expanding the line with new models that were more modern and more powerful than the curved dash. More engineers and draftsmen were needed to design the new models. Shown is a drawing room in 1905. Open windows and awnings were the only form of air conditioning at the time, so it's not surprising that some of the men have removed their suit coats on this warm day. **2.** Although the basic design and $650 price remained the same, the curved-dash Oldsmobile underwent major revisions for 1904. The new model was slightly bigger, heavier, and looked more substantial. The wheelbase grew from 60 inches to 66. Weight increased from 700 lbs to 800. To handle the extra weight, the bore of the single cylinder was increased and horsepower rose from four to seven. In spite of the improvements, curved dash production declined to 2306. Combined with other models, total Olds production reached 3412—still the highest in America. **3.** The 1905 Model C Buick had an overhead-valve two-cylinder engine that developed 22 hp from 159 cid. That power rivalled many larger four-cylinder cars. Thanks to their good performance and reliability, Buicks did well in hill climbs and races. The publicity from those exploits helped sell 750 cars for 1905, placing Buick ninth in U.S. sales. The Model C Cost $1200 without the optional top.

1

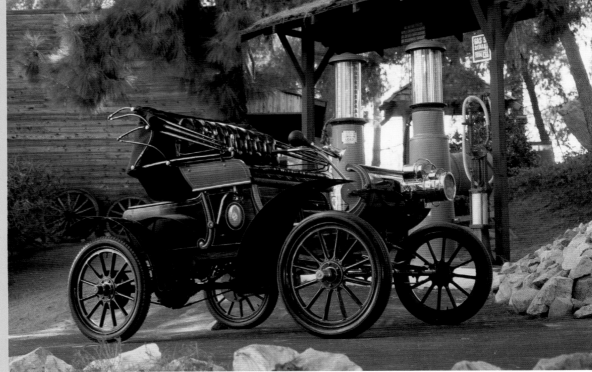

2

3

1

2

3

1. The 1906 Oldsmobile Model S Palace Touring cost $2250. The price included two acetylene headlights, two oil cowl lights, a horn, and a tool kit. A top was optional. This was Olds' first four-cylinder car and was a big move upmarket from the $650 one-cylinder curved dash. **2.** The 1905 Model E was a development of Cadillac's first car, the Model A. The one-cylinder engine remained under the seat while under a dummy hood was storage space and a water tank for the radiator. In the early years of the 20th century it was rapidly becoming fashionable to have a front-mounted engine. Some makes added false hoods to make their mid-engined cars appear modern. One-cylinder Cadillacs were simple, inexpensive cars, but because of the quality and precision of construction they were refined and reliable. **3.** The 1907 Model K was a further development of the single-cylinder Cadillac. The popularity of one-cylinder cars was declining and Cadillac had added four-cylinder cars to the line in 1905.

CHAPTER TWO

1908-1919

"That Which Deserves to Live—Lives"

Billy Durant, wrote auto editor Jim Mateja of the *Chicago Tribune,* was "an empire builder who, if offered a penny for his thoughts, surely would have found a way to make a nickel on the deal— only to let it drop through a hole in his pocket."

Gluing together General Motors took only 100,000 pennies: one thousand dollars, according to Arthur Pound's *The Turning Wheel.* The rest of it was paper: shares of stock, manipulated under the guise of acquisition, elevating GM's worth from $1000 to $3.75 million. No sooner had he succeeded than he let the company go for lack of cash. Then he reorganized and got it back again.

Buick would be the heart of Durant's empire, incorporated in New Jersey on September 16, 1908. Durant had owned Buick since 1904; folding it into General Motors was like selling it to himself. But few took notice of the empire abuilding. Chris Sinsabaugh, an auto editor at the *Chicago Tribune*, knew vaguely that "the concern was to be some sort of holding company, with Buick and Oldsmobile the first blue chips tossed on the table, the deal having been made possible by an exchange of stock rather than the paying out of real cash."

How did the swashbuckling Durant parlay nothing into something? GM began, his biographer Larry Gustin wrote, with a 1907 phone call from Benjamin Briscoe, Jr. in Chicago. Briscoe, the founder of Maxwell, was a sheetmetal and parts manufacturer who had helped sell Buick to Durant three years earlier (conveniently erasing Buick's considerable debt to Briscoe). A lot of car manufacturers owed him money, and Briscoe figured his books would be a lot blacker if he and his pal Billy could roll them all into one. According to Gustin's *The True Story of General Motors,* the conversation went this way:

Briscoe: "Hello Billy. I have a most important

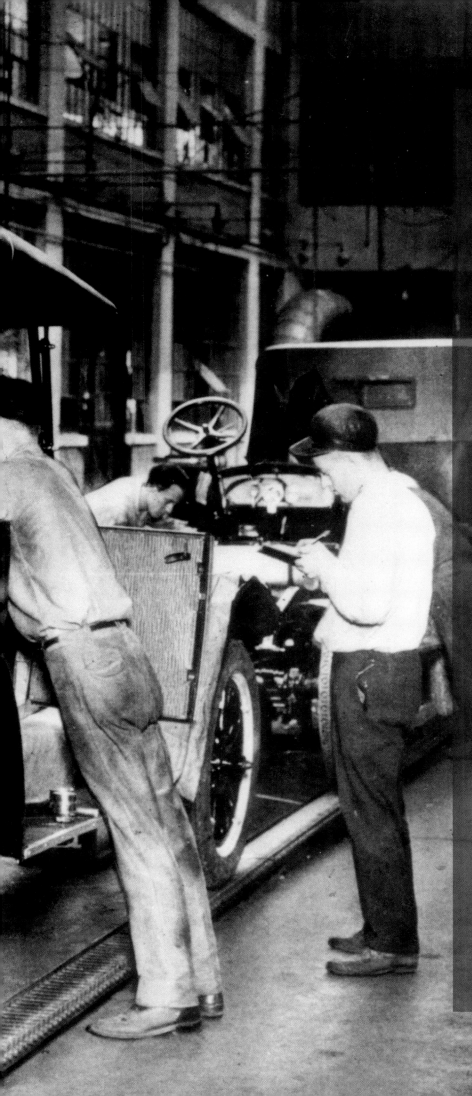

matter to discuss with you and want you to take the first train to Chicago."

Durant: "What's the big idea, Ben?"

Briscoe: "Don't ask me to explain; it's the biggest thing in the country. There's millions in it. Can you come?"

Durant could not, so Briscoe took a train to Flint. By January 1908, Gustin continued, "the talks were at a serious stage."

Briscoe was on to an old idea called "economies of scale": in this case, merging the resources of Buick and other companies to diminish unit costs and lower overhead. The problem was that Briscoe wanted to merge companies which mainly built the same kinds of cars: Packard, Peerless, Pierce-Arrow (the vaunted "Three Ps," at that time the cream of the American auto industry), along with Stoddard-Dayton and Thomas. Durant knew that a combination of luxury makes wouldn't work: Sales and growth would be limited by high prices and competitive overlap. Moreover, their plants were scattered from New York and Buffalo to Cleveland and Dayton to Detroit.

Durant saw mass production as the key to success, and he wanted to do it mainly in Michigan. He suggested combining one or two higher volume producers, Ford and Reo. Acquiring Ford was a "no-brainer"—if it could be done. Acquiring Reo—named for Ransom Eli Olds, who founded it after he left Oldsmobile in 1904—would provide product diversity, plus Ransom Olds. With his curved-dash Oldsmobile, Olds had virtually invented the production line. His expertise was desirable.

Briscoe got Durant, Ford, and Olds together, but nothing came of it. Henry Ford had no interest in joining a combine—though he would have been happy to sell Ford for $3 million. (Imagine automotive history had that happened.) Durant believed that Ford without Henry was not worth much. Ransom Olds didn't see the combine as useful and quietly backed out, and some of Durant's financial backers questioned his vision. When Billy said that "a million cars would some day be in demand," they thought him demented.

Financier J. P. Morgan had backed Durant at Buick and had faith in his star. Why not, he suggested, start by merging Buick together with Briscoe's Maxwell? That bubble burst when Morgan lawyers expressed doubts about trading Buick stock for shares in General Motors, as Durant, true to form, wished to do.

Obviously, Durant would have to go it alone if he hoped to make Buick part of something much bigger. And with the resourcefulness for which he was renowned, Durant did just that in the space of two months. Two weeks after organizing GM on the aforementioned shoestring, Durant put Buick into its basket. Six weeks later he acquired Oldsmobile, exchanging GM stock for a 75 percent controlling interest in the Lansing, Michigan, firm.

George E. Daniels was GM's first president—he lasted four weeks, from September 22 to October

20. Durant, the real boss, sold more stock and raised capitalization to $12.5 million. While promoting GM stock by personally underwriting some issues, Durant prevailed on his Durant-Dort Carriage Company in Flint to invest $1 million in GM.

This was still modest for a big-time firm, and while there was no doubt about Buick's value, Oldsmobile was heavily in debt. The luxury cars it had been producing were consistent money losers. Durant had paid $3 million for a company whose assets were a well-loved name (popularized by the 1905 tune "My Merry Oldsmobile") and a string of billboards around the country—"a helluva price to pay," he admitted, "for a bunch of road signs." But he was hopeful about the company that pioneered mass production.

Olds desperately needed a new model, so Durant sent a Buick Model 10 to Lansing, along with a Buick engineer and production manager. In the workshop before startled Olds bigwigs, the Buick chassis was sawed across the middle and split down the center. Metal was added to make a new chassis with a longer wheelbase and wider track, to accommodate a roomier, higher grade body. Existing springs, axles, driveline, and engine were retained. The result was the new Olds 20, priced $250 more than the $1000 Buick 10 but undercutting the rest of the Olds line with a price more buyers could afford.

Late in 1909 GM acquired a 50 percent interest in Oakland, an outgrowth of the Pontiac (Michigan) Buggy Company, founded only a year before by A. P. Brush, who worked on the design of the original single-cylinder Cadillac. (Two decades later, Oakland would spawn Pontiac.) This too seemed like an odd purchase: Oakland could build only 3000 cars annually. But Durant wanted Brush's novel two-cylinder vertical engine, in which the pistons moved in parallel, which he thought (erroneously) might be useful. Secondly, Oakland's owners weren't that eager to sell, which only made him want it all the more!

General Motors has always done things big. By the end of its very first fiscal year, on September 30, 1909, it had captured nearly 20 percent of America's total car and truck market—not bad for a newcomer. While income from its 25,000 sales didn't exceed $30 million, the firm realized a healthy profit of $9,114,498.

By now GM had 15,000 employees, scattered among many small plants located mainly in Michigan, but Durant was still buying. In rapid succession he acquired a host of companies: the auto manufacturers Cartercar, Elmore, Marquette, McLaughlin, Rainier, and Welsh; and suppliers of motor castings, electrical products, and other components.

Though the multiple acquisitions seemed to some a willy-nilly exercise, Durant was attempting to assure GM's long-term viability. Some buy-outs were made to eliminate competitors, but others were made to assure supplies. As with Oakland, some offered a unique feature. Durant bought Cartercar for its stepless friction drive, Elmore for its two-stroke engine, Welch for its overhead-camshaft engine. He added Rapid, Reliance, and Randolph to get GM into the truck business. In 1912 they were bundled together to become the familiar GMC.

Attempted acquisitions that didn't pan out were E. R. Thomas, builder of the great New York-to-Paris Thomas Flyer; Willys-Overland, for many years second to Ford in the annual production race; and Goodyear Tire and Rubber. In 1910 Durant had another go at Ford, but Henry Ford now wanted $8 million in cash on the spot, and the deal fell through again.

Durant also needed a spark plug supplier and wished to hire French-born Albert Champion away from the company he had founded. Champion accepted Durant's offer to set up a new spark plug company with the inventor's initials: AC.

The jewel in the crown was Cadillac, which became part of GM on July 27, 1909. Cadillac founder Henry Leland, the "master of precision," wanted a tall price: $4.75 million—in cash. Cadillac had survived the 1907 business recession and had launched the popular four-cylinder Model 30; Leland was not going to give it away.

Durant could be disarming when he wanted something badly enough, and he dearly wanted Cadillac. The price was fair, he told a surprised Henry Leland—if Henry and his son Wilfred would take a portion of it in GM stock instead of cash. And, the silver-tongued Billy added, they could continue running Cadillac without interference, with comfortable salaries and bonuses based on corporate profits. The Lelands couldn't refuse. They received $500,000 from the sale, and Cadillac brought GM a $2 million profit in its first year.

But rapid expansion soon caused problems. Many of Durant's acquisitions were losing money, and the situation worsened in 1910 when Buick, the original star of the cast, came close to not meeting its payroll. With the help of Wilfred Leland, who naturally wanted to save Cadillac, Durant talked the bankers into a $15 million loan, enabling GM to survive, Buick to concentrate on overhead valve engines, and Cadillac to continue its successful Model Thirty.

But the bankers had a price: Durant was unceremoniously yanked from management, though he retained a seat on the board. Financier James Storrow became GM president in November, handing over to businessman Thomas Neal in January 1911. GM's corporate headquarters shifted from New York to Detroit. After the loan went through, the bankers asked Durant to name a replacement. Billy wisely picked Charles W. Nash, who had been Buick's production manager. To fill Nash's post, Storrow chose another name later to become famous: Walter P. Chrysler.

Oldsmobile and some of the lesser firms continued to struggle; GM was still a loose amalgam of companies without a sense of corporate identity and unity of purpose. But temporary setbacks were eclipsed by new model introductions and technological breakthroughs, the first of which was the electric self-starter.

When Byron Carter of Cartercar died following complications after an accident with a hand crank, Henry Leland vowed to develop a self-starter. Credit for it usually goes to Charles F. Kettering, an engineer with National Cash Register who developed an electric motor that replaced the cash register's hand crank. Kettering left National Cash Register to set up Dayton Engineering Laboratories Company (DELCO) that supplied ignition systems to Cadillac. Leland asked Kettering to work on a self-starter. Herman G. C. Schwarze, Cadillac's own electrical genius, was also involved. The GM starter followed Kettering's cash register principle: Since the electric motor had only to run for a few seconds each time, it could be undersized and overstressed. By June, Cadillac had ordered 5000 electric starters for its 1912 Thirty, which also now featured electric lights and ignition.

In December 1912 Charlie Nash, who had been a Durant protégé, became president of General Motors. No-nonsense Walter Chrysler became president of Buick. The Flint company sailed into 1912 with five low-priced offerings from $950 to $1280, all with Buick's reliable ohv four, on wheelbases of 91 to 108 inches. The lineup reflected Nash's and Chrysler's cost-cutting product rationalization, with unnecessary engines and slow-selling luxury models eliminated; Buick production hit nearly 20,000, the $1000 Model 35 being most popular.

In Lansing, Oldsmobile struggled, having too many luxury models, including the fabulous Limited, which it could not sell in quantity. Olds fought back with a new, lower-priced Olds Model 42, powered by a new undersquare engine rated at 35 hp. Hoping that Olds could be salvaged, GM made Charlie Nash president of the company, a post he would hold through 1916.

In Pontiac, Oakland rebounded with new models and added self-starters in 1913. That year saw Oakland's first six, the 6-60 or "Greyhound," a handsome roadster, touring and close-coupled touring riding an expansive 130-inch wheelbase. Priced at only $2550, with a smart new vee'd radiator and sleek new fenders, it was just right. Oakland rebounded, selling nearly 9000 cars in 1913.

Though Europe went to war in 1914, President Woodrow Wilson assured Americans the USA would stay out, and it was a solid year for the auto industry. Now run by Chrysler, a former railroad man, Buick was like a locomotive pulling the rest of General Motors along. Production reached nearly 33,000. Cadillac's Thirty was also selling well, and lower prices boosted Oldsmobile's sales to 14,000. Oakland's Light Six and Big Six showed that Oakland was GM's most dynamic outfit when it came to updating models. Oakland was now building well over its capacity when Durant bought it.

The irrepressible Billy had not been idle since he'd let GM slip out of his grasp, and now he had a banker on his side: Louis G. Kaufman of New York. In 1914, the two began quietly buying GM shares. They acquired stock in small blocks, often through third parties, one of whom turned out to be chemical-industry tycoon Pierre S. Du Pont. It wasn't long before Du Pont was part of Durant's circle, accumulating GM shares in vast quantities. Billy planned to attend the board meeting of October 1, 1915, when GM would pay its final $2.5 million to the banking consortium, disband its loan trustees and elect a new board of directors. What's more, Durant was bringing a sweetener to the deal: Chevrolet.

After losing control of GM, Durant had started over, founding what he called Republic Motors and raiding Buick for personnel. One of his hires was racing driver Louis Chevrolet, who dreamed of building a car under his own name. Durant bought the Mason company to make engines, a defunct factory to assemble cars, and established the Little Motor Company, headed by former Buick general superintendent William H. Little, to produce a lightweight four. In 1911 he incorporated Chevrolet Motor Company, with Louis Chevrolet as consulting engineer, Bill Little as president, and the talented A.B.C. Hardy as general manager. The first Chevrolet was a 3350-pound blunderbuss on a 120-inch wheelbase, powered by a big six and selling for $2500. After several false starts, Chevy settled in Flint, near Buick.

Chevrolet soon absorbed both Little and Republic, but Durant's infatuation with Chevrolet did not extend to Louis, who left company in October 1913. The following year, with the help of more Buick people, Durant announced the first low-price Chevy, the H Series, comprising the exotically named "Baby Grand" five-passenger touring and "Royal Mail" two-seat roadster.

Powered by an efficient four, these pretty cars sold for $750-$875, the cheapest Chevrolets to date. They were first to wear the famous Chevrolet "bow tie" emblem, which has since become a widely recognized trademark. A year later, Chevrolet introduced the yet-cheaper "490," which stood for its price tag—$490 just happened to be what Henry Ford was charging for the now mass-produced Model T. The Ford-Chevy rivalry had begun.

Chevrolet had been building scarcely more than 10,000 cars a year up to now, but the 490 brought volume to 63,000 in 1916—big league production vying with Studebaker, Maxwell, and Dodge. It was a power to be reckoned with, an important factor in Durant's plan to regain control of General Motors.

Armed with massive blocks of GM stock, Durant, Louis Kaufman, and Pierre Du Pont took control of GM on schedule in October 1915. For his own peace of mind, Billy didn't cease buying GM shares until he held a majority interest, financing the purchases simply by issuing more Chevrolet stock. The patented Durant method still worked.

Banner year 1915 also saw the successful new Cadillac V-8, the first such engine offered as standard equipment by a volume manufacturer. It took competitors completely by surprise, many of them dismissing the new engine in their advertising. Cadillac's response was the famous advertisement, "The Penalty of Leadership," penned by Theodore MacManus of its ad agency: "In every field of human endeavor, he that is first must perpetually live in the white light of publicity....When a man's work becomes a standard for the whole world, it also becomes a target for the shafts of the envious few....If the leader truly leads, he remains the leader....That which deserves to live—lives."

Nineteen-sixteen saw President Wilson sign the Federal Aid Road Act, providing $75 million for construction of new highways: the first federal financing of highway transportation. With working capital of $44 million and net earnings of nearly $30 million, GM stock hit $460 a share. But there were also disappointments. Unable to get on with Durant, Charles W. Nash departed; purchasing the Jeffrey Company in Kenosha, Wisconsin, and launching the first Nash in 1917. Walter Chrysler was also grumbling, but a boost in his annual salary to $600,000—incredible at that time—kept him aboard for another three years.

America's belated entry into World War I, and the diversion of resources to war production, did not affect GM's burgeoning fortunes. By the end of the teens, the company we know today had emerged. Losing companies had gradually been weeded out, and the product mix was a refined blend of offerings in every price field except the highest.

Buick, with its pioneering overhead-valve engine, had coined the phrase "valve in head—ahead in value." Delco electric lighting and starting, a Cadillac innovation, had been standard on Buicks since 1914, and six-cylinders predominated by the end of the decade. In 1916, before the war effort damped down production, Buick built 125,000 cars and ranked third in production behind Ford and Willys-Overland. With the war's end production rebounded and hit 120,000 in 1919.

Cadillac's V-8 proved a triumph for the company, sending even Packard scurrying to trump it with a V-12, even though Packards then sold for considerably more. Cadillac production ranged around 20,000, except during the war year of 1918, and for a luxury maker Cadillac had a respectable place in the annual production race. During 1915, the V-8's first year, it had finished seventh.

Get the right product mix and you can't lose. There was no need to change Chevrolet's 490, except to add closed bodies in 1917. By 1919, Chevy had leapfrogged Willys, Dodge, and Buick into second place behind the seemingly ageless Model T. Chevrolet and Ford would exchange first and second place finishes in every annual production race from 1927.

In 1917, the Chevy Series H was replaced by a new prestige model, the Series F, which initially continued the romantic model names of Royal Mail and Baby Grand. Late in 1917 Chevrolet began building a V-8 of its own, the long and svelte Series D roadster and touring. But GM luxury cars were being addressed elsewhere, and for a decade following 1919 all Chevys would be fours.

Oakland had prospered since 1914. Its ohv "Sensible Six" was introduced in 1917 and from 1918 to 1923 was the only model in the Oakland line. It captured increasing numbers of buyers: Production topped 33,000 in 1917, 28,000 in 1918, and 50,000 in 1919. Oakland had certainly come a long way from the days when its total capacity had been 3000 a year.

Oldsmobile's volume by 1919 was almost 40,000. After the ups and downs of the early decade, prosperity had returned to Lansing with the moderately priced four-cylinder Model 42 and a sidevalve V-8 that looked like a big Fiat but sold for only $1700. Olds would continue to offer this engine through 1923.

Durant and his colleagues made some questionable acquisitions in 1919, but other moves were more important. First, McLaughlin and Chevrolet of Canada were merged to become GM of Canada. Then came General Motors Acceptance Corporation, a way to expand sales by bringing car ownership within the reach of lower-income people through time payment plans. Finally, in September, GM acquired a 60 percent share of the Fisher Body Corp.—an example of "vertical integration" in which the supplier was absorbed by its major client.

The balance sheet for 1919 showed a net of $60 million, $22 million paid out in dividends, and the rest plowed back into facilities, research, and new products—a policy characteristic of GM that largely explains its rise to industry dominance.

Ben Briscoe's 1907 premonition had turned out right. Automotively, GM had become "the biggest thing in the country."

1. Introduced in 1908, the four-cylinder Buick Model 10 was an immediate success with over 4000 sold that year. Its $900 price and 22.5-hp rating were similar to Ford's new Model T. In the early years, Buick was General Motors' highest volume division, offering the corporation's least-expensive cars. **2.** A gas tank was concealed under the Buick Model F's hood, while its 22-hp two-cylinder engine was under the front seat. **3.** The Buick Model G was a two-passenger version of the Model F and cost $1150. **4.** The Cadillac Model G limousine cost $3000. Cadillac would join General Motors in 1909.

1

2

3

4

5

6

5. William Durant started buying interest in the Rapid Motor Vehicle Co. in 1908. Rapid, along with Reliance and Randolph trucks, became the GMC truck division in 1912. This truck, probably a 1907 model, not only climbed Pikes Peak but carried baggage on Glidden Tours. The Glidden Tour was a grueling long distance trial to prove the reliability of early cars.
6. The Oldsmobile Model M had a 40-hp four-cylinder engine. Olds was pursuing the luxury market but would later be priced below Buick.

1

1. Buick team driver Bob Burman raced and defeated an early airplane on the long sand beach at Daytona, FL. Burman said of his Buick racers, "It either holds together and I win running wide open, or it breaks and I lose." **2.** The successful Marquette-Buick featured a modified Buick engine mounted in a racing chassis influenced by a Benz competition car.

BUICK RACING

Buick's efficient overhead-valve engines did well in competition. William Durant was quick to realize that racing was an effective form of publicity and allocated the impressive sum of $100,000 to form a racing team in 1908. The team included top drivers of the day such as the Chevrolet brothers (Louis, Gaston, and Arthur), Lewis Strang, and Bob Burman. Buick regularly beat larger and more expensive cars. By 1910 the team had won 500 trophies. Durant lost control of General Motors to a group of bankers who disbanded the team in 1911.

2

3. The Buick Model 16 was powered by a 32-hp four and cost $1750. **4.** The Oakland Model 40G had a 40-hp four-cylinder engine and cost $1600. Oakland would add Pontiac as a companion make in 1926.

3

4

5. The Oldsmobile DR roadster cost $2750. As late as 1905, Olds had held first place in sales, but increased competition and a switch from inexpensive to luxury cars decreased sales.

5

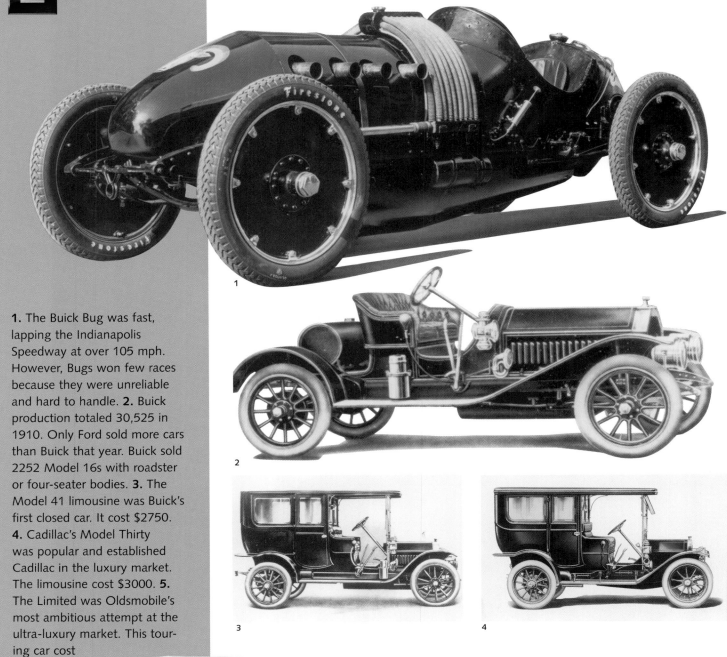

1. The Buick Bug was fast, lapping the Indianapolis Speedway at over 105 mph. However, Bugs won few races because they were unreliable and hard to handle. 2. Buick production totaled 30,525 in 1910. Only Ford sold more cars than Buick that year. Buick sold 2252 Model 16s with roadster or four-seater bodies. 3. The Model 41 limousine was Buick's first closed car. It cost $2750. 4. Cadillac's Model Thirty was popular and established Cadillac in the luxury market. The limousine cost $3000. 5. The Limited was Oldsmobile's most ambitious attempt at the ultra-luxury market. This touring car cost $4600. The Limited was so tall, it required two levels of running boards.

1

2

3

1. The Buick Model 26 roadster cost $1050. Powered by a 25-hp four-cylinder engine, the car had good performance for its price. **2.** The Cadillac Model Thirty was as comfortable and smooth-running as some other luxury cars costing far more. Thirty prices started at $1700, but this rare coupe cost $2200. Early closed cars were much heavier and more expensive than open cars. Not until the end of the Twenties would closed cars outsell open cars. Fisher Body Co. built this coupe. Fisher would later become part of General Motors and build all their standard bodies. **3.** Oldsmobile sold only 1000 Limiteds during a three-year run that ended in 1912. Large 42-inch wheels ensured generous ground clearance for the rutted dirt roads of the period. With a 60-hp six, the big car was capable of 75 mph.

1. Charles Kettering demon-strates a self-starter on a Buick. Buick would offer electric start-ing in 1914. **2.** Cadillac was the first car to offer an electric self-starter. Driving was no long-er restricted to those strong enough to crank an engine.

1

2

CHARLES FRANKLIN KETTERING 1876–1958
"BOSS KET"

Charles Kettering didn't look like his famous moniker. One's first impression was of a bookish, retiring engineer, whose only topic of conversation was how technology could solve the world's problems. He had poor eyesight, an introvert's disposition, and a wife whom he always referred to as "Mother." In today's parlance he would be a nerd.

Why then "Boss Ket"? Oliver Allen explained in *Invention & Technology Magazine*: "He was opinionated and in many ways unyielding...anyone who hesitat-ed to carry out one of his orders might be fired on the spot. He could be petulant, threatening to resign if not given his way, and he tended to nurse old grudges."

Born on a family farm in Loudonville, Ohio, Kettering displayed an early aptitude for elec-tronics. He worked his way through Ohio State, graduating with an electrical engineering degree in 1904. Joining Dayton's National Cash Register Company, he developed NCR's OK Charge Phone, which allowed charge account sales to be processed by cash registers; then he electrified the cash register itself, eliminating the old hand crank.

Kettering took an early interest in the new auto industry. In 1908, when a friend at Cadillac told him the Lelands were unhappy with magneto ignition systems, Kettering conceived of a battery-powered circuit with a timing device, a distributor, and an engine-driven gen-erator. The innovation was developed in an old barn at the home of Ket's NCR friend Edward Deeds. Cadillac's Henry Leland ordered 8000 "Delco" systems. The acronym Delco stood for Kettering's Dayton Engineering Laboratories Company.

Two years later, after Leland had determined to develop an alter-native to the crank starter (see main chapter), Kettering added the

electric self-starter to the Cadillac Thirty's features. A year later, the Delco system of starting, lighting, and ignition won Cadillac its sec-ond Dewar Trophy.

The inherently balanced V-8 engine was another Kettering con-tribution. Its two-plane crankshaft eliminated a peculiar roughness period found on earlier V-8s, even Cadillac's. Later, in a quest for ultimate performance, Ket helped develop the fabled Cadillac V-16. Two more standards were thus set by Kettering for the company already known as the "Standard of the World."

Boss Ket held more than 300 U.S. patents, including freon-based air conditioners; his 1914 home Ridgeleigh Terrace, outside Dayton, was the first house in America with air conditioning. During World War I he designed an aerial torpedo. Exhibiting his versatility, he also invented a treatment for venereal disease, an incubator for prema-ture babies, and the use of magnetism in medical diagnostics. His great and lasting contribution was the Memorial Sloan-Kettering Cancer Center, a combined cancer research and treatment facility in New York City.

After World War I, as sales boomed, GM production lines began to slow because of ancient painting methods, which required more than a month to finish each body completely. Boss Ket wanted the job done in hours! Working with DuPont, he developed nitrocellu-lose lacquer, suitable for paint sprayers, eliminating all the previous hand applications. The new paint, christened Duco, dried quickly to a glossy, quartz-like finish.

In 1916 Delco was sold to General Motors, where it evolved into Delco-Remy, GM Research Corporation, and Delco Electronics. Kettering was a GM vice president from 1920 through 1947, help-ing to develop ethyl gasoline for higher compression car engines and producing the diesel engine which powered railroad locomotives.

When his hometown outside Dayton was incorporated in 1955, it was named "Kettering." Boss Ket died three years later. In his later years, Charles Kettering had even begun to investigate the potential of solar energy. He was a man of his time—and before it, and after it.

3

3. The first electric starter is on the right, with a more mod-ern unit on the left. **4.** The Oldsmobile Autocrat speed-ster had minimal bodywork to reduce weight and increase speed.

4

1-2. After his ouster from General Motors, Durant organized the Little Motor Co. with William H. Little, a former Buick executive, as president. The Little roadster shown here sold for $690 and was meant to compete with Ford's Model T. The first Chevrolet shared factory space with the Little car. 3. Louis Chevrolet was one of Buick's best race-car drivers. Born in Switzerland but educated in France, Chevrolet came to the U.S. in 1900 and became a successful driver. Durant offered Chevrolet the chance to build his own car. Chevrolet, working with French engineer Etienne Planche, designed a car that he was proud to put his name on. Chevrolet had a fiery temper and left the company after a falling out with Durant. Legend has it that Durant wanted Chevrolet to smoke cigars instead of cigarettes.
4. Although considered a 1913 model, the first production Chevrolet left the factory in late 1912. William Durant stands to the left of the windshield while his son Clifford is at the wheel in this early publicity photo.

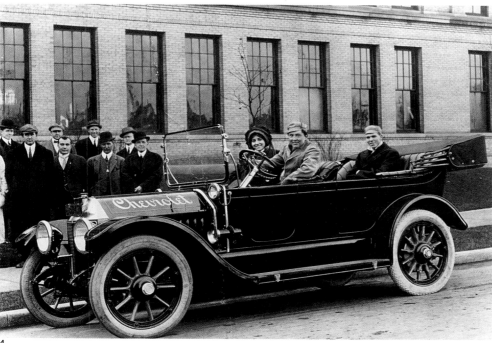

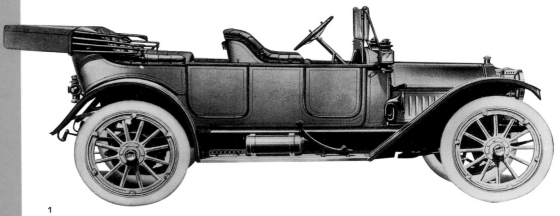

1

1. After a slump in 1911, Buick sales rebounded and the company sold 26,666 cars in 1913. Buick's most popular car was the Model 31, of which it built 10,000. The car sold for $1285 and had a 201-cid four-cylinder engine. Electric cowl- and taillights were used, but headlights were gas lit.

2

3

2. This Cadillac limousine had a custom body with more formal lines than the standard limo.
3. The Cadillac Torpedo cost $1975. In 1913 Cadillac won its second Dewar Trophy for the electric self-starter. Cadillac won its first Dewar in 1908 for the precision of its interchangeable parts. The prestigious trophy was presented by the Royal Automobile Club of England. Cadillac considered the award justification for its "Standard of the World" slogan. 4. The first Chevrolet, the Six Type C Classic, was not a popular-priced car; at $2500, it was more expensive than a Cadillac. It had a 50-hp six that provided a top speed of 60 mph and allowed the car to cruise comfortably at 50.
5. Replacing the Olds Limited was the Model 53. Price for the touring car was $3200—down from the 1912 Limited's $5000 tariff. It was powered by a 50-hp six. Electric starting and lighting were standard.

4

5

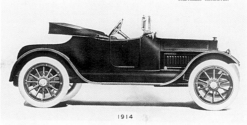

1914

1. Buick sold only 50 of its first coupe. In 1914, Buick adopted electric starting and left-hand steering. Many early American cars had right-hand drive before left became standard practice in the Teens.

HENRY MARTYN LELAND
1843–1932
"STAMPED WITH THE SEAL OF GENIUS"

Henry Leland—machinist, inventor, engineer, and founder of Cadillac—was known as the "Master of Precision" for his foremost contribution to the American automobile: interchangeable parts. In England in 1908, three Cadillacs were disassembled, their parts mixed, and three "new" cars reassembled from the bits and pieces. To the amazement of onlooking members of the Royal Automobile Club, each started and ran perfectly. The feat won Cadillac the RAC Dewar Trophy for "the greatest achievement of the year."

Born in Barton, Vermont, in 1843, Leland was a picture of fitness who eschewed tobacco and drink, and a lifelong Republican (after leaving GM in 1917 he would name his new company after Abraham Lincoln). Wearing a distinctive white beard, his subtle New England humor was laced with a dry bite.

Young Henry's early years were spent as an apprentice at the Federal Arsenal at Springfield, Massachusetts. There, and later at the Colt Arms Company and Brown & Sharpe, he was attracted to the concept of interchangeable parts in all things mechanical, an idea first advanced by Eli Whitney.

In 1890, Leland set up a machining factory in Detroit and soon was doing work for the borning horseless carriage industry. One of his first assignments was building engines for Ranny Olds' curved-dash Oldsmobile, America's most popular car in 1903–05.

One of many struggling new firms at that time was Detroit Automobile Company, founded in 1899, which had been reorganized under Henry Ford in 1901. Leland was hired as an adviser in 1902 and immediately clashed with Ford over shop management. The firm's directors took Leland's side, and Ford was shown out. Leland persuaded them to recapitalize, with his own company supplying precision-made single-cylinder engines. Their first effort, appearing in September 1902, was the Cadillac Model A, so well-received that the firm was renamed the Cadillac Motor Company the following year.

At Cadillac, Leland pioneered many modern manufacturing processes, among which interchangeability was merely the most famous. Left in charge after the GM purchase, Henry and his son Wilfred, an equally fine engineer, began to consider a V-8. Such engines had been seen before, but the Cadillac was the first to make one commercially viable.

The Lelands left Cadillac in 1917 in a dispute over the war effort. Cadillac had played a notable role in developing the Liberty aircraft engine, and Henry and Wilfred now wanted to build them, using a converted Cadillac body plant. William Durant, a pacifist, refused. The patriotic Lelands resigned on the spot and founded the Lincoln Motor Company to build aero engines. Ironically, William Durant changed his mind and put Cadillac itself into the Liberty business, trying to convince the Lelands to return. But by then they were on to greener fields.

After World War I, the Lelands turned again to automobiles with the beautifully engineered Lincoln motorcar, but its staid styling did not attract many buyers. In 1922 Lincoln entered receivership, and at the sale of assets, Henry Ford's $8 million was the only bid.

Like Durant at GM, Ford promised the Lelands they would remain in charge, and Wilfred remained Lincoln president. But Henry Ford quickly brought in his own product, engineering, and financial people, and by June he was asking for Wilfred's resignation. Henry Leland walked out with his son.

The old Vermonter remained a spry and salty Detroit figure until his death at 89. Maurice Hendry records that on his eightieth birthday in 1923, "he walked downstairs from his office to accept flowers and gifts from friends on the ground floor, then walked back upstairs to his office again. It was on the twenty-second floor of the Dime Building."

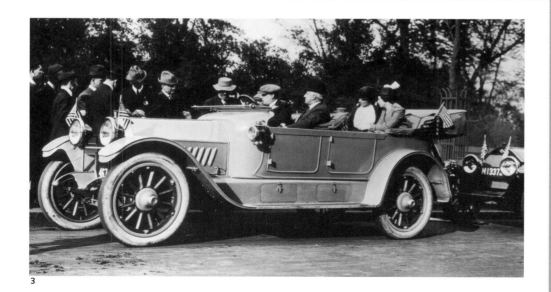

2. Cadillac also moved its steering wheel to the left in 1914. A standard two-speed rear axle with overdrive was added to reduce engine speed for more relaxed cruising and better fuel economy. The roadster cost $1975.
3. The Oldsmobile Model 54 was well-built and used good materials. Standard equipment was extensive for the time and included an air compressor for inflating flat tires—a common problem given the tire technology of the day.

1. The Chevrolet Baby Grand touring car replaced the Little Four. Durant realized that Little was a bad name for a car while Chevrolet, with its racing image, was good for sales. The base Baby Grand cost $875, or $1000 with electric starting. Its overhead-valve four-cylinder engine had better performance than the Little's sidevalve four.

2. The Chevrolet Light Six touring car replaced the Little Six. The $1475 Light Six retained a version of the Little's sidevalve six and was the only sidevalve engine Chevrolet ever built. Overhead-valve engines tend to produce more power per cubic inch than sidevalve engines. Buick (and later Chevrolet) touted the fact that they built only overhead-valve engines. 3. The Chevrolet Royal Mail was a roadster version of the Baby Grand. It cost only $750. The low-priced Royal Mail and Baby Grand proved popular and Chevrolet established itself as a Ford competitor.

1

2

3

1. The least-expensive Buick was the Model C-24 roadster for $900. Although sporty, the barrel-shaped external gas tank was considered old-fashioned by 1915. Most roadster buyers wanted a luggage compartment or rumble seat in the rear deck. Buick discontinued this model after 1915. **2.** The Type 51 Cadillac sedan cost $2800. The central-entrance sedan was similar to a two-door sedan except that the doors opened to the back seat instead of the front. Front-seat passengers had to squeeze between the two front seats. This body style disappeared after the Teens. **3-5.** Cadillac leapfrogged its six-cylinder competition in the luxury-car field by jumping from a four cylinder to the world's first mass production V-8. Cadillac developed its V-8 under tight security and surprised the competition. The V-8 engine had the advantage of being more compact than an inline six. By the mid-Fifties, the majority of American cars would be powered by a V-8. Cadillac's first V-8 was smooth-running, quiet, and reliable. It developed 70 hp from 314 cid. Open Cadillac V-8s were capable of 65 mph.

4

In spite of the addition of four more cylinders, Cadillac V-8s started at $1975 for the five-passenger touring car—the same as the four-cylinder version cost in 1914. The seven-passenger touring car shown here cost $2075.

5

1

2

1. The Chevrolet Royal Mail roadster cost $750, but the car shown has optional electric lights and starting, which raised the price to $860. Chevrolets sold well, and Durant started trading Chevrolet stock for General Motors stock. By 1916, Durant had enough GM stock to temporarily regain control of the corporation. **2.** Chevrolets had a conventional three-speed transmission with a center shifter. Many cars of that time mounted the shifter by the driver's door. Meanwhile, Ford's Model T used a two-speed planetary transmission that was shifted with a pedal. To drive in low gear, a Ford driver had to keep the transmission pedal pushed to the floor.

1

1. Buick introduced its first sedan in 1916 on a D-47 chassis powered by a 55-hp six. Buick built its first six-cylinder car in 1915, and by 1919 would sell exclusively sixes. The $1800 sedan was the most expensive in the Buick line; only 881 were sold.
2. More successful was the Buick D-44 roadster with more than 13,000 built. It used a smaller 45-hp six and sold for $985. Buick built 124,834 vehicles to take third place in sales for 1916.

2

3. The Chevrolet 490 touring car cost $490—the same price as the Ford Model T tourer. Chevy was now a serious competitor of Ford's, even though its sales were only a fraction of that of the Model T.
4. The four-cylinder Oldsmobile Model 43 roadster cost $1095. It sported a rumble seat that folded out of the rear deck, a feature that was gaining popularity in the Teens.

3

4

1. Cadillac joined the fight in World War I when their seven-passenger touring cars became the standard staff car for the U.S. Army. Cadillac was selected after a grueling 7000-mile Army test through the rough terrain of Southern Texas. The V-8 impressed with its power and durability. The English and French military also used Cadillacs—over 2000 were shipped to Europe.

1

2. The D-34 was Buick's least expensive car. The four-cylinder roadster cost $660. Buick would soon abandon four-cylinder cars to concentrate on more-expensive sixes. **3-4.** The Chevrolet Model D touring car was powered by Chevy's first V-8. The Model D was offered with roadster and touring bodies. Both versions were mounted on a long 120-inch wheelbase and sold for $1385. That price was at the upper end of the medium-priced field. Chevrolet had established itself in the low-priced field, and the Chevrolet name didn't have the prestige to sell a car as expensive as the V-8. Although the Model D was a marketing blunder, the car itself was quite good. The eight provided satisfying performance, and the body was well finished with polished mahogany trim. While the V-8 didn't sell well, the low-priced Chevrolets had a good year with production up by over 50,000 units. A total of 125,882 cars were built—including Canadian units. Chevrolet was closing in on Buick for top GM sales honors.

2

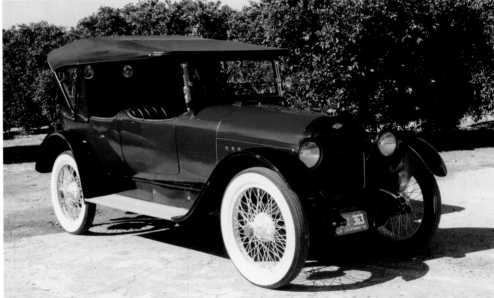

3

4

FIRST CHEVROLET V-8

Although many people believe that Chevrolet's first V-8 was the famous "small-block" introduced in 1955, Chevy sold a V-8 in 1917–19. Advanced in design, the engine had overhead valves and detachable crossflow cylinder heads for more efficient breathing and therefore more power per cubic inch. A counterweighted crankshaft allowed higher rpms and contributed to smoother running. Displacing 288 cid and utilizing a Zenith two-barrel carburetor, it developed 55 hp at 2700 rpm, running on 4.75:1 compression. The engine also looked good with polished valve covers. Chevrolet abandoned its first V-8 after building only around 3000. The postwar small-block V-8 became a legend and has sold more than 90 million units, while the 1917–19 V-8 is all but forgotten.

1. Oldsmobile realized its line of expensive luxury cars wasn't selling in adequate numbers and added a line of reasonably priced four-cylinder cars in 1914. Sales improved thereafter. For 1917, Olds replaced the entry-level four-cylinder car with a six and the division moved up to 10th in national sales. This was the first time Olds had been in the top 10 since 1907. The Model 37 touring car cost $1185. Its six-cylinder engine had overhead valves and developed 40 hp. It cost only $90 more than the four-cylinder car it replaced.

1

1

2

3

4

5

1. The Buick E-46 coupe was powered by a 60-hp six. It cost $1695. **2.** The Cadillac Model 57 Landaulet rode a 132-inch wheelbase that provided generous room for jump seats in the rear. A folding top could be raised to completely enclose the rear compartment. The chauffeur was covered by a solid roof, but he had to erect side curtains for complete protection from the elements. The $4295 Landaulet was an example that Cadillac was moving up in the luxury car market. **3-4.** The Chevrolet Model D-5 V-8 touring car was virtually unchanged from the previous year, although the price rose from $1385 to $1550. The mahogany dashboard included amp meter, speedometer, oil pressure gauge, and clock. **5.** The Chevrolet 490 touring car cost $685—far more than its 1916 introductory price of $490. The 490 was popular despite the price increase, and Chevy sales exceeded Buick's for the first time. **6.** The Oldsmobile Model 45-A club roadster cost $1700 and packed a 58-hp V-8. Olds had introduced its L-head V-8 in 1916. It proved more popular than Chevrolet's V-8, and more than 8000 were sold in 1918. Olds kept the V-8 in production through 1923. Olds' next V-8, the Rocket V-8 of 1949, would be even more successful.

6

1. The H-50 seven-passenger sedan was Buick's most expensive car at $2585. All Buicks were powered by a 242-cid six. Buick sold 119,310 cars in 1919, but only 4003 were closed cars. Buick was third in the national sales race, behind Ford and Chevrolet. **2.** The Chevrolet FB-50 touring car was a descendent of the Baby Grand. Post World War I inflation drove its price up to $1235. The FB was Chevrolet's most expensive car after the Model D V-8, which was dropped midyear after sales of only 71 cars. The FB's overhead-valve 224-cid four-cylinder engine developed 37 hp. **3.** The Chevrolet 490 roadster cost a reasonable $715. Its overhead-valve four-cylinder engine put out 26 hp. The wire wheels shown here were an aftermarket accessory. The 490 sold well, and Chevrolet made few changes to its winning formula for 1919. **4.** Oldsmobile finished the decade with healthy sales of 39,042—up from only 1075 in 1912, when Olds was concentrating on luxury cars. Olds was ninth in national sales. The 37-A sedan cost $1895. The two-door sedan was unusual in that there was a door for the front seat on the left side of the car and a door for the back seat on the right side. The 37-A retained the 44-hp overhead-valve six from the previous year.

GM

CHAPTER THREE

1920-1929

"Fortune favors the brave"

—Virgil, The *Aeneid*, ca. 29-19 B.C.

The Teens passed into the Roaring Twenties quite momentously at General Motors, for 1920 marked a definite end to an era. First, founder Billy Durant, who had regained control of the company in 1915, lost it again, this time for good. But the fates would smile upon GM, as new talent arrived to create a corporate monolith that would dominate the American auto industry for 50 years.

Many thought Billy Durant's spendthrift ways would be his undoing, and so it proved. In 1917, he had earmarked $20 million for a new Detroit headquarters building—in the words of author Malcolm Bingay, "as though ordering the construction of a chicken coop." In 1920 he authorized $20 million more, for Cadillac, the Hyatt ball-bearing division, and a new frame plant. However, Walter Chrysler—now VP-Operations as well as president of Buick—had negotiated for frames from an outside source at a lower cost than the new frame plant could deliver them. Infuriated, he walked out in March 1920, soon to parlay the old Maxwell-Chalmers Company into Chrysler Corporation, which would become a formidable GM rival over the next quarter-century.

By October 1920, with the stock market sliding and GM shares at five percent of their postwar high, Durant found himself with $200 million worth of unsold cars. Financier J. P. Morgan was willing to meet the deficit but demanded Durant's head in return. Billy resigned in November; Pierre Du Pont reluctantly took his job, searching for new, younger talent. A year later Du Pont named Alfred P. Sloan executive vice president, and with that, GM's future was assured.

It would take some assuring. The almost unchanged 1920 Buick and Chevrolet took a pasting from a resurgent Dodge. Cadillac sales were also down. Oakland's cars looked much the same, as did Oldsmobile's. Du Pont installed

Harry Bassett to take Chrysler's place at Buick and George Hannu to replace Fred Warner at Oakland, hoping for the best.

But it was Alfred Sloan himself who made order out of chaos with his progressive product hierarchy. When he arrived, the GM makes had overlapping prices and competitors: Chevy was competing not against Ford but Willys-Overland. Ignoring Ford for now, Sloan envisioned Oakland as a rival for Dodge, Maxwell, and Hudson's Essex. Buick would go against the big Hudson, Nash, Studebaker, and Reo in the $1200-$1700 price field; Oldsmobile would work the $1700-$2500 class; and Cadillac would compete against luxury makes. Sheridan and Scripps-Booth, along with the money-losing Samson Tractor Company, were sold or liquefied. But Sloan's logical approach didn't happen overnight, owing to changes in the economy, buyers' habits, and the moves of competitors.

As the market continued sluggish into 1921, financial expert Donaldson Brown introduced the concept of "standard volume," meaning the minimum production needed to make a profit. Dealer prices were set on this basis. Brown brought in Albert Bradley, who evolved Sloan's theories with the "pyramid of demand": at its base were the cheapest cars with the broadest appeal; at its apex were the elite. GM was now able to forecast sales volume, which was a huge advantage that enabled it to respond quickly to market changes.

Cadillac's 1921 Model 59 was little changed from 1920, for Cadillac was preoccupied moving into a new home on Clark Avenue. The move to this large and modern plant cost volume but paid off, enabling Cadillac to consolidate its scattered operations. Production also fell at Oakland and Oldsmobile, though Olds brought out a good new Model 47, its long-stroke V-8 producing 53 horsepower. Riding a 115-inch wheelbase, this new "light eight" was offered as a $1695 touring and three closed bodies listing for $2395.

As unimaginable as it seems today, Chevrolet nearly expired in 1921, when consultants Sloan had called in said it would never be a Ford beater! Sloan had faith in Chevrolet president Karl Zimmerschied, but the breadwinner 490 was still unchanged, and volume was down significantly from the previous year's.

By 1922, things had started to calm down. Buick brought out a new four-cylinder line; the engine was essentially two-thirds of the existing six. Starting at only $895, the new line boosted volume to more than 123,000, close to 1916's all-time high. Cadillac lowered prices for its spruced-up Model 61, which now spanned a range from $3100 for the two-seat roadster to $4600 for the seven-passenger limousine. Significantly, closed cars now accounted for half of Cadillac's production.

Although Chevrolet found itself second to Ford (by a long way) in 1922, its strong showing had more to do with economic recovery than with any new model. Attesting to the importance GM attached to Chevy, Pierre Du Pont himself temporarily became its president when Karl Zimmerschied suffered a nervous breakdown. When it became clear that Zimmerschied would not recover, Sloan started searching for another Walter Chrysler, and found him in a young Dane named William S. Knudsen (see sidebar, page 88). It was Knudsen who would build Chevrolet into a best-seller.

Oakland phased out its old Model 34 in favor of a more stylish and reliable 6-44, on the same 115-inch wheelbase and powered by the established overhead-valve six. Though the package underneath was pretty much the same, Oakland gave it a higher hoodline, new radiator, curvier fenders, a windshield visor on closed models, and drum headlamps on all models except the sport touring. Spanning prices from $1120 to $1785, Oakland accounted for 20,000 units in 1922.

Oldsmobile, likewise a holdover design, enjoyed a sprightly new model: the midyear Super Sport, a fancy tourer with black fenders, brown body, maroon upholstery, cast-aluminum step plates, glass wind wings, steel disk wheels, nickel-plated bumpers, and deluxe Motometer. It took $1825 to own one.

In 1923, Pierre Du Pont handed the presidency to Al Sloan, whose first challenge was the "Copper Cooled" Chevrolet—one of Pierre Du Pont's few excursions into product design and, altogether, one he would have preferred to forget. Carried away with the idea of air cooling, a development he thought would eclipse water-cooled engines, Du Pont had encouraged Charles Kettering's experiments with such models, especially adapting them for the low end of the market. The result was the "Copper Cooled" Chevrolet, named for its jackets of radial copper vanes (for heat conductivity) that surrounded each of the four cylinders.

Right from the start, Knudsen didn't like it. According to Norman Beasley's 1947 Knudsen biography, Bill told Boss Ket: "This car isn't any good. You and the people you have working on it down in Dayton…aren't automobile people. This car isn't strong enough, the rear axle isn't any good, and even if you get these things worked out so they are good, the car will cost too much for Chevrolet to make."

To save costs, they plopped the 22-hp "Copper Cooled" engine into stock Chevy bodies. It proved woefully inadequate. Chevy had planned to produce 50,000 units, but production ended after 759, most of which were rounded up and destroyed. Bill Knudsen proclaimed good riddance.

Other than that, 1923 proved a decent year. Buick set a new production record at more than 200,000 units. Cadillac built 41,000. Spiffy new styling on Chevrolets saw sales surpass 300,000—still a long way from the Model T (1.8 million), but gaining.

Oakland also had a much improved car in the 6-44 and enjoyed a good blip in production. Oldsmobile brought back a six-cylinder line with the long-lived Model 30, which sold handsomely. Olds quickly recovered, and would build only sixes for the next several years.

Product plans for 1924 reflected two industry trends: the low-priced closed car and the low-priced six (to challenge the rough-running four). Closed bodies already accounted for 43 percent of industry production and would rise to 85 percent by 1927.

Oldsmobile's new "light six" competed in unaccustomed market territory between Chevrolet and Oakland, a hole later plugged with the 1926 Pontiac. To avoid overlap with Oakland, Buick would soon discontinue its four-cylinder lines. Sloan's model strategy was beginning to take shape.

Cadillac's 1924 Model V-63 was almost completely new, with a reworked V-8, four-wheel mechanical brakes, a beefed-up frame, and a new 138-inch chassis for longer models. The engine prefigured all future GM V-types. Engineers W. R. Strickland, Roland Hutchinson, and T. P. Chase created the first balanced, two-plane crankshaft, improved valve timing, and added a new camshaft with 16 lobes instead of eight. They worked under the great Ernest Seaholm, who had become chief engineer in 1923. Under the aegis of chief body engineer William Davis, Cadillac bodies

were also improved, with longer hoods, two-piece "VV" (ventilation and vision) windshields, and more-rounded fenders.

Appalled by the disgrace of the Copper-Cooled Chevrolet, division chief Bill Knudsen sat down with Ormond Hunt to send Chevy in new directions. By 1925, a flashy-looking new Chevy Superior was on the market, and sales rebounded to surpass 1923's record.

Al Sloan favored overseas expansion. In 1925 he bought England's Vauxhall, more or less as an experiment; it grew to become General Motors UK. Hoping also to stabilize commercial vehicle production, he acquired Yellow Cab in Chicago.

Buick, now committed to sixes, added the smaller Standard Six, priced as low as $1150, to its Master Six line in 1925. The result was nearly 200,000 cars, the second-best year in Buick history.

At Cadillac, new general manager Lawrence Fisher launched a $5 million expansion plan. Engineers Seaholm and W. R. Strickland produced a new, more powerful V-8 for the 1925 models, and Cadillac continued its alluring "custom-built" Fisher bodies.

Oakland continued while Oldsmobile also stayed with its previous Model 30, now designated 30D, identifiable mainly by a styling shuffle. Having turned Olds around with the program of all six-cylinder models, A.B.C. Hardy retired as general manager, replaced by Irving J. Reuter, a mechanical engineer.

The most important product development in the last half of the Twenties was the 1926 Pontiac, a six-cylinder offshoot of Oakland, made possible by Knudsen's expansion of Chevrolet. Ford's Tin Lizzie was aging fast now, and Knudsen—sensing an opening—wanted Chevy to be capable of building a million cars a year. Moving into Ford territory would leave a gap that only Oakland had the capacity to fill: ergo the Pontiac.

Pontiac's engine was a technical trailblazer and a huge influence on future designs: a short-stroke L-head that developed peak power at relatively low rpm. Much "squarer" than the engines in rivals like Essex and Erskine, it was designed for low stress levels, low piston speeds, and long engine life. Offered as a coupe or coach, the Pontiac rode a 110-inch wheelbase, and its $825 price placed it right between a Chevy and an Oldsmobile. Nearly 77,000 were sold in 1926; from 1927 through 1933 the division was a steady fifth, giving GM three of the top five producers.

The most important corporate development in these years was the advent of styling as a discipline equal to engineering in the design of automobiles. It came about because Cadillac chief Lawrence Fisher was dissatisfied with his car's appearance. One of his favorite dealers was the Don Lee agency in Los Angeles, which supplied Hollywood celebrities with swoopy custom bodies made in their own shops. Don Lee's most imaginative designer was a lanky 30-year-old named Harley Earl.

Intrigued, Fisher invited Earl to Detroit to help develop a junior Cadillac he'd been planning that was to carry the name LaSalle. Rather than cause unrest among house body engineers, Fisher gave Earl an office and shops on the third floor of the GM building in downtown Detroit. Earl christened it the Art & Colour Section—using British spelling for snob appeal. Initially entrusted with Cadillac and Chevy design, Art & Colour gained departmental status and responsibility for all corporate styling in 1930.

Starting at $2495, $500 less than the cheapest Cadillac, the Earl-designed LaSalle was one of the most beautiful cars of the Roaring Twenties. It was also quite fast. With a light frame and a 303-cid V-8, it ran 951 miles in only ten hours at the Proving Grounds, an astonishing average for its day. The 125-inch-wheelbase chassis offered a coupe, convertible, roadster, phaeton, dual-cowl phaeton, Victoria, and town sedan; a 134-inch chassis carried long-wheelbase models.

The decision to aim Chevrolet at Ford, to create the all-new Pontiac and LaSalle, and to vest the "corporate look" in a young stylist from California were all chancy moves involving money and risk. But once again, fortune favored the brave. In 1927, with Ford factories idle while switching from Model T to Model A production, Chevrolet's restyled Capitol Series ("the Most Beautiful Chevrolet Ever") set a historic record: more than 1 million. The car GM almost abandoned in 1921 was now firmly established as "USA-1."

GM was now buying most of its tires from U.S. Rubber, a third of which was conveniently owned by the Du Ponts. The corporation had also merged Kettering's Dayton Engineering Lab with Remy Electric to form Delco-Remy. Through such suppliers, the firm was now beginning to make money selling products to itself—an enviable position for any mass manufacturer.

Buick, Oldsmobile, Pontiac, and Oakland spent most of 1927 with unaltered lines, and Pontiac, "The Chief of the Sixes," was already pulling away from its parent, with about three times as many sales. Oldsmobiles was setting sales records, and Buick was good for a quarter-million units.

Buick celebrated its 25th anniversary with fresh styling marked by headlamps in bullet-shaped pods along with lower, more rakish bodies. Wheelbase was still on the short side, but hydraulic shock absorbers, adjustable steering column, and temperature and fuel gauges were significant new features.

Cadillac's 341 V-8 powered 1928 models, which were mounted on a longer, 140-inch-wheelbase chassis with a new suspension system and torque-tube drive. They were the first Caddys styled by Harley Earl, who said he was inspired by the Hispano-Suiza. A handsome new radiator was announced by bowl-shaped headlights and smooth, well-integrated fenderlines. Fifty body styles were catalogued by Fisher and Fleetwood—the latter a Pennsylvania maker of svelte custom bodies acquired in 1925. Cadillac prices started at about $3300, leaving plenty of price-room for the "junior" LaSalle, itself little changed in its sophomore season. Cadillac and LaSalle combined for 56,038 units for model year 1928, a record not bettered until 1941.

Chevrolet outsold Ford again in 1928, partly due to the Model A just getting started. Also helping was Chevy's new "National" line of Harley Earl designs, longer from the cowl forward in anticipation of a new engine due the following year. Ormond Hunt added four-wheel mechanical brakes, while sales chief Dick Grant knocked the touring car down to $495, a Model T-like price.

As if to celebrate Pontiac's success, Oakland brought out a new model, the "All-American Six." It carried a Pontiac-based short-stroke L-head packing 60 hp on a 117-inch wheelbase and was priced about $200-$250 higher than Pontiac. The latter, now tagged the 6-28, got engine revisions that made for smoother operation. Styling was improved with a narrower radiator, recontoured fenders, and reshaped headlamps. Pontiac again far outsold its Oakland parent.

The aging Model 30, which had put Olds back in the black, dated to 1923; it was finally replaced in 1928 by the F-28, which carried a smooth, side-valve six of 197 cid and 55 hp. The line comprised seven models from $925 to $1205, sharply delineated by Sloan's rule that no GM product should compete in another's price class. Oldsmobile now had production capacity far beyond sales potential, but sales manager Dan Eddins was working on that, and in 1929 he helped Olds finish 9th, where it had not been since 1921.

For 1929, the F-28 was relabeled the F-29. Included in this successful 100,000-car year were 5000 Vikings, an Olds sister make. Not a junior car like LaSalle, the Viking was aimed at a gap between the most expensive Buicks and the cheapest LaSalles. Technically interesting, it was powered by the only GM V-8 outside the Cadillac/LaSalle family: a 260-cid unit with unusual horizontally set valves and triangular-shaped combustion chambers. It was rated at 80 hp, enough to coax a Viking to 75 mph. Body styles consisted of a convertible, sedan, and brougham, all on a 125-inch wheelbase. Dan Eddins hoped to sell 5000 Vikings a month. Outside factors would disappoint him.

Buick for 1929 offered three series named for their wheelbases. The all-new 116 had a 239-cid overhead-valve six with 74 hp and a healthy power/weight ratio. The 121 and 129 were essentially the old Master Sixes on longer wheelbases.

Buick got its first taste of Harley Earl styling in 1929, but the result met with mixed reviews. The cars seemed to have a bulge at the beltline from the hood to tail; they were immediately dubbed "pregnant Buicks." The fault was not his, Earl wrote later: "The factory…pulled the side panels in at the bottom more than the design called for…five inches was added in vertical height, with the result that the arc I had plotted was pulled out of shape in two directions." Whether or not for this reason, Buick sales were down to 196,000 for the calendar year.

Introduced as an early 1930 model was the Marquette, a junior Buick priced at around $1000. Marquettes rode a 114-inch wheelbase and were powered by a 68-hp six of side-valve configuration. Anathema to Buick, side valves were mandated by Al Sloan to hold the lid on price. Obviously built to a market formula, the Marquette was aimed at Chrysler's new DeSoto, but it was not nearly as successful and would prove short-lived.

Cadillac's 1929 offerings went on sale as the Series 341-B. They were fitted with a 92-hp V-8 and a brake system featuring three shoes per drum at the rear. But most notable was their new Synchro-Mesh transmission, which allowed clashless gear shifting—a technological "first" that would become a corporate-wide feature in the 1930s. Meanwhile, the 1929 LaSalle's V-8 was bored out to 328 cid, good for 86 hp. With Synchro-Mesh and four-wheel brakes, it was even more of a driver's car than before, and LaSalle production exceeded Cadillac's by a factor of 11 to 9.

The 1929 Chevrolet morphed from National to International and gained a six-cylinder engine, an obvious attempt to trump Ford's four-cylinder Model A. An L-head unit of 194 cid, it had three main bearings and delivered 46 hp. Chevy cut lots of corners to keep costs down. For example, it used iron pistons at a time when the industry was swinging to aluminum and soon earned the derisory nickname "Cast Iron Wonder." Wags spotted the quarter-inch slotted bolts that secured the cylinder head and dubbed it the "Stovebolt Six." Both names would linger long—but, to everyone's surprise, so did the engine!

Just as importantly, the six easily fit under the Chevy's hood; Bill Knudsen had wisely amortized new model costs by lengthening the chassis and body the year before. He now needed only modest changes—new cowl, hood, radiator shell, and fenders—for a fresh appearance. The International was promoted as "A Six at the price of a Four," though it sold for about $100 more than the Model A. Nevertheless, it was arguably a better buy.

At Oakland, manager A. R. Glancy spent $5 million on a new foundry but hardly changed his cars. The Oakland engine was enlarged to deliver 68 hp; the Pontiac 6-29's was unchanged. Both makes benefited from minor but effective restyling, and with combined sales of 211,054, it was a good year.

In October 1929, General Motors purchased a small Rochester, New York, company building electric starters and other components and renamed it Delco Appliance Division. In 1939, it was reorganized as Rochester Products Division. Further acquisitions included the Opel Company in Russelsheim, Germany; 24 percent of the new Bendix Aviation corporation; 40 percent of Fokker Aircraft Corporation of America; and the Allison Engineering Company. The latter would become famous for building fighter aircraft engines during World War II.

Overall, GM had done well this decade, solidifying the position of its leading makes, innovating widely, and acquiring key component suppliers and manufacturers at home and abroad. It all might have continued, had it not been for another October 1929 development with unexpected consequences. On Black Tuesday, October 29, stock prices dropped through the floor, triggering a financial panic on Wall Street and the start of the Great Depression. And GM was about to take casualties.

1. Few 1920 GM models showed significant changes in the face of new market competition and a national economic downturn, prompting some divisions to lower prices. That likely helped sales but didn't do much for profits. Buick's entry-level Model 44 roadster (shown) and Model 45 touring listed for $1495, a $100 price cut from 1919. Both rode a 118-inch wheelbase and carried a 242-cid six rated at 60 hp. The touring was far more popular, but both enjoyed healthy sales increases. **2.** Cadillac remained at the top of GM's price ladder, and despite bucking the trend by raising prices, the cars sold better than before. Aiding in that success was the $4750 Type 59

sedan, a closed bodystyle that was quickly gaining in popularity. It sat on a 125-inch wheelbase and, like all Cadillacs, was powered by a 314-cid 79-hp V-8. **3.** At $3590, the Type 59 roadster and its touring sibling were the least-expensive Cadillacs. This roadster shows off its pop-up cowl ventilator and available rumble seat. **4.** Oldsmobiles came with either a 177-cid 44-hp six or 246-cid 58-hp V-8. Closed models featured unusual front quarter windows, as shown on this 112-inch-wheelbase six-cylinder sedan.

1

2

1-2. Chevrolet's 490 roadster and touring remained the least-expensive cars in the 1920 GM portfolio despite an initial price increase that put the roadster at $795 and the touring (shown) at $810. Slow sales resulted in a midyear price cut to $720 and $735, respectively—essentially back to 1919 levels. New for 1920 were headlights that bolted directly to the front fenders, which now featured a reverse curve to flow smoothly into the running boards.

1. Buick switched from alpha to numeric model designations for 1921. The new Series 21 had a higher hood and radiator that were nearly level with the cowl, giving it a more modern look that helped the make vault to second in sales behind Ford. Closed models still cost significantly more than their open counterparts; this five-

1

ALFRED PRITCHARD SLOAN 1892–1966

The most notable early GM presidents were polar opposites. Billy Durant was the dreamer, the risk-taker, who made and lost several fortunes, several empires. Al Sloan also took risks, but there the resemblance ended. When Sloan acted, he did so on sound advice and sure judgment; Durant just winged it.

When the 29-year-old Sloan was named executive vice president in 1921, GM was alone in offering a range of cars in every price bracket, but they had no relation to one another—like an orchestra without a conductor. Each division carried on its own research and development, which led to conflicting or duplicated efforts. There was simply no overall corporate sales strategy.

Sloan sorted out the corporate stew through his idea of a progressive product hierarchy, which would retain the loyalty of customers as they aged and prospered. In his ideal, a young American would begin by purchasing a Chevrolet, then move up to a Pontiac, Buick, and Oldsmobile, and finally to a Cadillac. It worked like a charm for half a century.

Born in New Haven, Connecticut, Sloan graduated from Massachusetts Institute of Technology with a degree in electrical engineering. He was made president of troubled Hyatt Roller Bearing in 1899, turned the company around, and sold it to Durant (then head of GM) in 1916 for a steep $13.5 million.

Alfred Sloan became GM president in 1923, chairman of the board in 1937, and retired in 1956. Under his direction, GM became the largest industrial enterprise the world had ever known.

Sloan was also a generous philanthropist. In 1931, he sponsored the Sloan Fellows, the first university education program for management executives. In 1934, he established the Alfred P. Sloan Foundation, a grant from which funded what is now the Alfred P. Sloan School of Management at MIT. He is also remembered through the Sloan-Kettering Institute and Cancer Centre in New York.

passenger sedan cost $2895, while the five-passenger touring listed for just $1795. All Buicks carried a 242-cid six on either a 118- or 124-inch wheelbase. **2.** The move to a new factory in Detroit left Cadillac's Type 59 models little-changed for 1921. The popular seven-passenger touring remained on a 132-inch wheelbase and even listed for the same price: $3940. Power came from Cadillac's 314-cid V-8. **3.** Oldsmobile dropped its six-cylinder models for a four-cylinder line in 1921 and added this smaller V-8. Called the Model 47, it rode the same 115-inch wheelbase as the new four-cylinder car but carried a 234-cid 53-hp V-8 under its hood. Note the wire wheels, believed to be a factory option.

2

3

1

2

3

4

1. Buick "downsized" in 1922, introducing a new line of four-cylinder cars on a 109-inch wheelbase. In addition to open roadster and touring models that started as low as $935, two closed cars were offered: this $1295 coupe and a $1395 sedan. **2.** Buick continued its senior six-cylinder line with few changes on 118- and 124-inch wheelbases at prices ranging from $1495 to $2795. This five-passenger sedan used the shorter wheelbase and sold for $2435. A hand-operated windshield wiper was one of its standard features. **3.** Chevrolet's entry-level 490 carried on virtually unchanged. Huge price cuts the year before were matched by deeper cuts for '22: This coupe, which cost $1210 in early 1920, was now down to $850. **4.** An unusual-looking body style offered by Oldsmobile during the early Twenties was this four-passenger coupe; in six-cylinder Model 47 form, it sold for $1995. Note the angled hood vents that helped differentiate the six-cylinder models from the lower-priced fours.

1. Chevrolet restyled for 1923, reducing its portfolio to a single model line in the process. The former 490 and FB Series were compressed into the new Superior Series, which used 490 running gear on a 103-inch wheelbase, up one inch from the 490, down seven from the FB. Late in the model year, a DeLuxe version was offered (shown), which included windshield wind wings and disc wheels, along with classy

1

THE COPPER COOLED CHEVROLET

Many automotive executives had reason to drown their sorrows in the financially troubled early Twenties, but few managed to drown their mistakes. Such was literally the case, however, with the Copper Cooled Chevrolet.

It all started when Charles Kettering, the GM engineer who had gained fame a decade earlier for championing the electric starter, began experimenting with air-cooled engines. GM chairman Pierre Du Pont learned of his work and decided an air-cooled powerplant in a low-cost Chevrolet would be just the ticket to give GM's largest division a leg up on rival Ford. What it ended up giving GM, however, was little more than a very expensive headache.

Kettering's "waterless" engine displaced just 135 cubic inches—vs. 171 for the convention Superior Series four—and was cooled by copper fins attached to its cylinders. The fins were covered by a shroud, at the front of which was a large fan. Air was sucked up from beneath the engine, drawn across the fins, and blown out through what looked like the radiator but was actually just a housing with horizontal shutters—a flow that seems oddly reversed, as air forced through the "grille" at speed would fight against the fan.

Because Du Pont didn't care for the term "air-cooled," the car was promoted as the "Copper Cooled," which arguably sounded more sophisticated. In the end, however, it really didn't matter.

When the first prototype was delivered to Chevrolet, division chief "Big Bill" Knudsen—who hadn't been in favor of the idea in the first place—found it decidedly lacking. Not only was the small engine underpowered, but other parts of the car didn't seem up to the task. Nevertheless, Du Pont pushed the idea through, largely on the argument that the new engine would go into the redesigned Superior Series, which would—at least at first—also be offered with a conventional four-cylinder engine carried over from the previous 490 model.

It didn't take long for Big Bill's concerns to be justified. Overheating was the biggest issue, and so badly was the car's image tarnished that just 759 production examples were built before GM pulled the plug on the Copper Cooled engine. Those cars aleady shipped were recalled, but somehow, at least two slipped through GM's fingers and are now in private collections. The rest, according to legend, were unceremoniously dumped into Lake Erie. How ironic that cars specifically designed to be "waterless" would end up spending eternity in the drink.

nickel-plated radiator shell and bumpers. Touring models started at $525. **2.** Many manufacturers used durability runs to promote their products, but this one by Oldsmobile was a bit unusual. Running coast-to-coast in high gear must have proved stressful for the clutch—not to mention the driver, none other than famed endurance racer "Cannonball" Baker.

2

1. Buicks underwent their most radical update in nearly a decade when the 1924 models debuted with four-wheel brakes and restyled hood, radiator, and cowl. Four-cylinder versions remained otherwise little changed on their 109-inch wheelbase, but sixes got a larger 255-cid engine developing 70 hp and now rode either a 120- or 128-inch span. Pictured is a six-cylinder touring, which started at $1295. **2.** Oakland had originally been scheduled to get a six-cylinder version of the Copper Cooled engine for 1922, but when the design proved unworkable, the division fell back on its little-changed standard models. It wasn't until 1924 that Oakland had much new to crow about, when the Model 6-54s appeared with rounder bodies painted in a durable, high-luster Duco finish, along with solid steel wheels, four-wheel brakes, and a simpler flathead six in the same 177-cid size as the previous overhead-valve version. This coupe went for $1395. **3.** Note the arched radiator shell and slanted windshield that identifies this Olds coupe.

1-2. Buick dropped all four-cylinder offerings for 1925, replacing them with smaller six-cylinder models. These Standard Six Series cars had a 191-cid, 50-hp engine and a wheelbase of 114.3 inches. The larger models were renamed Master Six Series and retained a 255-cid, 70-hp engine on 120- and 128-inch wheelbases. Shown are the $2125 Master Six coupe (above) and the $1475 Master Six enclosed touring (below). The latter had sliding windows and a lined soft top permanently bonded to its frame. Some Buicks looked more substantial this year with meatier tires on smaller-diameter wheels.

3. Superior Coach Corporation of Lima, Ohio, built its first Cadillac-based ambulance in 1925 and continued building the combination until the late Seventies.

1

2

JUST *SLIGHTLY* AHEAD OF ITS TIME...

In 1925, General Motors hired Fabio Sergardi (driving) to design what would today be termed a subcompact car. Considerably smaller than standard cars of the day, it was intended for export but never saw production.

3

1. Chevrolet's 1925 models carried the Superior Series K moniker, along with a revised engine, strengthened driveline, and improved suspension. All were finished in high-quality Duco paint and available with steel wheels. 2. Chevrolet's two-millionth car, a 1925 two-door coach, was sent on a promotional tour of the United States. Here it's shown with Chevy's assistant general sales manager C. E. Dawson (left) and company president William S. Knudsen. 3. Bodies meet their chassis on a 1925 Chevrolet assembly line.

1

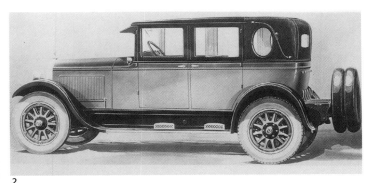

2

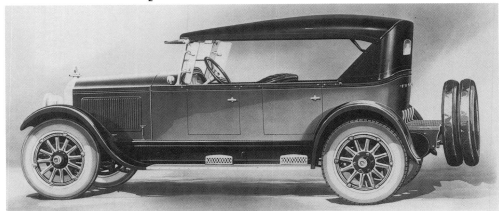

3

1-2. Buick sales hit a record for 1926, vaulting the company into third place behind Ford and Chevrolet. Both the Standard Six and Master Six lines got larger engines—the Standard growing to 207 cid from 191, the Master to 274 from 255—along with some other mechanical refinements and minor styling revisions. Also, the beefier tire/smaller wheel combination optional in 1925 became standard in '26, leaving all models riding on 6.00 x 21 rolling stock—and looking the better for it. Pictured are a $1795 Master Six coupe (left) and a $1925 Master Six Brougham touring (right). **3.** For the first time, closed cars were more popular than open cars in the Buick line, but that certainly wasn't the fault of the attractive $1525 Master Six Sport touring. **4.** Chevrolets were known as Superior Series V for 1926, and the line was anchored by this $510 roadster. **5.** At the opposite end of Chevy's price spectrum was the new $765 Landau Sedan, with dummy landau irons mounted to the rear corners of the fabric-covered steel roof. Like the vinyl tops that became popular in the 1960s, this was an attempt to mimic convertible styling on a hardtop body. What's odd is that in 1926, open cars were still generally less expensive than their closed counterparts. Note the solid steel wheels, a more conventional upmarket item.

4

5

1. Not to be outdone, coupe versions of Chevrolet's Superior Series V came standard with the dummy landau treatment. Steel wheels were included in the $625 price. 2. For those steeped in tradition, wood spoke wheels were still available, though they were standard only on Chevy's least-expensive models: the open roadster and touring, and closed two-door coupe. 3. Though a mild-mannered Chevrolet would seem an odd choice for a sporty "Boat Tail"

conversion, that didn't stop the Mercury Body Company of Louisville, Kentucky, from creating Speedster sheetmetal for this 1926 Superior Series V. The kits were installed at the dealership and included a folding top, side curtains, and related hardware, all of which could be stored in the sleek, tapered trunk. This was about as close as Chevy dealers would get to offering a sports car until the Corvette appeared for 1953.

1-2. Oldsmobile's offerings carried into 1926 with few changes, still wearing the squared-up radiator shell that had replaced an arched shell the year before. Sharp eyes might notice the cars sat a bit lower thanks to a one-inch roof chop and slightly lowered suspension, but that would hardly seem to account for a sales increase of more than 20 percent to a record 51,988, good for a hop from 13th to 12th in the industry. Chrome plating began replacing nickel in late 1925, and this sedan sports the shiny surface on its radiator shell and bumpers, the latter being part of the deluxe package that also included the motometer atop the radiator. The natural wood-spoke wheels were an option to the standard painted wheels, as were steel disc wheels. Newly available were two-tone Duco color combinations. The four-door sedan started at $1025 in standard form, $1115 in deluxe trim.

1

2

1. Oldsmobile coupes added landau irons for 1926. Prices were $925 for a standard version, $990 for the deluxe (shown). Looking very similar to the Olds was the new-for-1926 Pontiac. Sold by Oakland dealers, it carried a 36-hp 186.5-cid six in a 110-inch-wheelbase Chevrolet chassis. Only two versions were offered: a two-passenger coupe **(2)** and a five-passenger coach **(3)**. Both sold for $825.

1

2

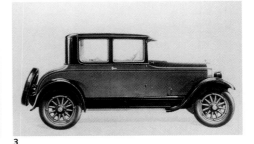

3

1. Some minor changes to the engine and engine mounts prompted Buick's 1927 sales slogan "Vibrationless Beyond Belief." Buick's most popular car was the $1495 Master Six sedan. Master Six models were built on either a 120- or 128-inch wheelbase; this sedan rode the shorter span. **2.** Built on the longer 128-inch chassis was the Master Six Brougham, at $1925. **3.** Buick's Standard Six line rode a 114.5-inch wheelbase. It's represented here by the $1275 coupe.

4

5

6

7

4-5. Styling changes that included a new radiator shell and bullet-type headlights helped Chevrolet's 1927 Capitol Series become the most popular car in America. Also helping was that Ford shut down its plants for several months to re-tool for the upcoming Model A. Best-seller of Chevy's line was the $695 coach, shown with newly standard steel disc wheels.
6-8. Buyers who didn't need a rear seat could get a $625 coupe, shown with optional bumpers and nickel-plated landau irons. A similar-looking car called the Sports Cabriolet hosted Chevy's first trunk-mounted rumble seat.

8

1

1. Just as Oakland dealers had been given the lower-priced Pontiac a year earlier, Cadillac dealers welcomed the new "downmarket" LaSalle in 1927. It marked the first time a stylist was called in to help design a car (see sidebar). LaSalles were mounted on 125- and 134-inch chassis and powered by a 75-hp 303-cid V-8. Prices ranged from $2495 for a four-passenger phaeton to $4700 for a Town Cabriolet. This convertible listed for $2635.

HARLEY EARL
1893–1969

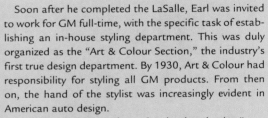

The first LaSalle will be forever famous, not only as a beautiful car, but for its impact on Cadillac and General Motors as a whole. Its designer, of course, was Harley Earl, the Californian who signed a consultant's contract with Cadillac early in 1926, drawn up specifically with the LaSalle in mind.

Harley Earl earned a strong reputation as chief designer for the Don Lee studio in Los Angeles, which specialized in building custom-bodied cars for Hollywood's elite. Cadillac general manager Lawrence P. Fisher was impressed with his "total approach" to car design. Earl created complete automobiles—the main body, hood, fenders, lights, and other parts were designed in relation to each other, blending into a unified whole. This was in contrast to most contemporary custom body designers, who usually worked from the cowl back, while leaving the area forward as a "given." Moreover, Earl used modeling clay to evolve the form of various body components—in those days clay was a highly unusual material for that purpose.

The 1927 LaSalle was the first mass-produced car to be deliberately "styled," at least in the way we use the term today. Its lines were somewhat reminiscent of the Hispano-Suiza—no surprise, really, since Earl was quite familiar with contemporary European design trends. In contrast to its square-cornered contemporaries, the LaSalle had graceful "tablespoon" fenders and smooth contours. The hood and cowl were sometimes painted a darker shade than the main body. The result was a gracefully handsome car, a fact not lost on GM's astute management.

Soon after he completed the LaSalle, Earl was invited to work for GM full-time, with the specific task of establishing an in-house styling department. This was duly organized as the "Art & Colour Section," the industry's first true design department. By 1930, Art & Colour had responsibility for styling all GM products. From then on, the hand of the stylist was increasingly evident in American auto design.

In 1938, Earl created another landmark: the "concept" or "dream" car, built to forecast future production ideas and whet (or test) the public's appetite for them. This was the famous Buick "Y-Job," with concealed headlamps and the toothy grille that prefigured production designs. Future concepts he either helped design or influenced toured the country in the Fifties as the fabulously successful Motorama, and he is credited—along with Alfred Sloan—with the annual model change.

Like all famous designers, Earl later became more of a manager and a judge of what to approve than a designer himself, and for this reason he has been credited with both more and less than he personally created. But without him, cars built between 1930 and 1958 would have been different. And not nearly as exciting.

Earl saw his career in simple terms: "All my life, my main purpose has been to lower and lengthen the automobile....oblongs are more appealing to the eye than squares." He also valued his anonymity. So he would probably be amused that in 2003, certain commercials began featuring an actor impersonating him, "the da Vinci of Detroit," returned on behalf of Buick. The cars were shown with his trademark fedora on the hood and the caption, "Harley Earl was here." And, in a way, he was.

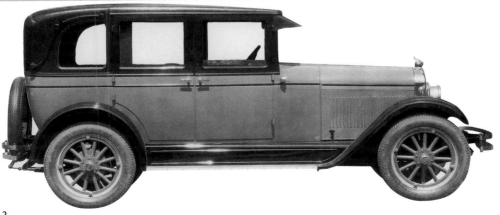

2

2. Added to Pontiac's line for 1927 was the make's first four-door model, the $895 Landau sedan. It featured a leather-covered rear roof section with dummy landau irons along with rear window shades and a foot rest for rear passengers. Like other Pontiacs, it sat on a 110-inch wheelbase and had a mildly tuned 36-hp 186.5-cid six-cylinder engine.

1-2. Buick's $1795 Country Club coupe (right), with its canvas-covered hard top and dummy landau irons, was in its final year. Its restyled fenders, radiator shell, hood, and headlights were shared with other 1928 Buicks, including the $1525 Master Six Sport Touring (below), the first Buick to carry side-mounted spare tires.

1

2

3. To combat Ford's new Model A, Chevrolet introduced the National Series AB for 1928. Wheelbase was stretched four inches to 107, all of it going beneath an elongated hood that gave the car a more powerful appearance—though the engine remained the old 171-cid four. The most notable mechanical improvement was the addition of front brakes, making this the first Chevy to have brakes on all four wheels. The Sports Cabriolet with standard rumble seat (shown) went through an interesting transition during the year. On early versions, which listed for $665, the canvas top was stretched over a fixed frame and thus didn't go down. At midyear, the model was given a proper folding top along with a $695 price tag.

3

1. Perhaps the most prestigious model in Chevrolet's 1928 lineup was the $715 Imperial Landau with its dummy landau irons. 2. Chevy's $595 coupe wore the fabric top and landau irons of the Cabriolet but lacked a rumble seat. 3. Despite a $495 starting price, sales of Chevy's touring model were a fraction of what they'd been early in the decade.

4-5. Now in its second model year, the LaSalle changed little except for the substitution of 28 narrow hood louvers for the previous 12 wide ones. This sporty convertible coupe listed for $2550. Unlike many LaSalles of the period, its body is all one color; others were painted so that the hood and cowl were a different hue than the rest of the car. It was built on a 125-inch wheelbase, seven inches shorter than that of its comparable sibling over at sister-division Cadillac. A longer 134-inch chassis was employed by LaSalle for its large five- and seven-passenger sedans, a span four inches shorter than on similar Cadillacs.

1

1. Oaklands grew considerably for 1928 in both size and power. Wheelbases were up four inches to 117, while the six-cylinder engine went from 185 cid and 45 hp to 212 cid and 60 hp. Oddly, prices actually dropped, with most models listing for $20 to $100 less than in 1927. An Oakland four-door sedan (shown) listed for $1145 vs. $1195 the year before. 2. Formerly known as a touring, the five-passenger Oakland phaeton went for $1075, $20 less than in '27. 3. Oldsmobiles were redesigned for 1928 on a 113.5-inch wheelbase. Three-inch-wider bodies provided more interior room, and beneath the hood lay a new 197-cid six with 55 hp. A distinctive styling element was a molding that ran along the bottom of the hood, curved up the side of the cowl, then arched toward the front of the car to meet with its mate at the radiator. This $925 coupe was the least expensive car in the line.

2

3

THE POWERS THAT BE—AND WOULD SOON BE

A photograph taken at the Delco-Remy Division plant in Anderson, Indiana, in 1928 captured several luminaries who had made a name for themselves in the hallowed halls of General Motors—or were soon going to. In the first row, third from left, is Alfred P. Sloan, Jr., then president of GM. Next to him, in the white suit, is C. E. Wilson, general manager of Delco-Remy, who would become GM president in 1941. Next to Wilson—in derby and spats—is William S. "Big Bill" Knudsen, a long-time GM man who was then vice-president and would be named president in 1937. At far left in the back row is the bespectacled Charles F. Kettering, the man behind the ground-breaking electric starter introduced on Cadillacs in 1912, as well as the ill-fated Copper Cooled Chevrolet of 1923.

1. Buicks were redesigned and renamed for 1929. The former Standard Series was now called the Series 116 and was fitted with a new 239-cid six rated at 74 hp. Meanwhile, the Master Series cars (on two wheelbases) were christened the Series 121 and Series 129 and were powered by a new 310-cid six developing 91 hp. In all cases, the Series number related to wheelbase length, which was up about one inch in all models. Shown is the rakish Series 129 "close coupled" Model 51 four-door sedan, which sold for $1875. The trunk, bumpers, side-mounted spares, and wood-spoke wheels cost extra.

1. For its otherwise little-changed 1929 line, Cadillac introduced an industry first: the Synchro-Mesh transmission. It was a major innovation, as it eliminated the gear clashing that traditionally accompanied shifts from one gear to the next. The feature would quick-

SYNCHRO-MESH: SHIFTING WITHOUT TEARS

In the early years of the 20th century, the typical three-speed manual transmission contained free-spinning gears that had to be "synchronized" by the driver in order to mesh without nasty crunches, usually by "double-clutching" and careful applications of engine speed. Shifting was thus somewhat of a demanding process that proved cumbersome and well-nigh impossible for many to learn. That all changed after Earl A. Thompson, a college professor and inventor from Oregon, developed the synchromesh transmission.

Working strictly on his own, Thompson came up with a grind-free, easy-shifting transmission with all gears constantly in mesh. Only one pair of gears at a time was locked to the shaft on which it was mounted; the others simply freewheeled. The locking mechanism for each gear was a "dog collar" mounted to the shaft that slid to mate the teeth on its inner surface with teeth on the outside circumference of the gear hub, thereby locking the gear to the shaft. Brass cones served as clutches to help match the gear speed to the shaft speed before the

collar locked in place. With synchromesh, what had previously been a tricky, comparatively time-consuming process could suddenly be accomplished smoothly and quickly by virtually anyone.

Using this concept, Thompson built a crude prototype gearbox, installed it in a Cadillac, drove the car to Detroit, and convinced Cadillac's chief engineer, Ernest Seaholm, to take a test drive. Seaholm was impressed and had a group of engineers develop the concept for production. Thompson initially served as a paid consultant, then as a staff member, and eventually Cadillac's assistant chief engineer.

Cadillac introduced Synchro-Mesh transmissions for 1929. The concept was quickly adopted in one form or another by the other General Motors divisions and then by rival manufacturers. By the end of the Thirties, synchromesh (one word, lower case when used as a generic term) was in widespread use. Today we take it for granted, but in 1929, Synchro-Mesh was a miracle and a major development in the history of the automobile.

ly be adopted by the entire industry. **2-4.** Chevrolets were called the International Series AC for 1929, and though they sported minor styling changes that left them looking lower and beefier, the real news was under the hood. Replacing the long-running 171-cid four-cylinder engine was a new 194-cid six—which would carry on even longer. Advertised as "The Six for the Price of a Four," the International Series sold in record numbers. A $645 Sport Coupe is shown with standard rumble seat and optional wire wheels and side-mounted spares. Its six-cylinder engine would become known as "The Cast-Iron Wonder." In initial 1929 form, it produced 46 hp—a substantial 11-hp increase over the outgoing four.

1. LaSalle's V-8 engine went from 303 cid to 328 cid for 1929, prompting a name change from Series 303 to Series 328. A $2595 sedan shows off that year's new fender-mounted parking lights. 2. Oldsmobile sales set a record in 1929 despite few changes to the model line. Helping little in the total tally was the $945 phaeton, of which fewer

than 80 were sold. 3. Pontiacs received significant styling changes for 1929, including a split radiator shell and a concave feature line running beneath the side windows. They also got a boost from 36 hp to 48. 4. Just as Oakland had done with the Pontiac and Cadillac with the LaSalle, Oldsmobile adopted a companion make for 1929. But unlike the others, this one was more expensive. The Viking rode a lengthy 125-inch wheelbase and came with a 260-cid V-8. This convertible listed for $1770, while the most expensive Oldsmobile cost less than $1200. As it turned out, it was hardly what Olds dealers needed, as the Roaring Twenties' high-flying financial plane was about to crash.

CHAPTER FOUR

1930-1939

"Brother, can you spare a dime?"
—E. Y. Harburg, 1932

No one who lived through the Great Depression would ever forget it. "You'd return from work on Fridays, wondering whether you'd still have a home to return to," said one New Yorker, recalling the rampant foreclosures that followed the Wall Street crash and relentless decline in wages and employment. By 1933, over a quarter of the U.S. workforce was idle.

Alfred Sloan took a wait-and-see attitude to the crash, and ironically, like several others, GM produced some of its most memorable products in the early Depression. Notable among these was the Cadillac Sixteen, top of the Cadillac line from 1930 to 1939; and the 1932 Chevrolet Confederate, the most beautiful Chevy produced up to then.

In the Twenties, luxury automakers spoke of "multi-cylinder" engines, hoping for more smoothness and power from the low octane fuels then available. Cadillac chief engineer Ernest Seaholm, apprised of upcoming Packard, Pierce, and Lincoln V-12s and the Peerless V-16, decided to meet the challenge. Assigned to the project was Owen Nacker, a young Detroiter who had worked for Buick and Brush before joining Cadillac in 1927. His V-16 was a work of art.

Every bolt and pipe of the engine was chromed; the exhaust manifold was finished in contrasting black porcelain. Rocker covers were finned and made of polished aluminum with a black enamel finish. With a bore and stroke of 3×4 inches, its 452 cubic inches gave 175 hp and an incredible 360 pound-feet of torque; the car could be driven off from a dead stop in top gear. With the right rear-axle ratio a Sixteen would do 0-60 in less than 20 seconds. Nacker also created the companion Cadillac Twelve (1931–36) that had wide parts inter-changeability, and used it to disguise his main purpose: drawings and requests for price quotes

carefully referred only to the V-12, so the V-16 took the industry by surprise. The majestic new Cadillac offered a vast array of special-order Fisher and Fleetwood coachwork, in addition to standard bodies, priced up to $9000. Production was limited, totaling just 3250 for the 1930 model year. By contrast, the Cadillac Eight ($3295-$5145) saw 11,000 copies.

The companion LaSalle racked up nearly 15,000 sales in the 1930 model year, thanks to new styling that gave it a visual relationship with the senior cars, and a V-8 displacing the same as the 1929 Cadillac. Thirteen factory body styles were catalogued, arrayed in Fisher and Fleetwood groups and priced at $2490-$3995.

Buick spent its energy restyling so people wouldn't call its 1930 models "pregnant." Chief engineer "Dutch" Bower stressed ride comfort and more horsepower, while adding vacuum-servo-assisted brakes and thermostatically controlled radiator shutters. But the cars arrived at the wrong time and sales were off by a third, including only 12,000 Marquettes, the last of the companion make.

The 1930 Chevrolet was mechanically improved, with a stronger bottom end and 50 horsepower. The rear axle was also stronger; Lovejoy hydraulic shocks were standard. Prices were now within $65 of Ford, which Chevy outsold, though its tally was under 620,000.

During 1929, Oakland general manager A. R. Glancy concluded that Pontiac was adequately covering his six-cylinder market and fitted the 1930 Oakland with an 85-hp V-8: a powerful, short-stroke L-head with horizontal valves, a feature borrowed from Oldsmobile's Viking. This new Oakland looked similar to the previous six but was quicker, topping out at more than 70 mph. Pontiac's 1930 6-40B had a larger, 220-cid engine, the "New Series Big Six," with 60 hp squeezed out by engineer Ben Anibal.

Oldsmobile faced the Depression with a handsome restyle, the F-30, riding a lower chassis and smaller wheels on an unchanged wheelbase. The best model was the Patrician sedan, with twin sidemount spares and wire wheels. But Oldsmobile's price class was the first to feel the economic downturn. Barely 50,000 were built, including some 2000 Vikings, the last of that line.

Hard times continued in 1931, but Alfred Sloan was now making changes. He created the GM Engineering Staff, under Ormond E. Hunt, to develop and evaluate new production concepts. It had taken Sloan ten years, but finally there were clear lines of technical responsibility, an infrastructure on which the divisions could rely.

Starting in 1931, Buick built only eights: 207- to 274-cid overhead valve engines producing 77 to 104 hp, designed by recent Italian immigrant John Dolza. They were nice cars, but Buick was hurting even more—only 88,417 were built in 1931.

Cadillac, although now offering a V-12, relied on its V-8 as the breadwinner. LaSalle was a best buy, since it carried the 1930 353-cid Caddy V-8, and with prices slashed, you could own a LaSalle for as little as $2195. Yet the division built only 15,012 Cadillacs, the worst tally in ten years. LaSalle was just over 10,000.

For his new chief engineer, Chevy general manager Bill Knudsen picked James Mark Crawford, 47, who had been Hunt's assistant. Succeeding Richard Grant as sales manger was Harry Klinger, brought over from Delco. Though demand was falling, Chevrolet was not as vulnerable to the Depression as its sister makes, and the 1931 Chevy "Independence" managed to maintain production close to its 1930 level.

The last year for Oakland was 1931: Its V-8 had sold reasonably well but was a case of too much car in a crowded field. Pontiac, meanwhile, was treated to longer bodies on a new 112-inch-wheelbase chassis, Synchro-Mesh transmission, one-piece crowned fenders, and a crisp-looking radiator.

Oldsmobile cut back to Standard and DeLuxe series for the 1931 F-31 line; wheel diameter was reduced for a longer look, though styling was little changed. Olds too now had Synchro-Mesh and more power. Production totaled close to 50,000.

By 1932, manufacturers were going out of business left and right. Durant Motors, Billy's last empire, collapsed, along with Stutz, Marmon, and Peerless. Studebaker and Willys-Overland were headed for bankruptcy. GM was hanging on, though its plants were operating at 30 percent of capacity.

"Big Bill" Knudsen became executive vice-president in 1933, and Chevy sales manager Harry Klinger was named general manager of Pontiac. To lower overhead, the Operations Committee combined Chevrolet and Pontiac manufacturing and melded Buick and Oldsmobile production management. Sloan reinforced his electrical supply line by buying Packard Electric at Warren, Ohio.

Design-wise, 1932–33 marked an important watershed between the more upright classic forms and the age of streamlining. The '33s were noticeably smoother and more rounded, with raked windshields and radiators, teardrop-shaped headlamps, and deeper, skirted fenders.

Buick restyled in 1932, adopting a more rounded body, modern but still conservative. Available on all Buicks was a new "Wizard Control," a combination of freewheeling and an automatic. But with dealers going out of business in droves, production plummeted to 41,522.

Cadillac began hinting at streamlining in 1932, with longer front fenders and a beautiful "tombstone" radiator. A tasteful but mild facelift graced the 1933 models. Most significant was a redesigned 1932 gearbox, with constant-mesh helical gears for all forward speeds and ball bearings instead of rollers. A vacuum-operated clutch permitted clutchless shifting.

Wisely, Lawrence Fisher didn't cut Cadillac's engineering budget. Maurice Olley was working on his revolutionary "Knee-Action" independent front suspension, Synchro-Mesh inventor Earl Thompson on automatic transmission. Fisher's vision and perseverance in new developments would enable GM to come roaring back when prosperity returned.

Thanks to Harley Earl, Chevrolet was never more beautiful than in 1932, when it seemed like a scaled-down Cadillac Sixteen. Smaller wire wheels imparted a lower stance for the new Confederate Series, which offered twenty models at $490-$640. The 1933 Eagle series was more streamlined, but in a coy sort of way, with diminutive fender skirting. The Eagle name (which later wound up on a Willys and then a Chrysler product) was eventually replaced by the name that would stick: Master. A lower-priced line called Mercury was offered in March 1933.

Although Chevrolet was up against the V-8 Ford, it was the first GM make to show an upturn in the Depression. Against 1932's rock bottom 307,000, production rose to 486,000 in 1933. And Knudsen's loss as general manager had been made good by the able Marvin Coyle, the former comptroller, who had joined Chevy in 1917.

Oldsmobile's new chief engineer, Charles McCuen, had designed the Olds six; now he produced the new L-32 straight eight. Olds styling followed that of the other divisions: smoother body contours, more flowing fenders, hood ventilator doors, slightly slanted windshields.

Pontiac Motor Division continued an ersatz "Oakland" with the Pontiac 302 V-8 series, smoothly styled and sold alongside the six, but sales were bad. Under Harry Klinger in 1933, Pontiac altered its image completely, dropping both the V-8 and the six and positioning itself nicely as the first step up from Chevrolet with a solid, reliable sidevalve eight. Compared to 1932's production of 42,633 cars, Pontiac built close to 90,000 in 1933.

The middle Thirties were a time of stabilization at General Motors, with production and sales returning to the control of each division. Chevrolet seesawed with Ford for sales leadership and finally achieved it for a 20-year stretch starting in 1936; Oldsmobile, Pontiac, and Buick held fifth, sixth, and seventh positions behind Chevy, Ford, Plymouth, and Dodge.

A key 1934 innovation was Maurice Olley's new "Knee-Action" independent front suspension, consisting of upper A-arms and lower transverse control arms inboard of the forward chassis side rails where they could pivot, a coil spring on each side. Next, in 1935–36, came all-steel "Turret-Top" construction, making for more-solid and quieter cars throughout the lines.

In 1933 the redoubtable Harlow Curtice was named to head Buick, which he shook up fiercely (see sidebar, page 72). Output rose from 79,000 to 179,000 between 1934 and 1936, thanks to good looking, successively more powerful models. In 1935 Curtice introduced now-famous model names: the Series 40 Special, Series 50 Super, and Series 90 Limited. That "factory hot rod," the 1936 Buick Century, packed a 120-hp eight into a light chassis for 100+ mph and lightning acceleration. Roadmaster, another famous luxury model, also began in 1936.

As Curtice took the reins of Buick, the capable Nicholas Dreystadt relieved long-serving Lawrence Fisher at Cadillac. At age 35, Dreystadt had gone to work for Caddy in 1916 and was running the Clark Avenue plant by 1932, when he convinced management not to drop Cadillac in favor of LaSalle (a fortunate move). Division production pushed 30,000 by 1936—now thanks to Harley Earl convincing Sloan and Knudsen not to drop LaSalle! Dropping either make at this time would have been a mistake. The 1934 LaSalle, styled by Julio Andrade and Jules Agramonte, evoked the streamlined age with "pontoon" fenders and "biplane" bumpers, "porthole" vents in the hood sides, and a beautifully tall, slim radiator. There was one catch, Dreystadt was told: It must cost much less than previous LaSalles. So it emerged with a chassis and powertrain shared with Oldsmobile.

Cadillac in 1934 acquired a new monobloc V-8 (322 and 346 cubic inches), the first new engine in eight years, and, in 1936, a lower-priced Model 60, to plug a gap between Caddy and LaSalle. With Cadillac's refined styling, X-frame chassis, new hydraulic brakes, and improved three-speed transmission, the 60 completely overshadowed the '36 LaSalle.

Chevrolet built its ten-millionth car in November 1934; a year marked by an improved six. (A V-8 to compete with Ford was considered but rejected.) Turret-Top all-steel bodies and a Master Deluxe arrived for 1935, hydraulic brakes (which Ford still didn't have) for 1936, a colossal year for Chevy, which saw close to one million vehicles built.

Oldsmobile in the middle-Thirties rose from its dreadful low of 1933 to nearly 200,000 cars per year. In 1935–36, general manager C. L. McCuen added plant capacity and handsomely designed models. Pontiac, similarly placed to do well as the economy recovered, held pat in 1934 and restyled in 1935, the first year of the famous "Silver Streak" design hallmark, brainstorm of a young stylist named Virgil Exner. By 1935, Pontiac had replaced Studebaker as the world's largest producer of straight eights.

Despite a loss-causing strike, GM was breathing easier in 1937, thanks to Alfred Sloan, whose management sense and feel for talent had served the corporation well. In May of that year, Sloan became general manager, succeeding Lammont Du Pont, though the Delaware family remained GM's majority stockholders. There was no doubt as to who would be named president: William S. Knudsen (see sidebar, page 88).

A sharp, unexpected recession blunted the nation's economic recovery in 1938, but because of its size, financial reserves, and economies of scale, GM weathered the setback better than its rivals. Recovery began in 1939, when Curtice's Buick did so well as to finish fourth in production behind the "low-priced three," a position it would generally hold in the years ahead.

Engine designer Harry Smith was responsible for Buick's new 100-hp straight eight for the 1937 Special and a larger eight with a counterweighted crankshaft, revised camming, and carburetion. In 1938 Buick achieved two industry firsts: coil-spring rear suspension and the first of what came to be known as the "dream cars."

The friendly relationship between Harlow Curtice and Harley Earl resulted in a 1938 Roadmaster-based special known only as the "Y-Job." This low, two-passenger roadster, largely designed by George Snyder, featured hidden headlamps and door hinges, front fenders extended back into the door area, a long rear deck evoking the boattail speedster, and a toothy vertical bar grille. Though nobody knew it then, the Y-Job accurately forecast future production styling.

Buick took on a new look in 1939 by reskinning its bodies and adopting a lower, roughly triangular grille. On coupes and convertibles, rumble seats gave way to cramped rear "opera" seats.

The '37 LaSalle edged closer to its parent by acquiring the 1936 Cadillac 60's 322-cid V-8, while the 60 itself gained the 346-cid Cadillac engine. As LaSalle production doubled, nobody noticed that Cadillac had given up on the Twelve and was relying almost entirely on the V-8. Twelves had always outsold Sixteens, whose production was only 464 in 1937, but a new Sixteen was now being planned.

Cadillac surprised the industry again in 1938 with a styling tour de force and an all-new Sixteen. The former was the magnificent Sixty-Special, a handsome sedan that made the reputation of young William L. Mitchell. Its significance cannot be overstated. It was the first American car conceived as a total design, rather than a collection of elements. The Sixty-Special cost 25 percent more than conventional 60s but was "longer, lower, and wider," the vernacular of the future. Many of its ideas influenced other Cadillacs, including the new Series 90 Sixteen, powered by a surprise development: an all-new L-head engine. It was better than its predecessor in every way. A sidevalve design, it was partly dictated by cost and ended up with half as many parts as the original V-16.

Chevrolet was completely new in 1937: a clever, low-cost restyle on the old chassis with smoother, sleeker bodies, more glass, and better-integrated fenders and grille. Its new engine offered 85 hp; there was a hypoid bevel rear axle and a lighter three-speed gearbox with simplified Synchro-Mesh. The Chevrolet truck line also benefited significantly from passenger car styling.

Chevrolet made only detail changes in its '38 models, continuing with the solid-axle Master and the independent-front-suspension Master Deluxe. A cowl-forward '39 facelift inspired by Cadillac (Earl liked to spread divisional styling ideas around) made the cars look longer and lower, even though the wheelbase hadn't changed. This year saw an end to Chevy's trunkless "beaver-back" sedans, and rumble seats gave way to inside seating on coupes and convertibles. A wood-body four-door, eight-passenger station wagon built by Midstates Body Company was new this year.

Oldsmobile set a record of 212,000 vehicles in 1937, leveled off in 1938, then rebounded in 1939. Styling was on the corporate mold with extended hood lines, shorter grilles, and lower ride height. Oldsmobile for 1939 was an expanded line with fresh styling, a more conventional-looking front end, and numerical model designations.

At Pontiac, both 1937 L-heads were much as before but with larger displacement and horsepower. The public was seduced by the good-looking '37s, and production was well over 200,000. The line stood pat in 1938 but came back strong in 1939 with a new low-end series called the "Quality Six," carrying the same engine as the Deluxe Six but on a smaller wheelbase and including a woody wagon. The Deluxe Eight continued as before. Pontiac styling was similar to LaSalle's and Oldsmobile's, but the Pontiac "face" was a complex amalgam of vertical-bar sub-grilles and a horizontal-striped center that blended into the "Silver Streak" trim and the by-now de rigueur Indian head hood ornament.

America entered the Forties in a hopeful mood. The worst of the Depression was over and prosperity was "just around the corner," as Herbert Hoover had promised in vain in 1932. At General Motors, Sloan and Knudsen breathed a joint sigh of relief, deciding that the Forties could be a very good decade indeed as long as nothing happened to change it.

1. This lavish GM auto "Salon" display, staged in the ballroom of the Old Astor Hotel in New York, was a predecessor of the GM Motoramas of the 1950s. **2.** Buick's new Series 50 consisted of just two models, a four-door sedan and this handsome $1510 four-passenger coupe. **3.** Top-of-the-line Buicks were the new Series 60 models. The Country Club Coupe mimicked ragtop styling with its fabric-covered top and dummy landau irons.

1

2

3

4. A beltline molding and lower stance minimized Buick's "pregnant" look, as on this 1930 Series 40 phaeton. Its 258-cid six developed 81 hp. Priced at $1310, only 1100 were sold. **5.** Cadillac surprised the automotive world with the industry's first V-16. This V-16-powered seven-passenger sedan is one of just 47 built. **6.** Then as now, celebrities demanded glamorous transportation. This Cadillac V-8 town car was more than enough luxury car for actress Delores Del Rio (pictured left).

4

5

6

1. V-16 Cadillacs were available in a plethora of body styles; some 33 variants were listed, starting at a pricey $5350. Convertible coupes like this one started at $5900. Only 100 were made. 2-3. Cadillac utilized Fleetwood bodies constructed in two plants: one in Detroit, one in Fleetwood, Pennsylvania. The vee'd windshield on this V-16 all-weather phaeton indicates it was built in Pennsylvania.

4. Chevrolet's biggest seller in 1930 was the $565 coach, a two-door sedan model that attracted 255,027 buyers. Options included wood-spoke wheels, sidemount spare tires, spare-tire covers, and a cigar lighter. 5. Chevrolet's 194-cid "stovebolt" six was introduced in 1929. For 1930, it was updated to put out 50 horsepower, a four-hp boost. The $615 sports coupe saw sales of 45,311. 6. The $515 Chevrolet sport roadster, equipped with rumble seat and wire wheels, outsold the $495 standard roadster 27,651 to 5684.

1. For 1930, all LaSalles rode the same 134-inch-wheelbase chassis and were powered by a 90-hp, 340-cid V-8. This convertible coupe wears LaSalle's unique two-tone paint treatment on the body moldings and windshield frame. 2. This Oldsmobile convertible roadster is accessorized with sidemount spares and a touring trunk. 3. All Oaklands, this jaunty sport roadster included, used an 85-horsepower, 250 cubic-inch V-8 engine with a 180-degree crankshaft.

1

2

3

4

4. Oldsmobile's most popular body style for 1930 was the four-door sedan (shown here), which accounted for just over 19,000 sales. A higher-level Patrician sedan was also introduced, with broadcloth upholstery and fancier interior trimmings. 5. Topping Pontiac's 1930 "Big Six" line was the $785 Custom four-door sedan. The sole Pontiac engine was a 200-cubic-inch six that made 60 horsepower. "Big brother" Oakland models got a 251-cid V-8 with 85 hp.

5

1. Buick's new top-echelon Series 90 models, like this $1620 Phaeton, used the division's largest, most-powerful engine: a 104-hp, 344.8-cid straight eight. 2. The roadster was the lightest and the cheapest of the V-16 Cadillacs, but it still tipped the scales at a whopping 5310 pounds and cost a princely $5350. 3. Popular bandleader Paul Whiteman, the self-proclaimed "King of Jazz," poses with a handsome Cadillac V-16.

3

4. This $650 Special sedan was one of two four-door sedans in this year's Chevrolet line. The other was a less fancy $635 standard sedan. The headlight buckets and tie bar now came chromed for all Chevrolet passenger cars. 5. The coach remained Chevrolet's best-selling model in 1931 with 228,616 built. This example wears some popular accessories of the period: dual sidemount spares, whitewall tires, luggage trunk, radiator guard screen, and quail radiator ornament. 6. Chevrolet introduced a new "five-passenger coupe" model for 1931. Its "bustleback" bodystyle was comparable to Ford's Model A Victoria, but Chevrolet's version boasted a small decklid for external trunk access. Ford Victoria owners had to pull the rear seatback forward to access the trunk. Sales of the five-passenger coupe reached 20,297.

4

5

6

1. The 1931 Chevrolet passenger cars boasted a wheelbase lengthened by two inches to 109, plus new styling highlighted by a taller, larger radiator and more hood louvers. Wire wheels displaced the previous disc wheels as standard equipment. Deluxe Phaetons like the one pictured here started at $510 and saw sales of just 852. **2.** In 1931, Chevrolet was eight years away from offering its first "woody" station wagon, but aftermarket firms built them on the $355 commercial-car chassis that Chevrolet offered separately. This example was built to replicate a body originally constructed by the Mifflinburg Body Company. **3.** Functional top irons quickly distinguished Chevrolet's cabriolet from the similar-looking sport roadster. Both were four-passsenger models with a standard rumble seat. The cabriolet started at $615, but this example wears numerous extra-cost factory accessories including bumpers, whitewall tires, trunk rack, and sidemount spare.

1

2

3

4

4. Pontiacs got a double-bead beltline molding and single-bar bumpers for 1931. Two-door sedans like this one cost $675. **5.** Oakland business coupes started at $895—$220 more than a comparable Pontiac. Sales of the upstart Pontiac brand were handily outpacing those of its corporate "parent" Oakland, leading GM to discontinue the Oakland nameplate after 1931.

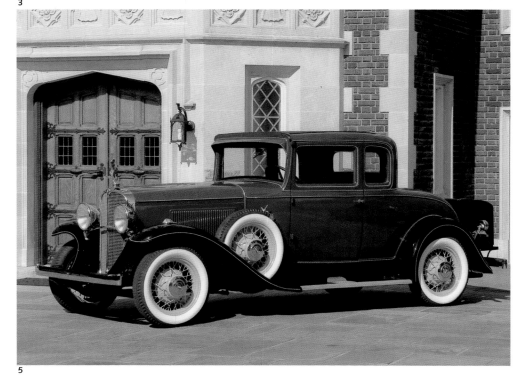

5

1. At \$935, the Series 50 business coupe was Buick's most affordable car. A new five-window body replaced 1931's three-window design. The wood-spoked wheels seen here were dropped at the end of the model year. **2.** The \$1310 five-passenger sedan was the most popular car in Buick's midlevel Series 60 line. The Series 60 straight-eight engine produced 95 hp from its 272.6 cubic inches. **3.** Buick's top level Series 90 lineup featured this handsome five-passenger convertible phaeton bodystyle, which started at \$1830. Only 269 were produced. **4.** The glamorous Cadillac Series 370B all-weather phaeton weighed 5385 pounds and cost \$4195. Its 368-cubic-inch V-12 put out 135 horsepower.

5. The \$2945 Cadillac V-8 convertible rode on a 134-inch wheelbase. This was the shortest chassis that Cadillac offered, but even these "junior" Cadillacs were about a foot longer than the typical nonluxury car of the day.
6. This V-16 four-door sedan is one of several special-edition "Madame X" models Cadillac produced in the early 30s. Its unique coachwork includes a rakishly sloped windshield and slender chrome door and windshield moldings.

1. Only 419 Chevrolet DeLuxe phaetons were built for the U.S., but foreign coachbuilders increased the count. This Holden-bodied right-hand-drive version was native to Australia. **2-3.** The Chevrolet DeLuxe cabriolet started at $610, $95 more than a DeLuxe coach. **4.** A LaSalle convertible sold for $2345, but chromed hood shutters added another $18. **5-6.** Oldsmobiles were available with either a straight-six or a new straight-eight engine. When equipped with sidemount spares, the six-cylinder two-door sedan started at $920, while its four-door counterpart sold for an even $1000. **7.** At 3335 pounds and $1025, the V-8 Custom sedan was Pontiac's heaviest and most expensive model for 1932.

1

2

3

4

5

6

7

1. This GM building was erected for the Century of Progress exposition in Chicago in 1933 and '34. 2. Like other 1933 GM cars, Buicks received substantial restyling that included fuller, skirted fenders and more-sweeping body curves. Pictured here, the $1030 Series 50 sports coupe. 3. The rumble-seat-equipped Chevrolet

sport coupe started at $535. Production was 26,691. 4. This Cadillac V-16 Fleetwood-bodied sedan weighed more than 6000 lb. Art-deco four-bar bumpers were exclusive to V-16s. 5. A routine road test for a 1933 Chevrolet at GM's 1268-acre proving ground in Milford, Michigan, gets bumpy.

1

1. Chevrolets used an enlarged "Stovebolt" with 206.8 cid and a claimed 65 hp, 10 fewer than Ford's year-old V-8. The $535 sport coupe came standard with a rumble seat. Note the pivoting vent windows, an across-the-board new feature on GM's 1933 lineup. 2. Skirted fenders and a vee'd grille were new to LaSalle for 1933. The rumble-seat-equipped coupe sold for $2245, but this example wears extra-cost sidemount spare tires and Duplex Pilot Ray driving lights. LaSalle also offered a five-seat town coupe, a sedan, and a convertible—plus a trio of sedans on a six-inch-longer 136-inch wheelbase. 3. Oldsmobiles were available in two series for 1933: the eight-cylinder-powered, 119-inch-wheelbase L-Series, and the six-cylinder-powered, 115-inch-wheelbase F-Series. With 7194 sales, this $825 F-Series four-door sedan was the most popular six-cylinder Olds. For $30 more, F-series shoppers could opt for the four-door touring sedan, which featured a "bustleback" body with an integral trunk. 4. At Pontiac, six-cylinder and V-8 engines were dropped in favor of a new straight eight that displaced 223.4 cid and put out 77 horsepower. Restyled bodies featured vee'd grilles, four-louver hoods, and streamlined fenders. Two-door sedans like this one started at $635.

2

3

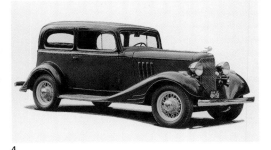

4

HARLOW HERBERT "RED" CURTICE 1892–1962

If anyone represented the spirit of unbridled optimism that typified General Motors in its glory years, from the mid-Thirties to the mid-Sixties, it was Harlow Curtice, the Michigan native who began his meteoric rise as a bookkeeper for the AC Spark Plug Division in 1914.

By 1929, aged only 36, he was AC's president; under him, AC's employment actually *rose* during the Depression. His performance was a feat of derring-do that could not fail to impress Al Sloan and Bill Knudsen. Curtice worked harder than anyone who worked for him, colleagues said; he was at his desk for long hours every day. Curtice's promotion to head Buick in 1933 was a novel event. Hitherto GM had relied on mechanics, engineers, and production people to run its divisions, whereas Curtice was a "bean counter."

Yet he possessed an uncanny feel for what customers wanted. It was Curtice who coined the famous model names Roadmaster and Special and Curtice who pushed the idea of

dropping a big eight into a light chassis and naming it after the greatest train in the world: the Century.

Curtice's efforts brought Buick to a 1000 percent sales increase in his first ten years, record volume, and fourth place in the industry when he left to become a vice president in 1948. Buick was hot on the heels of third-place Plymouth, which it actually outproduced in 1954.

Curtice succeeded Charles Wilson as GM president in 1953 and retired in 1958, having been named *Time*'s "Man of the Year" in 1955. During his presidency, GM became the first industrial corporation to make a $1 billion profit. Curtice, who often expressed a desire to "be out on the floor," made countless factory visits.

A critic described him as "Billy Durant reborn—given to quick decisions, disposing of problems with lavish hand and absolute authority...." Curtice was frank to assert, "The best committee is the committee of one." If Curtice typified the aloof arrogance of mighty corporations, he also typified that spirit of American enterprise that built the greatest economy in the world. Emerson said, "Build a better mousetrap and the world will beat a path to your door." Curtice did that.

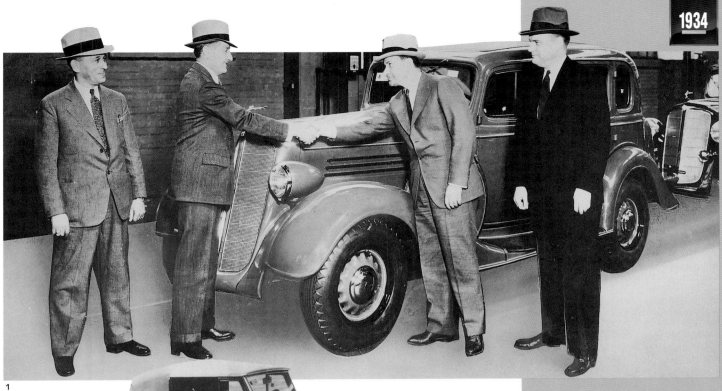

1

2

3

4

1. Buick general manager Harlow Curtice shakes hands with chief engineer F.A. Bower in front of a Series 40 four-door sedan. **2.** The rarest Series 60 Buick was the convertible coupe. Just 263 were built. **3-5.** After a highly successful showing at the Chicago Century of Progress exhibition, the stunning Cadillac V-16 Aero-Dynamic coupe was put into limited production. Only 20 were built between 1934 and '37; this 1934 model is one of only three.

5

1. Restyled Cadillacs featured lower, more-streamlined bodies and "Knee-Action" independent coil-spring front suspension. The V-8 town sedan was available on a 128-inch-wheelbase chassis for $2695, or in 136-inch-wheelbase form for $200 more. The 353-cid V-8 put out 130 hp, up 15 from '33.

1

2

2. The least-popular Chevrolet in 1934 was the phaeton, with just 234 produced. Phaetons were available in Standard trim only and sold for $495. Standard models used a 181-cid, 60-hp six. **3.** Upscale Master series Chevrolets, like this four-door sedan, got a 206.8-cid, 80-hp "Blue Streak" six; ads trumpeted "80 mph from 80 hp." "Knee-Action" independent suspension was available at extra cost on all Chevrolet models this year.

3

1

2

3

4

5

6

1. LaSalle was on the verge of extinction, but Harley Earl reportedly saved the division with a dramatic presentation of the mocked-up '34 model. Nonetheless, LaSalle's roster was whittled down to just four models for 1934, all with Fleetwood-built bodies. The four-door sedan, club sedan, and convertible coupe all started at $1695, while the coupe (shown) had a base price of $100 less. **2.** Oldsmobile continued to offer six- and eight-cylinder cars in 1934, in F-33 and L-33 series, respectively. The $780 F-series coupe came standard with a rumble seat, but covered side-mount spare tires were optional. **3.** Although they were shaped like a two-door sedan, Oldsmobile called these five-passenger, trunk-back cars "touring coupes." In F-series form, they weighed 3135 pounds and sold for $730. Rated horsepower of the 213.3-cid six was up four to 84, while the L-series straight eight output was unchanged at 90 hp. **4.** Pontiac two-door sedans sold for $705, while a new-for-'34 trunkback version could be had for $45 more. As a Deluxe-equipped model, this two-door sedan wears an Indian-maiden radiator-cap ornament. Standard-trimmed cars had a brave's head-within-a-circle ornament. **5-6.** All 1934 Pontiac models continued to use the 223.4-cid straight eight from 1933, but carburetion and cylinder-head improvements boosted horsepower from 77 to 84. The $725 sport coupe (shown here) came standard with a rumble seat. A five-window "business" coupe was available for $50 less. A single rear-mounted spare was standard, but dual side-mount spares were optional.

1. The 1935 Buicks were largely carryover models with only minor trim and color changes. The Series 60 convertible sold for $1495 and saw sales of just 111. **2.** Buick called its open Series 60 four-door a convertible phaeton in 1935. This example wears a striking two-tone finish, albeit in non-factory colors. **3.** Cadillacs were mostly unchanged from 1934, though closed Fisher-body models got all-steel "Turret-Top" roofs. The slender "bi-plane" bumpers of 1934 were nixed in favor of more substantial single bar units. The V-8 five-passenger town coupe cost $2495. **4.** The Fisher-bodied Cadillac V-8 two-passenger coupe was available on a 128-inch wheelbase for $2345, or a 136-inch span for $200 more.

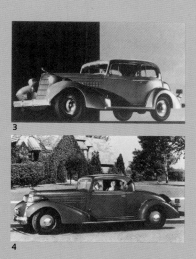

5. A Cadillac V-12 seven-passenger town cabriolet had a base price of $6295, but the extra equipment on this example pushed its original selling price to $7000. **6.** Chevrolet president Marvin E. Coyle (left) and Charles E. Wetherald, divisional vice president and general manufacturing manager, inspect the ten-millionth Chevrolet, a 1935-model Standard four-door sedan that came off the line on November 13, 1934.

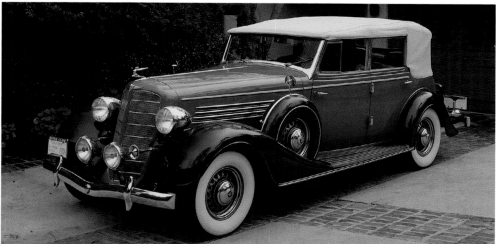

1. Chevrolet Master Deluxe models, like this $660 four-door sedan, wore streamlined new styling. 2-3. Chevrolet Standard models made do with facelifted 1934 sheetmetal. The Standard four-door sedan outsold its roadster sibling 42,049 to 1176. 4. Oldsmobile didn't produce a "woody" wagon model for 1935, but at least one prototype was built.

5-6. The 1935 Pontiac models ushered in the division's long-running "Silver Streak" styling motif. Pictured here are the Improved Eight two-door Touring sedan ($805) and sport coupe ($780). All regular production '35 Pontiacs wore rear-hinged "suicide" doors.

1. Buicks were totally redesigned for 1936. Buick built 534 Series 80 Roadmaster chassis for coachbuilders, one of which ended up as this Brewster-bodied town cabriolet. 2. Buick Centurys had 320-cid straight-eight power in a relatively small package. Here, the $1090 touring sedan.

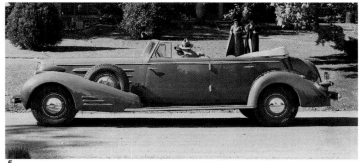

3. This $765 Special business coupe was the only Buick with a base price under $800. At 3150 lb, it was also the lightest Buick. 4. Cadillac V-16 sales had slowed to a trickle; only 52 were built this year. This V-16 town cabriolet saw military service during World War II, when it was assigned to U.S. Navy Fleet Admiral Ernest J. King. 5. The side view of this Cadillac V-16 convertible sedan shows off its lengthy 154-inch wheelbase. 6. Eager to quell the exodus of sales to Packard's One Twenty line, Cadillac introduced the lower-priced Series 60 lineup for 1936. All three Series 60 models—the coupe, convertible, and touring sedan (shown)—started below $2000.

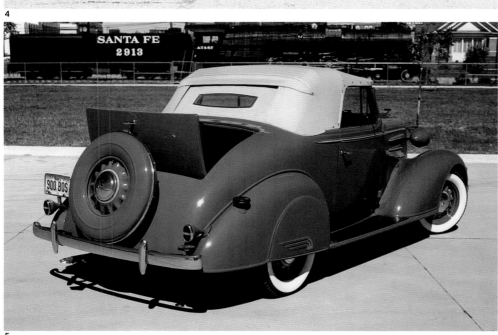

1. The 1936 Chevrolets got a new "fencer's mask" grille shell carrying headlights moved up from the fenders. Four-wheel "Perfected Hydraulic Brakes" were newly standard for all Chevys. Wire wheels, as seen on this Master DeLuxe coupe, were now an option.

2. The $590 Master DeLuxe sport coupe was the year's only closed rumble-seat model. This example wears accessory foglights, covered side-mount spares, a spotlight, and fender skirts. **3.** At $495, the Standard coupe was the lowest-priced 1936 Chevy. Sales reached 10,895. The five-window body style was the only coupe available in the Standard series; three-window fanciers had to step up to the Master DeLuxe sport coupe. **4.** It took a second look to distinguish 1936 Standards from Master DeLuxes, though the former's shorter wheelbase was apparent. This is the $535 Standard town sedan, the line's most-popular model with 220,884 sales. **5.** After a year's absence, a cabriolet returned to the Chevrolet line, somewhat surprisingly as a member of the Standard series. It was Chevy's only open model for '36. Despite a bargain price of $595, the revived cabriolet drew only 3629 orders, leaving Chevy barely ahead of Plymouth in ragtop sales among the "Low-Priced Three."

1-2. LaSalle continued to offer just four models for 1936, all with minor styling changes. The grille pattern was revised, but the unique "chevron" front-fender badges were carried over. The hoodside portholes of 1935 were replaced by a horizontal louver panel. The two-passenger coupe (shown) was the most affordable LaSalle, with a base price of $1175. LaSalle faced tough competition not only from the Packard One Twenty and new Lincoln Zephyr, but Cadillac's lower-priced Series 60 models. **3.** At nearly 70,000 units, the F-36 four-door touring sedan was by far the most popular Oldsmobile. The new trunk-back sedans were broadly favored over their fastback kin. **4.** Stylists tweaked Pontiac's "Silver Streak" motif for '36. The "waterfall" grille got narrower, and slimmer headlight buckets were mounted on the grille shell instead of the fenders. The beam front axle just visible on this cabriolet identifies it as an entry-level Master Six. The cabriolet was the most expensive body style in each series; the Master Six version cost $760. **5.** Pontiac Deluxe Sixes got Knee-Action independent front suspension. Sport coupes like this one came standard with a rumble seat for $720 to start.

1

2

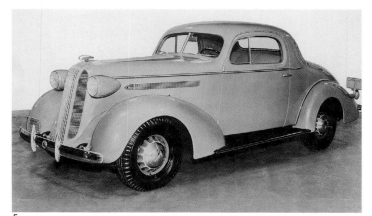

3

4

5

1. Buicks got handsome restyling for 1937 by designer Franklin Hershey; updates included a split horizontal bar grille and longer fenders with blunt trailing edges. Trunkbacked four-door touring sedans retailed for $1233 and were the most popular Buicks in the Series 60 Century line—production totaled 21,140. This Hampton Grey example wears accessory fog lights and side-mount spares.

2. The Buick Series 40 Special's straight eight was enlarged to 248 cid, which boosted power by seven to 100 hp. Sport coupes like this one sat four via small opera seats behind the front seat. **3.** Buick now offered a convertible phaeton in its 1937 Century and Special series, as well as a more costly $1856 Roadmaster (shown), which had debuted a year earlier. The 320-cid engine used in the Century, Limited, and Roadmaster models gained 10 horsepower, to 130. Specials and Centurys now boasted all-steel body construction, but Roadmaster and Limited models still utilized composite wood and steel bodies. **4.** Cadillacs received minor styling updates, such as an eggcrate grille and revised hood trim. The entry-level Series 60 lineup expanded to include this $2120 convertible sedan. All Series 60 models got an upgrade to Cadillac's 135-hp, 346-cid V-8.

1

1. Cadillac's majestic V-16 models were were image-boosting "halo" cars that sold in miniscule numbers. This Series 90 seven-passenger Imperial Sedan is one of just 49 V-16 Caddys built for 1937. The '37 model year would be the last for Cadillac's original ohv V-16 engine; a more-advanced L-head V-16 would replace it for 1938.
2. After four years of fielding two distinct car lines, Chevrolet consolidated all 1937 models around a new 112.3-inch-wheelbase chassis and "Diamond Crown" styling by General Motors designer Jules Agramonte. Master and Master DeLuxe models now shared the same body, chassis, and engine, but Master DeLuxes got extra enhancements, including Knee-Action suspension. Pictured here, the $788 Master DeLuxe sport sedan. **3.** The price leader among 1937 Chevys was the $619 Master business coupe.

2

3

1

2

3

4

1. The $725 Master cabriolet was Chevrolet's rarest 1937 model. Only 1724 were built. **2.** After three seasons with an Oldsmobile straight eight, LaSalle turned to a 125-hp, 322-cid V-8 in 1937, borrowed from the prior year's Cadillac Series 60. Convertible coupes like this one went for $1350. **3-4.** Oldsmobiles were completely restyled for '37; six-powered F-37 cars got bold horizontal grille bars, while eight-powered L-37 models wore a more-subdued "waffle-grid" pattern. Shown here are the $840 L-37 business coupe and the $1060 L-37 touring sedan. **5-6.** With a base price of $685, the F-37 business coupe (left) was the cheapest '37 Oldsmobile. Its club coupe sibling (right) offered four-passenger capacity via rear opera seats for $55 more.

5

6

1. Pontiacs got a new "face" for 1937, with horizontal grille sections bisected by the "Silver Streak" waterfall chrome trim. Phaetons were fading from the automotive scene in the late 1930s, so it seems odd that Pontiac saw fit to add a convertible sedan to its lineup. Available in both DeLuxe Six or DeLuxe Eight form (shown here) for $1197 or $1235, respectively, the body style was available in 1937 and '38 only.

2. Pontiac interiors featured clean, streamlined dashboards with an attractive rectangular gauge cluster. Note the unique spherical ashtray on the glovebox door. The convertible sedan's center door posts were removable when the top was lowered for open-air motoring.

3. "Silver Streak" decklid trim was available on Pontiac convertible sedans. An "8" insignia in the decklid badge identifies this example as a Deluxe Eight.

4. Both Pontiac engines gained horsepower and displacement for '37. The six now put out 85 hp from its 222.7 cid, while the eight now displaced 248.9 cubic inches and made 100 hp. The Master Six line was dropped, leaving only DeLuxe Six and DeLuxe Eight models. The $781 DeLuxe Six coupe (shown) was the most affordable Pontiac.

1

2

3

4

1

2

3

4

5

1. For 1938, Buicks received a minor facelift that included a more vertical grille with thicker grille bars, a longer hood, and updated trim. This one-off Buick Roadmaster-based "opera brougham" town car was originally built for a Polish countess. Famed designer Howard "Dutch" Darrin was responsible for the custom coachwork. The intricate "canework" section on the doors is actually painted on. **2.** Roadmaster sales were sliding downward; with 6100 cars produced, the Series 80 accounted for only 3.6 percent of Buick's total output. A Roadmaster four-door touring sedan went for $1645. **3.** Series 60 Centurys were still the hot rods of the Buick line— Buick engineers pushed one to

103 mph. The $1297 Century four-door sedan was the most popular Series 60 Buick; 12,673 were sold. **4.** The Special four-door touring sedan was Buick's most popular model, with 82,191 produced. **5.** The less-popular, non-trunkback Special four-door sport sedan saw sales of 11,341.

1-2. Designed by 23-year-old William Mitchell, the new Cadillac Sixty-Special broke new styling ground with its concealed running boards, extended rear deck, and thin, chromed window frames. Just one body style was offered, a $2090 four-door sedan.
3. Series 60 Cadillacs, like this $1730 four-door sedan, kept their former shape for '38, adding a column gearshift.

1

2

3

4

5

4. A new engine and new styling injected new life into the Cadillac V-16 for 1938. Prices were dropped, too; while the '37 Series 90 had started at a towering $7450, the '38 version started at $5200, and no body style cost more than $7500. The convertible sedan (shown) had a base price of $6000. **5.** As before, the V-16s were the rarest and most exclusive Cadillacs in the line. This seven-passenger town car is one of just 11 built. Total 1938 Series 90 production was just 311 cars. **6.** The seven-seat Imperial sedan was the most popular Cadillac V-16 body style, with 95 produced.

6

1

2

3

1. The 1938 Chevrolets got a minor facelift that included a horizontal bar grille and enlarged hood louvers. A Master convertible sold for $755. Despite the recession, demand for this relatively pricey model was up this year; 2787 were sold. 2. The Master coupe-pickup carried a unique trunk-mounted pickup bed. The car could be converted to a regular business coupe by removing the bed and attaching a decklid. 3. The two-door sedan remained the most popular model in Chevy's entry-level Master series; with 95,050 produced, it outsold

4

its trunkless companion model by a margin of 29-to-1. 4. For an additional $61, a Chevy shopper could have the Master DeLuxe version of the town sedan, which included such standard niceties as dual wind-shield wipers and taillights. 5. Even though it held just two passengers, the $714 Master DeLuxe business coupe vastly outsold its $750 rumble-seat-equipped running mate. The fuel filler on business coupes was mounted in the right body side; on other '38 Chevys, it was located in the right rear fender.

5

1. A rakish wraparound grille and fender-mounted headlights highlighted Oldsmobile exterior styling changes for 1938. The side profile view of this $1056 L-38 two-door touring sedan shows off its integral trunk. As before, eight-cylinder cars rode a 124-inch-wheelbase chassis, while sixes used a 117-inch chassis. **2.** Of the approximately 1600 Oldsmobile convertibles built for 1938, a scant 475 were the eight-cylinder L-38 variant. **3.** Olds interiors boasted a smoothly contoured "safety dash" with most controls clustered out of harm's way behind the uniquely styled steering wheel. "Automatic Safety Transmission," a semi-automatic precursor to true automatic transmissions, was again optional for $100.

1

2

3

SIGNIUS WILHELM KNUDSEN 1879–1948

In 1899, at the age of twenty, Signius Wilhelm Poul Knudsen arrived in New York from Denmark with $30 in his pocket to assure U.S. Immigration that he would not become a public ward. In 1901, Knudsen joined the John R. Keim Mills in Buffalo, where he took quickly to production management: In short order in 1905, he whipped out 4000 brake drums for the Olds Motor Works. Keim soon became a major supplier of automotive steel pressings, castings, and tubes, and Henry Ford bought the company in 1911.

Two years later, with the newly married Knudsen now making $150 a week, Ford moved Keim to Detroit. "Big Bill" Knudsen laid out new Ford assembly plants as they opened and accelerated production of Model Ts. He quit in 1921, fed up with being countermanded by Henry Ford, with whom he developed a severe antipathy. Ford historian Ed Cray wrote, "wanted men about him who neither smoked nor drank,

and certainly did not profane the Lord. Knudsen did all three."

After a frustrating ten months managing a small car parts supplier with limited horizons, the big Dane applied for work with C.S. Mott, an Alfred Sloan protégé who was vice-president of GM Accessories Division. "Big Bill" was a bluff, hearty giant who stood no nonsense. As president of Chevrolet, where Sloan installed him, he pushed for volumes of price-competitive, conventional cars and took personal delight in going out after his old company, Ford.

Knudsen was heir-apparent to Sloan as president General Motors in 1937, but no sooner was he installed before a debilitating strike occurred. In June 1940, Knudsen resigned to serve as a consultant on the Advisory Commission on National Defense. Knudsen died in 1948 at the age of 69. His son, Semon E. "Bunkie" Knudsen, rose to head Pontiac in 1956 and Chevrolet in 1961.

1

2

1. The mildly facelifted 1938 Pontiacs wore a new grille design with thicker grille bars and revised hood-side louvers. A DeLuxe Six two-door touring sedan sold for $891 and offered 17.5 cubic feet of luggage space. 2. Pontiac cabriolets sold for $993 in six-cylinder form, or $1057 when powered by an eight. Both came standard with a rumble seat. Sidemount spare tires were available only on DeLuxe Eights, but all Pontiacs wore unique stamped steel wheels with ten cooling slots. 3-4. Pontiac interiors featured a redesigned instrument panel. Though this example sports the standard floorshift, a "Safety Shift Gear Control" column-mounted gearshift was newly available this year. "Woody" wagons started at $1110.

3

4

1. Buicks wore all-new bodies with a radical "waterfall" split grille for 1938. The $2350 Limited touring sedan was the most-expensive Buick outside of the Limited limousine. All Limited models rode a 140-inch wheelbase. **2.** Buick's attractive new convex dashboards could have a "Sonomatic" push-button radio. The control for the new standard turn signals was mounted on top of the steering-column gearshift lever.

3. (Left to right) Alfred P. Sloan, GM's board chairman, Harlow Curtice, Buick's general manager, and Albert Bradley, vice-president in charge of Financial Staff, admire the new 1939 Buick. **4.** This Buick Century convertible is one of just 850 built for 1939 at a base price of $1343. It has several rare options such as sidemount spares and "streamboards," which replaced standard running boards for a more streamlined look. The '39 Centurys upheld the line's reputation as "the banker's hot rod" with a 320-cid straight eight that put out 140 horsepower. That was one more than Cadillac's most powerful V-8...a fact resented by the Cadillac division.

1

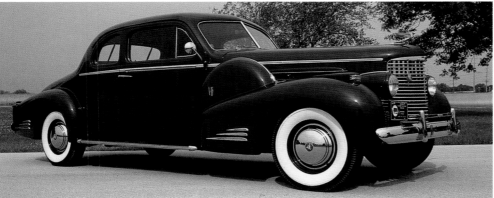

2

3

1. Most Cadillacs adopted a more-streamlined, prow-like front appearance for '39, but V-16s pressed on with carry-over styling and minor detail changes. Shown here is a $5440 V-16 convertible, one of only seven built. 2. The heart of the 1938–40 Series 90 Cadillac was a 431-cid L-head V-16 good for 185 horse-power. This $5440 V-16 coupe carried fold-down rear jump seats for five-passenger capac-ity. 3. LaSalles rode a wheel-base four inches shorter than in 1938 and gained new bodies with a slender, fine-bar grille and large "catwalk" subgrilles. Metal rocker panels appeared for the first time, but running boards were still available as an option. The $1240 coupe was the most affordable LaSalle.

1

1-2. Chevrolets got handsome new "Aero-Stream Styling" for 1939. The $628 Master 85 business coupe was the most affordable, while the $883 Master DeLuxe "woody" wagon was the most expensive. 3-4. Oldsmobiles had new, lower profile bodies and were now available in three separate series. Shown here, the $838 Series 60 two-door sedan and the $1119 Series 80 convertible.

2

3

4

1. New-for-'39 Pontiac DeLuxe Six and DeLuxe Eight bodies wore wider "pontoon" fenders and streamlined noses with chromed "catwalk" grilles. A new low-cost "Quality Six" line debuted, wearing a Chevrolet bodyshell with Pontiac front sheetmetal. The $1046 Deluxe Eight convertible shown here was the only 1939 Pontiac to break the $1000 barrier. Rumble seats were no longer available. 2. Pontiac didn't produce commercial vehicles for sale in the United States but offered sedan delivery models like the one pictured here in Canada. 3. External running boards were mandatory on baseline Quality Six models, but DeLuxe buyers could specify chrome-trimmed "body skirts." The DeLuxe Six four-door touring sedan started at $922.

CHAPTER FIVE

1940-1949

"I'll be seeing you in all the old familiar places...."

—Billie Holiday; lyrics by Irving Kahal

During the 1940s, GM was evolving a superior product. By the end of the decade, World War II notwithstanding, the corporation had introduced the modern high-compression V-8, the hardtop convertible, the progenitor of muscle cars, and the all-steel station wagon—all of which played vital roles for the next 40 years. About the only thing they failed to do was launch a "compact," although Charles Wilson tried his best with his pet project, a small Chevrolet tentatively dubbed Cadet. It was designed to sell for less than $1000, but GM executives shot it down, citing that small cars were a death sentence to corporate profits.

Rationalizing the product line became crucial. With the Depression over, there was no real need for the LaSalle as a prop to Cadillac. The last LaSalle was the '40, a handsome car with a 322-cid V-8 on an expansive 123-inch wheelbase. There were two models, one Cadillac- and one Buick-based. And it sold—the second best run in LaSalle history. But the high-end LaSalle listed at just $80 more than a Buick Roadmaster, and that just wouldn't do: they were too close. So for 1941, Cadillac reverted to a single-make luxury car division.

For 1940 Cadillac set a new Series 72 between the Sixty Special and the Series

75: a long sedan and limousines on a 138-inch wheelbase. More significant was the arrival of what became Caddy's breadwinner, the Series 62, replete with convertible coupe and sedan along with closed models. The year witnessed another funeral besides LaSalle's: the last of the famous Sixteen. Only 61 were built in 1940.

Cadillac came back with dramatically restyled '41s, a little chrome-happy, but not really garish. Here arrived as well the first Cadillac eggcrate grille, a hallmark that would survive half a century. It was created by the talented Art Ross, who had been with Art & Colour since 1936. All Caddys were now powered by the same engine, the reliable 346, with higher compression and 150 hp.

Cadillac spent big money on a dramatic 1942 facelift, with pontoon fenders on all models but the 75 and a grille evolved from 1941. The body lines worked especially well on the new Series 62 sedanet (fastback coupe) more so than on the second-generation Sixty Special notchback, riding its own 133-inch wheelbase.

Torpedo styling was in vogue at Buick, which expanded its bodies with fastback "Streamlined" sedans, torpedo sedans, and coupes. Exclusive to the Super was Buick's first factory station wagon: a four-door woody at $1242. Styling was little changed but headlamps were now faired into the front fenders—a styling trend that soon swept the industry. Buick set a record 300,000 cars for calendar 1940, enjoying another fourth-place finish behind Chevy, Ford, and Plymouth.

Buick fine-tuned its '41 product line, splitting the Special into two series, one on a light, 118-inch wheelbase, while dropping the top-line Series 80 Limited in deference to Cadillac. The woody wagon was now a Special, while the Century lost its open and coupe models. Chassis were updated with an Olds-like X-member frame developed by engineer V. P. Mathews.

Buick continued to emphasize fastback styling in the handful of '42s produced before car production ended. The Super and Roadmaster grew longer, but the Special and Century didn't, and with 165 hp from its 320 straight eight, the Century remained as hot as ever. Unfortunately, it would not immediately return after the war.

Chevrolets came in two series for 1941: the Master Deluxe, including a woody wagon and more sporty body styles—the Special Deluxe workaday models. All models now had "Knee-Acton" independent front suspension, wider-spaced springs for better ride stability, more efficient cooling, and higher-voltage electrics. Model year production was well over a million cars, a third more than Ford and a new record.

The following year, Chevrolet added a third Fleetline subseries including an interesting notchback four-door (Sportmaster) and fastback coupe (Fleetline Aerosedan). Priced under $1000, they cost roughly $100 less than the convertible or woody wagon. By contrast, the price-leading Master Deluxe business coupe came in at only $760. Despite the war-shortened production run, Chevrolet remained first in volume with over 250,000 cars. Chevy

would continue to provide "blackout" coupes and sedans during the war for military staff use. Registered as 1943–45 models, they were '42s in every respect.

Oldsmobile chief designer George Snyder styled the 1940 models; the 1941–42s were by Edmund Anderson (later of American Motors fame) and John Oswald. The wider, fresh "face" of the '40 Olds was the work of Lewis Simon. There were three models, six cylinder F-40 and G-40, eight-cylinder L-40, each with a coupe, sedan, and convertible, plus business coupes and two-door sedan for the six cylinder models. They were the first cars with the Hydra-Matic transmission, a development for which Oldsmobile won deserved fame.

The following year, Olds doubled its lineup by offering the six- or eight-cylinder engines as options across the board, deploying a confusing array of names, such as "Custom Cruiser Eight Model 98." Such nomenclature is of interest only in tracking the origin of the famous postwar 88 and 98.

Olds entered 1942 in patriotic fervor, advertising new, stronger "dreadnaught" frames, "firepower" engines, and the bomber-like series designation B-44. Styling was more changed than specifications, with Cadillac-like pontoon fenders and a complicated two-tier grille with double bumpers connected by large vertical guards. This design would not be seen after the war.

Pontiac started the 1940s with its own version of the corporate C-body and a new top-of-the-line series called the Torpedo Eight, a coupe and sedan riding 122 inches of wheelbase. Power came from the little 249 eight. Subtract two cylinders and you had the DeLuxe Six: coupes, sedans, and a cabriolet. At the bottom was the Special Six, derived from Chevy on a slightly longer wheelbase.

Pontiac held the lid on price, which helped set a calendar year record at 250,000 in 1940. Back it came the following year with each line doubled: six separate series encompassing two wheelbases, two engines, and three body shells, all bearing the "Torpedo" name.

Sensible rationalization controlled the revised 1942 lineup, which was more orderly—just four series in two groups: 119-inch A-body Torpedo, 122-inch B-body Streamliner, each available with a six or an eight. The price hierarchy ran from Torpedo to Streamliner to Streamliner Chieftain, the latter simply a fancier trimmed Streamliner that cost $50 more.

Like its GM brethren in 1942, Pontiac updated its appearance with longer, flow-through front fenders, tapered rear fenders, and gaudier grillework. Mechanical changes were notable by their absence. The advent of war blunted an encouraging upward sales trend of the previous three years.

A postwar strike got GM off to a slow start in 1945, and for 1946–47 all customers saw were warmed-over versions of the prewar designs—which, after all, GM had scarcely introduced when the war had cut production off.

Cadillac continued with its 61, 62, Sixty Special, and 75, the latter carrying long-wheelbase sedans and limousines; all were clearly related to the stillborn 1942 models. Buick's 1946–48 cars comprised the Special, Super, and Roadmaster, with convertibles and wagons in the upper two ranges and Specials starting at $1800. They were distinguished by a bold, buck-toothed grille comprising heavy vertical bars, which would become a Buick hallmark for several years. Chevy stayed with slightly facelifted prewar bodies for its Stylemaster and Fleetmaster powered by the familiar Stovebolt Six.

Only Pontiac and Oldsmobile fielded broad arrays of cars, though in fact their specifications were pretty much the same. Oldsmobile's standard- and Deluxe-trimmed 66/68, 76/78, and 98 (there was no 96) rode just two wheelbases (119 and 125 inches) and came with only two engines: the 100-hp six and 110-hp eight. Pontiac's situation was similar. Although it offered standard and deluxe Torpedo and Streamliner sixes and eights, they were rode just two chassis (119 and 122 inches), with the 93-hp six or 108-hp eight.

By the end of the decade, GM's handsome new cars, in the words of the war-time hit song, were "seen in all the old, familiar places."

Many individuals have taken credit for the fabulous 1948 Cadillacs, including Bill Mitchell, Frank Hershey, Julio Andrade, Ned Nickles, and a dozen others. A recent article in *Collectible Automobile®* probably came nearest the mark simply by crediting the work to Harley Earl. Although Earl did not necessarily put the actual lines on paper or translate them into clay—Art & Colour was, after all, a group enterprise—it was he who had the final word before management saw the proposals.

The P-38-inspired tailfin was the finishing touch on a totally beautiful Cadillac. The traditional grille shape was retained, emphasized by a more curvaceous hood, roof, and fender lines, clean and perfect from every angle. Inside, a huge ornate drum-like panel housed all the instruments and most controls. It proved expensive, however, and was replaced by a more conventional dash in 1949.

Cadillac rightly concluded that dramatic new styling was more than enough for 1948, so the specifications remained unaltered. Although it took $2833 to buy an entry-level 61, more than 66,000 Caddys sold, and more than 80,000 the following year.

In 1949, Cadillac added its second trump card: a new overhead-valve, high-compression V-8, proclaimed "the greatest automobile engine ever built." Lighter, more compact, easier on gas, and far more powerful than the previous flathead, the 331-cid engine set the standard for everyone else to shoot for—everyone except Oldsmobile, which simultaneously released a winner in its 307-cid Rocket V-8. This powerful engine so transformed the performance of the 98 that Lansing made the decision to put it into a lighter body. The result was the "Rocket 88," the first "muscle car," which dominated NASCAR auto racing from 1949 to 1951.

Another important development, by Cadillac, Buick, and Oldsmobile in 1949, was the "hardtop convertible," a closed coupe with the pillarless roofline and deluxe interior of a convertible. Each division gave its hardtop a special name: Roadmaster Riviera, 62 Coupe de Ville, 98 Holiday. Hardtops, usually with two-tone paint jobs to mimic the look of a convertible, were lavishly equipped with hydro-electric power seats and windows, radio and heater, turn signals, back-up lights, fender skirts, full wheel covers, and wool rear carpets.

Buick did not adopt aircraft styling until 1949 but made news the previous year with "Dynaflow Drive," standard on Roadmasters and a $200 option on other models. Dynaflow used a torque converter that depended on induced rotation of a drive turbine through an oil bath by a facing turbine driven off the crankshaft. Smoother than Hydra-Matic, its underwhelming performance caused wags to dub it "Dyna-slush." In 1953 it would be replaced by much improved Twin/Turbine Dynaflow.

At the direction of Harlow Curtice, Buick now introduced an offbeat styling innovation that would survive into modern times: the famous "Ventiports" or "mouseholes," as some called them, on front fenders. Four were on Roadmasters, three on Supers. This was apparently another Ned Nickles innovation; punching holes in the sides of his own car, he'd fitted them with small colored bulbs hooked to the distributor and firing in sync with the cylinders! They seem trivial and decadent, but Ventiports were just a signature—soon to be as well-known on Buicks as the three-pointed star on the Mercedes-Benz.

Chevrolet restyled for 1949. Two series comprised the Special Styline and fastback Special Fleetline at the low end, and the more luxurious Deluxe, mainly Styline models, at the upper end. Among the Deluxes was Chevy's most important development of the Forties: an all-steel station wagon. It outsold the woody version by nearly two to one and became the only available Chevy wagon in 1950. Pontiac and Oldsmobile also offered steel wagons and, like Chevy, abandoned woodies in 1950.

Nineteen forty-nine was opening year for NASCAR's "Strictly Stock" series. Of the eight races, Oldsmobile's Rocket 88 won five of them, Red Byron becoming the first driving champion. "Futuramic" styling, which had debuted on the 1948 Olds 98, was now applied across the board, and Olds racked up nearly 300,000 sales for the calendar year.

In the restyle of 1949, Pontiac fared well. For its new, 120-inch chassis, Art & Colour developed a smooth body with full-width bar-grille and traditional silver streaks. The Pontiac line comprised a Silver Streak Six and Eight, each available in standard (Streamliner) and deluxe (Chieftain) trim. Engines were unchanged from 1948, but a new high-compression head boosted horsepower slightly.

The end of this decade and the start of the next ushered in an era of boundless prosperity, and with it came a decision that a 49-percent market share, established for years as GM's upper limit, could be exceeded with impunity. For GM and the rest of the auto industry, that decision would prove significant.

1. Buick largely targeted loyal, upper-class buyers with its products. In 1940, Buick offered six series of cars, from the low-priced Special to the top-of-the-line Limited. The rarest of the Series 40 Specials was the sport phaeton. Priced at $1355, only 597 were built. 2. All Buick Special and Century models rode on a 121-inch wheelbase. At $895, the Special business coupe was the lowest-priced car in Buick's stable that year. 3. Styling on all models, including the Special four-door sedan, was refreshed from 1939. One adjustment was the position-ing of the headlamps into the front fenders, resulting in a slightly lower appearance. Complementing this change was a more prominent grille with bolder horizontal bars. 4. The 126-inch-wheelbase Centurys ran Buick's 320-cid, 141-hp straight eight, making them some of the best-per-forming cars of the day. Lower-line models had the 248-cid, 107-hp eight.

CHARLES ERWIN "ENGINE CHARLIE" WILSON 1892–1962

"...for years I thought that what's good for the country is good for General Motors, and vice versa."

—Wilson at his Senate confirmation hearings, 1953

When GM president Bill Knudsen resigned in 1940 to advise the Council on National Defense, he was replaced by "Engine Charlie" Wilson, whose nickname had nothing to do with his personality. It had simply been invented on Wall Street to distinguish him from Charles Edward Wilson, president of General Electric. Perhaps predictably, the latter came to be called "Electric Charlie."

Born in Minerva, Ohio, Wilson graduated from Pittsburgh's Carnegie Institute of Technology in 1909, moving across town to Westinghouse, where he was soon involved with the production of automotive electrical components. During World War I, he oversaw dynamotors and radio generators for the military. In 1919 he moved to Remy Electric, the GM subsidiary that merged with Delco in 1926.

When Alfred Sloan named Wilson GM's vice president for manufacturing in 1929, he demonstrated his trust in a letter to the organization advising all departments "to consult Mr. Wilson" before proceeding to develop "all new projects." Thus Wilson signed off on the many important GM developments of the 1930s; when America went to war, he spearheaded the defense effort. For his work he received the Medal of Merit in 1946.

Like most executives, "Engine Charlie" feared a return of the Depression after the war. To prevent it, he declared, the United States needed "a permanent war economy." He had only just begun the expensive conversion to civilian car production when GM was faced with demands for a 30 percent wage hike by the United Auto Workers. This lead to a strike that wasn't settled until March 1946.

Wilson had brought GM forcefully back to the production, engineering, and styling pinnacle when, in 1953, Dwight Eisenhower nominated him for Secretary of Defense. Then came his famous reply to a senator who asked if, as Defense Secretary, he could make a decision that adversely affected General Motors. What he said is at the top of this report, but it was quickly rephrased as "What's good for General Motors is good for the country."

Engine Charlie was confirmed anyway, and to the surprise of some detractors he cut spending and trimmed fat, ironically enabling Senator John Kennedy to run for president to the right of Richard Nixon in 1960, claiming defense deficiencies and a "missile gap."

Wilson retired in October 1957, Dwight Eisenhower remarking: "the strength of our security forces has not only been maintained but has been significantly increased...[he has managed the Pentagon] in a manner consistent with the requirements of a strong, healthy national economy." What was good for the country had been good for Charlie Wilson.

HYDRA-MATIC: SHIFTING WITHOUT SHIFTING

"The greatest advance since the self-starter"
—Oldsmobile advertisement, 1940

If any single development contributed to the reputation of Oldsmobile as "the experimental division of General Motors," it was Hydra-Matic Drive, which went into production in May 1939 for the 1940 models first shipped the following October. By the mid-Fifties, Hydra-Matic was an under-license option on such rival makes as Hudson, Nash, Frazer, Kaiser, and even Lincoln.

Oldsmobile general manager Charles L. McCuen, who retired shortly after it entered production, is the father of Hydra-Matic, having been involved with it from the late Thirties, when he realized that the Automatic Safety Transmission (1937–39) was not the ultimate solution to shift-free driving. Engineering had always been McCuen's passion, even as general manager. He personally held 16 patents related to suspension systems, oil coolers, crankcase ventilation, radiators, and manifolds.

Though Earl A. Thompson laid the actual groundwork for Hydra-Matic, it was Harold N. Metzel, a mathematics whiz and former football player from Illinois, who led the development effort. Joining Oldsmobile out of Bradley University, as a test driver in 1928, Metzel moved up to head of dynamometer testing in 1930, then to development engineer in 1935 and transmission engineer in 1939. One of his first tasks was to shepherd 5000 Hydra-Matic-equipped Oldsmobiles around the country for evaluation.

Hydra-Matic was offered as an across-the-board option on all 1940 Oldsmobiles, priced at only $57—a subsidized figure designed to win over a large number of customers. (In 1941 it was raised to a more realistic $100.) Its initial form was essentially a combination of the Automatic Safety Transmission and a fluid coupling, which replaced a friction clutch and eliminated the clutch pedal and all shifting. It had four forward speeds plus reverse, affording a wide range of torque multiplication. Hydra-Matic Oldsmobiles equipped carried a 3.63:1 final drive ratio, versus 4.30:1 on manual transmission models, which enabled Olds to claim a 10-15 percent fuel economy improvement for the new transmission. (Axle ratios being equal, it was, of course, less economical than a stickshift.)

Though Oldsmobile built the experimental units, it did not have the production facilities to cope with expected demand for the new two-pedal drive system. At Bill Knudsen's instigation, therefore, GM organized the Detroit Transmission Division in 1939 to manufacture Hydra-Matic for any division that wanted it. Cadillac added it in 1940, Pontiac in 1948; Buick and Chevrolet opted to develop their own automatics, respectively Dyna-flow and Powerglide. In 1953, GM bought the huge, mile-long ex-Kaiser-Frazer plant in Willow Run, Michigan, to expand further its Hydra-Matic production.

The biggest complaint customers had about Hydra-Matic was jerky shifts, and several semi-successful alterations were made to cure this. In 1956, a smoother but more costly automatic was developed and named Jetaway. Jetaway later evolved into the less-complex Roto-Hydramatic. Then, in 1964–65, Hydramatic was replaced on passenger cars by the three-speed torque-converter Turbo-Hydramatic.

1

1. Cadillac's new Series 62 rode on a 129-inch wheelbase, three inches longer than the Series 61 it replaced. Coachbuilding firm Bohman and Schwartz customized a pair of Series 62 coupes, turning them into dashing convertibles.

2. The Sixty Special Fleetwood returned with minor styling tweaks compared to the previous model year. A predictive, if rarely ordered, option was a sliding metal sunroof, called the "Sunshine Turret Top Roof."

2

A MAJOR MILESTONE

On January 11, 1940, a Chevrolet Master DeLuxe Town Sedan rolled off the assembly line. This car had the honor of being the 25,000,000th vehicle produced by General Motors. It was only fitting that this milestone car be a Chevy. The division enjoyed another record sales year. In total, it turned out 895,734 vehicles, with a gratifying 775,073 as passenger cars. Chevy had a commanding lead over a faltering Ford, which could manage no better than some 542,000 cars for the model year. GM's production has increased a bit since then. In 2006, the company, as a whole, produced 9.1 million vehicles, which were sold in 33 countries.

3

1. For Chevrolet, 1940 brought some notable changes, including "Royal Clipper" styling that provided more flowing lines and Buick-like grilles. New Chevrolet chief designer Kenneth E. Coppock can be credited with these styling revisions. Despite the exterior changes, these cars were little changed mechanically. They retained the 113-inch wheelbase of previous years. Special DeLuxes, like the one shown here, were the new top-line models. 2. Exclusive to the Special DeLuxe was a convertible body style. Though the Special DeLuxe was new, it proved to be Chevrolet's best-selling series for 1940. The convertible alone racked up an impressive 12,000 sales. 3. All Chevrolets were powered by a 217-cid, 85-hp "stovebolt" six-cylinder engine. This Master DeLuxe business coupe had an open luggage area behind the front seat; sport coupes had a rear bench seat. Sedan spare tires were mounted vertically against the front trunk wall; coupes mounted them horizontally on the trunk floor.

1. LaSalle entered its swan-song year in 1940. Though it was the brand's last year, it wasn't about to go quietly. Modified styling marked a high point in LaSalle's 14-year history, plus the make's first two-series lineup in a decade. The design leader was the plush new Series 52 Special bearing Harley Earl's latest "torpedo" look. The 52s joined the carryover Series 50. Most elegant among LaSalles were the Special convertible coupe (pictured) and sedan, both of which arrived midyear. Under the hood, minor engine changes boosted output of the 322 L-head V-8 to 130 hp from 125. **2.** By 1940, LaSalle had been crowded out of its once-exclusive price niche. It's true that the 1940 lineup was broad, running from the $1240 Series 50 coupe to the $1440 Series 52 Special sedan (pictured) to the $1895 Special convertible sedan. Contrast that with Series 62 Cadillacs that could be had for as little as $1685 or Buicks that ranged from $895 to $2199. The LaSalle brand tallied 24,130 sales in 1940. Among other luxury makes, it ranked only slightly ahead of Lincoln and far behind Packard. LaSalle felt the squeeze from Cadillac at the top and from Buick at the bottom, which eventually led to the make's demise.

3. Oldsmobile gave its cars new grilles and fenders for 1940. The Series 90 replaced the Series 80 this year, and wheelbases increased to 124 inches from 120. The most popular Olds of 1940 was the $1131 Series 90 four-door sedan pictured here. The big news at Oldsmobile this year was Hydra-Matic, the industry's first fully automatic transmission.

1

2

3

1. The Custom Cruiser designation made its debut on top-level Oldsmobile Series 90s, all of which ran a 257-cid, 110-hp inline eight-cylinder engine and featured the Cadillac C-body. Here, a $1069 Series 90 club coupe. The one-millionth Oldsmobile (since November 1933) rolled off the assembly line during the 1940 model year.

2. Pontiacs also benefited from a facelift for 1940. The Special Six woody station wagon sold for $1015 and came standard with a fender-mounted spare tire. Special Six and DeLuxe Six models used a 223-cid, 87-hp inline six-cylinder engine.

3. The Special Six two-door touring sedan was based on the Chevrolet A-body and rode a 117-inch wheelbase. Special Six models replaced the Quality Six at the low-end of the Pontiac model range.

1. Buick sold more convertibles than any automaker except Ford in 1941. Series 40A models, such as this ragtop, rode a 118-inch wheelbase. **2.** Among 26 body styles Buick sold in 1941 was the SE Special four-door shown here. The fastback body was a new addition. **3.** Supers equipped with the 248-cid engine got a horsepower boost to 115 from 107 this year thanks to the new "Turbolator" piston that provided better compression of the fuel/air mixture.

1

2

3

Buick's other 1941 innovation was "Compound Carburetion." This feature was optional on the 248-cid "Fireball 8" engine and standard on the larger 320-cid eight-cylinder. Essentially two carburetors working in series, the primary unit handled part-load driving, with the secondary opened during full-throttle acceleration. This setup allowed for maximum horsepower with little impact on fuel economy. So equipped, the 248 produced 125 hp, while the 320 delivered 165 hp. **4.** Supers (sport coupe shown) shared the Series 40 121-inch wheelbase. **5.** Engine-turned metal panels flanked a central radio speaker. The steering wheel was made out of plastic, which had a tendency to crack over time. **6.** The 1941 model year was the last for Buick's convertible phaeton body style.

4

5

6

1. New front-end styling introduced Cadillac's trademark rectangular eggcrate grille. The Fleetwood Sixty Special sported front fenders that flowed into the doors. This styling cue began a trend that would be widely copied. 1941 was the final year for the unique Sixty Special in its original William Mitchell-designed 1938 configuration; the '42 was a more mainstream car. This example was a show car that featured the newly available Hydra-Matic automatic transmission. Another ahead-of-its-time feature was a set of fully electric windows. **2.** Series 62 Cadillacs went down slightly in wheelbase and price but up dramatically in sales, out-distancing 1940's output by a factor of four. This convertible coupe cost $150 less in 1941 than in the previous model year. The ragtops now worked with the aid of vacuum assist. **3.** Cadillac interiors set the standard for all General Motors cars to emulate. Symmetry played a big part in dashboard design, with a passenger-side clock offsetting the driver's speedometer. Air conditioning was introduced as an option this year, but few buyers ordered it. **4.** Convertible sedans were fading fast industrywide, and '41 was the last year for Cadillac's version; sales reached only 400. Like all 1941 Cadillacs, the gas cap was hidden under the left taillight. **5.** The new Series 63, which was available only as a four-door sedan, filled a price void between the Series 62 below it and the Series Sixty Special above it. All of these cars, as well as the Series 61, rode on a 126-inch wheelbase.

1

1. With more than 1 million cars produced in 1941, Chevrolet led the industry. This Special DeLuxe convertible coupe features optional fog lamps, stainless-steel fender trim, chrome wheel-trim rings, and an accessory hood ornament. 2-3. Chevrolet's second redesign in as many years stretched the wheelbase to 116 inches, concealed the running boards, incorporated the headlights into the fenders, and gave the front and rear windows a greater slope. Shown here are a Special DeLuxe coupe and four-door sedan. 4. With a new roof that lacked rear quarter windows, the Fleetline four-door sedan was styled like a Buick Special. Introduced midyear as Chevy's most expensive sedan, Fleetline garnered a respectable 4162 orders. 5. White ash and mahogany woody station wagon bodies were provided by Cantrell or Ionia Manufacturing. Only available in Special DeLuxe trim, the wagon was the costliest of all 1941 Chevrolets, selling for $995.

2

3

4

5

1. Oldsmobile entered 1941 with new hoods, grilles, and longer wheelbases. Series Sixty Special coupes came in two forms: club and business, the latter of which lacked a back seat. **2.** Forward-thinking fastback styling was featured on series 70 Dynamic Cruisers. **3.** Priced at $1575, the 98 convertible sedan was the most expensive Olds in '41. **4.** Olds offered wagons only in the 50 series. All had second- and third-row seats that could be removed easily. **5.** The front-fender badge indicates that this six-cylinder Oldsmobile 96 Custom Cruiser sedan is equipped with Hydra-Matic.

1. The Pontiac DeLuxe Torpedo Eight convertible cost $1048, $25 more than the Six. 2. Pontiac Streamliners, like this four-door sedan, utilized Olds/Buick B-bodies with fastback styling on a 122-inch wheelbase. 3. Six-cylinder cars could be distinguished from Eights by their trim. Sixes had "Pontiac" lettering in the hood trim; Eights said "Pontiac Eight." DeLuxe models, like this coupe, used Chevy's A-body on a 119-inch wheelbase. 4. The Custom Torpedo Eight station wagon was the most-expensive Pontiac at $1250.

338-323
NORTH CAROLINA 42
1

2

3

4

UNTIL TOTAL VICTORY, WE DEDICATE OURSELVES TO THE OBJECTIVE... "WHEN BETTER WAR GOODS ARE BUILT, BUICK WORKMEN WILL BUILD THEM."
5

1. Unlike most makes for 1942, Buick came out with a brand-new body that followed the lead of Harley Earl's 1938 Y-Job show car. The new styling brought the Super four-door sedan's front fenders into the doors. **2.** Estate wagons were among the rarest '42 Buicks, with only 327 produced during the shortened model year. **3.** Buick's waterfall grilles and huge bumpers were very modern. Roadmasters rode a 129-inch wheelbase. The convertible sold for $1675 and came with a power top. **4.** Supers (sedanet shown), Roadmasters, and Limiteds were powered by the Fireball 8, which remained unchanged at 320 cid and 165 hp. The government mandated that cast-iron pistons replace the aluminum units in Buick's 248-cid straight, taking horsepower down to 110, or 118 with Compound Carburetion. **5.** A Special "blackout special" was the final Buick built before factories were completely converted to defense work on Feb. 3, 1942. All General Motors cars sold after January 1 that year were blackout specials with exterior trim that was painted, rather than chromed.

1. Series 75 models were the only 1942 Cadillacs to maintain squared-off fenders with triple chrome trim. This basic body would remain in production until 1949. **2.** A mere 1742 Special DeLuxe convertibles were built before Chevrolet's civilian car production ended on February 9, 1942. **3.** The U.S. government placed restrictions on stainless-steel- and

chrome trim, as this Chevrolet Special DeLuxe Fleetline "blackout special" displays. **4.** The 1942 Oldsmobile 98 line was down to three models, including this four-door sedan. **5.** Nearing war, Oldsmobiles bore the "B-44" designation, marking the division's 44 years in business. This year, there was a name change from the Olds Motor Works to the Oldsmobile division of General Motors. **6.** Pontoon-style fenders extended into the doors of 1942 Pontiacs. This is the Torpedo Six sedan, which started at $985.

A quarter of all aircraft engines produced by America during the war were made by GM. Among the 206,000 that left GM plants were numerous V-12 Allison V-1710s that powered Lockeed's tough P-38 Lightning. Each 1710 was fitted with a General Electric turbo-supercharger and pro-duced 1475 horsepower, which gave the Lightning the speed (414 mph, max) and the climb-ing capability (2850 feet per minute) the U.S. Army Air Corps demanded. A fighter, bomber escort, attack, and recon aircraft, the P-38 was the only single-seat, twin-engine airplane to be mass produced during WWII.

GENERAL MOTORS AT WAR

Everything from seniority rights to year-end bonuses was put aside as General Motors mobilized to join what Franklin Roosevelt described as "the arsenal of democracy." With its vast engine, design, and production resources, GM became a major supplier to the wartime manufacturing industry.

More than 113,000 GM workers left to serve in the armed forces. The corporation hired replacements, many of them women, immortalized by "Rosie the Riveter," and spewed forth $12.3 billion in aircraft, tanks, vehicles, and armaments. GM produced 854,000 trucks, including the amphibious DUKW or "Duck"; 198,000 diesel engines; 206,000 aircraft engines; and 38,000 tanks, not to mention vast quantities of guns and ammunition. It would be impossible to list all of GM's wartime activities, but here are a few examples from the various divisions.

Buick general manager Harlow Curtice received a call from former GM president Bill Knudsen in Washington. The military needed an endless supply of the 1200-hp Pratt & Whitney radial aircraft engine. "We can do it," said Curtice. Knudsen asked for 500 a month; Buick was soon producing 1000 and then 2000 a month. To make the cylinder heads, Curtice built Buick's own aluminum foundry. Starting at 25,000 heads a month, the Flint division was turning out 125,000 a month by 1945.

Buick also built a specialized "tank destroyer," the lightly armored, tracked "Hellcat," with torque-converter automatic transmission, 37mm cannon, and 360-degree turret. Buick built over 2500 and turned the transmission into the "Torqmatic" unit for the heavy Pershing tank.

Cadillac's Cleveland tank plant, which had been producing the M-5, upped production to as many as the Army needed, powering them with L-head V-8s mated to a tank version of Hydra-Matic transmission; the same chassis was adopted for the self-propelled M-8 howitzer.

In Indianapolis, GM's Allison Division had designed the V-1710 air-craft engine, which powered the famous Lockheed P-38 Lightning and P-51 Mustang fighter. The famous Owen Nacker, together with John Gordon and a young engineer named Ed Cole, developed the turbocharged V-12, probably the most advanced aircraft engine of World War II.

At Cadillac itself, C. F. Arnold, a 15-year employee, took charge of developing the M-24 tracked vehicle that Caddy would begin building in 1944—a project that ultimately involved no fewer than 17 GM divisions. Cadillac also produced M-19 self-propelled anti-aircraft guns.

Chevrolet was 100 percent converted to war production by mid-1942, producing shells, gun parts, and aircraft engines. Chevy produced 3000 of the four-wheel-drive "Staghound" armored car, a light-armored half-track that saw action with General George Patton in North Africa, along with 1 ½-ton trucks and ambulances for the Army.

Oldsmobile employed 11,218 workers at the height of the war effort, winning the Army-Navy E pennant with three stars for exceptional perfor-mance. Between April 1941 and September 1945, the Lansing division manufactured 48 million rounds of artillery ammunition, 140,000 air-craft machine guns and tank cannons, nearly 350,000 high-precision air-craft-engine parts, and 175 million pounds of forgings for trucks, tanks, guns, and aircraft.

Pontiac converted rapidly from cars to military production, thanks to the efforts of P. H. MacGregor. In March 1941, Pontiac had received an order to produce the Oerlikon 20mm anti-aircraft naval cannon. The division's next assignment was a U.S. Army order for Bofors automatic field guns. Pontiac cleared more than 200,000 square feet in its sheet-metal plant for the high-precision machinery needed to make the Swed-ish-designed weapon.

When Pontiac was asked to participate in supplying front axles for Cadillac's M-5 tank, it built not only all that were needed but parts for the large, two-stroke Detroit Diesel engine that was in such demand for stationary and marine use by the Army and Navy.

Not the least of Pontiac's efforts was production of aircraft-launched torpedoes for the Navy—an intricate assignment because of the weapon's complexity. Each torpedo contained 5222 separate parts and 1225 different assemblies—within a thin envelope less than 20 feet long! Pontiac easily handled this challenge, fulfilling every requirement with ease.

After the war, cynics sneered that it was all done on a "cost-plus" basis and that the various divisions reaped huge profits. When we stop and consider how much of its civilian-car production infrastructure GM destroyed in order to meet the demand, and that nobody else could have done it—not to mention the many GM people who served, and those who did not return—the true greatness of the company's achievement becomes obvious.

1

2

3

4

5

1. The Fisher Body plant in Trenton, New Jersey, built Grumman Avengers for the Navy. Forty percent of GM's $12.25 billion in war material was aviation related.
2. General Motors produced a total of 854,000 trucks for wartime use, including these near-ready light-duty models. Cadillac, among others, earned an Army-Navy "E" Award for its military production efforts. **3.** Some top executives did more than contribute to the war effort from home. William S. Knudsen served as a lieutenant general.
4. Developed by the GMC Truck and Coach Division, the amphibious "Duck" saw duty worldwide during World War II, carrying troops on land and water. All five GM passenger-car divisions also turned their facilities over to the war effort. Many M-24 tanks used Cadillac V-8 engines and Hydra-Matic transmissions.
5. Conversion to all-out military production began right after war was declared. Eight million artillery shells came out of Chevrolet plants. Here, ordnance inspection takes place at the Chevrolet-St. Louis Shell Division.

1. Substantially redesigned for 1942, the '46 Buicks looked fresher than most competitors. The first "gunsight" hood ornaments appeared, above a revised grille. Century and Limited models were discontinued, body styles were fewer, and no more exotic customs were issued. Compound Carburetion didn't return either, meaning the 320-cid V-8 engine dropped to 144 hp from 165. That was still 9 hp more than its closest competitor, however. Four-door models, like this $2110 Roadmaster sedan, got full-length "Airfoil" fenders like their two-door kin. **2.** The '46s had less trim than '42s, and the new grille had fewer teeth spaced farther apart. Supers, like this convertible, rode 16-inch tires, as did Specials; Roadmasters used 15s. **3.** Cadillac got rolling after the war on October 17, 1945, but not for long. A United Auto Workers strike shut down all GM production for more than four months. Cadillac's Sixty Special line was reduced to one model, this five-passenger, four-door sedan without a division window. New "Cadillac" block letters adorned the front fenders, and the chrome fender louvers of '42 were gone. **4.** The Series 62 club coupe, with its fastback styling, returned, but not until a few months into production. Grille changes were minimal. The parking lights became rectangular instead of round, and the bars were slightly heavier and spread farther apart.

1

2

3

4

1. The $1250 Chevrolet Fleetmaster four-door sport sedan was the division's second-best seller in 1946. 2. General sales manager D. E. Raltson and general manager S. E. Skinner (standing) greeted the first postwar factory-produced Oldsmobile as it rolled off the line. 3. Oldsmobile produced 117,623 vehicles during the 1946 model year. Here, the 100,000th 1946 Olds rolls off

the assembly line. 4. A shot of Ransom Eli Olds in 1946. The founder of the Olds Motor Vehicle Company would die four years later. 5. Oldsmobile Custom Cruiser 98 mechanicals remained the same as prewar models: a 127-inch wheelbase with a 257-cid, 110-hp straight-eight engine. Priced at $1492, the four-door sedan was the most popular of this series. The division produced more than 11,000.

1

2

3

1. Occupying the middle of the model range, Oldsmobile's Dynamic Cruiser lineup came in two-door- and four-door-sedan body styles. The 76 models had a 238-cid six-cylinder engine that produced 100 hp. The 78s had a 257-cid straight eight that made 110 hp. All rode a 125-inch wheelbase and ranged in price from $1184 to $1413. **2.** Pontiac was 6th in model-year production for 1946, outpacing Oldsmobile by about 20,000 units, despite its products being warmed-over '42s. With the war over, thoughts turned to play. Pontiac, like many automakers, issued factory photos that depicted its products with active-lifestyle folks. Here, the $1335 Torpedo Eight convertible coupe is shown with horseback riding aficionados. Torpedoes used GM A-bodies on 119-inch wheelbases. **3.** The Pontiac Streamliner Eight four-door sedan sold for $1538, $478 more than the '42. Streamliners ran the GM B-body on a 122-inch wheelbase. A spear-shaped hood-side nameplate replaced the '42's full-length side trim and revealed which engine lurked under the hood.

1

1. Buicks in 1947 were basically '46s with new grilles. Two-tone paint was an attractive extra-cost option on all models. The Roadmaster sedanet listed at $2131. 2. The only convertible Cadillac produced in 1947 was the Series 62, priced at $2902. 3. The block "Cadillac" lettering on the front quarter panels changed to script in 1947, and bright chrome "sombrero" wheel covers became available on all models. 4. The Cadillac Series 62 club coupe sat five passengers and was available with the extra-cost Hydramatic Drive automatic transmission.

2

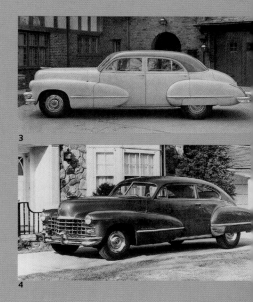

3

4

RIDING THE RAILS

General Motors ordered construction of the "Train of Tomorrow" after World War II. It consisted of the locomotive, chair car, dining car, and sleeping car. Passengers could sit up high in the "Astra Dome" roof and enjoy an expanded view of passing scenery. The train was delivered in 1947 and toured the country until 1950. The Union Pacific Railroad then purchased the train for the city of Seattle.

1. Though they didn't look much different, 1947 Chevrolets cost 15 to 20 percent more than their 1946 counterparts. For $149.50, consumers could buy a Country Club wood trim kit and have it installed by the dealer. The kits were Chevy's answer to the wood-sided Ford Sportsman. 2. The $1893 wood-bodied Fleetmaster station wagon was the costli-

est and least popular 1947 Chevy. Only 4912 were sold. 3. Much more popular was the two-door Aerosedan, of which more than 159,000 were produced. 4. Many municipalities bought low-end Chevy Stylemasters for use as police cars. Apparently, the state of Idaho had money to spare, as it used the uplevel Fleetline Aerosedan for highway patrol duty. 5. On November 13, 1947, Chevrolet announced a production milestone. The sedan pictured here was the division's 20,000,000th vehicle. It was made at the Flint, Michigan, assembly plant. Shown here (left to right) are Nicholas Dreystadt, the Chevrolet division general manager; T. H. Keating, general sales manager; and Hugh Dean, general manufacturing manager. In 1947, Chevrolet produced 671,546 vehicles, good enough to reclaim first place in the industry.

1

2

3

4

5

6

1. Without innovation or a new design to sell, Olds touted convenience features for its 1947 cars. Priced at $1433, the two-door club sedan was the most popular Series 66 Special; a total of 23,960 were sold. **2.** For $121 more than the six-cylinder Series 66 club sedan, buyers could get an eight-cylinder Dynamic Cruiser 78.

3. The revised grille of 1947 Pontiacs lost its vertical bars and sported a new Indian-head emblem. New teardrop-shaped hood side trim on all cars no longer identified the engine choice. **4.** Accessories on this Asbury Green Pontiac Torpedo Eight convertible include a radio, turn signals, fender skirts, and bumper wing guards. The wraparound bumpers introduced in '46 carried over for '47. **5.** Classified as a Streamliner, the wood-bodied station wagon came in standard or DeLuxe trim. Eight-cylinder Pontiac wagons sold for $2282 or $2359 with the DeLuxe interior appointments. This year, straight-eight models outsold sixes for the first time. **6.** Harley Earl (center) stands with the GM "Parade of Progress" truck. The brain-child of Charles F. Kettering, the parade was a nationwide tour designed to showcase the company's latest technologies. This event kicked off in 1936, ran for 20 years, and covered millions of miles through American cities and towns.

1. Externally, not much changed for Buick in 1948. Buick again sold more convertibles than most automakers, but overall ragtop sales were down about 25 percent. The big news was the addition of the Dynaflow automatic transmission that was introduced as a $244 option on Roadmasters. Dynaflow included a hydraulic torque converter that provided fully automatic shifting. It was originally developed by Buick during the war for the Hellcat tank destroyer. Not as effi-

2

cient as the Cadillac and Olds Hydra-Matic, it was dubbed "Dyna-slush" by some. The 320-cid inline eights of cars so equipped came with six extra horsepower (150 vs. 144) to make up for the new transmission's tendency to slip. **2.** The only difference between this '48 Roadmaster Estate Wagon and its '47 counterpart is the script on the front fenders. **3.** Cadillacs got a total redesign for 1948, complete with tailfins inspired by P-38 Lightning aircraft. These were among the first all-new postwar cars from any Detroit Three automaker. Due to the redesign, production got a late start, shortening Cadillac's model year to just nine months. Series 62 models had stone shields behind the front wheel openings and bright rocker sill moldings.

1

3

1

2

3

1. Chevrolet retained its spot as the top producer for model-year 1948, with 696,449 vehicles rolling off assembly lines, a 3.7 percent increase over 1947. Part of the Fleetline Sportmaster sedan's appeal was its similarity to GM's senior line cars. Sales increased 18 percent over '47, but it was still outsold by the Aerosedan by more than three-to-one. Chevy produced slightly more than 64,000 Sportmaster sedans but almost 212,000 Aerosedans. 2. Convertible sales were down 28 percent, but the Fleetmaster convertible coupe was still appealing, so much so that it paced the Indianapolis 500 race. Convertible boots matched the top color. Chrome-plated gravel shields were optional on all models. 3. The only Chevy priced higher than $2000 was the Fleetmaster woody wagon at $2013. Despite the relatively steep price tag, wagon production more than doubled to 10,171 units, setting a company record. Wagons would become much more popular in two short years, as GM converted to steel bodies. 4. Spearhead-shaped hood-

4

side trim identified the series of all Chevys. The Fleetmaster four-door sport sedan had sliding rear quarter windows. They started at $1439 and were the most popular of the series. In addition to sport sedans and woody wagons, the Fleetmaster line included the two-door town sedan, sport coupe, and convertible coupe. All had a 116-inch wheelbase.

1. Along with Cadillac, Oldsmobile was the first GM brand to get redesigned cars after the war. The 98 lineup got "Futuramic" styling midyear and rode a 2-inch shorter wheelbase. Futuramic styling included slab-sided, flow-through fenders, and a lower, wider appearance. This 98 Deluxe convertible coupe helped Olds ragtop sales outdistance Buick convertibles 12,914 to 11,503. Topless Buicks had outsold their Olds counterparts three-to-one in 1947. **2.** The 98 club sedan

1

2

3

was the least expensive of the senior series cars at $2078. The DeLuxe version (shown) cost another $104. **3.** A combination wood and metal Fisher body replaced the Ionia unit on Olds 60 series station wagons for '48. These were by far the most expensive models in the 60 series lineup. A six-cylinder model cost $2456, and the straight-eight version went for $2514. These prices were up to $1000 more than standard coupes and sedans. It's little wonder less than 2000 woodies were produced in '48. **4.** The 98 series became Oldsmobile's best seller for the first time. Its straight-eight engine produced 115 hp, up from the previous year's 110. This would be the last year for the straight eight.

4

1. Pontiac carried over its pre-war car designs for 1948. The automatic Hydra-Matic Drive transmission was a new option this year. Hydra-Matic was popular, as roughly three-quarters of '48s were so equipped. Streamliner coupes were available in standard trim, starting at $1677. An additional $89 bought this DeLuxe version, which on all '48s included front-fender trim, full wheel covers, and bright-metal gravel guards in place of the

standard rubber units. 2. This convertible is the Pontiac Silver Streak. Its inline eight-cylinder engine had 104 hp, an increase of one over '47. 3. You can spot a base-model 1948 Pontiac by its unadorned fender sides, as this Torpedo Eight two-door sedan demonstrates. Pontiac's model-year production increased two percent to 235,419, good for a ranking of 5th in the industry.

1-2. Buick completely redesigned the Roadmaster line for 1949, giving it a shorter wheelbase. The new Roadmaster Riviera shown here, with its pillarless hardtop, became a style leader as soon as it hit showrooms late in the model year. Riviera production for 1949 was only 4343 units, but that would grow drastically in the next two years. **3.** The second-most-popular Buick was the Super two-door sedanet.

1

2

Dynaflow automatic transmission was newly available on Supers; Supers so equipped came with 120 hp, five more than non-Dynaflow models. **4.** Estate wagons came in Roadmaster (shown) or Super form. Overall, wagon sales were down, partially due to price; the Roadmaster wagon cost $3734, about $500 more than the Riviera hardtop coupe. **5.** "VentiPorts," more commonly known as portholes, made their debut with the '49s; Roadmasters had four and Supers and Specials had three. Buick claimed the holes helped cool the engine, and they actually did for the first few months. GM plugged the holes shortly thereafter, making them a purely cosmetic touch.

3

4

5

1

1. Cadillac's biggest news came from under the hood with the introduction of a 331-cid, overhead-valve, short-stroke, high-compression V-8 engine. It produced 160 hp. High-style convertibles were especially popular, with sales jumping to 8000 units. **2.** A late-year release, the Series 62 Coupe

2

3

4

de Ville hardtop earned accolades for its styling. **3.** The three chrome strips below the taillights of the '48 Series 62s were gone in '49. Here, the $2966 Series 62 two-door fastback club coupe. **4.** Cadillac's best seller in a record year was the Series 62 four-door sedan. Stone shields behind the front wheel wells and chrome rocker moldings differentiated 62s from Series 61s. The division produced its 1,000,000th vehicle on November 25, 1949.

1. Though Chevrolet's production for 1949 set a company record at 1,010,013 units, the division fell behind Ford for overall sales. Chevy only offered convertibles as DeLuxe Styleline models; prices started at $1857. **2.** Fleetline no longer designated Chevy's top series; instead it meant fastback styling. **3.** Styleline denoted bustle-back or notchback styling, as seen on this $1508 DeLuxe sport coupe.

1

2

3

4. All Oldsmobiles adopted Futuramic styling for 1949. The division offered two types of four-door sedans in the 76 and 88 series, a fastback (shown) and a notchback. **5.** Olds supplied two Rocket 88 pace cars for the '49 Indy 500, one white, the other maroon. **6.** Oldsmobile's best seller, the 98 four-door sedan, combined for sales of 57,821 in standard and Deluxe trim. **7.** The Olds Rocket V-8 (along with Cadillac's new V-8) changed the way the industry thought about engines. With a 90-degree overhead-valve design, a short stroke, and a high compression ratio, the new 303-cid engine put out 135 hp. It was designed to take advantage of the high-octane fuels that were on the way. **8.** The 76 woody wagon sold for $2895. Olds sold 76- and 88-series wagons.

4

5

6

7

8

1-2. These two Oldsmobiles were the least popular of the division's 98 series lineup. The $2426 club sedan (left) sold 3849 copies while the $2973 Deluxe Holiday hardtop coupe (below) moved only 3009 units. The most popular 98 series car was the $2594 Deluxe four-door sedan, which accounted for 49,001 sales. Overall model-year production of 288,310 was good enough for Oldsmobile to take 7th place in the industry. 3. Pontiac's cars

were redesigned for 1949, with flow-through-fender styling similar to that of the new-for-'48 Cadillacs. This Chieftain four-door sedan shows the '49s lower profile, due in part to the switch from 16- to 15-inch tires. 4. Streamliner four-door sedans started at $1740 with a six-cylinder engine and $1808 with the eight. 5. A small amount of wood was still used in Pontiac wagons, but unlike previous designs, most of the '49's doors were steel. Later in the model year, steel panels covered with simulated wood replaced this last remaining cabinetwork. Streamliner DeLuxe wagons ranged in price from $2622 with the six to $2690 with the eight.

CHAPTER SIX

1950-1959

"The independents' troubles are of their own making. Ever wonder what they did with the rich profits of the war years? Did they plow them back into the company? We didn't drive them under; they drove themselves."

—Harlow Curtice, president & CEO 1953–58

In the Fifties, the keys to every General Motors vehicle bore the legend, "Your Key to Greater Value." There was truth in that. As the industry's most efficient automaker, GM could offer competitive prices and still earn more money per sale than any rival. Bob Bourke, designer of the famous 1953 Studebaker Starliner, priced that car with a friend at Chevrolet and found that GM could have sold it profitably for $300 less than Studebaker did. GM also led Detroit in trade-in values. In 1955, for example, a five-year-old Packard Custom Eight was worth $380 versus $1105 for a Cadillac Sixty-Special of the same age—and the Caddy sold new for $200 less.

Every GM division seemed unstoppable in this decade. In 1950, Buick sold more than 300,000 of its low-priced Specials to spurt ahead of third-place Plymouth for the first time. Unmistakable with its big chrome grille teeth, portholes, bodyside sweepspears, and "gunsight" hood ornament, the Special was a threat to Oldsmobile's market sector. But Olds still had the hot V-8 and Hydra-Matic, while Buick made do with Dynaflow and inline eights.

Cadillacs saw only detail changes in the early Fifties but remained surprisingly fast. Durable, too. Briggs Cunningham proved both points when he entered a near-stock Coupe de Ville in the 1950 Le Mans 24 Hour race that finished 10th overall against formidable foreign competition.

Chevrolet and Pontiac added hardtop convertibles for 1950. At $1741, Chevy's Bel Air was the industry's lowest-priced hardtop, and nearly 77,000 were sold that first year alone. Chevrolet also an-

nounced two-speed Powerglide automatic for 1950, optioned on 300,000 cars.

When the Korean War broke out, the government fixed auto prices and production for 1951–52. GM was assigned 41 percent of the market, nearly 25 percent less than it held in 1950. With that and the mandated defense work, GM's total car production fell to 80 percent of 1950 levels in '51 and to 65 percent in 1952.

Buicks continued with little change except for horsepower, as the Roadmaster straight-eight was pushed to 170. Even with production curbs, Buick again pressed Plymouth for third place.

Cadillac was the only GM division to post higher 1951 sales—setting a new record in the process—despite military production of replacement transmissions, M-24 tank parts, and the new Walker Bulldog light tank. The '52 models were little changed, yet Cadillac finished 11th in the production race, a new high. And except for 1953, Cadillac would run 10th or 11th right into the 1970s, when it occasionally rose as high as eighth.

Chevrolet served the war effort through its aircraft-engine assembly plant and a tank-transmission factory. But the division also managed to introduce a new "stop-and-go" delivery truck, which could be driven standing up, and sold more automatic transmissions than anyone else. The '52 lineup, almost the same as 1951's, included the last fastback Fleetline models, whose sales had dried up.

On paper, 1951 looked bad for Oldsmobile. Volume fell by 125,000, allowing Dodge and Mercury to move ahead in the production race. But some of the loss was due to general manager J. F. Wolfram, who decided to move Olds up into the profitable $2000-$3000 market—the middle of the middle-priced field. To get there, Wolfram dropped station wagons and the six-cylinder Series 76 and added a more-deluxe "Rocket 88," the Super 88. Though all '51 Oldsmobiles were just slightly facelifted, the Super's color-keyed interiors, extra brightwork, and exclusive 120-inch wheelbase helped make it the most popular Olds line, earning many "conquest sales" from Dodge, Mercury, Hudson, and Packard Clipper.

Pontiac had one of its best years in 1951 despite production lost to defense work (amphibious army vehicles, 40mm cannon, and 4½-inch rockets). Bob Critchfield took over as general manager the following year, when the division dumped Streamliner fastbacks and watched Chieftain Eights outsell Chieftain Sixes by 11 to one.

Dwight Eisenhower moved into the White House in 1953 and made good on his campaign promise to go to Korea. Hostilities soon ended, and all GM divisions prospered as the industry returned to business as usual. A jealous Ford Motor Company tried to close the sales gap with GM by flooding dealers with cars, whether they'd been ordered or not, forcing deep discounts to move the metal. GM reacted in kind, and the resulting sales battle crippled the independents. Within two years, Kaiser and Willys abandoned the U.S. car market. Others were forced into mergers: Nash with Hudson, Studebaker with Packard. When the dust settled, GM, not Ford, was Detroit's undisputed sales leader.

The price war continued into 1954, when Buick, Olds, and Pontiac finished 4-5-6 in industry production and Cadillac bested every independent for the first time. But Ford edged Chevy in model-year output, and volume was down for all GM brands except Buick, whose new-for-'53 "Fireball" V-8 was giving the brand a "hot car" reputation.

After years of thinking about it, Chevrolet introduced a sports car in 1953, but with only six cylinders and Powerglide, the Corvette was a mild performer. To hold costs down, the body was made of fiberglass. Styling was pure Motorama show car, with a toothy grille, wraparound windshield, and rocketship taillamps. This first-year Corvette was a virtual prototype (only 315 built) and not much liked by sports-car purists, but the two-seat Chevy would soon command respect.

Also new for 1953 were the Cadillac Eldorado, Buick Skylark, and Oldsmobile Fiesta, each a jazzy, high-priced, limited-production convertible intended more to glorify their showroom siblings than to make money on their own. Cadillac, Buick, and Olds all restyled for 1954, increasing wheelbases and adopting new square-rigged styling with wrapped windshields. The Fiesta disappeared, but Eldorado and Skylark became more like regular convertibles, which allowed lower prices and helped sales.

Pontiac had no limited edition and was still stuck with an inline eight, but a heavy facelift served it well for 1953–54. Sibling Chevrolets also looked more "important" and regrouped into 150 Special, 210 Deluxe, and 240 Bel Air series. Typical of the age was a new option for senior GM brands called "Autronic Eye," the first automatic headlamp dimmer.

For 1954, Buick revived its prewar "factory hot rod," the Century. Combining the smaller Buick body with the big Roadmaster's 322 V-8, these cars could do 0 to 60 in 11 seconds and easily top 100 mph. V-8 power also transformed Buick's Special, which stole more customers from Plymouth and Ford in 1954: a rousing 200,000 sales.

With model-year 1955, the auto industry "exploded," as *Ward's Yearbook* put it, producing 9,188,574 vehicles including nearly eight million passenger cars. For the first time, a good economy combined with unprecedented capacity and a host of new models and features from almost every nameplate.

Cadillacs showed the least change among GM makes but were still recognizably new. The Eldorado gained distinction by adopting pointed "shark fins"; other models retained the traditional modest, upturned rear fenders. Model-year production set another new record at 140,000. Cadillac management had planned well. With advanced engineering, styling that was just new enough each year, and careful attention to buyer wants, GM's flagship division now claimed a 55 percent share of the luxury market, almost double its 1950 penetration. This was partly due to the decline of Packard and lackluster Lincoln sales, but the real credit was to Cadillac engineers, designers, and executives.

The 1955 Buick and Olds lineups focused on more flash, color, and power. With the market crazy for hardtop coupes, both makes took the next logical step and added hardtop sedans at midseason, forcing rivals to play catch-up again.

Chevrolet was arguably 1955's biggest sensation, boasting the division's first modern V-8 and terrific all-new styling. The V-8 was designed under Ed Cole (see sidebar, page 158), while the handsome exterior was the work of a team led by Clare MacKichan. Designer Carl Renner, who created the new Chevys' Ferrari-like grille, also conjured up a distinctive two-door "hardtop" station wagon, the Bel Air Nomad. Pontiac lobbied for and got its own version, the Star Chief Safari. Alas, both models were impractical for wagons and thus slow-sellers, but high style and low production have since made them coveted collector cars.

As ever, Chevy and Ford vied for "USA-1" sales supremacy in 1955, but that year's Ford, with a radical facelift, couldn't compare. Nor could Plymouth, despite a flashy redesign of its own. Suddenly, the reliable but dull Chevrolet was not just a beauty but a genuinely

exciting V-8 performer. Chevy ads rightly called it "The Hot One."

Pontiac also joined the V-8 ranks for 1955 with a lively new "Strato Streak" engine producing 173-200 horsepower. A full redesign really jazzed-up appearance—as startling a change as Chevrolet's—but not everyone liked the blunt front end. Quotable road tester Tom McCahill said the car looked "like it was born on its nose." Nevertheless, Pontiac built a record 553,000 cars in 1955 and would not have a better year until 1963.

No one expected 1956 to be another red-hot year, but sales were still good—the fourth best in Detroit history—at 5.8 million cars. Luxury makes suffered least in the inevitable industry slowdown, but Chevrolet increased its share of the low-priced market.

Buick built 635,000 cars in '56, selling on price rather than radically changed looks. Cadillac introduced its first four-door hardtop, the Sedan de Ville, which was popular from the first. One negative aspect was Cadillac's newly bored-out 365 V-8, notorious for "soft" valves and resultant engine problems; this wasn't really cured until a stroked 390 V-8 debuted for 1959.

Chevrolet played up its impressive performance in NASCAR racing by offering its "Turbo Fire" V-8 with a much as 225 horsepower. Four-door Sport Sedan hardtops and freshened styling also made '56 news.

So did a clean-sheet Corvette. It returned with V-8 power, a '55 addition, but more of it. And a three-speed manual transmission was newly available to take full advantage. Chevy also got serious with Corvette styling: now beautifully sculpted and much cleaner. Though GM almost killed the Corvette in 1955, the redesigned '56 began a sales revival that would earn the "plastic" sports car a permanent place in the Chevy line.

Olds prospered in 1956, partly at the expense of Pontiac, which was hampered by an undistinguished facelift. But the Oldsmobiles were nicely styled, and up to 240 horsepower was available across a broad model slate.

The 1957 season was more difficult. First, GM's facelifted cars looked dated next to Chrysler Corporation's all-new "Forward Look" designs with their high-flying tailfins and low silhouettes. Though Detroit built 7.2 million vehicles this year, GM's market share was 46.1 percent, down from 52.8 in 1955. Stronger Chrysler competition was a factor, but so was a recession that began during the model year. That hurt all Detroit producers while boosting buyer interest in small, economy imports like the Volkswagen Beetle.

GM's senior makes all restyled for '57, becoming longer, lower, wider, and chromier. Yet despite all-new bodyshells, they were less dramatic than Virgil Exner's Chrysler fleet. Buick and Olds added pillarless four-door hardtop station wagons, the Caballero and Fiesta, but they did little for sales. In fact, Buick general manager Ed Ragsdale was disappointed by his division's losses to Mercury, DeSoto, and the Chrysler Windsor. Meanwhile, Plymouth made a powerful comeback, sending Buick down to fourth place again.

Leading the 1957 Cadillac line was an opulent newcomer, the $13,000 Eldorado Brougham. Descended from recent Motorama concepts, this compact four-door hardtop boasted center-opening doors, Caddy's first quad headlamps, a brushed stainless-steel roof, a lush interior, and air suspension. It was another "ultimate car," corporate grandstanding to rival Ford's year-old Continental Mark II. But the air suspension caused no end of trouble, and Cadillac lost a bundle on every Brougham sold. Production totaled only 704 for 1957–58 combined. After 200 more were built in Italy for 1959–60, the model was dumped.

Against all new '57 Fords and Plymouths, Chevrolets offered a three-year-old basic design with a heavy restyle marked by a big new bumper/grille and tailfins that imparted a strong Cadillac flavor. Though Chevy edged Ford in model-year production by 130 cars, Ford won the calendar-year race by a whopping 165,000 units. Nevertheless, the '57 Chevys have since become among the most popular collector cars in history, partly because they were better built than Fords and Plymouths, of which far fewer survive.

Leading the engine lineup was a bored-out 283 V-8 offering up to "one hp per cubic inch" with optional Rochester fuel injection. This was also available for the Corvette, which added an optional four-speed manual gearbox and more factory "competition" equipment for road and track alike.

The '57 Oldsmobiles were cleanly styled, blending another gaping bumper/grille with longer, lower lines. Lansing built close to 400,000 of them, including station wagons, back for the first time since 1950. These Fiestas came with or without door pillars in the 88 series and as a Super 88 hardtop. But buyers were largely unmoved by pillarless wagons, and Olds phased them out after 1958, as did Buick.

Over at Pontiac, Semon E. "Bunkie" Knudsen, son of the famous "Big Bill," was now general manager, intent on transforming the brand's image just as Ed Cole had done with Chevrolet. The immediate result was the first performance Pontiac, the flashy $5782 Bonneville convertible, offering Tri-Power (three two-barrel carbs) or fuel injection and able to run a quarter mile in 16.8 seconds. Though fuel injection was problematic and expensive, and its high price precluded many sales, the Bonneville signaled Pontiac's ultimately successful shift from "deluxe Chevrolet" to brawny, good-looking performance machine.

If 1957 had been a mixed Detroit sales year, 1958 was an unqualified disaster. The deepening recession was bad enough, but GM compounded its woes with overblown, overstyled cars that were out of step with a public now thinking more about gas mileage than horsepower. As a result, Chevrolet built 1.25 million cars, its worst showing since 1952. Pontiac and Buick had "captive imports"—British Vauxhalls and German Opels—but these small cars were curiosities to the people who typically patronized those brands. American Motors' George Romney taunted the Big Three, especially GM, for building "dinosaurs," even as his compact Ramblers bucked the down market with higher sales versus '57.

Critics chided the "B-58" Buicks as a perfect example of Detroit's "wretched excess," the revived Limited series in particular. Buyers agreed, and production slipped to 240,000 as Buick fell to fifth place behind Olds. The Limited, really just a senior Roadmaster, accounted for just 7600 sales.

Oldsmobile styling fared little better than Buick's. Stylist Alex Tremulis, who later admitted to conjuring equally repulsive dishes at Ford, lampooned Oldsmobile's four rear-fender chrome strips by drawing one with a clef and a few notes of music. Pontiac, meanwhile, received a new body, but it was the wrong year to offer one, and volume dropped to just over 215,000.

Cadillac, America's luxury leader, suffered less from 1958's economic setbacks, but its 125,000-unit output was the smallest since '54. Even Caddy buyers must have been put off by the chrome-laden Eldorados and Sixty-Specials. Perhaps the same cars would have done fine in 1955, but their slow sales caused much anxiety at Cadillac headquarters.

Harley Earl, who had led GM styling since his arrival in 1927, retired in 1958. Taking over was Bill Mitchell, who preferred the clean-cut "extruded" look to Earl's more rounded—and lately overchromed—forms. "I'm out to change our tarnished image," Mitchell brashly declared, determined to move away from mere decoration to cleaner, purer, original shapes. The Mitchell era would produce some of GM's most beautiful cars.

Against the needless gimmickry of GM's upper divisions, Chevrolet deserves credit for its relatively conservative 1958 redesign. Yes, the cars were lower, longer, wider, and heavier. Slower, too, despite a new 348 V-8. But all that was laid down in the boundless optimism of 1955, the year Ford began planning the Edsel. And by '58 standards, the Chevys looked pretty good, especially the lavish new top-line Impala convertible and two-door hardtop. Ironically, though, these cars and their Pontiac stablemates would last just one year, as both makes would look "all-new all over again" for 1959.

Even the Corvette couldn't escape GM styling "gorp," but the all-new '58 offered more power, speed, and convenience, offset-

ting a heavier, flashier look and modest dimensional increases. In fact, Corvette was one of the few Detroit cars to post higher '58 sales—a surprising 50-percent spurt from '57 to 9168 units. The future of America's sports car was now truly secure.

Harlow Curtice, "the last president of GM who really ran it" according to John Z. DeLorean, retired in 1958, as GM reverted to a separate president and chairman. The new chairman was 55-year-old Frederic G. Donner, who had joined GM as an accountant in 1926. That made him a bean counter, but as he insisted, "I am not taciturn. I am not shy, I am not afraid of people…. I don't even own a slide rule." Compared to the outspoken Harlow Curtice, however, Donner was invisible. The new president was John F. Gordon, a nuts-and-bolts engineer with a long, distinguished career at Cadillac. Respected throughout the company, he was credited with the 1959 body-sharing programs that completely transformed GM styling.

As a group, GM's '59s were the wildest ever, the result of a secret, fast-track effort by humbled designers to "outdo" Chrysler and regain industry styling leadership. Big Three compacts were still a year away, allowing Ramblers and Studebaker's new Larks to share nearly half a million sales. And Rambler shot past Buick, Olds and Pontiac into fourth, the first time an independent had placed among the top-five sellers since Hudson in 1934.

The '59 Buicks sported dramatic "delta wing" fins, less obvious brightwork, and new series names: LeSabre, Invicta, Electra, and Electra 225. The "linear look" Oldsmobiles were more conservative, with a simple dumbell-shaped grille and horizontal fenderlines. All were big, roomy cars offering fine performance and poor gas mileage, plus acres of glass.

Bunkie Knudsen's Pontiacs were arguably GM's best-looking '59s, wearing a split grille—soon to be a brand hallmark—modest twin-fin fear fenders, and a much-touted new Wide-Track chassis. Pontiac's V-8 was up to 389 cubes and 315 horses, but there was now a low-tune "Tempest 420E" version that returned 20 miles per gallon if carefully driven. Bonneville now topped the line as a full series, but midrange Star Chiefs and low-end Catalina were also popular. Pontiac deservedly won *Motor Trend*'s "Car of the Year" award. Knudsen had worked wonders in three years, nearly doubling division output and boosting Pontiac into fourth place behind Chevrolet, Ford, and Rambler.

By contrast, the '59 Cadillacs were real spaceships, with busy, chrome-encrusted grilles and the highest fins ever, capped by dual-bullet taillamps. Four-door hardtops offered a choice of rooflines, as at Buick, but all Cadillacs except the long Series 75 rode a unique 130-inch wheelbase. Elvis Presley drove a pink '59 Eldorado convertible that seemed a city block long, as symbolic of the times as any artifact could be.

The 1959 Chevrolets sprouted "batwing" tailfins as outrageous as Cadillac's, plus rear decks "big enough to land a Piper Cub," according to "Uncle Tom" McCahill. It was an incredible change from the sensibly sized Chevys of 1955–57. Wheelbase was up by four inches, length by a foot, width by seven inches, heft by 300 pounds. Impala expanded to a full top-of-the-line series, adding pillared and pillarless four-doors—and "every creature comfort that could be had." Also new for '59—complete with batwings—was the El Camino, a station wagon-based pickup answering Ford's two-year-old Ranchero.

General Motors marked its 50th anniversary in 1958, and despite the disappointments of that particular sales year, it had much to celebrate. Since 1908, the company had posted sales of $129 billion and profits of $11.3 billion. It had sold 56 million vehicles, 16 million refrigerators, and 20,000 diesel locomotives. GM had grown to become one of the world's top-four producers of diesel engines, bicycles, aircraft engines, air conditioners, water heaters, electric ranges, and ball bearings. Had an investor bought 100 GM shares in 1908 for the official price of $10,000, his stake would have been worth $10.6 million 50 years later—a thousand-fold increase.

Next on the agenda: taking on those pesky foreign economy cars…

1. Buick greeted the 1950s with redesigned bodies boasting fresh styling. The company's biggest barge for 1950 was the $2738 Roadmaster Riviera sedan, which rode a 5-inch-longer wheelbase than other Roadmasters. **2.** A snazzy Roadmaster convertible started at $2981. **3.** Buick's least-expensive four-door for 1950 was the $1809 Special Jetback sedan.

1

2

3

4

5

4. Cadillacs got one-piece windshields for 1950. Topping the company's standard lineup was the $3797 60 Special four-door sedan. It rode a regal 130-inch wheelbase, four inches longer than the midline Series 62. **5.** Cadillac's smallest and least-expensive sedan for 1950 was the 122-inch-wheelbase Series 61 four-door at $2866. **6.** The glamorous Series 61 hardtop coupe was the least-expensive Cadillac at $2761. Like all Caddys, it was powered by the division's advanced 331-cid overhead-valve V-8 rated at 160 hp.

6

1. Chevrolet produced nearly 1.5 million cars for 1950, a new record. The $1847 Styleline Deluxe convertible contributed 32,392 to that total. Newly available was Powerglide automatic transmission. 2. One of America's first hardtops was Chevy's $1741 Bel Air. 3. The most popular Chevy for 1950 was the $1529 Styleline Deluxe sport sedan, with 316,412 finding

buyers. 4. Oldsmobile's top seller for 1950 was the $2056 Futuramic 88 Deluxe sedan at more than 100,000 units. 5. Just $2294 bought a rakish Futuramic 88 convertible. 6. Oldsmobile offered Holiday hardtop coupes in both the midline 119.5-inch-wheelbase 88 series and the top-line 122-inch-wheelbase 98 series. Shown is the $2162 Futuramic 88 version; a 98 cost $2383. All 88s and 98s were powered by Oldsmobile's 303-cid 135-hp overhead-valve V-8.

1. One of the most significant labor deals in auto history took place in 1950 between GM and the UAW. The agreement promised five years of peace in GM plants across the country. **2.** The 3-millionth Oldsmobile came off the assembly line on February 15, 1950. It was a club coupe version of the top-line 98, which was restyled for 1950 with "flow through" rear fenderlines. Olds built a performance reputation during this era as the car to beat on race tracks. **3.** The 1950 Pontiacs shared bodyshells with their Chevrolet cousins but sat on a five-inch-longer wheelbase, at 120 inches. Pontiacs of the era were known for their bold, chrome hood streaks (which justified their "Silver Streak" moniker) and orange plastic chief's-head hood ornaments. Two engines were offered, both inline flatheads. The 239-cid six produced 90-93 hp, while the 268-cid eight was rated at 108-113 hp. Shown is the $2069 Chieftain Eight Deluxe Catalina hardtop coupe. **4.** A toothy grille differentiated the 1950 Pontiacs from the 1949 models, as shown on this $1908 Chieftain Eight Deluxe four-door sedan. **5.** A Streamliner Eight wagon listed for a lofty $2332, which included seating for up to eight passengers. **6.** GM's Motorama showcased the corporation's cars on lavish displays at such prestigious venues as New York's Waldorf-Astoria Hotel.

1

2

3

4

1. For 1951, Buicks got a front bumper that underlined their toothy grille. Supers, such as this $2728 convertible, had only three fender portholes, whereas top-line Roadmasters had four. Entry-level Specials and midline Supers had a 263-cid straight-eight engine producing 120-128 hp, while top-line Roadmasters got a 320-cid eight with 152 hp. **2.** A Buick Special Deluxe two-door sedan went for $2127. **3.** Cadillac's midline Series 62 hardtop coupe could be yours for $3436 in 1951. **4.** A Series 62 convertible tipped the price scales at $3987. **5.** Like all Cadillacs for 1951, the entry-level Series 61 four-door sedan came standard with Hydra-Matic automatic transmission. The Series 61 rode a shorter wheelbase than other Caddys (122 inches vs. 126 or 130), which might explain why the company's lowest-priced sedan saw just 2300 sales; perhaps it just wasn't stately enough. At $2917, it cost a whopping $611 less than the longer Series 62 sedan, which proved to be far-and-away Cadillac's best-seller with more than 55,000 built. With Series 61 sales so low, it's perhaps not surprising that 1951 would be the last year for the short-wheelbase model. In all, 110,340 Cadillacs found buyers in 1951, the division's best sales year to date.

5

1. Chevrolets got squared-off rear fenders for 1951, and sales dropped to a "mere" 1.2 million from nearly 1.5 million. At $1914, the Styleline Deluxe Bel Air hardtop was the second most expensive car in the Chevrolet line, exceeded only by the $2030 convertible. **2.** Chevrolet's Styleline Special two-door sedan listed for just $1540; only the $1450 business coupe cost less. **3**. Fastbacks were falling out of favor with the buying public, and 1951 would mark the last of Chevrolet's four-door Fleetlines, represented here by the $1680 Deluxe version. **4.** The Michigan State Police evidently found Chevrolet's old "Stovebolt Six" sufficient for highway patrol duties. The engine came in two sizes: 216-cid/92-hp with manual transmission, 235-cid/105-hp with Powerglide automatic. **5.** Oldsmobile's top seller in the top-line 98 series for 1951 was the $2610 four-door sedan. **6.** Optional on 1951 Oldsmobiles was a steering-wheel-mounted Maar self-winding watch. **7.** Offered in both standard and Deluxe versions was the Oldsmobile 98 Holiday hardtop coupe. Fewer than 18,000 were sold between the two trim levels, which listed for $2545 and $2882, respectively. The same body style was available in the new Super 88 line. Dropped for '51 were station wagons, which had previously been offered in the entry-level 76 and 88 lines.

6

1

2

3

4

5

7

LeSABRE

Harley Earl invented the Detroit "dream car" with the 1939 Buick Y-Job, but his 1951 LeSabre is far better known. Like the Y-Job, this two-seat convertible was built as a fully drivable testbed for GM's latest design and engineering ideas. A special 116-inch-wheelbase chassis carried an experimental 215-cubic-inch supercharged V-8. Horsepower was an impressive 300-plus on a required methanol/gasoline blend. Because Earl loved aircraft and the "jet age" had arrived, the LeSabre nodded to America's new F-86 fighter with a large, round "exhaust port" in back and a high-set oval "air intake" up front. The latter actually concealed the headlamps, which swiveled out when switched on. Other futuristic features included stationary wheel hubs and the wraparound "panoramic" windshield adopted for several 1953 production models. Of all his dream machines, the LeSabre was one of Earl's favorites, and he drove it regularly throughout the 1950s.

1

2

3

1-2. The new Oldsmobile Super 88 series was available in five body styles including the $2673 convertible and $2328 four-door sedan, the former being Oldsmobile's rarest model for 1951, the latter the company's most popular. In the entry-level 88 series, the six-cylinder engine was dropped, meaning all Oldsmobiles were now powered by the famed "Rocket V-8." **3.** Pontiac said a mouthful when it named the Chieftain Eight Super DeLuxe Catalina hardtop. At a starting price of $2320, it was one of the most expensive cars in the lineup. A non-"Super" Deluxe cost $2257, while six-cylinder versions of both trim levels retailed for $2244 and $2182, respectively. Even eight-cylinder models didn't sell so much on speed as on durability, because both engines remained "old fashioned" inline flatheads. **4.** A Chieftain Deluxe four-door sedan was offered as a six-cylinder for $2006; an eight cost $75 more—a small price to pay for the added power. Indeed, across the Pontiac line, eights outsold sixes by nearly six to one.

4

1. Buicks were little-changed for 1951, though power steering was a new option for upper-line models. Just $2115 bought a Special two-door sport coupe—the company's lowest-priced car—which still carried a 263-cid straight eight. **2.** The same 263-cid eight powered Buick's midline Supers, represented here by the $2869 convertible. **3.** Cadillac celebrated its 50th

anniversary in 1952 by offering power steering and boosting the horsepower rating of its 331-cid V-8 to 190—the highest in the industry. A flashy Coupe de Ville went for $4013. **4.** All Cadillacs came with dual exhaust tips in the rear bumper for 1952, including the stately $4323 Cadillac Sixty Special four-door sedan. **5-6.** Few changes marked the 1952 Chevrolet line, which included the $1761 Styleline Deluxe four-door sedan and the $2006 Bel Air hardtop coupe.

1

2

3

4

5

6

1. Oldsmobile boosted the power ratings of its 303-cid V-8 for 1952. The $2673 Super 88 Holiday hardtop coupe now offered 160 hp, an increase of 25, thanks in part to a four-barrel carburetor. Power steering was a new option. **2.** The V-8 in the lower-line Deluxe 88 was fitted with a two-barrel carburetor and carried a 145-hp rating, 10 more than before. A four-door sedan cost $2327. **3-4.** Oldsmobile's top-line series was now called the "Ninety-Eight" (rather than "98"). A convertible cost $3229; the popular sedan was $2786. Ninety-Eights shared the Super 88's engine. **5.** All Pontiacs featured a fresh face and new rear trim for 1952, and all body styles were offered in both six- and eight-cylinder form. This Super Deluxe Catalina hardtop coupe cost $2370 as a six, $2446 as an eight. **6.** The least-expensive Pontiacs were the two-door sedans, which started at $1956 for a six-cylinder version, $2031 for an eight. Eights outsold sixes by nearly eleven to one this year, and more than 80 percent of Pontiacs had optional Hydra-Matic.

1. A fire destroyed GM's Hydra-Matic plant in Livonia, Michigan, on August 12, 1953. Damages of more than $35 million set a U.S. record. Production resumed within 60 days, but in the interim some 1953 Cadillacs and Oldsmobiles were fitted with Buick's Twin-Turbine Dynaflow automatic, while a few Pontiacs received Chevy's Powerglide. **2.** Buick observed its 50th anniversary in 1953 with modest styling

updates and improved Twin-Turbine Dynaflow automatic. Senior models like this $3506 Roadmaster convertible also got Buick's first V-8. Called "Fireball," the 322-cid unit put out between 164 and 188 hp, depending on application. **3.** Only the entry-level Special retained straight-eight power for '53, carrying over a 263-cid engine. This Riviera hardtop coupe priced from $2295. **4.** The last Roadmaster "woody" wagon listed for a lofty $4031. Just 670 were built. **5.** The Super Riviera hardtop coupe was the second most popular '53 Buick. Starting at $2611, it drew a healthy 91,298 orders. **6.** Highlighting Buick's golden anniversary year was the limited-edition Skylark. Priced at a steep $5000 and based on the Roadmaster ragtop, it wore an exclusive chopped windshield, rakish full-length "sweepspear" side moldings, and no Venti-Ports. Just 1690 were built.

1-2. Cadillac's popular Coupe de Ville hardtop returned for 1953 with a $3995 base price. Literally prominent among the few styling changes for all models were bigger front bumper guards that were soon known as "Dagmars," after a buxom entertainer of the day. **3.** Cadillac's "carriage trade" Fleetwood 75 series again offered standard and division-window Imperial sedans in the mid-$5000 range. **4.** A genuine dream car come true, Cadillac's new 1953 Eldorado convertible sported a wrap-around windshield and a body-color metal top cover, two features taken from recent GM Motorama concept cars. A towering $7750 price insured exclusivity, and only 532 were built. Newly elected President

Dwight Eisenhower waved to the crowds from an Eldorado during his inauguration parade. **5.** TV's Dinah Shore literally sung the praises of Chevrolet's new 1953 styling, basically another reskinning of the 1949 design. This Bel Air convertible topped the line at $2175. **6.** The top-selling '53 Chevy, the Bel Air four-door sedan drew a rollicking 248,750 orders. This example wears popular options like two-tone paint and whitewall tires. All models adopted one-piece windshields.

1. Developed over some 30 months as project EX-122, the two-seat Chevrolet Corvette sports car wowed GM Motorama crowds in early 1953. Pleas for a showroom version prompted Chevy to begin production the following June in a corner of its giant Flint factory. 2-3. Only 300 Corvettes were built for 1953. The slow pace was dictated by the car's newfangled

1

2

3

fiberglass body, a first for a mass-market U.S. automaker. 4. The Corvette wasn't as fast as it looked, limited to a 150-hp version of Chevy's trusty "Stovebolt Six" and speed-sapping Powerglide automatic. Price was $3513, but Chevy reserved most '53s for promotional and VIP use. 5-6. The new 1953 Olds Ninety-Eight Fiesta ragtop cost $5717 and saw just 458 copies. Under the hood: a special 170-hp "Rocket" V-8.

4

5

6

1. Other Oldsmobiles added a few horses for '53, plus power steering and GM Frigidaire air conditioning as first-time options. Here, the 98 Holiday hardtop, which listed for $3022. **2.** The limited-edition Fiesta convertible fronts this view of the Olds exhibit at the 1953 Chicago Auto Show. Also on display there was the Starfire, a sporty concept convertible (just left of the sedan). It looked much like Chevy's new Corvette but could seat four and was strictly a one-of-a-kind Motorama exercise, though some of its styling touches would soon grace Olds showrooms. **3, 5.** Like Chevrolet, Pontiac adopted new outer sheetmetal to give its '53 models a more "important" look that included vestigial tailfins. Chieftain Six and Eight series reprised Catalina hardtop coupes as the glamour offerings, with prices starting at $2304 for the Deluxe-trim six-cylinder version. **4.** Pontiac Chieftain Eights outsold Sixes by almost 10 to 1 for 1953, a sign of the times. Four-door sedans like this drew the most sales in each line, but hardtop Catalinas claimed a surprising 20 percent of total volume.

1. Buick boasted an expanded 1954 lineup of longer, lower, wider cars with Motorama-inspired styling and more V-8 power. This Super convertible listed for $2964. **2.** The Buick Roadmaster Riviera sedan returned with four fender "port-holes," but most everything else was changed. Base price rose by $15 to $3269. **3.** Buick's prewar "factory hot rod" Century returned for '54 as a fleet four-model line with the division's larger V-8 in the lighter Special bodies. **4.** All-steel Buick wagons bowed for 1954 in Special and Century trim.

1

2

3

4

THE GM MOTORAMA

"A MOTORAMA IS MORE THAN A GOOD SHOW.... FRANKLY, IT MAKES MY STYLING JOB EASIER." —Harley Earl, 1953

The automobile show was invented in 1900 and soon became an annual convocation. Even during the Depression, the New York Automobile Show each January was as important on the calendar as the Academy Awards. In the optimistic postwar years, GM management had the idea of an auto show of its own—not only to hawk current products but to promote cars yet to come. Only General Motors was able to organize anything like these eight extravaganzas between 1949 and 1961. They bracketed an age when Americans thought nothing was impossible, and that when better cars were built, GM would build them.

Over 600,000 attended the 1949 "Transportation Unlimited Autorama" at New York's Waldorf-Astoria Hotel, which then traveled to Boston. Cadillac was the star, with three specials: the Embassy, Caribbean, and Fleetwood Coupe de Ville, all on the long Sixty Special chassis. The following year, more than 300,000 Autorama visitors were treated to the Cadillac Debutante, a 62 convertible with leopard skin upholstery. Lacking Motoramas in

1951–52, Cadillac sent several more specials on nationwide tours, including a convertible with a flush-fitting steel top cover that evolved into the limited-edition 1953 Eldorado.

In 1953, GM rechristened the event "Motorama" and made it a traveling show, with an orchestra and musical revue. Cars, performers, and musicians were displayed on "grasshoppers"—revolving, tilting disks that looked like they were borrowed from an amusement park. Putting the show on the road produced 1.4 million visitors, but required 100 trucks with choreographed arrivals, departures, and loading schedules. Still, business was thriving, and it seemed a good idea at the time.

GM stylists, led by Harley Earl and Bill Mitchell, began to mix with Motorama crowds, listening to their reactions and making notes. "By the time hundreds of thousands of these critics have examined your show and commented on your exhibits you have a firm idea of their likes and dislikes," Earl said.

Nineteen fifty-three was the year of the two-seater, the Motorama featuring the first production Chevrolet Corvette. Alongside it were 'Vette-inspired one-offs from the other divisions: the

Buick Wildcat, Oldsmobile Starfire, Pontiac La Parisienne, and Cadillac Orleans and Le Mans. The fiberglass Starfire displayed the combination bumper-grille that Olds would put into production in 1956. Caddy's Le Mans was another fiberglass two-seater, but closer to production was the Orleans, the world's first four-door hardtop.

The next Motorama, in 1954, hosted 1.9 million visitors, attracted by the first Chevy Nomad (production followed in 1955), and fiberglass specials with names soon to become familiar: Oldsmobile Cutlass, Buick Wildcat II, Pontiac Bonneville, Cadillac Park Avenue and El Camino, and GM Firebird.

Held in New York, Miami, Los Angeles, San Francisco, and Boston between January and April 1955, the next Motorama featured GM president Harlow Curtice himself, along with the production Nomad, the soon-to-be-production Eldorado Brougham, and a dream car called LaSalle II, a 'Vette-like roadster. Decades later, when Cadillac did produce a two-seater, fans wondered why they didn't honor tradition and call it a LaSalle.

1

2

1. Cadillac's familiar and popular styling was carefully evolved for 1954 with lower, sleeker bodies on new chassis with three-inch-longer wheelbases. All models now featured GM's trendsetting "panoramic" wraparound windshield, yet retained Caddy's expected dignified demeanor. This Sixty Special sedan rode an exclusive 133-inch wheelbase and listed for $4863. **2.** Cadillac's Eldorado convertible was less "special" for '54, but retained a metal top cover and added ribbed brightwork on the lower rear fenders to stand apart from the Series 62 ragtop. The '54 Eldo was also much more affordable at $5738, a whopping $2012 reduction from '53. Sales leaped to 2150 units. The 331-cid V-8 returned for all '54 Cadillacs, but mild retuning added another 20 horsepower, bringing the total to 230.

The 1956 Motorama set the attendance record with more than 2.2 million visitors. They saw the Eldorado Brougham town car, another Firebird, the Oldsmobile Golden Rocket, and Pontiac's Club de Mer. By now the repertoire was very professional: crowds jammed the lobbies, standing in long lines to ogle the cars of the future and the women of the present, glamorously presented and choreographed by the heads-up advertising department.

If Motoramas didn't send everyone home to buy the latest GM offerings, they certainly had impact—but exactly how much was always hard to measure. Although show cars returned in 1957, the Motorama didn't—and was really never the same again. The 1958 recession, and growing interest in economy cars like the Rambler and Volkswagen, perhaps suggested that an annual luxury car carnival might be passé.

GM did stage a small Motorama to mark the introduction of the '59 models in New York and Boston in October 1958. At it were a new Firebird and the Cadillac Cyclone, featuring rocket ship styling, a pop-up Plexiglas canopy top, and on-board radar. Attendance was low, and the company did not engage in the usual road show.

The Motorama went out with a bang, attracting one million visitors in New York, San Francisco, and Los Angeles in 1961.

More than ten million people attended the eight Motoramas between 1949 and 1961. Resolutely a product of simpler times, they vanished simultaneously with the first waves of doubt about Detroit's preeminence in the automotive world.

1. The Chevrolet Corvette saw a number of detail refinements during the '54 model run, though its basic concept was unchanged. In a significant move, production was shifted from Flint to St. Louis, where 3640 examples issued forth. Most were done in Polo White with red interiors, though alternate colors were newly available. Unlike the debut '53, the '54 Corvette was genuinely available to the public.

1

2

3

4

2. Chevrolet reprised three station wagons for '54, with the four-door 210 Handyman repeating as the top-seller. **3.** The 1954 Chevy line was the last to list nothing but sixes. Horsepower was up for the second straight year: to 115 with manual transmission, 125 with Powerglide automatic. This nifty Bel Air convertible priced from $2185. **4.** The companion '54 Bel Air Sport Coupe hardtop started at $2061. All models wore a light but effective facelift. **5.** Oldsmobiles were all-new for '54. Some think them some of the decade's best-looking Detroit cars. The top-line 98 convertible added the name Starfire and listed from $3740. **6.** Olds helped kick off the postwar "horsepower race," and its '54s were some of the quickest cars around. Super 88s like this Holiday hardtop coupe packed a 240-hp Rocket V-8, as did 98s, while 88s were now up to 230.

5

6

1. Olds wheelbases stretched two inches longer for 1954, bringing the spans to 122 inches for 88s and Super 88s and to 126 for top-line 98s. "Hockey stick" rear side moldings and a big-mouth grille with thick central bar preserved the established Olds identity on a lower-slung new GM B-body with trendy wraparound windshield. This $2868 Super 88 convertible was an ideal ride for a Saturday night. Still is.
2. Pontiac followed Chevrolet for 1954 with a mild facelift, and added a few more horses to its veteran inline eight. As before, the Chieftain Six and Eight lines listed Catalina hardtops in Deluxe and nicer Custom versions, but they were no longer the most glamorous Ponchos.

3. In profile, this 1954 Pontiac Chieftain two-door sedan looks rather like a stretched Chevrolet. That's because it was, riding a 122-inch wheelbase, seven inches longer than Chevy's. Bodyside chrome trim marks this as the uplevel Deluxe version. 4. But Pontiac was no longer content to be just a "big Chevy," so for 1954 it added four Star Chief Eight models on a 124-inch chassis. The line included this $2557 Custom Catalina hardtop with extended rear deck.

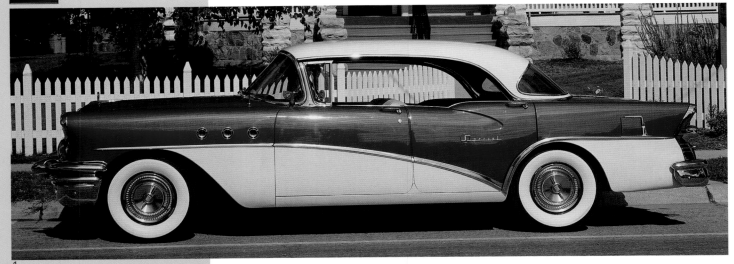

1. Four-door Riviera hardtops in Special and Century trim joined the Buick bunch at mid-1955. It was another GM first, shared with Olds. This Special version started at $2409. All '55 Specials retained Buick's 264-cid V-8, but horsepower was up to 188. **2.** The horse count was 236 for the 322-cid V-8 used in all other '55 Buicks. This Century wagon listed at $3175. **3.** Specials were the only '55 Buicks with three ventiports. This two-door sedan remained the line price-leader but now cost $2490 minimum. **4.** The 1955 Buick Century convertible listed at $2991 and drew a modest 5588 sales. **5.** All Buick prices were quite a bit higher for '55, with this Roadmaster two-door Riviera going for $3453. **6.** Broderick "Ten-Four" Crawford drove a speedy '55 Century two-door sedan in TV's *Highway Patrol*, but the real-life California Highway Patrol ordered some 270 specially equipped versions that easily reeled in scofflaw speeders.

1

2

3

4

1. Cadillac enjoyed record 1955 sales with a mild update of its all-new '54 design. This Series 62 convertible started at $4448. **2.** All '55 Caddys boasted 250 standard hp, up 20 from '54. Here, the $5047 Sixty Special sedan. **3.** The 1955 Cadillac Eldorado cost a princely $6286; a 270-hp engine was a $161 extra. **4.** Four "dream" hardtops starred at GM's 1955 Motorama shows (clockwise from lower left): LaSalle II, Chevrolet Biscayne, Oldsmobile Delta, Cadillac Eldorado Brougham.

1. Chevrolet was utterly transformed for 1955 with a ground-up redesign that replaced dull dependability with stylish sizzle. About the only things carried over from '54 were series names, wheelbase, and the basic "Stovebolt Six." Surprisingly for a low-priced brand, top-shelf Bel Airs were among the hottest '55 sellers. This Sport Coupe hardtop started at $2067 and drew a smashing 185,682 orders. **2.** Chevy built over 1.7 million of its '55

cars, beating archrival Ford by a quarter-million. Aiding the cause were big improvements to handling, brakes, steering, and interior room. This Bel Air convertible, wearing extra-cost fender skirts and lower-body trim, started at $2206. **3.** After decades of only sixes, Chevy made 1955 headlines with a lively new 265-cid "Turbo-Fire" V-8 offering 162 or 180 hp. Ads said every V-8 Chevy was "The Hot One." No wonder leadfoots rushed to buy. **4.** Also new for Chevy '55 was the Bel Air Nomad, a posh two-door wagon with "hardtop" styling. A lack of wagon utility held sales to a modest 8386. **5.** V-8 brawn made Chevy a new racing power in 1955, so it was fitting that a V-8 Bel Air convertible was chosen pace car for that year's Indianapolis 500 race.

1

2

3

5

6

4

1. GM marked a milestone in 1955 by building its 50-millionth car, a gold-colored Chevrolet Bel Air Sport Coupe hardtop. GM president Harlow Curtice gave it a smiling sendoff at Chevy's Flint factory, then sent it on a lengthy national publicity tour. **2.** Corvette volume plunged to just 700 units for 1955, but most had the potent new Chevy V-8, whose special 195-hp tuning did wonders for performance. The only exterior clue to its presence was an enlarged "V" in the "Chevrolet" front-fender script. **3-4.** Oldsmobile joined Buick in adding hardtop sedans during 1955, a four-door Holiday for each of its three series. All proved popular, in part because rear-seat access was easier than in two-door hardtops. This Super 88 Deluxe version started at $3140, just $71 more than its two-door sister. **5.** All 1955 Oldsmobiles wore a nicely evolved facelift of their all-new '54 styling. Entry-level 88s like this $2422 two-door sedan now claimed 185 standard horsepower. **6.** Again topping the Olds line for '55 was the ritzy Starfire convertible, which boasted 202 hp along with other 98s and Super 88s. It started at $3740 and saw just 8581 copies.

1

2

3

4

1. Pontiacs were redesigned for 1955 around Chevrolet's new bodies, but retained a longer wheelbase—now 122 inches for all models—and specific styling. Not everyone approved the blunted front end. Also like Chevy, Pontiac got a modern V-8 for '55, a 287-cid "Strato Streak" replacing all the old inline engines. Horsepower rose dramatically to 175-200. Catalina hardtops sold better than ever. This $2499 Star Chief Custom topped the 13-model line with 99,629 deliveries. **2.** Pontiac listed three mainstream wagons for '55. The most popular was this four-door Chieftain 870 with 19,949 sales. **3.** The 1955 Star Chief convertible listed at $2691. **4.** The Star Chief Safari was Pontiac's version of the '55 Chevy Nomad, but cost more and drew fewer sales—just 3760.

1

2

1. GM dedicated a new $100 million Technical Center in Warren, Michigan, northeast of Detroit, on May 16, 1956. Begun in 1945, the 330-acre facility is still home to GM Design, Research, and Engineering staffs. 2. The experimental Firebird II and single-seat Firebird I turbine cars front five 1956 Motorama concepts and their production sisters outside the Tech Center styling dome. 3. Buick styling evolved nicely for '56. The division again ran third in industry sales, remarkable for a medium-price make. This ragtop Special cost $2740. Just 9712 were built. 4. The open-air Roadmaster started at $3704; it drew only 4354 orders. 5. The grille emblem on all '56 Buicks named the model year—not great for resale values. Buick again offered wagons in Special (shown) and hot Century trim. Respective production: 13,770 and 8160. 6. The popular Buick Special four-door sedan drew 66,977 sales for 1956.

3

4

5

6

1

1-2. Cadillac's 1956 Eldorado added the surname Biarritz to stand apart from a new hard-top companion, the Eldorado Seville, which sold almost twice as well (3900 units versus 2150). Price was the same for either: $6556. **3.** The Coupe de Ville and other '56 Caddys boasted a newly bored-out 365-cid V-8 with 285 hp (305 for Eldos). **4.** The 1956 Cadillac Sixty Special started at $5047. **5.** Cadillac followed sister GM makes for '56 by adding a four-door hardtop. The Sedan de Ville promptly became the line's best-seller with 41,732 units.

2

3

4

5

1. Chevrolet's Corvette was redesigned for 1956, highlighted by more power and an optional liftoff hardtop. 2. Glitzier styling marked other '56 Chevys. This Bel Air Nomad is one of 7886 built. 3. Four-door Sport Sedan hardtops joined the '56 Chevy line in Bel Air (shown) and 210 trim. 4. The 1956 Bel Air Sport Coupe drew 128,382 sales. 5. The 210 four-door sedan topped '56 Chevy sales at 283,125. 6. The 150 two-door priced from $1826. 7. This disguised '56 Chevy 210 Sport Sedan set a new record for the Pike's Peak hillclimb.

1. Olds freshened its styling for 1956 with a distinctive "wide-mouth" bumper/grille, reshaped rear fenders, and revised trim. The 98 Starfire convertible remained the costliest model, this year priced from $3740. 2. The four-door 98 Holiday Sedan returned for its second season as the new sales leader in Oldsmobile's top-line series, drawing 42,320 orders. 3. Olds sponsored a popular late-1950s TV variety show starring "that singin' rage," Miss Patti Page, shown in this publicity photo with a new '56 and Olds workers. Though the vocalist was a great sales asset, Olds again ran fifth in the industry for 1956. 4. The Olds Rocket V-8 remained at 324 cid for '56, but more massaging lifted standard horse-

power to 230 for 88s—up a whopping 45 hp—and to 240 for other models—a gain of 38. Super 88s like this Holiday hardtop coupe used subtly different upper-body side trim versus 88s. 5. GM helped popularize two-tone paint jobs in the 1950s, and no brand did it better than Olds. Black-and-red was a hot 1956 combination all over Detroit, and this Super 88 convertible wears it well. Production for the model was fairly low: 9561 units. 6. Four-door Holiday Sedans led sales in every 1956 Olds series. This is the $2671 baseline 88 version, which drew 52,239 orders.

1

2

3

4

5

6

1

2

3

4

5

1. More chrome and cubic inches highlighted numerous updates for 1956 Pontiacs. All models now packed a "Strato-Streak" V-8 enlarged to 317 cid. Top-shelf Star Chiefs offered 216 or 227 horses. One Star Chief Custom Catalina hardtop coupe like this rolled out in late summer as the 6-millionth Pontiac built. **2.** Pontiac's modest tailfins were unchanged for '56—and still resembled the rear fenders of recent Packards. This year's Star Chief convertible priced from $2810 and saw 13,510 copies. **3.** Pontiac joined the industry swing to four-door hardtops with a Catalina in each 1956 series. As with many other makes, this Star Chief Custom was the top-selling model in its group at 48,035 units—which also made it the most popular '56 Pontiac. **4.** The Star Chief Custom Safari returned for '56 as a high-style "hardtop" wagon sister to the Chevrolet Nomad—and Pontiac's costliest model, this

year listed at $3129. Both verions wore bright "banana" tailgate trim. Though wagon sales were booming, buyers judged this pair too expensive and impractical, so '56 Safari sales totaled just 4042. **5.** Pontiac Chieftain 860s and midline 870s (four-door shown) offered 205 standard horses and up to 227 optional.

1. Redesigned bodies made 1957 Buicks look lower and sleeker despite unchanged wheelbases. New top-line Roadmaster 75 two- and four-door hardtops offered near-Cadillac luxury—and pricing: around $4400. 2. Buick's V-8 went to 364 cid for '57. Horses rose to 250 for Specials and to 300 for other models, including this $3270 Century Riviera hardtop coupe. 3. Buick joined a Detroit mini-fad for '57 by adding pillarless station wagons, the Century Caballero (shown) and Special Estate Wagon. Respective sales were modest at 10,618 and 6817. 4. Buick's reverse-slant 1957 fenders were shaped to suggest fashionable tailfins without gaudy period excess. This Century is one of three convertibles offered that year. Priced from $3598, it drew 4085 orders.

1

2

3

4

EDWARD NICHOLAS COLE 1909—1977

"The only really fortunate people in the world, in my mind, are those whose work is also their pleasure," said a young Winston Churchill. Ed Cole was exactly that sort of man. The son of a dairy farmer in Mendon, Michigan, he aspired to become an automotive engineer and enrolled in the GM Institute, only to leave for lack of money. It was 1933. Cole was 24. Before age 60 he would be president of General Motors.

Starting as a lab assistant, Cole worked his way up into engine engineering under Harry Barr and was a key figure in developing Cadillac's milestone 1949 V-8. In 1952, Cole's dream came true when he was named chief engineer of Chevrolet Division. His arrival signaled a powerful change in Chevrolet's product philosophy that would rock the industry.

Cole's first task at Chevrolet was a new engine, the eventual 1955 small-block V-8. He wanted five main bearings for smoothness and durability, oversquare cylinder dimensions and low reciprocating mass for high rpm, die-cast heads, aluminum "slipper" pistons, and a forged-steel crankshaft. He specified 265 cubic inches as the optimum size and designed around that. The initial result: 162 horsepower, 180 with Power Pack (four-barrel carburetor, dual exhausts). This engine was so "right" that its design principles survive in today's Corvette V-8.

Along the way, Cole worked with Zora Arkus-Duntov to transform the underpowered early Corvette into a serious high-performance sports car. By 1956 he was Chevrolet general manager.

Also involved with the stillborn Cadet project after the war, Cole advocated compact cars long before the market demanded them. The rear-engine 1960 Corvair, with its air-cooled "flat" six and fully independent suspension, reflected his engineer's thinking.

But Cole misread the market. The Corvair was too radical for economy-car buyers, forcing GM to launch the simple Chevy II to counter Ford's top-selling Falcon. And though the bucket-seat Monza uncovered a huge unmet demand for sporty compacts, Corvair sales were clobbered when the Ford Mustang came along (and not by Ralph Nader, as many believe). With that, GM halted further Corvair development, then dropped the car after 1969.

Meantime, Cole was appointed head of the GM Car and Truck Group in 1961, then executive vice-president in 1965. He became president in 1967, just in time to lead GM through some of its toughest battles in history. Yet through it all, he maintained his poise. He also eventually changed his mind about small cars, concluding that big ones were what people wanted at that time. To some extent, he was right.

Per GM policy, Cole retired on reaching age 65 in 1974, only to resurface as chief executive officer at Checker. The Kalamazoo, Michigan, cab company had dabbled with civilian versions of its practical but homely taxi. Many speculated that Cole had a plan for making Checker a much bigger player in the retail business. Whatever he had planned, Cole never got the chance to try it. Just before arriving to take charge, he was killed while landing his small aircraft in rain and fog outside Kalamazoo.

Those who knew him remember Ed Cole not only as a free-thinking engineer and competent manager, but as a straightforward and decent man. Although he was sometimes mocked by the failure of his hopes and the upsetting of his calculations, his guide was his conscience, his shield the rectitude and sincerity of his actions.

1. Though smaller than other 1957 Cadillacs, the new Eldorado Brougham hardtop sedan was America's costliest car yet at an eye-popping $13,074. Descended from recent Motorama dream cars, the Brougham used its own body with center-opening doors, stainless-steel roof, and quad headlights. A specific 126-inch-wheelbase chassis included an "air-ride" suspension that gave no end of trouble. But the interior was

lavish even for a Caddy, with built-in perfume bottle and silver beverage tumblers in the back seat. Such opulence had a limited market in '57, and only 400 Broughams were built for the model year. 2. Other '57 Caddys got new bodies with more squarish lines and much smaller grille "bullets." The Sixty Special four-door became a hardtop, priced at $5614. 3. Raymond Burr drove a 1957 Series 62 convertible in the first season of TV's *Perry Mason*— but not every week. A total of 9000 were built. 4. Non-Brougham Eldorados returned for '57 with "shark" fins atop newly rounded rear fenders. The Seville hardtop drew 2100 sales at $7286 apiece.
5. Eldorados gained 20 hp for '57 to reach 325. Other models had 300, up 15 hp. The Eldo Biarritz also cost $7286. Just 1800 were built.

1. Chevrolet could only counter all-new 1957 Fords and Plymouths with a heavy facelift of its three-year-old body. But buyers loved the new Cadillac-like styling, and that helped Chevy edge Ford in model-year production. All '57 Chevys have long been prized collectible cars, none more than Bel Air convertibles like this. It sold new for $2511. **2.** Ribbed aluminum rear side trim made 1957 Chevy Bel Airs easy to spot. Modestly finned rear fenders added eye appeal to all models—as well as extra length. Priced from $2364, the '57 Bel Air Sport Coupe was a big seller at 166,426 units. A good many survive today, but not nearly enough for all those who want one.

1

2

3. The Bel Air Sport Sedan hardtop was a little less popular, drawing 137,672 original sales. Like all '57 Chevys, it could be ordered with a new bored-out 283 V-8 in no fewer than seven states of tune. Horsepower ranged from 162 to 270 with carburetors. New "Ramjet" fuel injection delivered up to 283 hp—the hallowed "1 hp per cu. in." ideal—but found few takers at around $500.

3

1

2

3

4

1. Rear fender skirts dress up this 1957 Chevrolet Bel Air Townsman wagon, one of 127,803 built. **2.** Sales of Chevy's stylish Bel Air Nomad dropped to just 6103 for 1957, so the two-door "hardtop" wagon would not return. **3.** Two-toning and whitewall tires were an easy way to glam up a mainstream '57 Chevy like the popular 210 four-door sedan. How popular was it? Over 260,000 sold. **4.** The "fuelie" 283-hp 283 V-8 made for vivid performance, but high

5

6

cost produced few orders on 1957 passenger Chevys. Which makes this 150 two-door sedan a genuine "sleeper," marked only by small "fuel injection" badges on its rear fenders. **5.** Corvette looked much the same for '57 but got the new 283 V-8 as standard. With the top "fuelie" option and newly available four-speed manual gearbox, it could do 0-60 mph in as little as 5.7 seconds. **6.** Road tester Tom McCahill (left) gets a briefing on fuel injection from Corvette chief engineer Zora Arkus-Duntov.

1. Olds again ran fifth on lower 1957 sales despite fresh styling on longer-lower-wider new bodies. The famed Rocket V-8 went to 371 cid and 277 standard horses, with 300 optional via a new "J-2" power package. This Holiday hardtop coupe was part of a renamed Starfire 98 series. Priced from $3937, it drew 17,791 sales. **2.** Golden Rocket was the new first name for '57 Olds 88s and Super 88s. Ragtops remained

glamorous slow-sellers. This $3447 Super 88 found just 7128 buyers. **3.** Olds revived wagons for '57, including hardtop Fiesta models in Super 88 (shown) and 88 trim, but buyers were scarce here too. **4.** The 88 Holiday Sedan priced from $2932. **5.** Three-piece rear windows were a new gimmick for fixed-roof non-wagon '57 Oldsmobiles. This 88 four-door sedan was the line's top-seller at 53,293.

1

2

3

4

1. Pontiac's V-8 grew to 347 cid for 1957, then added fuel injection for a hot midyear ragtop, the 310-hp, $5782 Bonneville. Riding the Star Chief chassis, it was an effort by new division chief Bunkie Knudsen to liven up Pontiac's image. Only 630 were built. **2.** An accessory "continental" kit graces this '57 Pontiac Star Chief convertible. **3.** As with Chevy's Nomad, demand for Pontiac's two-door Safari wagon waned in 1957—only 1292 sold. The model would not be back. **4.** Knudsen also erased Pontiac's traditional "Silver Streak" trim for '57, as on this two-door Chieftain Catalina hardtop. **5.** A four-door "Transcontinental" Star Chief wagon bowed at mid-1957 to draw 1894 sales.

5

1. Buick went crazy with chrome for 1958—the grille alone used 160 bright squares resembling drawer pulls—and paid the price with much lower sales in a recession economy. This Century Riviera hardtop coupe started at $3368. 2. The longer Super version listed at $3644 and drew 13,928 sales versus 28,460 for its $3789 four-door sister. 3. Two hardtop wagons continued for the "B-58 Buick" line, but sales dropped to half of 1957's already modest levels.

This Century Caballero cost $3831 and attracted just 4456 buyers. 4. Replacing the Roadmaster 75 at the top of Buick's '58 line was a revived luxury Limited series, with 15 chrome slashes on extra-long rear fenders. This $5512 hardtop sedan was the most popular of the three models, though sales were just 5571. 5. The Limited con-vertible saw just 839 copies. Like so many '58 Detroiters, these Buicks were simply the wrong cars at the wrong time. 6. Cadillac's two V-8s each added 10 horses for '58, bringing Eldorados to 335. This ragtop Biarritz is one of only 815 built. 7. Other '58 Caddys claimed 325 hp. The Series 62 convertible scored 7825 sales. 8. The Sixty Special hardtop listed at $6233 and got 12,250 orders.

1

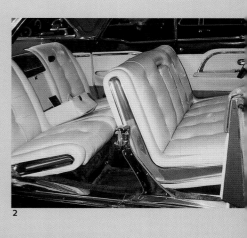

2

3

4

5

6

7

8

1-2. Cadillac's ultra-lux Eldorado Brougham was little changed for 1958 save lower sales—down a fourth to just 300 units. **3-4.** Despite the recession, Chevrolet sold over a million 1958 passenger cars, helped by tasteful new styling on an upsized package with a 117.5-inch wheelbase, up 2.5 inches from 1955–57. The redesign added weight, but that could be offset with a newly optional 348-cid V-8, borrowed from Chevy's truck line. Leading the fleet were a new Impala convertible and Sport Coupe with all of Chevy's literal best trimmings and prices that pushed into Pontiac's preserve. Even so, Impala was a popular move, drawing some 60,000 sales, mostly hardtops. **5-6.** Biscayne replaced 210 as the 1958 Chevy series below Bel Air, limited to two- and four-door sedans. Respective base prices with the good old "Stovebolt Six," still hanging on, were $2236 and $2290. The six-cylinder two-door accounted for some 75 percent of the line's 100,000 unit sales. **7.** Delray ousted 150 at the bottom of the '58 Chevy line and also offered only sedans. Chevy split off wagons into a separate model group. The lightweight V-8 two-doors found favor in police work. **8.** Chevy still offered a Sedan Delivery in '58. Badged as a Delray, it started at just $2123.

1

1. Corvette added inches and pounds for 1958, plus a four-lamp face, phony hood louvers, and trunklid chrome strips. Critics moaned, but the 283 V-8 returned in five versions, each with more power—up to 290 with fuel injection—so Chevy's sports car remained fast and, yes, agile. And for all the gilding—plus a steeper $3631 base price—sales improved some 45 percent to 9168. **2.** Olds

2

lost sales in 1958 but passed Buick to claim fourth in the industry race despite ladling on just as much chrome. This Super 88 four-door sedan was the year's third most popular Olds, drawing 33,844 orders. **3.** By contrast, the Super 88 convertible got only 3799 sales. **4.** In a stab at better mpg, Olds 88s like this two-door Holiday were detuned to 265 hp for '58. Other models had 300 standard, 315 with the rarely ordered J-2 option.

3

4

1. The 1958 Pontiacs followed Chevrolet's lead with longer and lower new bodies, but wheelbases stood pat despite a redesigned X-brace chassis. A two-door hardtop joined this Bonneville convertible to form a top-line series priced in the mid-$3000s. The ragtop accounted for 3096 of the combined 12,240 sales, far below the level of equivalent Chevy Impalas. 2. Pontiac's former top-line Star Chief was thinned to four models for '58. This two-door Catalina hardtop started at $3122. Another bore job took the Pontiac V-8 to 370 cid for all '58s. Horsepower ran from 240 to 310. 3. The Star Chief Custom Safari wagon was one of the rarest '58 Pontiacs: just 2905 built. 4. GM Design chief Harley Earl, "father" of Detroit styling, retired in 1958 after 30 years.

1. Buicks got a full redesign and new series names for 1959. All models sprouted canted quad headlights and big "delta wing" fins. Behind a still-complex grille sat a new 325-hp 401-cid V-8 as standard for Invictas, Electras, and top-line Electra 225s like this hardtop sedan. **2.** LeSabre denoted Buick's entry-level line for 1959. The six models

retained a 250-hp 364 V-8. **3-4.** An Electra 225 ragtop paced the 1959 Indy 500. "Deuce and a quarters" stretched 225 inches long. **5.** Cadillac redesigned its Eldorado Brougham for 1959 and outsourced production to Pininfarina in Italy. Price was still a whopping $13,075, but sales were poor: just 99 units.

1

2

3

4

5

1. Save the Chevy Corvette, GM's 1959 cars were starkly different, the result of a crash redesign to answer Chrysler's popular '57 styling. Cadillacs were unmistakable, wearing the tallest tailfins ever, though only this one year. Caddy sales improved a bit as the recession eased. This Series 62 convertible cost $5465 and drew 11,130 orders. **2.** Like Buick, Cadillac offered two hardtop sedan rooflines for '59: a flat-top "four-window" style and a sloping "six-window" type as on this Series 62. **3.** All '59 Cadillacs used a V-8 stroked to 390 cid. Eldorados like this Biarritz ragtop had 345 hp, other models 325. **4.** The 1959 Chevrolets added 2.5 inches of wheelbase to reach 119—and looked wilder than ever. The Impala Sport Coupe was now part of a full-line series. **5.** "Dog-leg" windshield posts were pushed forward on GM's redesigned '59s, which reduced the likelihood of banged knees on entry/exit.

1. The 1959 Chevrolets stoked controversy with their "bat-wing" fins and "cat's-eye" taillamps—which helped Ford win the model-year sales race. This hardtop Sport Sedan was one of eight models in the new top-line Impala series.
2. Chevy's new-for-'59 El Camino was a wagon-based light-duty pickup answering Ford's two-year-old Ranchero.
3. The midline Bel Air series was Chevy's top seller for '59. The mainstay four-door sedan listed for $2440 with the base six-cylinder engine.
4. The Corvette returned for '59 with an unchanged engine lineup, a few styling geegaws removed, and an improved chassis. Priced moved up to $3675, but sales also moved up, reaching 9670 units.
5. Olds touted "The Linear Look" for its redesigned '59s, which were little longer but much cleaner-looking than the fussy '58s. A bored-out 394 Rocket V-8 with 315 hp was newly standard for 98s like this $4365 convertible, as well as Super 88s.
6. Oldsmobile's 1959 four-door hardtops used the flat-roof Buick/Cadillac style and were called Holiday SportSedans. This top-line 98 model sold from $4162.
7. Four-door 1959 Olds sedans were dubbed Celebrity. This one's a 98.
8. Holiday SceniCoupe was the moniker for '59 Olds two-door hard-tops like this Super 88. GM's redesigns featured much-larg-er windshields and hardtop rear windows.

1. Before he retired in 1958, GM design chief Harley Earl had his troops prepare a final turbine-powered GM show car, the Firebird III. Revealed in '59, it was the wildest yet, with a "double-bubble" canopy and triple vertical tailfins. Here, the legendary designer poses with his three Firebirds. 2. A "Wide Track" chassis, potent new 389-cid V-8s and GM's cleanest 1959 styling vaulted Pontiac from sixth to fourth in Detroit sales. This Bonneville convertible was part of an expanded four-model top-line series, with Star Chiefs and entry-level Catalinas arrayed below. Bonnevilles now had 250/300 hp with manual/automatic transmission, but a rollicking 345 was newly available with "Tri-Power" triple carburetors. Priced from $3478, the Bonneville ragtop scored much higher sales of 11,426 units. 3. Pontiac didn't change wheelbases for '59, but length did increase. So did width, as wheels moved outboard for greater cornering stability. "Wide-Track Design" was one reason why *Motor Trend* named the entire Pontiac line its 1959 "Car of the Year." This Bonneville Vista hardtop sedan started at $3333. 4. The six-passenger Bonneville Custom Safari was Pontiac's flagship '59 wagon. The low-end Catalina line offered six- and nine-passenger versions.

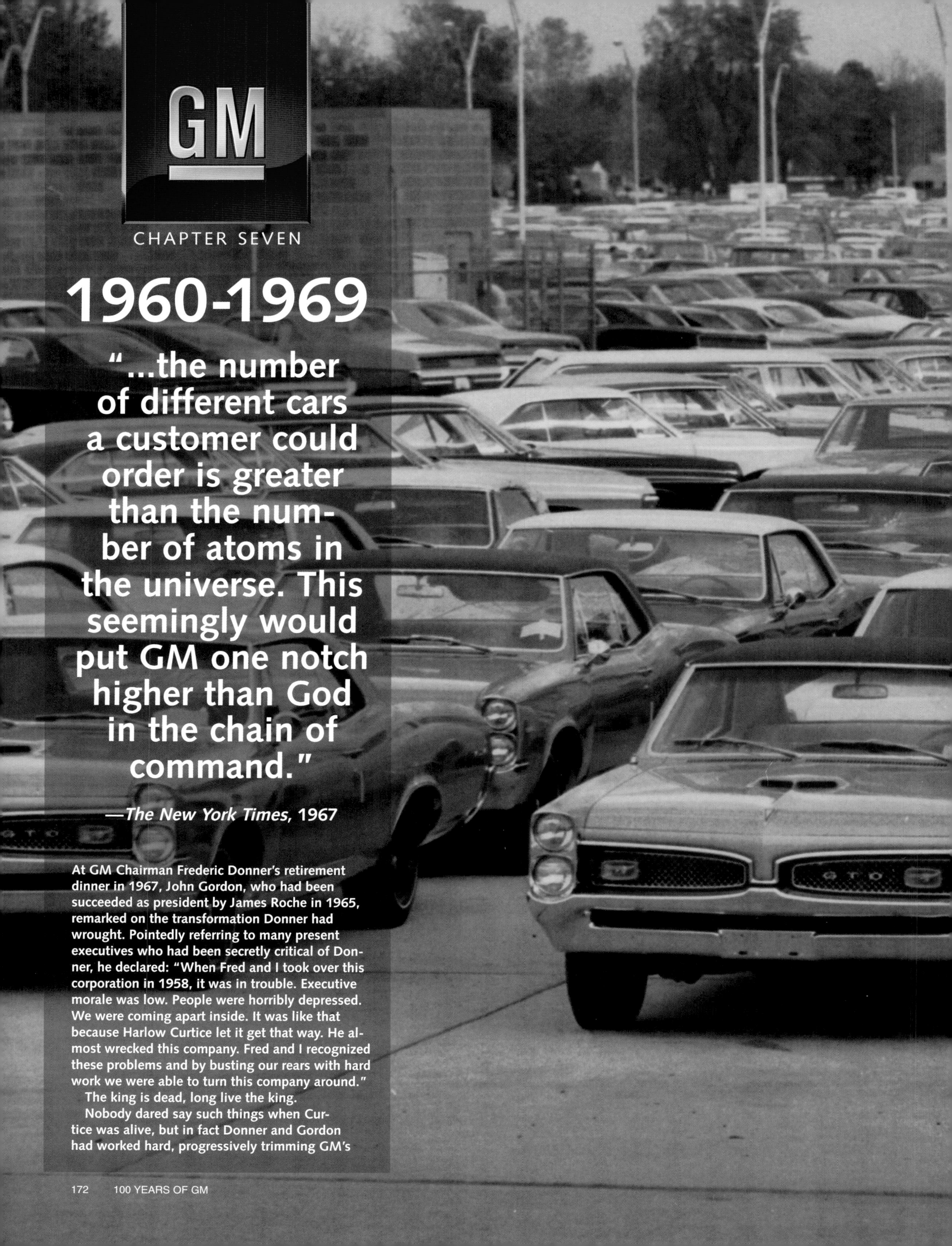

GM

CHAPTER SEVEN

1960-1969

"...the number of different cars a customer could order is greater than the number of atoms in the universe. This seemingly would put GM one notch higher than God in the chain of command."

—*The New York Times*, 1967

At GM Chairman Frederic Donner's retirement dinner in 1967, John Gordon, who had been succeeded as president by James Roche in 1965, remarked on the transformation Donner had wrought. Pointedly referring to many present executives who had been secretly critical of Donner, he declared: "When Fred and I took over this corporation in 1958, it was in trouble. Executive morale was low. People were horribly depressed. We were coming apart inside. It was like that because Harlow Curtice let it get that way. He almost wrecked this company. Fred and I recognized these problems and by busting our rears with hard work we were able to turn this company around."

The king is dead, long live the king.

Nobody dared say such things when Curtice was alive, but in fact Donner and Gordon had worked hard, progressively trimming GM's

jukebox styling, along with the authority of the divisions. Longtime managers who had spent their lives in one division naturally resented this, labeling Donner a "bean counter"; it took one of their own, engineer Ed Cole, to convince them that centralized engineering and marketing was required.

The fat years when Detroit could sell everything it produced were over. Rivals from South Bend, Kenosha, and Wolfsburg—the Lark, Rambler, and Volkswagen—were cutting into the Big Three's market share. The 1958 recession had bred new buyers, still interested in performance, but also in economy, safety, and clean styling. As suggested by the plucked tails of such cars as the 1961 Buick and Chevrolet, the tailfin era was ending.

One of Donner's and Gordon's first goals, the compact car, appeared in 1960. General Motors, Ford, and Chrysler each launched one: the Corvair, Falcon, and Valiant. The Corvair was by far the most interesting and innovative, with fully independent suspension and a rear-mounted, air-cooled, flat-opposed six that developed up to 95 hp, compared to Volkswagen's piddling 36. Unfortunately, the engine was 100 pounds heavier than planners had hoped and drastically affected handling, leading to the most famous safety challenge to an American car in history. In fact, as accident statistics eventually showed, the Corvair was not outstandingly dangerous. But GM buyers unfamiliar with such layouts, who ignored the owner's manual, got into trouble. (See sidebar, pages 218-219.)

Corvairs were offered in three series: 700 (cheap); 500 (very cheap); and 900 Monza, a luxus model with a difference. With colorful vinyl bucket seats, plush carpets and a coupe body style, the Monza held surprising appeal. Not many were sold in 1960, but a year later the Monza was leading the economy Corvairs by up to ten to one. Almost by accident, it had defined a new type of car, the "sporty compact" or "ponycar," whose most successful manifestation, unfortunately for GM, turned out to be the Ford Mustang.

Corvair continued with little styling change through 1964. Any handling problems it did have were cured with suspension modifications. In 1961, Chevrolet added a wagon called the Lakewood; a sleek convertible followed in 1962.

But the Corvair had disappointed as an economy car, and 1962 saw the launch of the conventional front-engine, rear-drive Chevy II, to defend against the high-selling Ford Falcon. Corvair production began to slide, ironically in 1964, which saw the quickest, best-handling model yet—the turbo-charged Monza Spyder.

Bill Mitchell, who famously declared that "styling a small car is like tailoring a dwarf," nevertheless worked magic with the new 1965 Corvair, which was smooth, Italianesque, virtually perfect from any angle. The turbo model was now the 180-hp Corsa, but against the small-block V-8 Mustang it didn't compete. The Corsa was dropped after 1966, and the last handful of Corvairs were sold in 1969.

Corvette came of age as a true sports car in the Sixties. The 1958–62 models were updated at the back end by Bill Mitchell in 1961. Then in 1963 came Mitchell's Sting Ray, a beautiful coupe as well as a roadster, with hidden headlamps, a "dual-cockpit" dash, a shorter wheelbase, far better aerodynamics, and a reworked chassis with independent rear suspension.

Then there was power! The first Mark IV V-8, in 1965, displaced 396 cubic inches, packing 425 hp and 415 lbs-ft of torque. Stiff front springs, a thick front anti-sway bar, a new rear anti-sway bar, a heavier clutch, and a more efficient cooling system handled its brute force. In 1966, a bore increase produced the legendary 427, which, with 4.11:1 gears, could do 0-60 in under five seconds and still hit 140 mph.

Corvette restyled in 1968. Though engineers had considered a mid-engine, the drivetrain remained conventional. The roadster, and a notchback coupe with lift-off roof panels, were shaped by a talented youngster named David Holls. Held over from 1967 was the mighty L-88 competition 427 V-8, which was underrated at 430 horsepower (the true number was more like 560). Mere mortals usually settled for the baseline 350-hp 327, or the 427 with 400 or 435 hp. Seven inches longer and 200 pounds heavier than the 1963–67 Sting Ray, the new Corvette was hugely popular, and in 1969 (rechristened "Stingray") it set a production record: almost 40,000 units.

The Mustang's success had taken Chevrolet by surprise. Its response was the 1967 Camaro, a sharp looking ponycar with flat nose, chiseled profile, chopped-off deck, and low roofline. A four-seater, Camaro offered exceptional handling and (per Mustang practice) a wide list of options.

The base Camaro was a $2466 six; you worked up through a 210-hp V-8 to the Super Sport (stiffer springs and shocks, Wide Oval Firestone tires, nose stripe). Soon the 396 V-8 and Turbo-Hydramatic became available. Of course there were bucket seats, extra instruments, a console-mounted shifter, and a Rally Sport package with hidden headlamps and special trim.

It would take Camaro three years to match the volume of the Mustang. The Z-28 package, created to win the Trans-Am racing series, helped win converts. The Camaro received modest facelifts through 1969. Because of a delay attending the all-new 1970 model, it was kept in production longer than usual, and nearly a quarter million were produced for the 1969 model year.

Chevrolet soon began planning something rather larger than a compact: the "intermediate." It arrived in 1964 as the Chevelle, conventional in layout but larger than the Chevy II—actually its dimensions were quite close to the '55 Chevy. Chevelle offered almost as much interior space as an Impala, an array of sixes and V-8s, body styles from sedans and wagons to hardtops and convertibles, and the usual array of Super Sport options. The V-8 convertible started at only $2857 and a six-cylinder hardtop cost only $2538. Chevrolet barely had the capacity to meet demand.

Chevelle received its first redesign in 1966, in a body shared with the comparable Olds Cutlass, Buick Skylark, and Pontiac Tempest. It was now substantially larger, riding two wheelbases: 116 inches on four-doors, 112 on two-doors. In 1968, the Chevy II/Nova was also enlarged slightly, given a 111-inch wheelbase, and restyled with smooth new bodywork.

Between 1960 and 1969, the full-size Chevy progressed from overstyled indulgence to clean, extruded looks, outselling rival Ford in most years. Mitchell dropped the tailfins in 1961 and further smoothed up the styling for 1962. Among engines, Chevy now offered a V-8 with an unprecedented 409 cubic inches.

Bunkie Knudsen, who had moved from Pontiac to Chevrolet Division in 1962, was responsible for most of these market initiatives but never forgot the bread-and-butter big cars: Biscayne, Bel Air, Impala, and later the Caprice. With bright colors, handling mods, stick shifts, and assorted engines, there was one for every buyer, from the baseline six or 283 V-8 to the 409 Impala Super Sport.

A sculpted body arrived for 1963, with Impala dominating divi-sion sales. In 1964, standard-size Chevys scored nearly 900,000 sales. Another redesign occurred in 1965 and was followed by a swoopy new body for 1967. Despite no change in the 119-inch wheelbase, the big Chevy was inexorably growing bigger.

Knudsen and his predecessors wrought well. In the decade of the Sixties, Ford bested Chevrolet in model-year production only twice: in 1961 (on the strength of the Falcon) and 1966 (with the help of the Mustang). In other years, Chevy typically fin-ished several hundred thousand cars ahead. As American Motors sales ebbed in the face of Big Three competition, and Studebaker disappeared, Chevrolet's competition fell away. By the end of the decade, its dominance was near-complete, except for the luxury sector where it did not compete.

Where Chevrolet was absent, the spoils belonged to Cadillac. Packard, the noble rival, had seen its last cars in 1958. Imperial, which had sold well in the Fifties, had not sustained its success, suffering from quality problems and dealer disinterest. Lincoln, which offered an outstanding new Continental in 1961, lacked dealer penetration and those long lines of Caddy loyalists who bought a new one every couple of years.

Cadillac had "out-finned" everyone in 1959 but just as rapidly "de-finned" in the Sixties. Chuck Jordan, moved to the Cadillac studio in 1958, was ordered to revolutionize the line's looks. His efforts matured in 1961 with the cleanest Cadillac in years—the grille reduced to modest grid, the wraparound windshield aban-doned (except on the 75). Product planners meanwhile thinned the model range, dropping the slow-selling Eldorado Brougham and Seville, while retaining a 325-hp Eldo convertible.

In 1962, tailfins dropped again slightly and Cadillac intro-duced front fender cornering lights. The next year, Cadillac finally replaced the V-8 that had been around since 1949. The new block was stiffer, yet 50 pounds lighter. The new engine added little in performance but was smoother and quieter. After all, a '63 could do 0-60 in ten seconds while hitting 120 mph and returning 14 mpg. With standard Hydra-matic, power steering, power brakes, remote rearview mirror, and six-way power seats, Cadillac re-mained the outstanding buy it had long been.

Cadillac's last true tailfins appeared on the mildly facelifted 1964 models. A new "Comfort-Control" heater/air conditioner was the first step toward modern climate control. The '65 restyle brought a longer, lower body sans tailfins, and the Sixty Special regained its special long wheelbase. Horsepower, at 340, gave Cadillac the highest power-to-weight ratio in the industry. The 75, which had continued with its 1964 look, adopted current styling in 1966, along with a full perimeter frame. Variable-ratio power steering, which provided progressively faster response as speed diminished, was standard.

Many management changes were occurring in the mid-Sixties. Longtime chief engineer Fred Arnold retired in 1965, succeeded by Carl Rasmussen. General manager Harold Warner retired in favor of Ken Scott; he was replaced six months later by Calvin Werner, who would remain general manager until mid-1969.

Cadillac built 200,000 1967 models, including a transformed Eldorado, now a big coupe with Olds Toronado front-wheel drive. More conservative-looking than the Toronado, it rode better and handled just as well, thanks to unique suspension tuning with standard rear leveling. Production (17,930) was only half that of the Olds, but the Eldo was established as a superb road machine.

Minor styling changes attended the 1968 Eldorado, while other Cadillacs got a longer hood, revised grille, and a new trunk lid to increase load capacity. The new 472 V-8 was not as economical but churned out impressive performance. A typical 1968 Coupe de Ville would squirt from zero to 100 mph in 27 seconds. And Cadil-lac was now outselling Rambler, which AMC President George Romney had predicted would replace all of Detroit's "dinosaurs" in the 1960s.

In 1969, Cadillac broke back into the top ten with another record year: 267,000 cars. The Eldorado front end was revised slightly;

the other models were restyled, with a square roofline, horizontal headlamps, and various trim shuffles. Cadillac prices ranged from $5500 for the Calais to more than $10,000 for the 75 limousine.

Newsmakers in 1961 were the second-wave compacts from Pontiac, Olds, and Buick, each quite different though sharing a common shell. The Pontiac Tempest had GM's first postwar U.S. four-cylinder engine, a radical flexible driveshaft, a rear-mounted limited-slip transaxle, and independent link-type rear suspension. *Motor Trend* called it a "prototype of the American car for the Sixties," which couldn't have been more wrong. No Detroit manufacturer copied the "rope shaft" and transaxle and not until the late 1970s was there a Detroit swing to four-cylinder engines.

The 195-cid slant four was essentially half of Pontiac's 389 V-8, installed with soft-rubber "doughnut" motor mounts and other measures to quell vibration. Optional, but rarely ordered, was a Buick-built aluminum 215 V-8 with 155 hp.

Both Oldsmobile's F-85 and Buick's Special compacts were less radical than the Tempest. Upmarket models, they carried the 215 V-8 standard. The bucket-seated coupes were respectively the Cutlass and Skylark. Special, F-85, and Tempest convertibles all followed in 1962. Also in '62, base Buick Specials offered the postwar industry's first passenger-car V-6, with 198 cid and 135 hp.

Optional on 1962–63 F-85 V-8s was the turbocharged Jetfire, which produced one horsepower per cubic inch, using liquid injection (water and alcohol) to prevent carbon buildup. Though the Jetfire was remarkably quick (0-60 in 8.5 seconds, 107 mph), its unreliable injection system saw it dropped after 1963. In 1964–65, GM compacts became less compact, adopting longer wheelbases (up to 120 inches on some wagons) and sharing bodies with the new Chevrolet Chevelle.

Next to the compact car, the most immediate problem Donner and Gordon faced in 1958 was Buick itself, which was following what writers Jan Norbye and Jim Dunne described as a "road to ruin." With busy and dated styling, large and thirsty engines, and no compact, Buick had slipped to 9th place in 1960, as low as it had done since 1905, when it built only 750 cars.

Edward D. Rollert, an engineer-manager from Harrison Radiator, was chosen to turn Buick around, and by mid-1957 he had Ned Nickles' design staff at work on the handsome '61s, with shorter wheelbases and finless styling—as attractive as any Buick since the war. The similar '62 successor saw Buick sell 400,000 cars that year, among them the Wildcat, a stylish hardtop based on the Invicta sport coupe, with special trim and a bucket seat interior. By 1969, Buick would be back in fifth place in the production race.

Because it had been doing so badly, and had more production facilities, Buick was selected over Cadillac to produce GM's new "personal luxury" car, the 1963 Riviera—an old name with a new look. Design chief Bill Mitchell said this glamorous coupe borrowed European ideas like the razor-edge lines of English custom coachbuilders. But the Riviera was quintessentially American, riding a relatively short 117-inch wheelbase, powered by a 325-hp 401 V-8, packing outstanding handling and performance. Buick sold a healthy 40,000 Rivieras in the model's first year. Few changes occurred for two years; then the big coupe was fully restyled in 1966, with equally beautiful, sculpted lines.

Buick built 600,000 cars in banner 1966, despite few changes other than the new Riviera. They began to bulk up again in 1967, when another half-million came off the lines, with a new 430-cid V-8 for the full-size cars and 400-cid variant for the Skylark muscle-car model, now named GS400. Buick ended the decade with a complete restyle for the LeSabre, Wildcat, and Electra, a new suspension system, three-speed automatic transmission, and variable ratio power steering—all of which helped the division break the 700,000 mark.

Elliot M. "Pete" Estes, Pontiac's chief engineer since 1955, replaced Knudsen as its general manager when the latter moved to Chevrolet in 1961, turning Pontiac into GM's most successful division. Assistant Chief Engineer John DeLorean said Pontiac

originated three-quarters of GM's innovations from 1962 to 1969, although some were dubious: a radio antenna molded into the windshield that didn't receive well, and concealed windshield wipers that iced up in an overnight snowstorm.

Full-size Sixties Pontiacs retained their crisp, attractive styling, a factor that helped Pontiac out-produce Rambler with half a million cars in 1962. The Grand Prix sport coupe was a new 1962 introduction, with more than 30,000 sales. Estes's key to winning never changed: clever engineering, high performance, a high level of luxury. Typical of this was the 1964 Tempest GTO, with the performance of a Ferrari at one-fifth the price.

The full-size Pontiacs were restyled and larger in 1965, when 800,000 Pontiacs of all kinds were built. In 1966 came the first high-performance straight six since the old Hudson Hornet: Pontiac's overhead cam Sprint, which could do 0-60 in ten seconds and cruise at 100 mph. With four-speeds and bucket seats, a Sprint had the look and feel of a true grand-touring car. Unfortunately, it quickly grew more bulky, and by 1969 the engine had been emasculated by emission controls.

The red-hot GTO was redesigned and promoted to its own model line for 1966; boffo sales of 96,946 helped it boost total Pontiac production to more than 830,000. In 1967, Estes launched the Firebird ponycar, with engines up to 400 cubic inches. Priced a notch above Camaro, it sold 82,000 copies, and overall Pontiac production topped 900,000. In 1969, Firebird introduced the Trans Am performance and appearance package, which evolved into one of the longest-lived performance models.

The '69 big cars were redesigned, while the intermediates wore a facelift; a new version of the GTO was the "Judge" coupe and convertible, with a blackout grille, functional ram-air hood scoops, a Hurst three-speed shifter, plus wild decals and striping.

Oldsmobile was GM's most consistent producer throughout the Sixties, never falling below seventh in annual volume and rising as high as fourth. The Sixties began with the familiar line of Dynamic (later Delmont) 88, Super 88, and 98; in 1961 the F-85 was added, along with the Starfire, a limited-edition convertible with bucket seats and console. A Starfire coupe was added for 1962. By 1964, Olds had a true performance model in the 4-4-2 and a junior Starfire in the 88-based Jetstar I coupe. The best year in Olds history to date was 1965, which saw 500,000 cars.

Traditionally the "experimental division," Olds produced the innovative 1966 Toronado, the first front-wheel-drive car from an American automaker since the prewar Cord. Deftly styled by David North, Toronado combined traditional big-car size and power with the handling of front-wheel drive.

Sticking to just two full-size wheelbases and a continuity of styling, the Lansing division ended the decade with a new record, close to 670,000 '69s. The teething troubles of the original F-85 were history, and Olds found increased strength in the midsize Cutlass, soon the most popular single model in the U.S. industry.

In 1965, Senator Abraham Ribicoff convened hearings to investigate the "fantastic carnage" on the highways, and GM Chairman Donner and new President James Roche botched their testimony. "What have you done about auto safety?" Senator Robert Kennedy demanded. "Door locks," Roche sweated, "have undergone constant improvement." "You made $1.7 billion last year?" Kennedy asked Donner incredulously. "Yes, sir." Then, on safety research, Kennedy asked: "And you spent $1 million on this?"

It was a disastrous performance, with painful implications for GM and the industry. In 1966, the National Traffic and Motor Vehicle Safety Act created a new federal agency, the National Highway Traffic Safety Administration, empowered to set safety standards and to order repairs to safety-related defects. There was a new wind blowing around the Motor City. It came from Washington, and it scared the trousers off of every self-respecting mogul. Or at least it should have.

1. Like other General Motors cars of 1960, Buicks were toned-down versions of the all-new 1959 models, though Buick's basic "delta-wing" design was still pretty wild. The facelift did revive Buick's trademark: front-fender "ventiports." Top-line Electras and Electra 225s had four of the decorative accents, versus three for midrange Invictas and entry-level LeSabres. The '60s also wore a prominent new "tri-shield" Buick logo. The Electra hardtop sedan (shown) priced from $3963, $337 less than its Electra 225 sibling.

1

2

3

2-3. The Invicta series debuted for 1959, taking over the Century's role as the "banker's hot rod." That meant it had Buick's biggest, most powerful engine, a 325-hp 401 V-8, stuffed in its smallest, lightest bodies. Shown here, the $3620 convertible and the $3447 hardtop coupe. **4.** The 1960 Buicks' voluptuous curves made even the station wagons look swoopy. Invicta station wagons started at $3841 with two-row seating, or $3948 with a rearward-facing third-row seat.
5. Cadillac ruled the luxury roost as the 1960s dawned, outselling Lincoln, Chrysler, and Imperial combined. This stately Series 75 limousine is one of just 832 produced. The price was an equally stately $9748.

4

5

1. Cadillac's 1959 styling was the pinnacle of Fifties flamboyance. Designers dialed back for the new decade, making the 1960 models more restrained, with lower tailfins and less-gaudy grilles immediately evident. With 1285 produced, the limited-edition Biarritz convertible was the best-selling Eldorado model. 2. The Biarritz's hardtop sibling, the $7401 Seville coupe, rounded

out the Eldorado line along with an ultralimited Brougham hardtop sedan. All Eldorados used 390-cubic-inch V-8s like other models but had a three two-barrel carburetor setup that netted 345 horsepower versus 325. 3-4. The 1960 Chevrolet Corvette looked nearly identical to the '59, but model-year volume set a record at 10,261. Engines were unchanged, but the suspension gained a rear sway bar and other revisions. Corvettes continued to rack up victories in SCCA competition.

1

1. Detroit's Big Three debuted compact cars for 1960. Chevrolet's Corvair was the most radical by far. Instead of using a water-cooled engine in front, Corvair used a unique air-cooled "flat" six-cylinder placed at the rear. Corvair bowed in coupe and four-door sedan models in plain 500 and slightly ritzier 700 trim. A full-perimeter chrome strip identified 700s like this four-door sedan, which carried a starting price of $2103. **2.** Corvair model-year sales totaled just 250,000. Of those, 36,562 were 700 club coupes like this one. **3.** Chevy's 1960 big-car styling softened the '59 rear-end look with reshaped and separated "bat-wing" tailfins, plus orthodox round taillamps. Suggested price for this 1960 Bel Air was $2384 with six, $2491 with base 283-cube V-8. **4.** Full-size 1960 Chevy four-door sedans retained their clean "six-light" roofline from 1959. Impalas like this one priced at $2590/$2697 with six/V-8. **5.** Impalas like this sport coupe returned to 1958's triple-light motif, with a backup lamp splitting pairs of stop/taillights on each side. This Impala sold new for $2704 with base V-8.

2

3

4

5

1

2

3

4

1. The 1960 Chevy's new look well suited the glamorous Impala convertible, which cost $2954 with base V-8 and garnered 79,903 total sales. **2.** Oldsmobile pried the tinsel off its all-new 1959s to create one of 1960's more attractive cars. Offerings again spanned Dynamic 88s, Super 88s, and top-line Ninety-Eights. Ninety-Eights rode an exclusive 126.3-inch wheelbase, versus 123 for the others. Dealers saw sales fall 10 percent in a compact-minded market. **3.** The Dynamic 88 four-door sedan was the volume leader of Olds' entry-level series, with sales of 76,377. **4.** The 1960 Olds lineup still embraced three convertibles. The one seen here is the mid-range Super 88, a $3592 offering that weighed 4134 pounds and found favor with 5830 customers.

1

1. The 1960 Pontiacs sold even better than the all-new '59s on which they were based. Fresh styling and new colors aided the cause. All '60 Pontiacs used a 389-cubic-inch V-8, which ranged from an economical 215 horsepower to 348 on Tri-Power Bonnevilles. Pictured here is the top-line Bonneville convertible, which started at $3476. Frugal ragtop shoppers could also choose the entry-level Catalina convertible for $3078. **2.** With their classy dashboards and multitoned "Morrokide" upholstery, Pontiac interiors were some of the most dazzling of the day. **3.** The Vista Sedan four-door hardtop, a body style that debuted for 1959, was again the most popular Bonneville for '60, with 39,037 sold. Its unique wraparound rear window design was shared with other GM four-door hardtops. **4.** Pontiac again promoted the virtues of its "Wide Track" design, a marketing gem that also enhanced the appearance of its cars. The Star Chief two-door sedan made its final appearance for 1960. Just 5757 were made.

2

3

4

1

2

3

4

1. The 1961 Buicks were fully redesigned with much cleaner "bullet-nose" styling. The most affordable droptop was the $3382 LeSabre convertible. **2.** At one time, all Buick hardtops were known as Rivieras, but for 1961, that distinction was reserved solely for the Electra 225 four-door hardtop. At $4350, it was the costliest Buick of the year, but sales still hit 13,719 units. **3.** The Invicta's use of a bright trim strip all the way around the side cove worked well to delineate a break for a two-tone paint scheme that was exclusive to the series. **4.** Rounding out the Electra 225 line for '61 was the $4192 convertible. All big Buicks except LeSabres had a 401 V-8 with 325 horsepower. LeSabres made do with a 364 V-8 that put out 235 or 250 horsepower.

1. Cadillac was all-new for 1961, shedding a few inches and pounds while gaining a crisp, chiseled look. Highlighting the new design were lower-body "skeg fins" and arched windshield posts—no more Fifties-faddish "doglegs" to bang knees. Regaining its flagship status with the demise of the Eldorado Brougham was the

Series 60 Special, a formal-roof hardtop costing $6233. **2.** Two-door hardtops came either as this Coupe de Ville, starting at $5252, or as the Series 62, beginning at $4892. **3.** The $5588 convertible was the priciest member of Cadillac entry-level Series 62 line. It saw sales of 16,833. Cadillac's sole engine was again a 390-cid V-8, though it now came only as a 325-hp four-barrel. **4.** Chevy's Corvette received a "taillift" with four round taillights and a "ducktailed" rear end for '61, its first major styling change since 1958. Up front, a simple mesh grille replaced the familar chrome "teeth." Engines were unchanged, but a 315-hp "fue-lie" with a four-speed manual shift could hit 60 mph in 5.5 seconds and top 130 mph.

1

2

3

4

1-2. Along with their corporate siblings, Chevy's 1961 "standards" were the first General Motors cars to bear the full imprint of corporate design chief Bill Mitchell. The result was a cleaner, more coherent big Chevy that was 1.5 inches shorter yet looked much trimmer despite an unchanged 119-inch wheelbase. These Impala sport coupes wear the optional Super Sport package that was a midyear addition along with the soon to be legendary 409 V-8. **3.** As in recent years, full-sized Chevy wagons had their own names for 1961, though still outfitted in parallel with the three non-wagon series. The Impala-level four-door Nomad remained at the top of the line. **4.** Corvair 700 four-door sedans like this one started at $2039 and saw respectable sales of 51,948. The real Corvair sales dynamo was the bucket-seat Monza coupe, which hit 109,945.

1

1. Oldsmobile remade its image in '61, shifting from performance to premium-car luxury. Its big cars looked crisper, more mature, and made better use of space. The best-selling Super 88 model was the $3402 hardtop sedan, with an output of 23,272 units. 2. The new flagship of the Olds line was the $4647 Starfire, a deluxe-trimmed convertible intended to compete in the emerging personal-luxury field. 3. The top-line Ninety-Eight series featured two four-door hardtops: the $4021 Holiday hardtop sedan and this $4159 Sport Sedan. 4. Even the cheapest full-size hardtop, the $2956 Dynamic 88 coupe, cut a sharp figure. In all, Oldsmobile built 317,548 cars for '61, a slight drop from '60 in an overall slow car market but enough to move up a notch to sixth in the industry. 5. Pontiac's compact Tempest debuted for '61 as a four-door sedan, station wagon, and later a coupe. Standard power came from a 195-cid four-cylinder derived from a bank of Pontiac's 389-cube V-8; a 215-cid V-8 was optional. Both engines were linked to a very unconventional drivetrain: a flexible-cable driveshaft connected to a rear transaxle.

2

3

4

5

1

2

3

1. Pontiac's redesigned fleet of big cars revived the split-grille theme on shorter and lower but roomier bodies. The $2702 Catalina four-door sedan was the most popular full-size 1961 Pontiac, with sales of 38,638. Total Pontiac output reached 340,635, allowing the division to retain fifth place in industry standings. 2. Pontiac two-door hardtops, like this $2971 Ventura, shared the new "bubble roof" with Chevy and Olds. Optional eight-lug aluminum rims, exclusive to Pontiac, combined wheel hub and brake drum. All big Pontiacs used the 389-cid V-8, which could be ordered with as much as 348 horsepower. Late in the model year, Pontiac unleashed the special-order Super Duty 421, rated at 405 horsepower with dual four-barrel carburetors. 3. Top-line Bonnevilles, like this $3331 Vista sedan four-door hardtop, got ritzier trim with flashy triple taillamps. The track of the full-sized '61 Pontiacs was reduced by 1½ inches, but that didn't dent the "wide track" advertising slogan. Thanks to the astute leadership of general manager Semon "Bunkie" Knudsen, Pontiac was poised for great success.

1. Big Buicks were restyled for 1962, but compact Specials retained the pointed-fender styling theme from '61. The premium Skylark model expanded from a single two-door pillared coupe to add a genuine two-door hardtop and this flashy convertible. Specials got a notable new powerlant: America's first mass-produced passenger-car V-6. The 198-cid engine made 135 horsepower. 2. Buick's Wildcat debuted midseason as a $3927 Invicta-based hardtop with a bucket-seat interior and 401 V-8 good for 325 hp. 3. The Electra 225 series grew to five models in '62 when it assumed the three body styles from the now-defunct Electra line. Among the

1

2

3

newcomers to Buick's top rung was the four-window four-door hardtop. 4. For 1962, the Estate Wagon station wagons migrated to the Invicta series from the LeSabre line. Prices for the three-seat version (shown) started at $3917, making it the costliest Invicta until the Wildcat came along later in the model year. In spite of the change in series, the '62 Estate Wagon wore rear styling that was changed only in detail from that of the 1961 car. The chrome luggage rack and whitewall tires seen here were extra-cost options.

4

1. Cadillac's 1962 styling was a more-conservative take on the new '61 look. Subtle styling tweaks included a revised grille texture, rectangular front parking lights, slightly subdued tailfins, and vertical taillight housings. The "entry-level" Series 62 convertible started at $5588. 2. Although it had lost its two-door hardtop stablemate after 1960, the Eldorado convertible for '62 still carried the Biarritz name. With a production run of just 1450 units and a base price of $6610, it was the rarest and most expensive '62 Cadillac outside of the specialized Series 75 models. 3. The Cadillac Series 62 four-

door sedan priced from $5213. The 1962 model year was a good one for Cadillac; the division assembled 160,840 cars to break a production record that had stood for more than six years—and better 1961 output by more than 22,000 units. 4. Corvette looked cleaner for '62 via less chrome and without the two-tone option, though bright rocker-panel trim was added. New 327-cid V-8s supplied the go. Corvette's base price broke the $4000 barrier for the first time this year, and the top 360-hp "fuelie" engine and four-speed transmission could add $700 to that tab. Still, sales jumped to another new record at 14,531.

1. Taking over for Corvair as Chevy's mainstream compact, the Chevy II was as simple and conventional as its targeted rival, the successful Ford Falcon. Topping the new line was the snazzy Nova 400 convertible, which saw 23,471 copies.
2. Chevy IIs in the midline 300 series, like this four-door sedan, could be had with a standard four-cylinder engine or a related 194-cubic-inch six with 120 horsepower. The fender skirts seen here were a dealer-installed option. 3. Corvairs got minor trim changes for '62. The Corvair Monza Spyder came in coupe or convertible form, both packing a turbocharged version of the 145-cid "flat" six that churned out 150 hp. 4. Corvair's Lakewood wagons returned for '62 but would not be back the following year, thanks to sluggish sales. Rarest of the lot was the new 1962 Monza Lakewood, offering all the sporty accoutrements of its coupe and sedan siblings starting at $2569. 5. Corvair Monza four-door sedans started at $2273—the same base price as the Monza coupe. 6-7. New outer sheetmetal gave full-size

1

2

3

4

5

6

'62 Chevys a more "important" look. Shown here are the $3026 V-8 convertible and the $2776 V-8 Sport Coupe. Both came standard with a 170-hp 283.

7

1

2

3

4

5

1. For 1962, Oldsmobile styling came in for a facelift that featured a protruding grille and squarer rear quarters, as seen on the $4459 Ninety Eight convertible. The new look helped Olds to its best sales year since 1956. **2.** New rear styling, as displayed on the $3273 Super 88 four-door sedan, featured oval taillights in a larger cove area. **3.** The bucket-seat Starfire became its own series and added a coupe. The $4131 hardtop outsold the convertible—at $4774, the priciest Olds—34,839 to 7149. **4.** The most popular model in Oldsmobile's top-echelon series was the Ninety-Eight Sport Sedan, which sold more than 33,000 copies despite its $4256 price tag. Standard power in Ninety Eights and Super 88s was the chrome-trimmed Skyrocket V-8, which was boosted to 330 hp for '62. **5.** Oldsmobile's F-85 compacts debuted for 1961. At midyear '62, Olds unveiled the innovative Jetfire, a bucket-seat F-85 coupe that was powered by a turbocharged 215-cid V-8. Available with manual or automatic transmission, the Jetfire could do 0-60 mph in a credible-for-the-day 8.5 seconds.

1. Pontiac's new-for-1962 Grand Prix—essentially a cleaned-up Catalina two-door hardtop with bucket seats and special trim—would help define the personal luxury field. Sales of 30,195 made it a hit. The $3490 base price included bucket seats and a 303-horsepower 389. 2. Nineteen sixty-two was a breakthrough year for Pontiac, when more than a half-million of the division's products were built, including more than 380,000 of the full-size cars. Catalinas like this $3172 convertible gained an inch in wheelbase and could still be optioned with triple two-barrel carburetion for the 389-cube engine. 3. Big Pontiacs got fresh new looks for '62 but retained their split-grille motif. The biggest Pontiac hardtop coupe was the $3349 Bonneville. 4. Pontiac station wagons, such as the nine-seat Catalina Safari, retained the 119-inch wheelbase introduced for '61. The Catalina hauler came in two- and three-seat versions. 5-6. Pontiac's compact Tempest got a facelift that included a tri-section grille that incorporated a Pontiac "arrow-point" crest at its center. The sportiest Tempests were the bucket-seat LeMans models: a $2418 coupe or $2741 convertible (the droptop bodystyle was new to the Tempest lineup).

1

2

3

4

5

6

1-2. The Buick Riviera was reborn as a stunning $4365 hardtop coupe artfully blending American and British style. Like most full-size Buicks, it came with a 325-hp 401 V-8, but a new 425 V-8 with 340 horses was an exclusive Riviera option. This svelte personal-luxury car changed Buick's stodgy image almost overnight. **3.** Buick's Invicta put in its last appearance for '63, by which time it had been reduced to a single Estate Wagon. **4.** Big Buick styling was crisper and more-formal for '63, as this Electra 225 four-door hardtop demonstrates. **5.** Having gotten by without an open-air LeSabre in '62, Buick restored a convertible to the line in '63. Almost 10,000 of the $3339 cars were called for.

1. Another redesign helped Cadillac to a new sales record of more than 163,000 for '63. Shown here is Cadillac's marquee car, the $6608 Eldorado Biarritz convertible. **2.** Cadillac's best-selling model, at 31,749 units, was this dashing $5386 Coupe de Ville. **3.** Chevy Corvair Spyders were in short supply for '62 but more readily available as '63 models. Priced at $317, the package was fit-

ted to 11,627 Monza coupes like this and 7472 Monza convertibles. **4.** In 1963, the Chevy II could be ordered with a $161 SS option package that added sporty trim. **5.** Brand-new body designs brought a crisp new look to full-sized '63 Chevrolets. Impala Sport Coupes started at $2774 with the standard 283 V-8.

1. Save carryover engines, Corvette was all-new for '63, gaining Sting Ray badges and stunning new styling. Ragtops started at $4037. 2. The Grand Sport was an all-out racing Sting Ray developed to beat Carroll Shelby's Ford-powered Cobras. 3. Joining the traditional 'Vette roadster was this sleek fastback coupe with a split rear window that hampered visibility but looked terrific.

1

1. Side sculpting gave way
to a slab-sided look on '63
Oldsmobiles. Starfires continued
as convertibles and hardtops with
a 345-hp, 394-cid V-8.
2. Ninety-Eights adopted rear
styling all their own; shown here
is the $4178 Holiday coupe.
3. This 1963 Olds family por-
trait includes the Starfire ragtop,
Dynamic 88 two-door hardtop,
F-85 Jetfire, and F-85 Cutlass
ragtop.

2

3

1. The Olds Dynamic 88 Holiday two-door hardtop saw respectable sales of 39,071. 2. Oldsmobile's turbocharged Jetfire closed out its second and final year of production with sales of just 5842 units. 3. All-new sheetmetal below the beltline gave the 1963 Pontiac Tempests a more upscale look. The rarest '63 Tempest was the base-model Safari wagon, of which 4203 were made. 4-5. The sporty LeMans became a separate Tempest series for '63 with a $2418 hardtop coupe and $2742 convertible.

1-2. Youthful and energetic, Pontiac's 1963 restyle was one of the era's benchmarks. The full-sized models' stacked headlights would be copied by other cars. The Grand Prix entered its sophomore season wearing handsome new sheet-metal with smooth bodysides, a concave rear window, and "hidden" taillamps. **3.** Pontiac's top-line Bonneville series consisted of six-passenger Safari wagon, four-door-hardtop Vista Sedan, two-door-hard-top Sport Coupe, and convertible models, all of which wore unique ribbed bodyside trim. At $3568 to start, the Bonneville convertible was Pontiac's priciest ragtop. **4.** The $3179 convertible was the flashiest member of Pontiac's mainstream Catalina line. Its sales hit 18,249. **5.** This all-business Catalina two-door hardtop packs a High Output 421 with Tri-Power carburetion and 370 horsepower. The Pontiac division saw its highest model-year production to date, 590,071, under the leadership of general manager E. M. "Pete" Estes.

1

2

3

4

5

1

2

1. Big Buick styling was further refined for 1964. Bright lower bodyside trim and new standard fender skirts accentuated the exclusive 126-inch wheelbase of Electra 225 models. Four-door hardtops started at $4194. **2.** Except for revised badging and detail trim, the Buick Riviera's appearance was unchanged for its second season. **3.** With the two-door sedan dropped from the line,

3

4

Buick's entry-level two-door was the LeSabre hardtop coupe, which started at $3061. **4.** The Special/Skylark line grew from compact to midsize proportions for '64. The handsome Skylark ragtop cost $2834 and drew 10,225 sales. **5.** The Skylark Sports Wagon boasted an airy raised roof section with four overhead windows for additional interior light.

5

1

1. Cadillac's once-soaring tailfins were down to modest blades for 1964—which made the cars look even longer and lower. A new grille with a body-color divider bar enhanced visual width, but exterior dimensions were basically the same as for '63. The division's most-prestigious two-door, the $6630 Eldorado convertible, could be identified by its full rear-wheel cutouts sans fender skirts—the only '64 Cadillac so styled. 2. The stately Cadillac Fleetwood Series 60 Special four-door hardtop started at $6388. 3. The Corvette Sting Ray coupe lost its "split-window" styling for 1964, but available horsepower hit a mighty 375. Four-wheel independent suspension aided on control in corners and on straightaways.

2

3

1. GM's answer to Ford's successful Fairlane was the Chevelle, Chevrolet's first mid-size car. In price as well as size and power, Chevelle slotted between the compact Chevy II and full-size Chevrolets. Buyers took to it right away. The topline Malibu series arrived with a snazzy SS option for the Sport Coupe (shown) and convertible. **2.** Chevy resurrected the El Camino on its new midsize platform. Buyers had a choice of six-cylinder or V-8 power and standard or Custom trim. **3.** Chevy II sales sank for '64, likely cannibalized by the new Chevelle. An entry-level 100 two-door sedan started at $2070 with six-cylinder power. **4.** Corvair's original 1960 design made its final bow for '64. All models, including this Monza Spyder Sport Coupe, offered improved handling via a "camber compensator" newly added to the rear suspension. **5.** The '64 Corvairs also got a larger 164-cid "flat" six with 95 horsepower standard, 110 optional; Spyder horsepower was unchanged. This ragtop Monza is one of 31,045; another 4761 were built as Spyders.

1. The big "Jet-Smooth" Chevys returned for 1964 with a more rounded look on the new-for-'63 bodyshells. Impala SS sales rose to 185,325 Sport Coupes (shown) and ragtops. Though still available with a six, most SS '64 Impalas were built with V-8s, which now involved two small-block 283s, three 327s, and burly 400- and 425-hp 409s. But big-block orders plunged to 8864 this year, as speed demons quickly saw the performance potential of the lighter midsize Chevelles. 2. Slightly more conservative styling was the 1964 direction for full-sized Oldsmobiles. Ninety-Eight continued as Olds's flagship line. The $4468 convertible was the series' rarest model, with a production run of just 4004 units. Olds's 330-hp "Skyrocket" 394-cid V-8 was standard in Ninety-Eights and Super 88s. 3. Jetstar 88 was introduced as a new economy line below the Dynamic 88 series. With bucket seats, standard 345-hp V-8, and a $3603 price tag, the Jetstar I was the sportiest and priciest model of this new entry-level series. 4. The F-85 ascended to GM's new 115-inch wheelbase and got a new performance-oriented 4-4-2 package. The name stood for four-barrel carb, four-speed manual gearbox, dual exhausts. A 310-hp 330-cid V-8 was included.

1

2

3

4

1

2

3

1. Big Pontiacs, like the $3578 Bonneville ragtop, got a handsome freshening that had them looking a bit huskier and "softer" for 1964. **2.** A 1963 Pontiac Catalina two-door hardtop cut a fine profile. This example packs a 330-hp Tri-Power 389. A 20-percent jump in overall production helped Pontiac strengthen its hold on third place in the industry. **3-4.** By stuffing its big 389-cube V-8 into its redesigned midsize Tempest, Pontiac created the first modern muscle car, the trendsetting '64 GTO. Three body styles were offered: a $3500 convertible, a $3250 two-door hardtop (both shown here), and a $3200 pillared coupe. GTO's magic was that it was the first "factory hot rod" marketed as an integrated performance package, with a key component being a carefully cultivated image. But it had the goods too, starting at 325 horsepower with the standard four-barrel carb or 348 with the optional Tri-Power setup. Demand instantly outpaced Pontiac's projections, and a performance legend was born.

4

1-2. GM restyled all its full-sized cars for 1965. Buicks fared well, gaining curvier lines without losing the brand's conservative upscale elegance. Pictured here are the $3325 LeSabre convertible and the $4206 Electra 225 hardtop sedan. **3.** Buick's Riviera looked better than ever for '65, with headlights newly concealed behind "clamshell" doors flanking the grille. **4.** Buick joined the blossoming muscle car trend in its own classy way with a performance version of the Skylark called Gran Sport. A 325-hp 401 was part of the option package.

1

2

3

4

1

2

3

1. Cadillac sales zoomed to nearly 200,000 for a banner 1965. Yet another redesign produced the trimmest Caddys in many a year, highlighted by stacked headlamps and gently curved side windows. Standard Cadillacs rode a 129.5-inch wheelbase, but the extra-posh Fleetwood Sixty Special mounted an exclusive 133-inch span. **2.** Deville convertibles tipped the scales at 4690 pounds and cost $5639. **3-4.** Further refinements marked the '65 Corvette Sting Rays. 'Vettes with the new big-block 396 option could be identified by their side exhaust pipes. Small-block V-8 power was unchanged, but all Corvettes got standard disc brakes to better rein in their muscle.

4

1-2. Chevy's Corvair was fully redesigned for 1965 with swoopy new styling. Chassis revisions made handling both more predictable and even sportier. Pictured here are the $2493 convertible and the $2422 hardtop sedan. **3.** Only 1528 Corvair Greenbriar vans were built for '65, the model's last year of production. **4.** The Chevy II again saw only detail changes for '65, but a 195-hp 283 V-8 option returned,

1

2

3

4

5

6

7

along with new 250- and 300-horsepower 327s. Most went into Novas like this SS sport coupe. **5-6.** Chevelle got the usual second-year cosmetic changes for '65. Malibu SS coupes (left) started at $2539 with six-cylinder power, or $2647 with the base V-8. Late in the model year, a limited run of "Z16" big-block SS396 coupes were produced (right). **7-8.** Chevrolet's redesigned big '65s were longer, wider, and roomier overall, enhanced by a fulsome, flowing new shape. As before, the sportiest models were the Impala SS Sport Coupes and convertibles (both shown here).

8

1

2

3

1. Full-sized Oldsmobiles adopted curvier lines with "hop-up" rear fenders for 1965. The Starfire two-door hardtop cost $4138 to start. 2. The showy Starfire convertible was again the most expensive Olds starting at $4778. Just 2236 were built. 3. Ninety-Eights adapted well to Oldsmobile's new design motif while retaining their unique styling features. Pictured here is the $4197 Holiday sports coupe, one of 12,166 built. 4. Cutlass was the top trim level for the subtly facelifted '65 Oldsmobile intermediates, and the king Cutlass was the $2983 convertible.

4

1. Big Pontiacs added inches and pounds for 1965 but hid their bulk nicely with new, flowing body lines. Shown here is the $3594 Bonneville convertible, which saw a production run of 21,050. **2.** Top-line Bonneville luxury was available to wagon buyers in the six-seat Custom Safari. The $3632 wagon was the least popular Bonneville, with 6460 sold. **3.** The year's most-popular full-sized Pontiac was the Catalina

two-door hardtop with 92,009 made. **4.** A $244 "2+2" option package endowed Catalina coupes or convertibles with special trim, bucket seats, heavy-duty suspension, and a standard 338-hp 421 V-8. **5-6.** Pontiac GTOs got vertical headlights and other styling updates for '65. The Tri-Power 389 gained 12 horsepower, to 360. Sales more than doubled, to 75,352. The GTO was already a bona-fide pop-culture phenomenon.

1

2

1-2. The Buick Riviera was redesigned for 1966 as an underskin cousin of Oldsmobile's new front-drive Toronado. Buick, however, stuck with rear-wheel drive. Parking lights were canted in at the front fenders; dual headlights flipped down from above the grille. Two versions of Buick's 425-cid V-8 were offered: one with a single four-barrel carb and 340 horsepower, the other with twin quads and 360 hp. **3.** Full-sized Buicks got no drastic change for 1966. Still, engineering tweaks improved quietness and ride comfort a bit, so that year's new "tuned car" ad slogan

3

4

wasn't all hype. Outside of the Riviera, the Electra 225 convertible was the priciest Buick at $4378. **4.** Updated trim kept the '66 Buick Wildcats as handsome as ever. A 325-hp 401 was standard. Here, a coupe in Shadow Turquoise. The changes in full-size Buicks were not enough to sustain the public's interest at 1965 levels. Model-year volume declined by nearly 50,000 units, to 553,870, and Buick slipped to seventh place, behind Oldsmobile, in industry standings.

1-2. A total restyling of all General Motors intermediate car lines was ordained for 1966. Like its corporate siblings, the Skylark Gran Sport was new all over. Buick signaled its commitment to the muscle car market by elevating the Gran Sport from a Skylark option package to its own series of two-door sedans, hardtops, and convertibles. Its 325-hp 401 V-8 delivered 0-60 mph in 7.6 seconds; a quicker 340-hp version was optional. **3.** The 1966 Cadillacs reprised the successful '65 formula, albeit with minor tweaks and two new options: variable-ratio power steering for sportier handling and heated front seats—another industry first. Cadillac's "affordable" droptop was the DeVille convertible, which started at $5555. **4.** The $5581 Cadillac DeVille hardtop sedan accounted for 60,550 sales. **5.** Cadillac's Eldorado retained its exclusive status for '66. Just 2250 of the $6631 ragtops were called for, though that was up slightly from '65.

1

2

3

4

5

1. Chevy's new 427-cid big-block V-8 replaced the 396 as Corvette's top 1966 power option. **2-3.** Reskinned Chevy IIs included frugal 100s (left) and spunky Nova SSs (right). **4-5.** Caprice debuted as a posh Impala trim option for '65. For '66, it expanded into a full three-model series comprised of a station wagon, hardtop coupe (both shown here), and hardtop sedan. **6.** This Corvair Monza convertible is one of 10,345 built.

1

1-2. A landmark automobile and one of the decade's most-important cars, the 1966 Oldsmobile Toronado reintroduced front-wheel drive to America and forecast the design revolution that would sweep the U.S. industry in the 1980s. Underhood was the most-powerful Olds V-8, a 425 with 385 hp. Toronado's groundbreaking styling bore hints of the classic 1936–1937 Cord 810/812. 3. Full-sized Oldsmobiles got a minor facelift, as seen on this Delta 88 ragtop, which listed for $3588 with the standard 310-hp 425 V-8. 4. Oldsmobile's Starfire lost its convertible model for '66, leaving only a $3564 hardtop coupe. Sales reached 13,019. 5. Olds intermediates were reskinned for '66, and the high-performance 4-4-2 was promoted to its own model line. The $2770 Holiday hardtop coupe (shown) was the most popular model in the upscale Cutlass line.

2

3

4

5

1

2

3

1. This year's slightly revised styling looked good on the 124-inch chassis of the Pontiac Bonneville and Star Chief. Lower-body trim on Bonnevilles got a ribbed texture for '66. Demand for the $3586 Bonneville convertible dipped to 16,299. 2. Pontiac's entry in the growing personal-luxury field continued to be the Grand Prix hardtop coupe, which was based on the Catalina chassis but featured distinct grille, roof, and rear styling. 3-4. Like Olds's 4-4-2, Pontiac's GTO was promoted to its own model line for 1966 and saw a production run of 96,946 units, the highest-ever total for a true muscle car. Redesigned bodies had a handsome "Coke-bottle" shape. Pillared coupes, hardtops, and convertibles were still offered, again with a 389-cubic-inch V-8; 360-hp versions did 0-60 mph in 6.5 seconds.

4

1. Full-size Buicks had a new look for '67, highlighted by flowing "sweepspear" body-side lines, a nod to 1950s Buick styling. LeSabre continued as Buick's entry-level full-size series, offering standard and Custom trim levels. Shown here is the $3172 Custom hardtop coupe. **2.** Rivieras saw little change on the outside for 1967 but got a new 360-hp 430 V-8 under the hood. Sales improved to 42,799. **3.** Buick's midsize performance lineup got a new "junior" muscle car in the GS340. Available only in white or silver, both with red accents, the GS340 packed a 260-hp 340 V-8. **4.** Buick's top midsize muscle car dropped the Gran Sport tag for GS 400 in honor

1

2

3

4

of its new engine, a 400-cid V-8 of 340 horsepower, 15 more than the old "nailhead" 401. The new mill was good for quarter-mile times in the high 14-second range. GS 400 ragtops cost $3271 and saw a production run of just 2454. **5.** All Buick intermediates got a mild-facelift for '67, station wagons included. Simulated wood paneling became an option for Sportwagons. At $3340, the three-seat Custom Sportwagon was the priciest model on Buick's intermediate roster. The base Skylark engine was a 225-cid V-6, but V-8s of 300 or 340 cubes were available.

5

1-2. Cadillac reserved the Eldorado name for a special car, and that certainly described the totally new two-door hardtop that bore the badge for 1967. Adopting the Olds Toronado's front-wheel-drive technology, Caddy fashioned a creased coupe on a 120-inch wheelbase (nine inches briefer than the rear-drive '66 Eldo and one inch less than Toronado). The $6277 Cadillac rode and handled better than the $4850 Olds, and its sales of 17,930 were just 4000 short of Toronado's. Like all '67 Caddys, the Eldo used a 340-hp 429-cid V-8. **3.** Though overshadowed by the reborn Eldorado, Cadillac's mainstream '67s offered fresh styling highlighted by a forward-raked grille and front fenders. The $5608 DeVille convertible was now Cadillac's only ragtop. **4.** Cadillac's entry-level Calais series shared bodies with DeVilles but made do with less-fancy fabrics and manually adjustable seats and windows. The $5040 Calais two-door hardtop was the cheapest 1967 Cadillac.

1-2. Chevrolet's new-for-'67 Camaro answered the Ford Mustang ponycar and was a solid hit itself. The sporty coupe (shown) and convertible offered a huge choice of options; hidden headlamps identified Camaros equipped with the Rally Sport appear-

1

2

3

4

ance package. **3-4.** Still regarded as one of the best 'Vettes of all time, the '67 Sting Ray got five smaller front fender vents, new rocker-panel trim, and slotted Rally wheels. Ironically, year-to-year sales eased for the first time in years, slipping to 22,940 units. **5-6.** The '67 Chevelles sported a crisp facelift. Power-bulge hood vents on SS396s looked great but weren't functional. **7.** Keeping to a two-year design cycle, full-sized 1967 Chevys got brand new bodyshells with flowing lines that made the cars appear longer, though overall length and wheelbase were unchanged. Even plain-Jane Impalas could get serious muscle; this two-door hardtop packs a 385-horsepower 427.

5

6

7

1-2. Chevy II Novas sported just minor trim changes for '67. Most coupes got six-cylinder power (left), but SSs (right) could be equipped with a potent 350-horsepower 327

V-8. **3.** Oldsmobile Toronados were updated with freshened front-end styling and new taillights. Toronado shared with all big Oldsmobiles a 425-cid V-8, though it had 385 hp to the others' 300-375. **4.** Full-sized Oldsmobiles got curvier for 1967 and were again led by the Ninety-Eight series. Here, the $4498 Ninety-Eight convertible. **5.** The most-popular member of Olds' midpriced Delta 88 lineup was the $3328 Holiday hardtop sedan, with 33,326 produced. **6.** Like other GM intermediates, the F-85/Cutlass line got a mild facelift for '67. The muscular 4-4-2 reflected Oldmobile's level-headed values and so was more a well-balanced performance machine than a barely tamed race car. Its 350-hp 400-cid V-8 could be outfitted with the optional W-30 performance package. That put air-induction scoops in the headlamp housings and returned 0-60 mph in 6.7 seconds. **7.** The Cutlass Supreme convertible started at $3026. Standard Cutlass Supreme engine was a 330 V-8.

1

1-2. Pontiac's big news for 1967 was the introduction of the Firebird ponycar. Though based on Chevrolet's new Camaro, Firebird had Pontiac engines and styling cues, plus slightly more upscale trim and pricing. **3.** Pontiac marked its sixth year as Detroit's third best-seller in 1967. Swoopy Bonneville hardtop sedans started at $3517. **4.** Grand Prixs stood apart from their Catalina kin with a hidden-headlamp nose and unique tail. **5-6.** GTOs got minor styling updates such as a mesh grille and resculpted tail, and a 400-cid V-8 replaced the 389. Of 782,734 Pontiacs built for '67, nearly 82,000 were GTOs.

2

3

4

5

6

1

2

3

4

5

1. The Buick Riviera got a more-massive look for 1968 via a restyled nose and tail. Sales were up slightly, to 49,284. **2.** Full-sized Buicks got minor trim changes and new grilles for '68. The most popular and affordable model in the mid-level Wildcat series was the $3416 four-door sedan. **3-4.** Government-mandated side-marker lights were among the few visual changes for Eldorados. **5.** Senior Cadillacs sported new grilles and, thanks to longer hoods, hidden windshield wipers. The demise of the Lincoln Continental four-door convertible left Cadillac and Imperial with the only soft tops among American luxury cars. By '68, the starting price of a DeVille convertible (shown) was up to $5736.

1

2

1-2. Originally planned for 1967 but delayed by development problems, the '68 Chevrolet Corvette wore a swoopy new body atop the 1963–67 chassis and dispensed with the Sting Ray name. It also dispensed with conventional door handles in favor of a pushbutton next to a hand grip covered by a spring-loaded metal flap. Though the styling was controversial at the time, Corvette production rose to 28,566, a new all-time high. Ragtops priced from $4320.

RALPH NADER AND THE CORVAIR

Born the son of Lebanese immigrants in Connecticut in 1934, Ralph Nader graduated from Princeton in 1955—the year he sold his last car—and from Harvard Law School in 1958. After a stint in the Army, he became a lawyer and professor of History and Government, moving to Washington under Assistant Labor Secretary Daniel Patrick Moynihan in 1964.

Nader is as closely linked to the Corvair as the word "failure" is to the Edsel, but the linkage is bedizened with ironies. His 1965 attack on the auto industry, *Unsafe at Any Speed*, contained only one chapter about the Corvair. (Other parts of it blamed manufacturers as insignificant as Packard for such errors as misplacing the "R" in automatic shift quadrants where drivers might shift into Reverse when they really wanted Low.)

Nader took aim at the most innovative and potentially revolutionary small car in postwar history, whose concepts might have accomplished much of what he sought: fuel-efficient, air-cooled, smaller and more-sensible automobiles. A final irony is that GM had decided to kill off the Corvair months before Nader's book was published.

Nader's case against the Corvair began with the assertion that GM had adopted a rear engine to exploit the "trendy sports car market," which is pretty silly, given that the only popular sports car with that configuration was the Porsche. In fact, what GM was looking for was efficiency and economy in a compact package. Nader did not criticize the car's swing-axle suspension (shared by that consumer paragon, the Volkswagen) but rather its weight distribution, which could produce violent oversteer, especially if drivers forgot about tire pressures. Both VW and

1

2

3

4

5

1. Full-sized 1968 Chevys wore a nice update of their '67 stylng. Here, the Impala wagon, which started at $3245. The standard V-8 for all big Chevys was now a more emissions-friendly 307 small-block with 200 horsepower. 2. The Corvair lineup shrank to just three models: a "500" coupe, Monza coupe (shown), and Monza convertible. 3. Like all '68 General Motors intermediates, Chevelle was fully redesigned on a brand-new "A-body" platform designed around two wheelbases. The shorter, 112-inch span was exclusive to two-door models like this $2899 SS396 Sport Coupe. 4-5. Chevrolet's Camaro wasn't much altered for its sophomore year, but optional four-wheel disc brakes arrived at midyear and were especially welcome on high-power models like the Z/28. This one wears the separately available Rally Sport appearance package.

Corvair required pressures on the order of 15 psi front, 26 rear, a strange combination for Americans used to front engines and rear-drive.

So...those who didn't bother to read the owner's manual or to check tire pressures now and then may have paid a price, at least with a 1960–61 Corvair. After that, a Regular Production Option of stiffer springs, shorter rear axle limit straps, and a front anti-sway bar was widely fitted, and on the 1964 models, Bunkie Knudsen insisted that a rear anti-sway bar be added as standard. The second generation (1965–69) models had an all-new and admirable independent rear sus-pension, but by then, alas, the Corvair's fate was sealed.

Worse gaffes were commit-ted by the General Motors man-agers who blundered after Nader like enraged bull elephants, trying to discredit him in the popular press, and at one point hiring prostitutes to compromise him sexually. The plots failed, Nader sued for invasion of privacy, and GM was forced to pay a settle-ment of $284,000 and to issue a public apology. The govern-ment responded by creating the National Highway Traffic Safety Administration, which after long investigation concluded that the early Corvair was no less safe or prone to rollovers than the average car of the early 1960s.

The most explosive and influential best seller of the decade!

ORIGINALLY $5.95 NOW ONLY $1.00

UNSAFE AT ANY SPEED

The Designed-In Dangers of the American Automobile

RALPH NADER

1

1-3. A curvaceous rede-sign for midsize Oldsmobiles agreed with the 4-4-2's classy image. Its 400-cid V-8 made 350 horsepower, or 360 with optional W-30 hop-ups. Convertibles started at $3341, hardtop coupes at $3150. W-30-equipped cars were good for quarter-mile times of 13.3 at 103 mph. **4.** Oldsmobile teamed with aftermarket shifter manufacturer Hurst to produce the limited-edition Hurst/Olds. It packed a 390-hp 455 Toronado V-8. **5.** The Olds Vista-Cruiser's new-for-'68 body design featured rear-quar-ter windows that rose higher into the roof than before. This example wears dealer-installed wire wheels.

2

3

4

5

1

2

3

4

5

1. Full-size Pontiacs picked up a protruding "beak" styling motif for 1968. The $3800 Bonneville convertible was the line's biggest and spendiest ragtop. **2.** Catalinas could be equipped with a Ventura option package that included specific badges. This example is equipped to move with eight-lug wheels, four-speed, and 375-hp 428-cid V-8. A 400-cid V-8 was the smallest engine available in full-size Pontiacs. **3.** Grand Prixs got a heavy new look for '68 that didn't sit well with some shoppers; sales declined 26 percent to a new low of 31,711. Fender skirts and hidden headlamps were standard; a "halo" vinyl top was optional. **4-5.** GTOs got a dazzling new shape with an energy-absorbing Endura front bumper for '68. Hidden

headlamps were so popular that most people didn't realize they were an option. GTO sales rose by about 6000 units, to 87,684. The $3101 hardtop accounted for 77,704; the $3227 made up the balance. Top GTO engine choice was the 366-hp Ram Air II 400.

1

1. All of Pontiac's 1968 inter-mediate models wore curva-ceous new styling on GM's new 112-inch-wheelbase chassis. The $2839 Tempest Custom convertible was the most affordable droptop in the line. As before, LeMans was a step up the model roster from Tempest. Engine choices for these midline midsize cars ranged from a 175-horsepower 215-cubic-inch six to a 320-hp 350 V-8. **2.** Like its Camaro cousin, Firebird lost its vent windows for '68 but changed little otherwise. The optional hood-mounted tachometer looked neat but was hard to read in rain or snow or when driv-ing with the bright sun at your back. **3.** As on other '68 Pontiacs, Firebirds satisfied the newly mandated side-marker-light regula-tions by employing illuminated Pontiac "arrowhead" badges on their rear fenders. With base six-cylinder power, Firebird coupes started at $2781, convertibles at $2996.

2

3

1. Buick's midsize models returned with few changes for 1969, though GS400s got functional hood scoops. This GS400 convertible is fitted with the optional Stage 1 package, which boosted the 400-cid V-8 from 340 horsepower to 345—on paper. The actual increase was probably more. **2.** Buick's dome-top Sportwagon models made their final appearance in 1969. Aside from woodgraining, this example is packed with optional comfort and convenience features, plus the extra-cost 340-hp 400-cid V-8. **3.** Rivieras didn't change much but sold better than ever, with a production run of nearly 53,000 units. As before, the front bumper's outer edges housed large parking/turn sig-

nal lamps. Hidden headlights powered down from the top of the grille. A standard 430 V-8 delivered 360 horsepower. **4-5.** Bladelike front fenders, ventless door glass, and wraparound taillights were elements of Cadillac's new look for '69. Accessory wire wheels dress up this DeVille convertible, which was one of 16,445 made for the year. All '69 Cadillacs used the same engine: a 375-horsepower 472-cid V-8.

1. Recontoured below-the-belt sheetmetal with racy rear-fender "speedlines" gave a huskier, more "performance" look to all '69 Camaros. Performance is the operative word for this unassuming Camaro coupe; it's one of just 69 produced with the all-aluminum ZL-1 V-8, one of Chevy's most exotic and powerful engines. 2. This convertible is one of 17,573 built

2

for the model year. Camaro would then do without a ragtop for the next 17 years. 3. For '69, Camaros were available with an even greater array of performance and appearance options for seemingly limitless personalization. This coupe sports the RS/SS packages, 300-hp 350 V-8, Cowl-Induction hood, and the Z10 striping package, which replicated the paint scheme of the '69 Camaro Indianapolis 500 Pace Car. 4-5. In a move that surprised no one, Chevrolet ended Corvair production on May 14, 1969, after five years of controversy and falling sales. Shown here are the $2641 Monza convertible and $2522 Monza coupe. The last Corvair buyers got a $150 credit toward the purchase of any new Chevrolet through 1974. 6. Chevelle's year-old styling was just mildly tweaked for '69. The line posted another healthy sales gain, led by some 367,100 Malibus like this Sport Coupe, which priced from $2601 with base 230-cid six, $2690 with base 307 V-8.

1

3

4

5

6

1-2. The '69 Corvettes revived the Stingray name and set another sales record with a production run of 38,762. Coupes outsold ragtops for the first time. This coupe packs the mighty 435-hp, triple-carb 427. **3.** The two-year-old styling of the full-size Chevys was handsomely updated for '69, announced by a broad loop-style bumper/grille and prominent bodyside bulges around the wheel openings. The Impala Super Sport made one final stand as a $422 package for the two-door hardtop and convertible (shown). Installations totaled just 2425. **4.** Big Chevy wagons again had separate model names for '69. Top of the line was the Brookwood Estate, trimmed to Caprice level and identified by woody-look side trim. The roof rack seen here was available over the parts counter. **5.** Full-size 1969 Chevrolets sported flow-through "Astro-Ventilation" that eliminated front-door vent windows. Small badges above the front marker lights indicated engine size. This Impala Sport Coupe is equipped with one of Chevy's most powerful engines for the year: the 425-hp L72 427 V-8.

1

2

3

4

5

1. Oldsmobile's Cutlass lineup got a modest facelift for 1969 and was again keynoted by the sporty 4-4-2, which started at $3395 in convertible form. All 4-4-2s had a wacky pitchman in the fictional Dr. Oldsmobile, the mustachioed, white-lab-coat-wearing "mad scientist" of Olds performance. **2.** The Hurst/Olds returned for 1969 wearing a wild airfoil decklid spoiler, racing-style mirrors, twin-snout hood scoop, and a "Firefrost Gold" and white paint scheme. At its heart was a 455-cid V-8 tweaked to deliver 380 horsepower. Production almost doubled, amounting to 906 two-door hardtops and a pair of convertibles designed for show duty. **3.** Though redesigned on a one-inch-longer wheelbase, the full-size Oldsmobile Delta 88 didn't look much different than before. The convertible moved from the departed Delmont 88 series to become a $3590 Delta 88. Base engine was a 250-hp 350 V-8; options ranged to a 390-hp 455. **4-5.** Bucking an industry trend, the redesigned 1969 Pontiac Grand Prix shrunk three inches in wheelbase (to 118 inches) and lost 360 pounds (now 3715). Yet the trimmer GP sported one of the longest hoods in autodom, and with V-8s up to a 390-horsepower 428 available, it combined muscle-car go with luxury-car comfort.

1. Pontiac's full-size cars were redesigned but looked very similar to the '68s. Catalinas rode a 122-inch wheelbase, while Executives and Bonnevilles had a 125-inch span—both one inch longer than before. Catalina ragtops started at $3476. 2. All the '69 Pontiac intermediates saw

modest trim updates. This $3064 LeMans ragtop sports the optional hood-mounted tachometer. 3. Pontiac added op-art decals, a rear spoiler, and a 366-hp Ram Air III 400 to create The Judge, a $332 option package on the GTO. 4-5. The Pontiac Trans Am debuted as a $725 midyear option package for the Firebird. Just 697 were built, including eight convertibles. All were painted Polar White with blue stripes. 6. Firebird ragtops started at $3045, but this one has the optional Sprint package, which added sporty touches and a 230-hp 250-cid six.

CHAPTER EIGHT

1970-1979

"If you started managing General Motors very, very badly today, ten years from now you'd hardly have seen the result."

—Tony Hogg, *Automobile Quarterly*, First Quarter 1972

Looking back, we may observe (with a wry paraphrase of Buick's famous boast) that when bad cars were built, non-car people would build them. When GM's chairman, Fred Donner (a former accountant), and its president, James Roche (a former personnel manager), sweated and stammered before the 1965 Ribicoff committee on auto safety—and then compounded the mess by trying to discredit Ralph Nader—they enabled government officials and safety advocates to become amateur car designers by law.

Real car guys, like GM presidents Ed Cole (1967–74) and Pete Estes (1974–81), could have testified to the safety features their industry had developed on its own: hydraulic brakes, all-steel bodies, independent suspension, radial tires. Since 1913, when statistics begin, the death rate per 10,000 vehicles had dropped from 23.8 to 5.1. Deaths per 100 million miles were 18.2 for 1922–27 versus 5.3 by 1960, despite there being three times as many vehicles on the roads. By 1970, after three years of federal safety regulations, the death rate was still 5.3.

The seat belt itself might have joined these innovations without mandates. Eighteen months after Ford introduced optional seat belts in 1955, it had sold 400,000 sets. Ford Vice President Robert McNamara remarked that no other option had "ever caught on so fast."

In 1973, Henry Ford II said that due as much to regulation as to inflation, an Opel Manta then

priced at $3500 would be selling for five figures within ten years. He was right. Costly errors passed along to consumers by regulators included the seat-belt interlock that disabled your car until you buckled up the box of groceries on the passenger's seat; the five-mph bumper that cost more per buyer than the damage it prevented; and the cumbersome two-buckle, three-point belts that relatively few people bothered to use.

Sensible regulations, like state inspection and child restraints, are perfectly good ideas. But 40 years after federal regulation began, we're still experiencing "fantastic carnage" on the highways, mainly because we've failed to deal with the real killer: the incompetent driver. And much of it stemmed from that hopeless appearance of GM's leadership in Washington back in 1965.

The Seventies started rough. In late 1970, during a two-month United Auto Workers strike (the first since 1946), GM lost $5.3 billion in sales. The settlement included a $500-per-month pension for workers aged 58, available retirement at 56, and an uncapped cost-of-living adjustment that cost the company dearly when inflation soared later in the decade.

Chairman Roche retired in favor of Richard Gerstenberg at the end of 1971. President Cole had been considered for chairman but had no financial background and a reputation for what some called "maverick ideas": the prototype Cadet compact from the late 1940s, the advanced Corvair compact of the 1960s, and the radical Wankel engine (dropped because of emission and mileage problems) of the 1970s. What GM wanted was standardization and cost cutting, dear to the hearts of bean counters. Gerstenberg, analytical and conservative, also moved to stem the snowballing recalls (6.7 million in 1965–69, for example, to fix defective motor mounts).

The threat of foreign cars was a worry. In 1971, President Nixon slapped a 10 percent surcharge on imports. But curiously to some in Detroit, the import market share slipped less than a percentage point, to 14.5. Against such competition, Alfred Sloan's old policy of strict demarcation between makes was abandoned; now it was every make for itself, competing for the same buyers. The Chevrolet Chevelle, Oldsmobile Cutlass, Pontiac LeMans, and Buick Skylark (later Century), for example, were all rival intermediates.

The first import-killer was the 1971 Chevrolet Vega, announced by Chevy's new general manager, John DeLorean, as the car of the future. Powered by a 2.3-liter aluminum-block four with a cast-iron head on a 97-inch wheelbase, it was the smallest Chevy in history—and a thoroughly bad car. The body was a notorious ruster, the engine leaked oil and suffered from warped heads, and build quality was poor. However, there was one interesting variant called the Cosworth Vega. Arriving for 1975, it carried a short-stroke version of the 2.3 that displaced just 2.0 liters but made up for it with fuel injection and a 16-valve double-overhead-cam head designed by Cosworth Engineering in Britain. Though quite exotic for an American-made engine at the time, it produced only 24 more horsepower than a regular Vega engine. Special trim and suspension tweaks rounded out the package, but at nearly $6000—more than twice the price of a standard Vega—it sold only 3508 copies over its two-year life span. Though the rest of the Vega line lasted through 1977 (by which time sales had dropped to just 78,000 from a high of 456,000), convention-minded GM managers were long before then pointing to it as proof that the future did not lay in dwarf cars to compete with VW for the imports' measly 15 percent of the market.

An abrupt change in attitude came with the Arab Oil Embargo of October 1973 its effects heightened by GM's then-corporate-average fuel economy of 12.2 miles per gallon. In a shift of unbelievable proportions, demand for compacts and subcompacts went from 22 to 50 percent in a year. Other buyers tended to favor intermediates, leaving sales of standard-size cars severely depressed.

Retirement age conveniently arrived for Gerstenberg and Cole at the end of 1974. Gerstenberg was replaced by Thomas A. Murphy, another executive cut from the same cloth. Cole's successor, Elliot M. Estes, said later: "We had to move fast, just like in a war."

Indeed they did. Facing the worst situation since the Depression, 1975 calendar-year production of 6.74 million vehicles was the lowest since 1961. Although GM retained its typical 43 percent, that was only 2.9 million. A contributing factor was "sticker shock," caused by increases in prices of petroleum-based commodities cars depended on (rubber, glass, vinyl), coupled to ever-expanding government safety and emission mandates. The little Chevrolet Nova, which started at $2377 in 1973, was more than $3200 by 1975.

The first visible response to the emergency came—rather unexpectedly—from Cadillac. Introduced for 1975 was the compact, Nova-based Seville. Despite its trim 114-inch wheelbase and astronomical $12,500 price tag (a standard 130-inch-wheelbase Sedan de Ville started at $9265), the Seville sold surprisingly well. Aimed at the Mercedes market, it was a fine road car, returning 18-20 mpg.

The next response was the 1976 Chevrolet Chevette, 17 inches shorter than the soon-to-die Vega and weighing as little as 1870 pounds. Derived from the newly released 1974 Opel Kadett, Chevette was GM's first "world car," built to metric measurements. It delivered up to 35 mpg, but against a renewed assault from abroad (including government-subsidized Japanese exports like Datsun and Toyota), the Chevette sold only about half its intended volume. Not until 1980 did it meet its target of 400,000 units per year.

Ironically, every time GM tried to respond to the changed market, the same politicians who had blamed it for building "dinosaurs" rose up to say that it was dangerously big and should be broken up. To forestall them, Fred Donner created the GM Assembly Division to manufacture bodies and standardized some 15,000 components for all five GM makes, resulting in such anomalies as Chevy-powered Oldsmobiles. It was now impossible to unravel the corporation, though by the Eighties, no one still wanted to. (By then, some would worry about keeping it afloat.)

Buick offered both mid- and full-size models, but large cars were still its focus. A redesign for 1971 made the big Buicks even bigger, with curved "fuselage" bodies, massive hoods, and broad expanses of glass. They carried on in this form through 1976, thirstier than ever (Electra's EPA city mileage was 8.7). The '71 Riviera also gained weight, with a swoopy Bill Mitchell "boat tail" rear end which did not appeal and was soon dropped.

As Pontiac had done earlier with its Ventura II, Buick and Oldsmobile in 1973 added badge-engineered compacts, the Nova-based Apollo and Omega. Only 30,000 Apollos were sold, but Olds peddled double that number of Omegas. After 1973, sales of the Apollo rose, but it would take time for other economical Buicks to hit sales floors. One bright light was captive import Opel, with its practical 1900 sedans and wagons, the striking Manta sport coupe, and the nimble Opel GT.

In 1975, Buick, Oldsmobile, and Pontiac borrowed the Vega shell from Chevrolet in a desperate attempt to get more salable products. The Vega had produced a sporty derivation, the Monza, and this is what was cloned by Buick as the Skyhawk and by Olds as the Starfire. Pontiac even built its own Vega, called Astre. The Monza was an interesting, good-looking notchback coupe or 2+2 hatchback, the latter with a sloping greenhouse reminiscent of a Ferrari.

Buick had devoted itself so heavily to big cars that observers were astonished at the changes wrought by 1977, the year all GM's standard-size cars were downsized. The longest wheelbase was now only 119 inches, and that only on the Electra; the new LeSabre was the same size as a Century and 200 pounds lighter. There was a 403-cid V-8 on the option list, but the emphasis was on a new Buick V-6 and small-block V-8. Riviera was also radically downsized, and these changes successfully rescued Buick, which produced 845,000 1977 models.

In 1978, GM downsized all its intermediates. Wheelbase dropped by four to eight inches, curb weight by 500-600 pounds, width by five to six inches, length by a foot or more. Buick's Century was accompanied by a personal luxury coupe, the Regal, which, with an optional turbocharged V-6, could deliver decent performance and 20-mpg economy.

Cadillac, so long reliant on the largest cars in the industry, also benefited from the wave of downsizing. The 1977 De Ville and Fleetwood Brougham, as much as a foot shorter and a thousand pounds lighter, also had a more miserly engine: a new fuel-injected 425-cid V-8. The wisdom of these changes was proven when another oil embargo, this time by Iran, sent gas prices spiraling upward again in 1979.

As always, Chevrolet was in the thick of every wave that swept over the corporation. Singular among 1970 models was the cleanly styled Monte Carlo hardtop coupe, which soon became an inexpensive T-Bird substitute. Then there was the fully redesigned 1970 Camaro, a coupe with fine, balanced styling, so timeless that it was still around with few changes ten years later.

Camaro, along with Pontiac's Firebird, encountered rough sledding in subsequent years, particularly their performance variations. But management refused to quit on them, and by mid-decade, they were the only true ponycars left. The federal five-mph bumper requirement that applied to both the front and rear ends of all cars for 1974 added ungainly girders to most, but Pontiac's designers met the standards with soft Endura bumpers for the Firebird that many thought actually improved the car's looks. In support of that opinion, Firebird sales rose by more than 50 percent after the Endura bumpers arrived. Similar bumpers were fitted to the Camaro for 1978, and it, too, enjoyed a healthy bump in sales upon their arrival.

By 1976, the Camaro and Firebird were working their way back into public affection. While the Z28 was temporarily dropped mid-decade, Pontiac retained its comparable Trans Am. By continuing the entire Firebird line, from base coupe to luxury Esprit, Formula, and Trans Am, Firebird built a loyal customer base.

Redesigned intermediates of 1973 brought "Colonnade" styling, which did away with the old hardtop convertible (as well as the convertible itself). Colonnades were really just the old pillared body style with "C" pillars set at a more rakish angle. Duplicated by the B-O-P divisions, they represented the end of the traditional American car: big on the outside, small on the inside, heavy, posh, and thirsty.

With their 1977 downsizing, standard-size Chevrolets lost up to 800 pounds. Good looking and much better built, they accounted for more than 600,000 sales. The long-running Nova had its final year in 1978; there was never anything exotic about it, but it had come to symbolize consistency, practicality, and economy to a lot of Chevy faithful. Chevrolet's sports car also remained true to its precepts: The 1968 Corvette body had proven very popular and lasted a long time. It received a new nose design in 1973 and a new tail in 1974.

Throughout these hard times, Chevy trucks continued to be "Built to Stay Tough." Sales had fully recovered by 1978, thanks in part to a 5.7-liter diesel engine and an all-new El Camino pickup based on the downsized Chevelle Malibu. Chevy truck registrations hit 1.275 million in 1978, and GMC crossed 300,000 for the first time ever.

Given that Oldsmobile is no more, it is hard to believe that not so long ago Olds ranked third in the industry. In the early Seventies, the Cutlass Supreme, Oldsmobile's popular intermediate, was beginning its rise to best-seller status. Olds' strength, while the market for them lasted, remained its broad variety of Delta sedans, hardtops, and wagons, bigger and more garish than ever. Likewise the Toronado, which was restyled in 1971 and enlarged to a 123-inch wheelbase.

Pontiac inserted the Grand Ville series of hardtops and a convertible ahead of the Bonneville as top-of-the-line in 1971. The Grand Prix continued with its smaller body, while the Catalina was the lowest-priced full-size Pontiac. All the former Tempests were grouped into the Le Mans series, on the 112/116-inch wheelbase intermediate chassis. The famous GTO, however, was down to only 10,000 units.

Under dynamic general manager John Beltz, Olds finished third for the first time in 1972, bolstered by the Cutlass Supreme. The big models were as large as they would ever get, though the mammoth 455 V-8 was now detuned and rated at only 185/220 net bhp. Pontiac did well too, but not as well as Oldsmobile, discontinuing the GTO as a separate series. Then, in 1973, Pontiac released one of its memorable failures: the Grand Am.

As its name suggests, the Grand Am was an attempt to combine Grand Prix luxury with Trans Am performance. Created by assistant chief engineer Bill Collins and chassis wizard John Seaton, it was a European-style sport sedan like the BMW Bavaria or Mercedes 280, at one-third their price. Unfortunately, the Grand Am was ill timed. When it arrived, buyers were interested either in basic transportation or as much glitz as money could buy. The following year the performance car market bottomed. After only 43,000 sales in '73, Pontiac built only 28,000 in 1974–75. Had the company brought it out in 1969, the Grand Am would have been a success. One car magazine advised readers to "get one quick before they change it." They should have suggested getting one before they drop it.

The 1975 model year would be remembered as the finale (temporarily) for convertibles at all GM divisions except Cadillac, which offered the Eldo ragtop for one more year. On word this would be their final fling, sales of all shot up, but their fate was already sealed.

As GM's emergency-bred products multiplied, things began to improve. Oldsmobile ran off nearly 900,000 cars in 1976, a quarter-million more than in 1975. Its great strength was still its intermediates, led by the Cutlass Supreme. The huge Delta 88 and 98 were now hardly more than footnotes.

Pontiac was also up strongly, by better than 200,000, pushing the Astre and Monza-derived Sunbird. The aging Ventura compact and LeMans intermediate sold modestly; Catalinas and Bonnevilles were rocks on the market. The Grand Ville was dropped after 1975, the Grand Prix carrying on as Pontiac's personal coupe, and almost singly holding up its big-car sales.

GM's British operation, Vauxhall, had washed out of the American market in the Sixties, and by 1976, a rock-hard Deutsche mark made importing Opels cost-prohibitive. For two years the Opel badge was worn by a small Japanese product, one of the variations of GM's "world car." It was built by Isuzu, GM's newest branch, previously devoted mostly to trucks; Isuzu had been building Chevy's semi-successful LUV (Light Utility Vehicle) pickup since the early Seventies.

With its full-size cars downsized for 1977, Oldsmobile maintained its lock on third place, enjoying its first model year with more than one million sales. While most GM intermediates (due for redesign in 1978) were waning in popularity, the Cutlass Supreme still appealed, accounting for 633,000 sales despite a design that now seemed almost antique.

The Toronado, continuing with its large body, was powered by a 403-cid V-8. A sporty 1977 variation was the Toronado XS (XSC for '78), with a huge rear window that wrapped around to the sides in a nearly unbroken sweep, a sort of throwback to the early postwar Studebaker Starlight coupe.

Fourth-place Pontiac improved volume by 100,000 in 1977, trading on its "smaller big cars." While Pontiac was not nearly as strong as Oldsmobile in the intermediate market, its other strengths were the Grand Prix, Firebird, and sporty Sunbird hatchback.

Oldsmobile and Pontiac were aided in 1978 when the GM intermediates were downsized. Olds enjoyed another million-car year on the shoulders of the new, smaller Cutlass. The Omega, Oldsmobile's Nova-clone, had never been a big winner, while the Starfire had languished—perhaps because its name had previously been associated with large opulent battle cruisers.

The Pontiac LeMans had been overdue for a redesign, and on paper, its lithe new body should have been a winner. Yet only 120,000 were built. Even the specialty Firebird sold better than that. The best looking 1978 Pontiac had to be the Monte Carlo-based Grand Prix, which once again contributed handsomely to division sales volume.

Once in motion, relentless downsizing was inexorable. Toronado and Eldorado, the senior front-wheel-drive models, shrank in 1979. The Riviera now adopted their new, smaller body, acquiring front-wheel-drive technology for the first time on a Buick. An unusual touch was independent rear suspension, a compact layout that allowed a shorter wheelbase without loss of passenger space. The new Riviera and Toronado were well received, accounting for more than 50,000 each, while the Eldorado was a runaway success at 67,000.

Cadillac, so long a winner, chalked up another record by producing 383,000 cars in 1979 and finishing eighth ahead of...Plymouth! The division was going all-out with options like dual electric remote-control door mirrors, retractable radio antennas, eight-track or cassette stereo tape players, and "Tripmaster" on-board travel computers. Oldsmobile, meanwhile, was committing heavily to diesel engines. As the '79 model year began, most Oldmobiles had diesel-engine options, and a 4.3-liter diesel V-8 with a fast-start system joined the larger 5.7.

The 1979 Pontiac line was highlighted by new styling for the Firebird, which now came in five variants, including the $10,000 Trans Am 10th Anniversary model. With 900,000 for the model year, Pontiac had another successful fifth-place finish.

By 1979, Murphy and Estes were feeling bullish again. Coming up was a new wave of compacts, the 1980 X-bodies: Chevrolet Citation, Pontiac Phoenix, Olds Omega, and Buick Skylark. Representing GM's first foray into front-wheel-drive volume cars, they would be introduced as '80 models in April 1979 and be greeted with great enthusiasm.

During the 1979 calendar year, GM held 60 percent of the domestic market. Trouble was, the domestic market was declining—and so, eventually, would GM's share of it.

Despite the hubbub attending such oxymoronic products as Chevy-powered Oldsmobiles, GM seemed to have weathered the crises of the Seventies and was again selling cars in record numbers. What eventually caught up to the corporation was not the salability, fuel economy, or quality of its cars. All these had dramatically improved. The problem was their sameness: the certainty (which every buyer knew) that whatever you found at your local Chevy store, you could easily find with a different grille or taillights, for a few dollars more or less, at the Buick, Olds, or Pontiac showroom down the street. It was a strategy that would have left Alfred Sloan shaking his head.

1. Buick's 1970 Electra 225 Custom convertible was built on a 127-inch wheelbase and powered by a 370-horse 455-cubic-inch V-8. Base price was $4802. 2. Even Buick's entry-level full-size LeSabre had a rag-top. Custom convertible prices started at $3700. The standard engine was a 285-horsepower 350-cubic-inch V-8. 3. For the first time since 1964, there was a full-size station wagon on the Buick roster. The Estate Wagon was built on a 124-inch wheelbase and available in two- and three-seat models. Total Estate Wagon production was 28,346. 4. Buick's heavily facelifted Riviera returned to fixed headlamps for 1970. Skirted rear wheels gave the flanks a massive look, but an optional bodyside molding put some "swoop" back in the design. The 370-horse 455 was standard. 5. GM lifted its 400-cubic-inch limit on intermediate cars for 1970. Buick responded with the Skylark-based GS 455, named for its 455-cubic-inch V-8 rated at 350 horsepower. During the model year, the GSX (shown) was unveiled. It added $1195 to the GS 455 and came in either Apollo White or Saturn Yellow set off by unique stripes and spoilers. GSX production totaled less than 700 units.

1

2

3

4

5

6

1. Cadillac set a model-year production record in 1970 of 238,744 units. The most popular model was this Sedan de Ville hardtop. **2-3.** The Chevrolet Corvette's 427 big-block became a 454 for 1970. All models got a crosshatch-pattern grille and front fender vents, plus deeper rear wheel-arch skirts. Starting at $4849, convertibles accounted for 6648 of the 17,316 Corvettes built for the year. **4.** Corvette coupes started at $5192. This one is powered by the optional solid-lifter LT-1 350 V-8 with 370 hp. **5.** Chevrolet's compact Nova now offered a "hide-away" antenna built into the windshield. Prices started at $2335. **6.** A late prototype for the 1970 Caprice hardtop coupe displays the rear fender skirts that were optional on production versions.

1

1. Monte Carlo was introduced for 1970 with the longest hood in Chevrolet's history—which the division was fond of pointing out. With a wheelbase four inches longer than that of a Chevelle coupe, the car was Chevy's entry into the "personal-luxury" market dominated by the Pontiac Grand Prix and Ford Thunderbird. Prices started at $3123, and assembly lines churned out 145,976 of the new models. **2-3.** Just 3823 Monte Carlos were fitted with the SS 454 package, which delivered a 360-horsepower version of Chevy's newly enlarged big-block V-8, plus uprated suspension and buckets-and-console interior. **4.** A 250-horse 350 V-8 teamed with Turbo Hydra-Matic was standard on Monte Carlos, and all sorts of luxury options were offered.
5. Chevelle received a handsome facelift, plus new engines that were mostly featured in hot Super Sport models like this Malibu-based Sport Coupe. The SS 454 package added $840 to the $2809 starting price.

2

3

4

5

1. Chevelle remained Chevy's mainstay midsize for 1970, represented here by the uplevel Malibu hardtop sedan that started at $2790. New standard features included fiberglass-belted tires, variable-ratio steering, and steel safety beams in the doors. 2. Besides the SS 454, there was still a Chevelle SS 396, though now its engine actually displaced 402 cubic inches. Either could be ordered with a cowl-induction hood. 3. The 1969 Camaro was carried into the next model year as an "early" 1970. The last of the first-generation Camaros were sold until the totally redesigned "1970½" Camaro went on sale in late February. 4. When it finally arrived, the new Camaro came only as a coupe with a sloping roofline. Although the long hood/short deck proportions and 108-inch wheelbase were retained, styling was vastly different. More in step with European Grand Touring cars of the era, the Camaro had a distinctly Italian flavor. Two different front-end designs were offered, and the four large, round taillamps suggested kinship with the Corvette—and contemporary Ferraris. The lineup included base Sport Coupe, Rally Sport, SS 350, SS 396, and the mighty Z28.

1. The 4-4-2 remained Oldsmobile's top entry in the muscle-car arena. This example is fitted with the W-30 package, which brought a 370-horse 455-cubic-inch V-8 and lighter, twin-scoop fiberglass hood. Quarter-mile times were in the low 14s. 2. F-85 and Cutlass two-doors could be ordered with option W-45, which turned them into Rallye 350s. Their "small" 350-cid V-8 put out a healthy 325 hp, making them quick enough to justify their gaudy graphics. 3. A 4-4-2 W-30 convertible was chosen as the Official Pace Car of the 1970 Indianapolis 500. 4. Full-size Oldsmobiles got slightly revised styling for 1970. The Ninety-Eight Holiday two-door hardtop had a 127-inch wheelbase and 365-horse 455 Rocket V-8. Base price was $4656. 5. This was the last year for the Ninety-Eight convertible. Just 3161 were sold starting at $4914. 6. Toronados now had exposed head-lamps. Fewer than 1000 were equipped with the one-year-only GT package that included special seats, a front console, and discreet ID emblems.

1

2

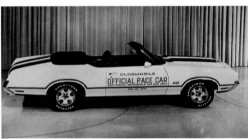

3

4

5

6

1

2

3

4

5

6

1-2. The Judge was back for a second year and continued to inject some pizzazz into the Pontiac GTO with its decklid airfoil and wild striping. This year, Judge production totaled 3629 two-door hardtops and 168 convertibles. **3.** The Executive Safari wagon came in six- and nine-passenger versions. Faux wood trim was included in the base price of $4015, but the roof rack cost an extra $84. Note the 1969 Firebird Trans Am in the background. Pontiac continued to sell the first-generation Firebird until the new one arrived. **4.** A full-size 1970 Pontiac Catalina convertible sold for $3604. **5.** Like Chevrolet's Camaro, the "1970½" Pontiac Firebird was all new and arrived in late February. The Trans Am's Ram Air 400-cid V-8 provided 345 or 370 hp. **6.** The base Firebird coupe started at $2875 with a 250-cubic-inch six. **7.** The handsome Grand Prix was little changed for 1970, continuing in J (shown) and SJ models starting at $3985. The top engine was a 370-hp 455.

1

1-2. Buick bulked up the Riviera personal-luxury coupe for the start of its third generation, giving it a distinctive—and controversial—"boattail" rear end. William Mitchell, GM's design chief, had ordained the first Riviera in 1963 and encouraged daring styling for the car. **3.** The Wildcat moniker gave way to Centurion for 1970, a name used on a 1950's show car. Centurion sat on the same 124-inch wheelbase as the Wildcat and, like its predecessor, came standard with a 455-cid V-8. **4-6.** All Buick Estate Wagons were fitted with a Glide-Away "clamshell" tailgate. **7.** The GSX became an option package available in a choice of six exterior colors. The potent Stage 1 option now offered 345 hp. **8.** Just 902 Buick GS convertibles were sold for 1971 starting at $3476.

2

3

4

5

6

7

8

1.

2.

3.

4.

1-3. Cadillacs received a smooth restyle for 1971 that gave them a massive look. The Coupe de Ville rode a 130-inch wheelbase and started at $6264. 4. Still driven through its front wheels, the Eldorado was also restyled for 1971 and gained a convertible version that took the place of the soft-top De Ville, which was no longer offered. 5. The "Heavy Chevy" was a midyear appearance option for V-8 Chevelles. 6-7. The SS 454 package was still available for Chevelles (convertible shown) and the related El Camino pickup.

5.

6.

7.

1

2

3

4

5

6

7

1. Full-size Chevrolets were redesigned for 1971 on a 2.5-inch-longer wheelbase. The Impala Custom hardtop coupe (shown) shared its formal roof with the top-line Caprice. **2.** Chevy's big full-size wagons got even bigger in their 1971 redesign, growing a whopping six inches in wheelbase. **3.** Chevrolet introduced the subcompact Vega for 1971 to battle imports from Volkswagen and Toyota. A Camaro-like front end decorated all three Vega body styles, including this best-selling hatchback coupe. Vega's 140-cubic-inch four used an aluminum block and cast-iron single-cam head. The standard engine offered 90 horsepower, while an optional unit increased the total to 110. **4.** In addition to the hatchback and a traditional two-door notchback coupe, Vega offered a nifty Kammback wagon that was also available as a Panel Express model without the rear side windows. Vega prices started at just $2090. **5.** Monte Carlo returned for its second year with few changes. This example carries the SS 454 package, which remained visually understated. **6-7.** Only a dozen 1971 Corvettes were fitted with the $1747 ZR2 package featuring a 425-hp 454 V-8—aka production option LS6—with aluminum cylinder heads, close-ratio four-speed transmission, heavy-duty brakes and cooling system, and uprated suspension.

1

2

3

1-2. Like many other GM models, Oldsmobile's Toronado got a full-bore restyle for 1971 that left it bigger and blockier than ever. Starting at $5457, it was the most expensive Olds offered. Built on a new 123-inch wheelbase, the front-drive Toronado now aimed at opulence rather than sportiness. 3. The Custom Cruiser was Oldsmobile's first full-size wagon since 1964. Two- and three-seat versions were available starting at $4776. 4. Vista Cruiser was Oldsmobile's most popular wagon. Its 121-inch wheelbase was five inches longer than that of the Cutlass wagon. Two- and three-seat versions started at $3866. 5. This was the last year the 4-4-2 was a separate series. The convertible cost $3743. 6. Buyers could save $236 by purchasing a Cutlass Supreme convertible.

4

5

6

1. Though their faces were vaguely familiar, Pontiac's full-size cars were all-new—and as big as the make's cars would ever get. Grand Ville was the new top model, edging past the Bonneville in plushness. The Grand Ville convertible started at $4706, and only 1789 were produced.

2. A new nose marked Pontiac's GTO in what would be its final year as a distinct series. The Judge (shown) continued with its flamboyant stripes, even though its 455-cid V-8 was down from 360 hp to 335. Meanwhile, the base GTO's 400 dropped to 300 hp.
3. At a base price of $3359, only 3865 LeMans Sport convertibles were sold.

4. Formula remained a step down from Trans Am among performance Firebirds, but Pontiac added new 350 and 455 models to join the carryover Formula 400.
5. A basic Grand Prix Model J started at $4557 with the standard 400-cubic-inch V-8. Front and rear styling was revised and single headlamps in square bezels were adopted.

1. Buick's LeSabre line included the $4291 Custom convertible. LeSabre production totaled 183,322, but only 2037 were convertibles. **2.** Biggest of the Buicks—and a strong seller—was the 127-inch-wheelbase Electra 225, shown here in posh Limited trim. The hardtop sedan started at $4890. **3.** This LeSabre sedan is a replica of a Buick cruiser the Peekskill, New York, Police Department used in the early 1970s. The LeSabre four-door sedan started at $3958 and found 29,505 buyers. **4.** The sharp-looking $4616 Centurion convertible attracted just 2396 buyers for 1972. Its 455-cid V-8 yielded 225 to 250 horsepower. Two- and four-door hardtops were also offered. **5.** Buick's big Riviera had a new power sunroof option. The dramatic "boattail" rear end made Riviera easy to spot. The base price eased slightly to $5149, and sales held steady at 33,728 of these controversially styled coupes. **6.** Although horsepower figures were down on all engines for 1972 due to new "net" ratings, Buick's GS remained a very hot number, its available Stage 1 455 V-8 putting out a healthy 270 hp. But the GS was in its final season, and just 852 convertibles and 7723 coupes were sold. **7.** Skylarks, like this Custom two-door hardtop, had a standard 150-horse 350 V-8. Hardtop coupes could become "Sun Coupes" with a fold-back cloth sunroof.

1

2

3

4

1. Beneath the Eldorado's hood sat the biggest engine on the market: a 500-cubic-inch V-8 generating 235 horsepower. **2.** Formal in form, the Fleetwood Sixty Special Brougham rode a unique 133-inch wheelbase. Cadillac sold 20,750 of them with prices starting at $7637. **3.** More than 95,000 Cadillac fans drove home a Coupe de Ville, which started at $6168. **4.** Chevrolet Monte Carlos earned a fresh grille that now held the parking lights. A 350 V-8 was standard, but buyers could still choose the big-block 454. **5.** Topping Chevy's full-size station wagon line was this Kingswood Estate. **6.** Shoppers who sought all the elegance Chevrolet could offer usually wound up with a Caprice. The four-door hard-top was the most popular with 78,768 sales. **7.** Impala four-door sedans might not have looked glamorous, but they attracted customers—helping Chevrolet return to the top in annual sales, ahead of Ford.

5

6

7

1. The $483 LT-1 option gave Corvette a small-block, solid-lifter 350 with 255 horsepower. **2.** Muscle cars continued to attract young folks—but wouldn't for much longer. Almost 25,000 Chevelle hard-tops came with Super Sport (SS) equipment—a $350 option. **3.** Chevelles, like this Malibu hardtop coupe, remained very popular with families on a budget. **4.** A Vega Kammback wagon started at $2285. Total Vega sales topped 390,000. **5.** Nova coupes that started at $2351 wildly out-sold their sedan counterparts that listed for just a few dollars more. **6.** More than 11,300 Camaros got the Rally Sport package for 1972. A crippling strike at Camaro's Norwood, Ohio, assembly plant resulted in drastically lower model-year production of just 68,656 units. **7.** Camaro buyers snapped up 6562 SS models, which would be the last of their kind until the 1990s.

1. Oldsmobile's 4-4-2 was now reduced to a Cutlass appearance/handling option package. This 4-4-2 ragtop packs W-30 equipment—a $648 option that included a 300-horse, 455-cid V-8 with air induction. **2.** This 4-4-2 hardtop also has W-30 equipment. All 4-4-2 models included a special grille. Production rose a bit, totaling 9845 units. **3.** A Hurst/Olds convertible served as Official Pace Car for the 1972 Indy 500. Oldsmobile built about 130 convertible and 499 coupe (shown) replicas for public sale. This car has the optional Hurst-designed sliding steel sunroof. **4.** Front-drive Toronados carried a special 455-cubic-inch V-8, whipping up 250 eager horses. **5.** Royale was the upscale rendition of the Delta 88 series. A hardtop coupe started at $4179. **6.** The most popular Ninety-Eight was the $5098 Luxury Sedan, with 69,920 sales.

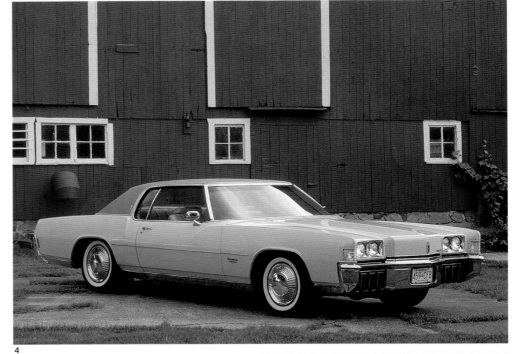

1

2

3

4

1. Performance-car fans continued to pay homage to Pontiac's Trans Am. Standard was a 455 H.O. V-8 good for 300 horsepower. **2.** An optional sliding fabric sunroof was a special touch available on a Ventura II coupe. The Pontiac compact was related to Chevy's Nova. **3.** The Luxury LeMans two-door hardtop wore a distinctive twin-cavity grille. **4.** Twin hood scoops helped direct air into the carburetor of this GTO hardtop. GTO was now a $344 option package for Pontiac's LeMans. **5.** Full-size Grand Villes received new slotted taillights and a Bonneville-style grille. The convertible had a $4640 base price. **6.** This year, about 60 limited-edition Hurst SSJ Grand Prix models were built.

5

6

1-2. All GM intermediates were given "Colonnade" styling for 1973 but remained on their former wheelbases. Buick brought back the Century name for its version. Still available was the Gran Sport version with a Stage 1 package, though it wasn't quite the fire-breather its ancestors were. 3. The formal-roof $3470 Regal coupe topped the Century line and was its most popular single model. 4-5. Available for the last time,

1

2

3

4

5

Centurions shared grilles and taillights with their LeSabre stablemates. The convertible listed for $4534. 6-7. Buick's Riviera wore a "boattail" deck for the last time, a slightly blunted version of the original design. A wraparound instrument panel gave the interior a cockpit feel. Still available was the GS package, which added $171 to Riviera's $5221 base price. Checking the box for the Stage 1 option added another $139. 8. Riviera's front end was also redesigned to accommodate newly required five-mph bumpers. Production totaled 34,080 units.

6

7

8

1

2

4

5

1. A midyear addition to the Buick stable, the compact Apollo was essentially a rebadged clone of the Chevrolet Nova. Three body styles were offered: coupe (shown), hatchback, and four-door sedan. Apollo sales totaled 32,793. **2.** Cadillac's Eldorado continued to appeal strongly to personal luxury-coupe buyers. The new five-mph front bumper was well-integrated into the styling, avoiding a "tacked-on" look. The 235-hp 500-cubic-inch engine remained standard.

3

3. The $7765 Fleetwood Sixty Special Brougham four-door sedan offered four more inches of rear leg room than a Sedan de Ville. Nearly 25,000 buyers felt that was worth an extra $1265. **4-5.** Chevrolet's Corvette Stingray had a smart new body-color nose that freshened the "Shark" appearance. It also satisfied the government's new requirement that front bumpers be able to withstand five-mph impacts without damage. The hood now extended back to cover the windshield wipers, and the rear window was fixed in place. Horsepower kept sliding: The base 350 V-8 withered to 190, while a 250-horse L82 replaced the LT-1. The lone big-block option, retagged LS4, made 275 net horsepower. All very disheartening, yet total sales rose again, to 30,464.

1-2. Chevelle joined other GM intermediates in a full restyle. No more midsize convertibles or pillarless hardtop coupes were built in the new "Colonnade" design. Shown is a $3010 Malibu V-8 coupe with the $243 Super Sport package, mostly a cosmetic reminder of better performance days. Of the 28,647 SS versions built, some 2500 were equipped with the 245-horse big-block 454 V-8, a separate $235 option. Additional body styles were a four-door sedan and wagon. Chevelle sales totaled 386,739, down about 7000 units from 1972.

3-4. Chevrolet's Monte Carlo coupe earned its own new Colonnade styling while retaining its "classic" countenance. Florid fenderlines, a marked midbody beltline dip, small rear "opera" windows, and a slightly vee'd hood and rear window were all part of the new look. The wheelbase held steady at 116 inches, but the car was four inches longer and two inches wider than before. Three sport coupe models were available: base, S, and Landau. Starting at $3415, the new car was more popular than ever with sales totaling 290,693 units.

1. Chevrolet's Caprice was renamed Caprice Classic for 1973. With 77,134 sold, the two-door hardtop was the most popular model. **2.** The Caprice line carried Chevrolet's only full-size convertible. Prices started at $4345. **3.** Oldsmobile's Cutlass Supreme Colonnade coupe was easily the best-selling Cutlass model; dealers moved 219,857 of them. Like all two-door Cutlass models, it was built on a 112-inch wheelbase, but Supremes had a crisp formal roof design with opera windows. **4.** Cutlass and Cutlass S coupes sported a semi-fastback roof. Both could be ordered with the 4-4-2 option package that included a distinct grille, bold stripes, and enhanced suspension. **5.** Four-door sedans like the base Cutlass had a 116-inch wheelbase. **6.** New to the Oldsmobile lineup for 1973 was the Omega, a badge-engineered variant of the compact Chevy Nova. The hatchback coupe started at $2762. A two-door coupe and four-door sedan rounded out the line. **7.** Hoods and fenders were revised on full-size Oldsmobiles, including the $4442 Delta 88 Royale convertible. Grilles, parking lights, and front bumpers were also new. **8.** Toronado coupes benefited from a reworked front end, plus a new back bumper and taillights. A 250-horsepower 455-cubic-inch V-8 was standard.

1-3. Based on LeMans, the Grand Am was a new model for 1973 that was offered as a coupe or sedan. Pontiac wanted to combine Grand Prix luxury with Trans Am performance to approximate a European-style "sport sedan." Grand Ams had a dent-resistant plastic nose, upgraded suspension, and a sports-luxury interior. With the standard 230-horse 400-cube V-8, it

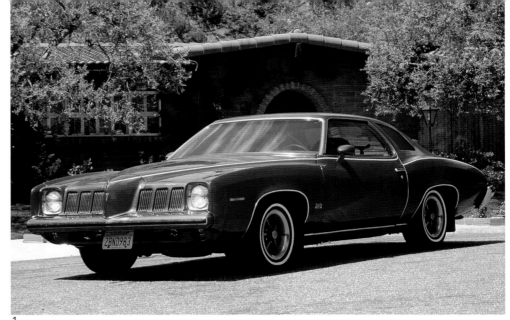

1

2

3

4

was a fine road car but cost at least $1000 more than a comparable LeMans. **4.** The GTO was now a $386 option package for the Pontiac LeMans and LeMans Sport Coupe. **5.** This Florentine Red Firebird Formula is optioned with a 250-horsepower 455-cubic-inch V-8. A twin-scoop hood was the Formula's trademark.

5

1

2

1-2. Pontiac redesigned the Grand Prix for 1973, and though it lost two inches in wheelbase, it was longer overall. Inside, drivers faced a new cockpit-style instrument panel. Sales of 153,899 set a record. 3. Venturas received new front-end styling for 1973. This Ventura Custom coupe was ordered with the $176 Sprint option package. Strictly for show, it included wider wheels and tires. The 350 V-8 was offered in 150- and 175-horse versions. 4. All full-size Pontiacs got a fresh front-end treatment and new bumpers for 1973. 5. Pontiac's Grand Safari wagon offered two- and three-seat versions starting at

3

4

5

6

$4674; adding the third seat cost $147 more. 6. Grand Villes came with rear wheelwell skirts that complemented the car's sleek lines. Also standard was a 455-cid V-8 rated at 215 or 250 hp. Hardtop coupes and sedans were offered in addition to the $4766 convertible, which, despite now being the sole ragtop in Pontiac's line, sold just 4447 copies.

1-2. Performance options weren't yet extinct in 1974 despite tighter emission standards, as shown by this Gran Sport with Buick's Stage 1 equipment package. For $558 extra, buyers got a modified 455-cid V-8 with dual exhausts and a dual-snorkel air cleaner. **3.** Buick restyled the Riviera for 1974, abandoning the controversial boattail rear end and fastback roofline for a more conventional profile. Interiors were fitted with a new dashboard and either cloth, ribbed velour, or leather upholstery. Despite the changes, sales dropped by 40 percent to just 20,129. **4.** The biggest Buick was the Electra 225, offered in base, Custom, or Limited trim. A new full-width eggcrate grille and more emphatic dual headlamp treatment highlighted its face. At the rear, taillights were placed below the decklid to minimize the effect of the new federally mandated five-mph bumpers. The base two-door hardtop started at $5260. **5-6.** Having carried on for three years with only subtle styling updates, Cadillacs received a substantial facelift for 1974. Bodyside sculpting was simplified, the obvious "point" at the rear giving way to a slab-sided appearance. Vertical bumper blades no longer housed the taillights. Slivers of lamps remained in the thinner new blades, but these functioned as side marker lights; the main taillamps were now horizontal strips below the trunklid, which sloped down to a new energy-absorbing five-mph bumper. In front, large parking lights now wrapped around the fenders, and inside was a completely redesigned instrument panel.

1

2   3

4

5

6

1

2

3

1-2. Cadillac gave the Eldorado new bumpers front and rear and a revised grille for 1974. Also new was the unloved seat-belt interlock that did not allow the car to start if the front-seat passengers failed to buckle their safety belts. Still standard was a 500-cubic-inch V-8, downrated this year to 210 horsepower. An Eldo convertible started at $9437—just $327 more than the coupe— yet sold only 7600 copies vs. nearly 33,000 closed versions. **3.** Corvette's face didn't change much for 1974, having adopted a sleek five-mph bumper the year before. Engine choices didn't change much either; both versions of the 350 V-8 returned, now with 195 or 250 horsepower, as did the big-block 454, which lost five ponies for a 270-hp rating. As it turned out, this would be the final year for a big-block option in the 'Vette. **4.** Corvette did see big changes at the rear, where the former "ducktail" and chrome bumpers were replaced by a tapered plastic end cap that met the federal five-mph bumper standards in unusually stylish fashion.

4

1. Chevy's full-size Caprice Classic convertible saw sales tumble from 7339 to just 4670 for 1974. All big Chevys carried a more formal-looking grille.
2. A Caprice Classic sedan displays the revised rear-end treatment that accompanied a new five-mph rear bumper.
3. America's bicentennial was still two years off, but Chevrolet came up with a "Spirit of America" Impala dressed in white with red and blue stripes. Impalas had slightly different front end styling compared to the ritzier Caprice Classic.
4. Chevrolet also offered a limited-edition "Spirit of America" Nova hatchback. Nova sales hit a record 390,537 units in 1974.
5. Vegas had new front and rear styling for '74. The hatchback offered Vega's take on the "Spirit of America" package. 6. Perhaps the most interesting Chevelle was the Laguna Type S-3 coupe, which replaced the previous three-model Laguna series and the SS option package.

1. In the Seventies, Oldsmobile's Cutlass Supreme coupe established itself as a true American favorite. For 1974, more than 172,000 Supreme coupes were built. 2. Oldsmobile and Hurst collaborated to create 380 Hurst/Olds Pace Car coupes to mark the special convertible that paced the Indianapolis 500. 3. Toronado suffered a huge drop in sales for 1974, possibly due to the fuel crisis. The $5933 coupe attracted just 27,582 buyers, half the '73 total. 4. Pontiac's Firebird had new front and rear styling for '74 that smoothly integrated the mandated five-mph bumpers. A dressy Esprit started at $3687. 5. The Firebird Trans Am offered an optional 290-horse Super Duty 455 V-8 that was installed in just 943 cars. 6-7. Grand Prix's revised front and rear styling was largely a result of adopting new federally mandated five-mph bumpers. Nearly 100,000 Grand Prixs were sold starting at $4936. 8. The name carried on, but the GTO—now a $195 option package for the compact Ventura that included little more than a hood scoop and distinct trim—was a mere shadow of its former self.

1

1. All full-size Pontiacs received new front and rear styling for 1974. Pontiac advertised its newly optional Radial Tuned Suspension (RTS) as a special set-up designed to take advantage of the benefits afforded by the new "radial" tires. An exclusive option for big Pontiacs was the adjustable foot-control system. This new comfort and convenience option allowed the driver to adjust the brake and gas pedals manually over a range of four inches. **2.** The most popular Grand Ville model was the $4939 four-door hardtop, though a coupe and convertible were also offered. The standard engine was a 215-horsepower 455 V-8, with a 255-hp version optional. **3.** All full-size Pontiac coupes wore a new roofline for 1974. Small rear quarter windows were retained, but extra glass area resulted in greatly improved rear visibility. Sales of the once-popular Bonneville plummeted in 1974, likely due to the fuel crisis. The Bonneville coupe—which attracted more than 23,000 buyers in 1970—lured just 7639 for '74 at a starting price of $4572.

2

3

1. Sales of Buick's posh Electra 225 Limited four-door hardtop continued to suffer from fuel-crisis jitters in 1975; at $6516, it sold just 33,778 copies, one-third of its 1973 volume. 2. The 1975 LeSabre Custom convertible marked the end of the line for Buick ragtops—at least for now. With the end in sight, sales of the $5133 droptop jumped dramatically to 5300 units. 3. Even with a Landau roof option, the $6420

Riviera failed to capture as many hearts as in the past. A GS option appeared for the last time. 4. Cadillac took a big risk betting that buyers would accept a compact—and very expensive—Caddy, but the "international size," $12,479 Seville proved a surprising success. By comparison, a full-size De Ville cost more than $4000 less. 5-6. Eldorado coupe and convertible sales remained healthy despite the fuel crisis. They retailed for $9935 and $10,354, respectively.

1. Cadillac's biggest boat for 1975 was the $10,414 Fleetwood Brougham, which rode a three-inch-longer wheelbase than De Villes.
2. Cadillac's bread-and-butter Sedan de Ville sold more than 63,000 copies starting at

$8801. Big Caddys still carried a 500-cid V-8. 3. Chevy's Monte Carlo enjoyed a healthy 259,000 sales for 1975. 4. A dressy Chevelle Malibu Classic Landau Coupe went for $3930. 5. Novas were redesigned for 1975 but retained a familiar silhouette. 6. New to the Chevy lineup was the sporty Monza, which evolved from the subcompact Vega. A 2+2 hatchback (shown) and notchback coupe were offered, as was V-8 power. 7. The new Cosworth-Vega had an exotic 2.0-liter fuel-injected twin-cam four and an equally exotic $5916 price tag. 8. The $6537 convertible would be the last 'Vette droptop of the decade.

1. Sales of Chevrolet's $5113 Caprice Classic convertible nearly doubled—to 8349—in what many realized would be its final year. 2. Chevy's best-selling big car was the $4548 Impala four-door sedan at 91,330 copies. 3. The Impala Sport Sedan hardtop cost just $83 more than its pillared counterpart but sold only half as well. It shared its roofline with the uplevel Caprice Classic. 4. Word got out that Oldsmobile's $5200 Delta 88 Royale convertible was in its final year, and buyers snapped up an amazing 21,038 of them—more than its Buick, Chevy, and Pontiac counterparts combined. 5. Oldsmobile's $6353 Ninety-Eight Regency was a truly big car in an era when size had become less of a selling point. 6. Despite new styling, sales of the Olds Omega fell for 1975.

1. High performance was thought to be dead in American cars, but Oldsmobile again worked with Hurst to produce a Hurst/Olds Cutlass Supreme coupe. Available only in white or black, the H/O had a standard T-top roof and W-30 equipment. **2.** The $4035 Cutlass Supreme coupe proved to be Oldsmobile's best-seller by far for 1975,

with nearly 151,000 customers drawn to its formal style. **3.** The most popular four-door Cutlass was the base $3818 sedan, with 30,144 sales. **4.** Astre offered the same three body styles as the Chevy Vega on which it was based: notchback sedan, hatchback coupe (shown), and station wagon. Base prices ranged from $2841 to $3071. **5.** Firebirds wore a new wraparound rear window for 1975. They again came in four varieties: base, Esprit, Formula (shown), and Trans Am. **6.** Beneath the rear-facing hood scoop of a Trans Am—now the best-selling Firebird—might be either a 185-hp 400-cid V-8 or a 200-horse 455. **7.** Grand Prix had few changes but, like all GM cars this year, got electronic High Energy Ignition and a catalytic converter as standard. Grand Prix prices started at $5296.

1. Pontiac gave the Grand Am one final shot for 1975 but allowed it few changes. A 170-hp 6.5-liter (400-cubic-inch) V-8 remained the standard engine, with a 200-hp 455 optional. Grand Ams continued to use the dashboard of the personal-luxury Grand Prix with its full array of gauges. The pictured car is wearing later-model wheels. **2.** Pontiac's last full-size convertible was the stately 1975 Grand Ville Brougham. The rectangular headlights were a new feature. Production totaled 4519 with prices starting at $5858. **3.** Four-door hardtops—now offered only as a Bonneville or this Grand Ville Brougham—received Colonnade styling this year. The small "opera windows" in their rear pillars improved visibility. **4.** Grand Safari wagons joined the Bonneville family for 1975 in both two- and three-seat versions priced at $5433 and $5580, respectively.

1. Buick's largest offering for 1976 remained the Electra 225, now in its final year on its stately 127-inch wheelbase. The four-door hardtop had a base price of $6527.
2. This upscale Electra 225 Limited wears Custom Landau trim. Electra coupes offered an optional all-metal electric sunroof.
3. Although Riviera's sporty GS version was discontinued for 1976, enthusiasts could still get much of the GS's ride and handling qualities by ordering the optional Rallye package. The standard engine remained a 205-hp 455-cid V-8. Despite the loss of the GS, sales of the $6798 Riviera perked up a bit this year, totaling 20,082.
4. Skylark S/R models were offered in sedan, coupe (shown), and hatchback

1

2

3

4

form starting at $4281, but combined production totaled only 8371.
5. A glass Astro roof could be installed on the subcompact Buick Skyhawk hatchback for $550 extra. Skyhawks came only with a 110-hp 231-cubic-inch (3.8-liter) V-6. With prices starting at $3903, production reached 15,768.

5

1

2

3

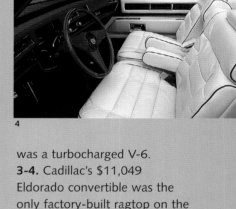

4

1. Midsize Buicks, including the new price-leading $3935 Century Special coupe, got a new look for 1976. 2. Wild graphics graced the Century Indy 500 pace car; underhood

was a turbocharged V-6. 3-4. Cadillac's $11,049 Eldorado convertible was the only factory-built ragtop on the market for 1976. Toward the end of the model year there was a special run of 2000 all-white "last convertibles." 5. Cadillac's Fleetwood Brougham continued on its long 133-inch wheelbase. 6. Cadillac's best-selling model remained the Coupe de Ville. 7. Sales of the compact Seville continued to grow. 8. Cadillac still cataloged nine-seat Fleetwood Seventy-Five sedans and limousines.

5

6

7

8

CHAPTER EIGHT: 1970-1979   265

1. The Chevrolet Chevette was essentially an Americanized version of the Opel Kadett "T-car" from GM's German subsidiary. The import-fighter arrived for 1976 as a two-door hatchback with a petite 94.3-inch wheelbase, feathery sub-2000-pound curb weight, and thrifty four-cylinder engines. Prices started at $2899. **2.** Monzas were visual reruns with shuffled engines. The Towne Coupe started at $3359. **3.** Vega was billed this year as "Built to Take It" but was still dogged by its early, well-publicized engine and rust woes. This rare Cosworth-Vega shows off the new grille that spruced up all Vegas. **4.** The $4621 Chevelle Laguna Type S-3 continued with the sloped nose adopted for '75. **5.** Malibu Classics gained visual flair by wearing the newly allowed square headlights in stacked pairs astride a mesh-type grille insert. **6.** Nova coupes still offered an SS option, but it was a pale echo of Super Sport's glory days. **7.** Monte Carlo's popularity spawned many competitors, including the Ford Gran Torino Elite, Chrysler Cordoba, and in-house rival Olds Cutlass Supreme. Even so, Monte Carlo sales jumped more than 36 percent to 353,272. Stacked pairs of rectangular headlights helped freshen the Monte's face. **8.** Camaro was little changed, though the LT gained a brushed-aluminum rear appliqué. With prices starting at $3762 and little competition from other quarters, sales continued to rise. **9.** Despite a coupe-only lineup for the first time in its history—and a near-$1000 price hike—Corvette sales set a record at more than 46,000. Horsepower outputs for the $7605 Stingray's 350-cid V-8 rose to 180 or 210.

1. The 1976 Oldsmobile Ninety-Eight Regency (shown) had a few more extras than the Luxury Series (LS). This $6544 coupe has the optional landau roof. 2. The brochure described the Ninety-Eight Regency's interior as having "plump and tufted loose-look cushions." Buyers could choose from velour or leather. 3. Lower-priced Ninety-Eight LS models were handily out-sold by the Regencys. Most of the differences were in the interior, where knit nylon fabrics or white vinyl were the upholstery choices. 4. The Cutlass received a waterfall grille and quad rectangular headlights for 1976. More than 186,000 Cutlass Supreme coupes were sold starting at $4291. Customer loyalty was very strong, and resale values were excellent. 5. Nineteen seventy-six marked the final year for the sporty Cutlass Salon sedan. Contoured seats and a floor console were standard.

1

2

3

4

5

6

7

1. Bonneville resumed its flagship role for 1976 by ousting Grand Ville as Pontiac's top full-size line. A $5246 base coupe is shown with vinyl roof and Rally wheels. **2.** The newest thing about the top-rung Bonneville Brougham was its name. Base price of the four-door hardtop was $5906.
3. A reshaped "shovel-nose" Endura front end gave all 1976 Firebirds a more aerodynamic look. This Starlight Black and gold Trans Am was one of 1947 built to commemorate Pontiac's 50th anniversary. Another 643 were converted by Hurst to include T-top roofs, the first Firebirds so equipped.
4. Firebird's taillamps and rear bumper were also modified. Trans Ams, like this one, carried a standard 185-horse 400-cid V-8. The big 455 with 200 horsepower remained available, except in California. **5.** An LJ luxury appointment group with velour buckets and two-tone paint could be ordered for the $4798 Grand Prix coupe.
6. A new 260-cubic-inch V-8 and five-speed manual transmission failed to stimulate sales of Pontiac's compact Ventura, shown in $3637 SJ sedan trim.
7. New this year, the subcompact Sunbird coupe was related to Chevrolet's Monza. Prices started at $3431. The Chevy Vega-sourced four-cylinder engine was standard, with Buick's 3.8-liter V-6 optional. First year sales were 52,031.

1

2

3

4

5

1. GM rocked the industry for 1977 with smaller, lighter full-size cars that were no less roomy inside than the gas-guzzlers of 1971–76. Buick offered the "downsized" coupes and sedans under its LeSabre and Electra banners. LeSabres and Estate Wagons were on a 115.9-inch wheelbase. Electras rode a 119-inch span. Engines shrank to match the cars; LeSabre came standard with a 231-cid V-6, while Electra got a 350 V-8. A new 185-hp 403 V-8 was optional on both. This Electra 225 coupe started at $6673. LeSabre and Estate Wagons racked up 215,801 sales, with the Electras adding 161,627 more. **2.** The padded vinyl roof and coach lamps are signs that this Electra 225 Limited sedan has the optional Park Avenue package. **3.** The downsized Riviera was related to the "B-body" LeSabre. Prices started at $7385. **4.** Centurys dropped the Colonnade tag and had revised grilles. This was the last year for the body style introduced in 1973. Like all GM "A-body" intermediates, they were now competing head-to-head with the downsized big cars. Special, base, and Custom (shown) coupes were offered. **5.** Buick's Skyhawk got a new grille for 1977. Prices started at $3981, and the only engine offered was a 105-horse 3.8-liter V-6. Sales totaled 12,345.

1

2

3

4

1-2. Billed as "The Next Generation of the Luxury Car," the new C-body Cadillacs shared a downsized platform with senior Buicks and Oldsmobiles. Curb weights were down about 900 pounds. De Villes and the closely related Fleetwood Broughams now shared a 121.5-inch wheelbase, while Fleetwood limousines rode a 144.5-inch span. The 500-cid V-8 was relegated to the history books, and 425-cubic-inch V-8 was now standard. Output was 180 horsepower; optional fuel injection raised the tally to 195. The $10,020 Sedan de Ville (shown) and $9810 Coupe de Ville saw their sales surge to 234,171 units. Fleetwood Broughams added another 28,000 sales. **3.** Seville sedans displayed only minor changes, including a new grille. Amber turn-signal lenses also contributed to its European-like demeanor. Because big Cadillacs had shrunk so sharply, the $13,359 Seville now weighed almost as much as a De Ville. **4.** Unlike its downsized companions, the $11,187 Eldorado coupe stuck to its overly abundant dimensions yet sold even better than before. With the 500-cid V-8 gone, the De Ville's 425 got the call.

1

2

3

4

5

6

1. Full-size Chevrolets looked clean and trim on 1977's smaller B-body platform. After the aggressive downsizing, this $5357 Caprice Classic V-8 sedan weighed less than a comparable midsized Chevelle. **2.** El Camino Classic shared its exterior styling, interior trim, and engine choices with the midsize Malibu. **3.** While Malibu sedans and wagons rode the same 116-inch wheelbase as the new downsized Impalas, coupes were still on a 112-inch span. Base and Classic versions were offered; the latter (priced at $3885) is shown here. **4.** The Malibu wagon was almost identical in size to the new full-size Impala wagon and also came in six- and nine-passenger versions. Malibu Classic wagon prices started at $5065. **5.** In its last year before being downsized, the $4968 Monte Carlo remained tremendously popular. **6.** At midyear, the legendary Camaro Z28 returned after a nearly three-year hiatus.

1

1. For 1977, Corvette lost its Stingray suffix and gained new crossed-flag emblems. Leather upholstery was now included in the $8648 base price—which was up by $1000 for the second year in a row. Nevertheless, sales set another new record at 49,213. A 180-horse 350 remained standard, with a 210-hp L82 version optional. **2.** The ill-fated Vega was in its final year as sales plummeted to just 78,402. This hatchback started at $3359. **3.** The classy Concours, available as both a coupe and sedan, continued to top the Nova line. With a bench front seat, Nova was a six-passenger car priced about $1400 less than the new Impala. **4.** Changes were subtle for the Chevette in its second season, and sales of the rear-drive subcompact hatchback faltered noticeably. A back seat was now standard on the bare-bones $2999 Scooter. **5.** Monza continued in coupe and 2+2 hatchback form. Spyder Equipment and Appearance packages could be teamed up to give 2+2 models mechanical and cosmetic upgrades.

2

3

4

5

1. Like other GM full-size models, the Oldsmobile Ninety-Eight earned a massive downsizing, losing 800 pounds and nearly a foot of length. **2.** The 4-4-2 appearance/handling option added just $169 to the $4351 price of a Cutlass S coupe. **3.** This prototype Toronado XSR had tinted glass panels that would retract toward the middle of the roof. The system was deemed too troublesome to put into production. **4.** The Can Am option for the LeMans Sport Coupe added Trans Am punch under the hood and appearance and handling enhancements throughout. **5.** LeMans Sport Coupes also had a GT edition with two-tone paint. **6.** Grand LeMans wore rear fender skirts. The coupe started at $4614.

1

1. Full-size Pontiacs shared the downsized platform with big Chevys, yet kept a distinct identity. This is the top-line Bonneville Brougham sedan; prices started at $5992. 2. The Bonneville Brougham was also offered as a $5897 coupe. 3. Full-size Catalinas shared the Bonneville's smaller size but were more modestly equipped. The four-door sedan started at $5050. 4. All three Grand Prix trim levels now enjoyed full model status. The SJ was the most expensive, starting at $5753. The T-tops that were part of the 1976 50th anniversary package joined the regular option list. 5. Esprit, the "luxury" Firebird since 1970, remained so when Pontiac's ponycar took on this handsome new quad-headlamp nose. 6. The Sunbird coupe started at $3659. Added was a new Sport Hatch based on the Chevy Monza 2+2 body. 7. Pontiac's Astre now had a 87-hp 2.5-liter "Iron Duke" four.

2

3

4

5

6

7

1. GM's 1978 intermediates were next up on the corporation's slenderizing schedule. All were built on a new 108.1-inch-wheelbase "A-body" chassis, and Regal was now a separate series of two-door coupes. Two conventional V-6s and a 305-cid V-8 were offered on Regal, but the top power option was a new turbocharged 3.8-liter V-6 churning out up to 165 hp. Cars so equipped wore a distinctive hood bulge. **2.** The Century coupe (shown) and sedan had new "aeroback" rooflines and could also be ordered with the turbo V-6. **3.** Century models like this four-door sedan lost a foot of length and 600 pounds. Also offered was a conventionally styled station wagon. **4.** A Riviera "LXXV" Anniversary Edition coupe marked Buick's 75th birthday. **5.** Skylark Custom coupes offered a Landau roof option. **6.** The LeSabre Sport Coupe was identified by flat black paint around the windows, a blacked-out grille, and "Turbo 3.8 Litre" badges on the front fenders. The 3.8-liter turbo V-6 came in 150- and 165-hp versions. **7.** Buick dealers still sold Opels, but now they were built by Isuzu in Japan. **8.** Buick's big Estate Wagon was little changed, and the front styling was borrowed from the Electra.

1. De Villes were marked with a bolder grille pattern for 1978. Coupe de Villes were the most popular Cadillac model with 117,750 sales. **2.** If a regular $12,842 Fleetwood Brougham wasn't quite comfy enough, the d'Elegance decor option added contoured pillow-style seats trimmed in Florentine velour. **3.** The limited-production Seville Elegante flaunted wire wheels and a choice of two-tone paint treatments: Platinum/Sable Black, or Western Saddle Firemist/Ruidoso Brown. Sevilles started at $14,161. **4.** At midseason, Seville gained an optional 120-hp 350-cid diesel V-8. **5.** Like other GM intermediates, the "personal luxury" Monte Carlo was downsized for 1978, ending up a foot shorter and 800 pounds lighter. Also lighter was the base price, though the $200 drop (to $4785) brought a V-6 in place of a V-8. **6.** Monte Carlo shared its 108.1-inch-wheelbase chassis with the newly downsized Malibu. The Landau coupe wore a "half" vinyl roof. A 145-hp 305 V-8 was optional. **7.** An all-new downsized Malibu made its debut for 1978, and the Chevelle nameplate was retired. Malibu was offered in coupe (shown), sedan, and wagon body styles.

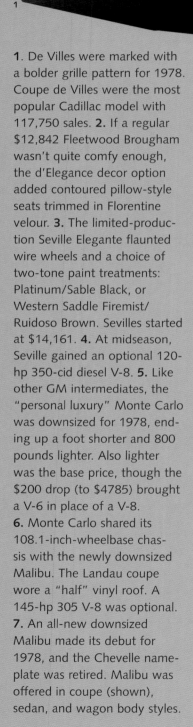

1

2

3

4

5

6

7

8

1. The Chevrolet Impala coupe was a rather rare version of America's best-selling car line. Just 33,990 Impala coupes and an additional 4652 Landau coupes were built for 1978 out of total Impala production of 287,744. **2.** El Camino was once again based on the intermediate line, so it carried the styling of the new, downsized Malibu. **3.** A new grille and slightly restyled taillights identified 1978's Caprice Classic. Shown is the popular $3686 V-8 sedan. **4.** Monza Sport models— offered in coupe (shown) and 2+2 hatchback body styles— wore a distinctive quad-headlight front end. **5.** "Regular" Monza models had a dual-headlight face. In addition to the 2+2 (shown) and coupe body styles, the old Vega hatchback and wagon bodies were also offered. All Monzas now came standard with Pontiac's "Iron Duke" four-cylinder engine. **6.** Corvette served as the Official Pace Car for the 1978 Indy 500. Pace car replicas often sold for considerably more than their $13,653 sticker. **7.** Camaro Z28's standard 350-cid V-8 gained 15 horsepower for a total of 185. Also added were nonfunctional front-fender vents and hood scoop. **8.** Chevette received a new grille along with a four-door hatchback version that quickly became the best-selling model.

1

1. A new vertical-bar grille was the extent of the external facelifting given the 1978 Oldsmobile Toronado, which marked the final appearance for the 1971-vintage platform. Demand dropped to 24,815, a scant 2453 of which were the $11,599 XSC (shown) with its wraparound rear window and powered glass sunroof.

2. Oldsmobile's dramatically downsized Cutlass Salon two-door coupe (shown) and four-door sedan used GM's new "aeroback" profile, a silhouette buyers did not embrace. Traditional notchback-coupe versions sold far better.

3. Neither truly a sporty car nor an economy car, the subcompact Oldsmobile Starfire hatchback coupe tallied some meager sales totals. Similar to Chevy's Monza 2+2, the Starfire was distinguished by a "waterfall" grille. Standard was Pontiac's Iron Duke four-cylinder engine, but a 3.8-liter (231-cid) V-6 and 5.0-liter (305-cid) V-8 were optional. It was about this time that Detroit started going "metric," expressing engine displacement in both cubic inches and liters.

4. Oldsmobile's Custom Cruiser station wagon came standard with a 350-cid V-8 engine. Options included a 403 V-8 or GM's 350-cid diesel V-8.

2

3

4

1

2

1. Offered in coupe or sedan form, Pontiac's sporty 1978 Grand Am was based on the newly downsized LeMans but came with a unique soft front end and two-tone paint. It came standard with a 301-cid V-8. 2. Downsized like other GM midsize models, Grand LeMans coupes kept a notchback profile. 3. The Grand LeMans sedan offered luxury in a midsized package. 4. Pontiac's Grand Prix rode a reduced 108-inch wheelbase, losing nearly a foot of length and at least 600 pounds. The coupes retained their traditional profile, including sweeping fenders. A padded landau top could be installed on the sporty Grand Prix LJ. 5. Trans Am offered a $1259 Special Edition package that included gold paint and trim. 6. Stylish Red Bird decor was optional on the Firebird Esprit.

3

4

5

6

1

1. The first front-wheel-drive Buick Riviera was introduced for 1979 on GM's downsized E-body platform. Wheelbase was tightened by only two inches, but overall length shrunk by about a foot. Base Rivieras held a 170-hp 350-cid V-8, but the new S Type offered a turbocharged V-6 that put out up to 185 horsepower. Prices started at $10,684, up nearly $1500 over the larger '78. **2.** Facelifted front and rear, a mid-level $9103 Electra Limited coupe was loaded with comfort and convenience features. **3.** Buick's LeSabre Sport Coupe again held a turbocharged V-6 engine. Optional bucket seats, console, and a floor shifter were offered, but only 3582 were sold. **4.** The $7169 Estate Wagon could be upgraded with Limited features for an extra $1853. **5.** Buick's little Skyhawk hatchback gained a sporty Road Hawk option for 1979. The package added sport wheels, a Rallye suspension, and flashy two-tone silver paint. Sadly, any semblance of "sport" ended there, as the only engine available was the standard 115-hp 3.8-liter V-6.

2

3

4

5

1. A 170-horse turbo V-6 added zest to Buick's 1979 Regal Sport Coupe, which started at $6497. 2. Buick had another enthusiast's car up its sleeve in the Century Turbo Coupe. It also packed the 3.8-liter turbo V-6. 3. This year's top-selling Century was the $5806 Custom wagon. 4. The fastback Century Limited now came only as a four-door sedan. 5-6. Downsizing dropped the Eldorado to the

size of a Seville and gave it a look that was the closest thing yet to a "sporty" Cadillac. Its 1100-pound diet allowed its equally downsized 170-hp 350-cid V-8 to provide ample thrust. A 350-cid V-8 diesel was optional. 7. Other than a whopping $2000 price increase, the Seville was virtually unchanged for 1979, the last year for its original 1975 design. 8. Seville's $2735 Elegante option featured black and slate two-tone paint plus wire wheels. 9. The poshest Fleetwood Broughams came with the d'Elegance option.

1

1-2. After its drastic restyle a year earlier, Monte Carlo was virtually unchanged for 1979, though the vinyl roof treatment on these Landau models now covered the front half of the roof rather than the rear. Prices started at $5333. **3.** Malibu Classics came four ways, including this $5215 four-door

2

3

4

5

sedan. **4.** This Malibu Classic wagon sports the "Estate" package, which included woodgrain side trim. **5.** The base $4161 Monza 2+2 hatchback was quite popular, selling 56,871 units. **6.** Refinements to the top-line Caprice Classic included a new grille with bold vertical accents and, on coupes and sedans, an update of the traditional tri-segmented taillights. Caprice Classic sedans started at $6323, a $700 bump over 1978.

6

1

2

3

4

5

1-2. A new and very popular addition to the Camaro line was the luxury-level Berlinetta. This high-style Camaro replaced the Type LT and included aluminum wheels and dual pinstripes. A custom cloth interior was standard. All Camaros had a redesigned instrument cluster. The $5906 Berlinetta was well received by the public, with 67,236 built. **3.** Chevette got a new grille design and rectangular headlights for 1979. Prices started at $3437 for the base Scooter two-door hatchback, but the best-selling four-door (shown) started at $4072. Still standard was a 1.6-liter four with 70-74 hp. **4.** Nova had a very short 1979 model year with production ending in November 1978. Even so, it got a revised grille with rectangular headlights. Nova was replaced in spring 1979 by the front-wheel-drive Citation. **5-6.** Painted black and gold or white and gold, the limited-production Hurst/ Olds was based on the Cutlass Calais coupe. The trademark Hurst Gold striping extended to two-toning on the front section of the roof, beltline, and hood. More gold paint was found on the sport mirrors and was used for grille and wheel trim. The only engine was a 170-horse Olds-built 350 that was labeled "W-30." The Turbo 350 automatic was controlled by Hurst's Dual-Gate shifter. The package cost $2054.

6

1. Oldsmobile's Toronado coupes slimmed down dramatically for 1979, losing 22 inches of length and 900 pounds of weight. What did not slim down was the base price: up $1300 over '78 to $10,709. A 350-cid gas V-8 was standard, a 350 diesel optional. 2. The Starfire hatchback got freshened styling for 1979. Introduced during 1978 was the Firenza option package, which included a rear spoiler, flared wheel openings, Rallye suspension, and special paint. 3. The entire lower body of a $6809 Cutlass Cruiser Brougham wagon could be covered with a woodgrain appliqué.

4. A Pontiac Grand Prix styling proposal included narrow vertical opera windows; production versions had wider panes. 5. The $6814 SJ remained the top Grand Prix model. 6. The $5430 Grand LeMans sedan was the most popular of Pontiac's midsize cars. 7. Woodgrain siding bedecks this $5931 Grand LeMans Safari wagon. 8. Despite offering European-style handling, Pontiac's $5530 Grand Am coupe attracted only 4021 buyers.

1. A facelift made the Pontiac Firebird's "beak" more pronounced, as rectangular headlamps moved into separate pods. Formula coupes had four-wheel disc brakes and a 301-cid V-8 standard. Total Firebird output soared past 210,000 to an all-time record. Obviously, the lack of Firebird's former super-hot engines didn't diminish its appeal. 2. Firebird's tail styling was also new, with a revised rear bumper, reshaped spoiler, and a full-width taillight panel. Taillights on Formulas and Trans Ams were hidden behind "blacked-out" lenses. A Formula coupe started at $6564. 3. Pontiac's Sunbird offered a choice of four-cylinder, V-6, or V-8 power. This hatchback has the Formula option, with a black grille, front air dam, rear spoiler, striping, and the expected high-visibility decals. Sunbird prices started at $3899. 4. Trim, color, and equipment shuffles were the only changes of note for this year's full-size Pontiacs, such as the $6718 Bonneville four-door sedan. As before, Bonnevilles used a 301-cid Pontiac V-8, while the lower-priced Catalinas had a 231-cid (3.8-liter) Buick V-6. Bonneville sold better than ever this year, attracting 179,416 buyers.

CHAPTER NINE

1980-1989

"Just because everything is different doesn't mean anything has changed"

—Irene Peter

When the 1980s opened, GM's U.S. market share was a commanding 46.5 percent, but the company faced two major challenges. A second energy crisis in 1979 had consumers thinking small again, and tough economic times were hurting new car sales overall.

GM had begun downsizing its large and intermediate cars for 1977 and had released its smaller, lighter, front-drive X-body compacts in April 1979 as 1980 models, but it wasn't enough. Even though the X cars—the Chevy Citation, Pontiac Phoenix, Olds Omega, and Buick Skylark— were breakout sellers, there was still room for smaller cars that sipped even less gas. That left an opening for the Japanese makers, who were simply better at building small cars than the Americans. Throughout the decade, GM and the other domestics would see their market share slip away to the Asian makers.

The aforementioned X-body cars were the stars of the 1980 product lineup, with Chevy Citation production topping 811,000 units (thanks in part to an extended 17-month model year), earning it best-selling car status that year. The honeymoon would be short-lived, however, as recalls and generally poor quality would cause production

to be cut in half for 1981 and decline each year thereafter. The subcompact Chevy Chevette was performing well, too, in 1980, with more than 450,000 units produced. GM's other small cars—Chevy Monza, Buick Skyhawk, and Olds Starfire—were in their last year, as a replacement was coming for 1982.

The intermediates were little changed for 1980, as they were due for a reskin in 1981. GM's biggest cars, such as Chevy Caprice, Olds Delta 88, Pontiac Bonneville, and Buick LeSabre, received a reskin for the 1980 model year. Minor aero changes were made, and the cars were built with lighter materials to take off about 150 pounds. A diesel engine, a 350-inch V-8 based on a gas engine of the same size, was also offered for the full-size cars. The diesels proved troublesome however, though GM would continue to market them through 1985.

At Cadillac, the Seville, introduced in 1975, received its first redesign. Most noticeable was the sloped "trunkback" rear end, a design element reminiscent of 1950s Rolls-Royces. A major personnel change occurred in 1981, when GM elected Roger B. Smith as its Chairman and CEO, replacing Thomas Murphy. Murphy had retired in 1980, after acting as top dog since 1974. Smith would attempt to prepare GM for the next century, but his reign would be a difficult one.

Also in 1981, GM bought five percent of Suzuki Motor Company, Ltd. and announced plans to develop future supply and distribution arrangements. The purchase would be one of many efforts by GM to reach out to foreign manufacturers for help building small cars.

Product news was light for 1981. The intermediate coupes—Monte Carlo, Grand Prix, Regal, and Cutlass—received a reskin that made them sleeker and more aerodynamic. With the growing popularity of small cars, nearly 500,000 Chevettes crossed dealer lots, and Pontiac was given a version of its own called T1000.

Engines made news at Cadillac this year. Standard on some Cadillacs was a 4.1-liter, 125-hp V-6 Buick. It was Cadillac's first-ever V-6. Also new was a V-8-6-4 version of Cadillac's 368-cid V-8. It was outfitted with a variable-displacement valve-selector system that allowed the engine to cut power to two or four cylinders depending on the engine load. Unfortunately, the system suffered from electronic problems, and it was discontinued after just one year.

Product news was more significant for 1982. GM released its all-new J-body front-wheel-drive compacts this year. The cars included the Chevy Cavalier, Pontiac J2000, Olds Firenza, Buick Skyhawk, and Cadillac Cimarron.

GM had a second series of front-wheel-drive cars ready for 1982, the A bodies. The offerings consisted of the Chevrolet Celebrity, Pontiac 6000, Olds Cutlass Ciera, and Buick Century. The cars used the X-body's 104.9-inch-wheelbase chassis and essentially the same powertrains.

The third-generation F bodies, the Camaro and Firebird, arrived in mid 1981 as 1982 models. Their wheelbase was down seven inches to 101, overall length was 10 inches shorter, and weight was down by 500 pounds.

Though 1982 was a down year for most manufacturers, including GM, the company managed to net a $1 billion profit. The economy was picking up by 1983 and so were car sales. GM topped four million sales for the year, after slipping to just more than three million in 1982. The company also celebrated its 75th anniversary on September 16.

The corporation made two important business moves during the year, both involving small cars. In November, Chairman Roger Smith and president F. James McDonald announced the Saturn Project, a developmental program to build a new family of subcompact cars to compete with the Japanese makes. The project would use "start-to-finish" innovations and include a union-management partnership. As if to hedge its bets, GM also reached out to Toyota. In February, GM and Toyota announced the formation of New United Motor Manufacturing, Inc. (NUMMI), a joint venture to produce a small Chevrolet car in the Fremont, California, assembly plant formerly operated by GM. The plant would produce its first car, the Chevrolet Nova, in late 1984 as an '85 model.

On the product side, Chevrolet went without a Corvette for 1983, as it was busy readying its first all-new model since 1968 for the '84 model year. Chevrolet introduced a convertible version the Cavalier, the marque's first droptop since the mid 1970s.

Buick general manager Lloyd Reuss aimed at making Buick the American BMW by offering sporty T Type versions of every model but the LeSabre and Electra.

Chevrolet made the biggest product splash for 1984 with an all-new Corvette, but Pontiac wasn't far behind with a sporty car of its own. Everything but the engine in the Corvette was new. The 350-inch V-8 (now described by its metric displacement of 5.7 liters) was capable of moving the car from 0 to 60 mph in just over seven seconds.

Vette-like with its plastic skin was Pontiac's new two-seat Fiero. The mid-engine runabout was meant to serve as a sporty commuter, being both frugal and fun. In other news from Pontiac, the 2000 was renamed Sunbird and the Impala-clone full-size Parisienne was added to the lineup.

Also in 1984, Cadillac added a convertible to the Eldorado lineup, its first since 1976. The droptop would make it only two model years.

The Saturn Corporation was born in January 1985 as a separate brand subsidiary, giving GM six North American passenger car marques. Saturn would have its own plant, its own employees, and its own contract with the UAW. The plant would be located in Spring Hill, Tennessee, in part to allow Saturn to develop its own corporate culture separate from the rest of GM.

While Saturn was weened, NUMMI bore fruit. The first car born of the NUMMI deal with Toyota appeared as a 1985 model. It was called the Nova, but it was actually a Toyota Corolla in Chevy trim. The Nova would last until the 1988 model year.

GM continued downsizing its cars, putting two product lines on a diet for 1985. The new C bodies, which included the Cadillac DeVille/Fleetwood, Buick Electra, and Olds

Ninety Eight, rode a 110.8-inch wheelbase, down 8.2 inches from the previous year. Despite the smaller size and six-cylinder power (only the Cadillacs offered a V-8), they were still billed as full-size cars. The other new front drivers were the N-body Buick Somerset, Olds Calais, and Pontiac Grand Am. They replaced the unloved X cars.

There was also some performance news this year. Chevrolet introduced the Camaro IROC-Z, a higher performance version of the Z28 that was capable of 0-60-mph times in the seven-second range.

GM also missed with an attempted answer to Chrysler's new-for-'84 minivans. The Chevy Astro Van, unlike the Chryslers, was rear-wheel drive and drove more like a truck than a car. And while more than 130,000 were sold in its first year, Chrysler enjoyed sales in excess of 240,000 with its vans.

In 1986, GM bought into CAMI, a joint-venture auto manufacturing plant in Ingersoll, Ontario. The project was half-owned by GM of Canada and half by Japanese auto-maker Suzuki. It was another attempt by GM to assimilate Japanese manufacturing know how. CAMI would go on to build small cars and trucks sold under the Chevrolet, Geo, and Suzuki banners.

While opening one plant, GM announced plans to close 11 other U.S. plants that had become redundant as a result of plant modernization pushed by Chairman Roger Smith. Plant closures in Flint, Michigan, would later give GM a black eye, thanks to Michael Moore's 1989 documentary *Roger & Me.* The film depicted the economic effects of the plant closures and portrayed Roger Smith as uncaring.

This was a year of transition for GM's full-size car offerings. While some models remained on the rear-drive B-body platform, others moved to a new front-wheel-drive H-body. The Chevy Caprice, Oldsmobile Custom Cruiser, Pontiac Parisienne, and the Estate Wagon versions of Buick's LeSabre and Electra remained B-bodies. Coupe and Sedan versions of Buick's LeSabre and Oldsmobile's 88 switched to the new H-body. The E-body personal luxury coupes (Olds Toronado, Buick Riviera, and Cadillac Eldorado), as well as their Cadillac Seville K-body spin-off, were all-new and much smaller. Unfortunately, these shrunken premium cars didn't seem premium to buyers, and sales dropped dramatically.

In small-car news, Chevy now offered three Japanese-built models, the Nova, Spectrum, and Sprint. Nova came from the NUMMI project, Spectrum was built by Isuzu, and Sprint was assembled by Suzuki.

GM introduced a new six-year, 60,000-mile powertrain warranty, and 100,000-mile corrosion warranty for most of its cars and trucks in 1987, just in time for a pair of new compact Chevrolets. The Corsica sedan and Beretta coupe shared a new L-body platform that was exclusive to Chevrolet. A late arrival limited sales for '87, but production for each exceeded 275,000 the following year. Camaro was now available as a convertible for the first time since 1969. Pontiac made bigger news in 1987 with the return of Bonneville. The new Bonnie was now front drive and

shared its H-body design with the Buick LeSabre and Olds Delta 88.

The most interesting new car for 1988 was Cadillac's Allanté. Built on a version of the Eldorado platform, the Allanté was a two-seat convertible aimed at the Mercedes-Benz 560SL. With a body designed by Italy's Pininfarina, the Allanté was a good-looking car, but its $54,000 sticker price led to a modest model-year sales total of 3065. *Automotive News* named Allanté its "Flop of the Year."

Buick also got a premium two-seater for 1988, the Reatta. Initially offered only as a coupe, a convertible Reatta would follow for 1990. All Reattas used a version of the Riviera platform. Like Allanté, Reatta was a sales dud. Buick produced only 4700 in its first year.

A more important line of cars debuted for 1988. General Motors spent some $7 billion to develop its GM10 line of midsize front-wheel-drive cars, the most it had ever put into a development project. Known as W-body cars, the first three to appear were the 1988 Buick Regal, Oldsmobile Cutlass Supreme, and Pontiac Grand Prix, and all were two-door coupes. Chevrolet wouldn't get its first W body until the release of the 1990 Lumina.

Also on the product front, GM introduced the Geo brand of small cars for 1989. The lineup included Metro, Prizm, Spectrum, and Tracker. Metro and Tracker (a Suzuki Sidekick clone) were built at the CAMI assembly plant in Canada. Prizm replaced the Chevrolet Nova as the Toyota Corolla clone built at the NUMMI plant in California. Spectrum was built by Isuzu. It was only sold as a Geo in 1989 (it had been a Chevy for the 1985-1988 model years) and was replaced by Storm for 1990.

To give the E-body luxury coupes (Eldorado, Riviera, Toronado) a more premium look this year, GM lengthened the cars some 11 inches. Sales increased, but the totals were still less than half of their mid 1980s highs. At Cadillac, driver's side airbags became a linewide option.

Through the decade, GM had made moves to modernize. The company spent billions to downsize its cars and change over to front-wheel drive. Partnerships were struck with Japanese makers to learn more efficient assembly methods.

GM started the 1980s on a low note, losing money for the first time since the 1920s. The company soon bounced back, though, and made a record $3.7 billion profit in 1983. By the mid 1980s, sales were peaking and times were good. As the 1980s drew to a close, though, sales suffered, due mostly to products that didn't resonate with the buying public. Oldsmobile, for instance, sold 1.17 million cars in 1985, but just 534,000 in 1989. Buick, which enjoyed high times in the mid 1980s as it moved toward sportier cars, returned to its heritage as a maker of "Premium American Motorcars" and watched its sales drop by almost half. GM was criticized for not focusing enough on product, and by decade's end, market share was down from 46.5 in 1980 to 35 percent. That wasn't the end of the trouble, though, as another recession and poor sales would leave GM on the brink of bankruptcy in the early 1990s.

—*Kirk Bell*

1. Arriving in spring of 1979, General Motors' 1980 X-body cars were compact, fuel-efficient, and instant hits with the buying public. The front-wheel-drive coupes, hatchbacks, and sedans were available from every GM division but Cadillac and GMC. Skylark, Buick's version, was 19 inches shorter and 700-800 pounds lighter than the car it replaced.

2. This Skylark Limited sedan has the optional 2.8-liter V-6. So equipped, base price was $5951. Buick sold 265,654 Skylarks during the model year. **3.** The Electra Limited Coupe received updated body styling this year, resulting in improved aerodynamics. The front fenders still had Buick's traditional "ventiports." For the first time, Electra had a standard V-6, a 4.1-liter unit with 125 horsepower. Gas and diesel V-8s were optional. **4.** Riviera was little changed and remained Buick's highest priced model with a base price of $11,640. **5.** Cadillac Coupe de Ville was restyled this year, sporting a more formal roof and a nearly upright rear window. Also new was a 6.0-liter V-8 that offered optional "digital" electronic fuel injection. Base price was $12,899. Caddy produced 55,490 1980 Coupe de Villes.

1

2

3

4

5

6

7

1. The Seville was all new with a $20,477 starting price. It was based on the Eldorado's front-wheel-drive mechanicals and boasted an all-indepedent suspension with automatic self leveling. Standard features included a 5.7-liter diesel V-8 and four-wheel disc brakes. **2.** The most controversial aspect of the Seville's new look was the sloped "trunk back" rear end. **3.** New the previous year, Eldorado was little changed for 1980. This car wears the new standard wheel covers. Note the lack of the popular available vinyl top. **4.** Chevrolet's Corvette entered the new decade with cleaner, more contemporary styling. The integrated front and rear spoilers were among the changes. **5.** This Caprice Classic coupe shows off the smoother, lower nose and rear end revisions made to improve aerodynamics and thus fuel economy. Also with a nod to better gas mileage, a more efficient 229 V-6 replaced the old 250 straight-six. **6.** Though little changed, Chevette sales rose to 451,000 in the aftermath of the second energy crisis. Base price was $4736. **7.** For Chevy's sporty Monza 2+2, 1980 was its last year. This example boasts the optional Spyder package.

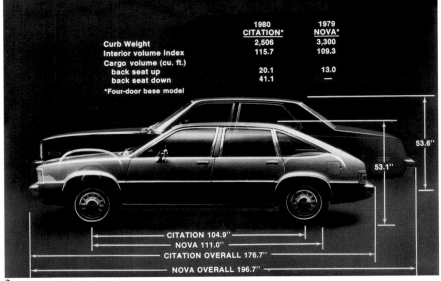

	1980 CITATION*	1979 NOVA*
Curb Weight	2,506	3,300
Interior volume index	115.7	109.3
Cargo volume (cu. ft.)		
back seat up	20.1	13.0
back seat down	41.1	—

*Four-door base model

53.6"
53.1"

CITATION 104.9"
NOVA 111.0"
CITATION OVERALL 176.7"
NOVA OVERALL 196.7"

1. Citation was the name given to Chevrolet's version of GM's new X-body compacts. This hatchback includes the X-11 package that added sporty styling details and improved the already good handling.
2. Citation was the most popular of the X-body quartet (Buick Skylark, Oldsmobile Omega, and Pontiac Phoenix were also offered) with 1980 model-year sales of more than 811,000. The four-door hatchback was most popular, finding 458,033 buyers. **3.** Though aging, Camaro Z28 kept V-8 performance alive at Chevy. **4.** Omega was the Olds version of GM's X-cars. This Brougham sedan was the most

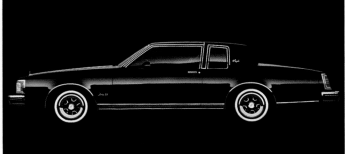

popular model with 42,289 sales. **5.** This Ninety-Eight Regency coupe shows off the car's revised-for-'80 side profile. **6.** Also sporting a tweaked silhouette is Olds' Delta 88 Royale coupe. **7.** Cutlass Supreme coupes received new quad-rectangular headlights.

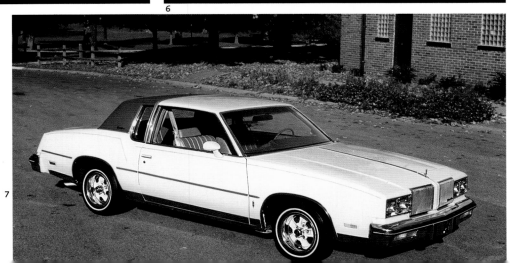

1

2

3

4

5

1. Pontiac also received a version of the GM front-wheel-drive X-body. This is a Phoenix LJ hatchback sedan. Pontiac's "Iron Duke" 2.5-liter four-cylinder engine was standard; a Chevrolet-built 2.8-liter V-6 was optional. **2.** The only other Phoenix body style was this two-door coupe. This example has the sporty SJ option package that included a black grille and headlamp bezels, vinyl bucket seats, Rally wheels, Rally RTS suspension, and an accent color on the lower body and bumpers. A four-speed manual transmission with floor shift was standard on all Phoenix models. **3.** Base price of this Bonneville Brougham sedan was $8160. **4.** Pontiac's Firebird Turbo Trans Am served as the Official Pace Car for the 1980 Indianapolis 500. This pace car replica shows off this model's unique graphics. The turbocharged 210-horsepower 301-inch (4.9-liter) V-8 was new this year. Turbo models also featured a specific hood with an offset scoop. **5.** The Pontiac Grand Prix was little changed. Three models were offered: base, luxury LJ, and sporty SJ. Base and LJ models had a 231-inch V-6 standard. The 301 V-8 was standard on the SJ, except in California where a 305 V-8 was included. **6.** This Firebird Turbo Trans Am is unusual because it does not have the very popular "T-Top" roof option. A 3-speed automatic transmission was standard on all Trans Am models.

6

1. Electra Limited entered this year with few changes, but Buick's traditional front fender "ventiports" were eliminated. **2.** LeSabre Limited had a new grille and revised taillights. Base price was $8101. **3.** This Electra Estate Wagon has the optional 5.7-liter diesel V-8 engine. **4.** This Buick Regal Sport Coupe shows off this year's handsome restyling. A turbocharged 3.8-liter V-6 engine was standard on Sport Coupe. **5.** Buick Century was only available with this notchback four-door sedan body. **6.** Unique smoked taillight lenses were standard on the Skylark Sport Coupe. **7.** Eldorado Biarritz had a new grille and Cadillac's short-lived V-8-6-4 engine. Total Eldorado production for the year was 60,643. **8.** Chevrolet's Camaro Berlinetta was easily identified by the chrome grille and standard wire wheel covers. **9.** This was the final year for the second-generation Camaro, introduced in 1970. This Z28 had a 165-hp 305-inch V-8 standard. A 175-hp 350-inch V-8 was optional.

1

2

3

4

5

6

1. Chevrolet Corvette lost about 100 pounds this year, the result of thinner door glass and a new plastic mono-leaf rear spring. Base price was $15,248. **2.** All Malibus received a new grille for 1981, while sedans also enjoyed a revised roofline. **3.** GM's 350-inch diesel V-8 was now available on all full-size Chevrolet models, including this Caprice Classic. **4.** Monte Carlos were restyled with an eye toward better aerodynamics. **5.** The Citation coupe was dropped, so the X-11 package was now only offered on the hatch-back. **6.** Chevy added GM's Computer Command Control electronic engine management system to the Chevette's 1.6-liter four-cylinder engine. It was still pretty slow.

1981

1. Oldsmobile Ninety-Eight Regency buyers could choose from three engines. A 4.1-liter V-6 was standard, with 5.0-liter gas and 5.7-liter (350-inch) diesel V-8 engines optional. All engines were mated to a standard four-speed automatic transmission. The diesel engine offered EPA estimates of 21 mpg city and 33 mpg highway. **2.** The subtle spoiler stamped into the trunklid was designed to improve fuel economy. An Oldsmobile advertisement described the Ninety-Eight Regency as "A beautiful way to experience luxury and acknowledge the realities of today." **3.** Toronados were basically unchanged, but Oldsmobile was able to reduce curb weight by 147 pounds. Base price was now $12,148. Production totaled 42,604. **4.** The standard Toronado engine was the 4.1-liter V-6 teamed with a three-speed automatic transmission. The 5.0 gas and 5.7 diesel engines were optional. **5.** Cutlass coupes had attractive new styling. They were available in Supreme, Supreme Brougham, and Calais versions. Shown is a Cutlass Calais with a base price of $8004. Calais was the most expensive Cutlass coupe and also the least popular with production of just 4105. Total Cutlass coupe sales this year: 285,835.

1

2

3

4

5

1

1. Cutlass Cruiser Brougham received this new grille with quad headlights. Buyers had three upholstery choices at no extra cost: all vinyl, all fabric, or a combination of fabric in front and vinyl in the back. 2. The Oldsmobile SportOmega was a $669 option package for base coupes. The front fenders were molded from plastic using a new process. Production totaled only 696 units, all

2

3

4

white with orange and red stripes. 3. Now in their second year and selling well, Omega sedans were little changed. 4. This Omega Brougham sedan has the optional vinyl top and a base price of $6855. 5. The Pontiac Firebird's base engine was a 110-horse 3.8-liter V-6. 6. The Pontiac Grand Prix was treated to new body styling. Base price for this LJ was $7803. 7. This Firebird Trans Am has the base 150-horse 4.9-liter V-8 engine. The 200-hp turbocharged 4.9-liter V-8 was optional. Trans Am production was 33,493 for 1981.

5

6

7

1. Regal was now Buick's only rear-wheel-drive midsize offering. Coupes, like this Limited, were little changed. Sedan and station wagon models were new additions to the lineup.
2. Buick Regal Estate Wagon production totaled 14,732 for the year. 3. Base price of the Regal Limited sedan was $9364. 4. A Regal Grand National package was offered for the first time. The first Grand National was powered by a 125-horsepower 4.1-liter V-6. 5. Buyers could choose a 5.7 diesel V-8 engine for their Electra Estate Wagon. 6. This Skylark Limited sedan displays this year's new front-end styling. 7. Buick's Century was completely redesigned, riding now on GM's A-body front-drive chassis. Shown is the Century Limited sedan with the optional 4.3-liter diesel V-6.
8. Century was also available as a two-door coupe. 9. Riviera was little changed, but Buick made news midyear with the announcement of a convertible version of its big coupe.
10. This Cadillac Seville Elegante has the optional 5.7-liter diesel V-8. Prices started at $23,433.

1. Like most of this year's Cadillac models, the Fleetwood Brougham coupe had a new standard engine, the HT4100. The small 4.1-liter V-8 featured digital fuel injection and was mated to a four-speed automatic transmission. **2.** Driving enthusiasts welcomed the sporty Eldorado Touring Coupe. The only available color combination was Silver with a gray leather interior. **3.** Cimarron was Cadillac's version of GM's new J-body front-drive subcompact. Unfortunately, Caddy styling tweaks did little to hide its economy-car origins. **4.** Chevy's "J-car" offering was the Cavalier. This CL wagon was the most expensive model, starting at $8452. **5.** The sporty Cavalier hatchback coupe had a unique sloped nose. **6.** Cavalier was offered in four body styles. All were powered by an 88-horsepower 1.8-liter four-cylinder engine. Total sales were just over 195,000. **7.** All Citation models now had throttle-body fuel injection instead of carburetors. Bad publicity and recall problems helped limit 1982 sales to 165,647. **8.** Chevette continued to be available in two- and four-door (shown) versions. A 1.8-liter four-cylinder diesel and low-priced Scooter models were still offered. The smallest Chevy suffered a 50-percent drop in sales, to 232,808.

1. Also new from Chevy was Celebrity, a front-drive intermediate built on the GM A-body platform. Celebrity shared Citation's wheelbase, suspension, and four-cylinder and V-6 powertrains. The notchback body was available in two- and four-door versions. **2.** Chevy's full-size line was trimmed for 1982. Impala and Caprice Landau coupes were dropped, as was the two-seat Caprice wagon. Total sales were fairly healthy at 188,189. **3.** With the new Celebrity around, Malibu models were pared to this Classic sedan and a companion wagon. **4.** Camaro was downsized, now on a 101-inch wheelbase. Shown is the Z28. Total Camaro sales for the year were 182,068. This was more than a 40-percent increase from the 1981 tally. **5.** The top engine option for the Z28 was a 165-horse 305-inch V-8 with "Cross-Fire" fuel injection. The hatch rear window lifted up for access to the usefully large cargo area. **6.** The Berlinetta proved to be the least popular Camaro model with sales of just 39,774. **7.** For the third time, Camaro was chosen to pace the Indianapolis 500. Chevrolet built 6360 replicas—all were

Z28s. **8.** As a farewell to the long-lived "shark," Chevy produced 6759 Corvette Collector Edition models with lift-up rear glass, unique wheels, and special trim. The 350-inch V-8 now had standard "Cross-Fire" fuel injection. Total Corvette sales for the year were 25,407.

1

2

3

4

5

6

7

8

1. Oldsmobile's flagship Toronado sported a revised grille. A 4.1-liter V-6 was standard at the $14,462 base price. 2. Oldsmobile's version of GM's J-body was the Firenza. Two-door hatchback coupe and four-door sedan body styles were available. This Firenza S started at $7413. 3. The full-

size Custom Cruiser wagon was powered by a standard 5.0-liter V-8, with the 5.7 diesel V-8 still optional. Production this year was 19,367 units. 4. The Oldsmobile Ninety-Eight received a new grille this year but had few other changes. This Regency Brougham sedan was the new top model. 5. The Cutlass Cruiser was now down to a single model. Prices started at $8905 with the base 3.8-liter V-6. 6. This Cutlass Supreme sedan has the optional vinyl roof and sail panel opera lamps. Two diesel options were offered, a 4.3-liter diesel V-6 and 5.7-liter V-8. 7. Oldsmobile's version of GM's front-drive A-body was the Cutlass Ciera. An available 4.3-liter diesel V-6 earned impressive EPA estimates for Ciera. With the diesel, city mileage was rated at 27 mpg, and on the highway at 44 mpg. First year sales totaled 101,320.

1-2. The big news at Pontiac was a completely redesigned Firebird. Offered in base, SE, and Trans Am models, Firebird shared most of its body with the new Chevrolet Camaro. Stylists were able to maintain a distinctive Firebird look using a low-profile nose with shallow twin grilles and pop-up

1

2

3

headlights. At the back, a full-width taillight lens maintained the look introduced for 1979. This pre-production Trans Am has T/A emblems on the front fenders instead of the Trans Am lettering found on production models. **3.** The Firebird Trans Am had a base price of $9658. **4.** J2000 was Pontiac's version of the front-drive J-Car. The sporty SE was only offered as a $7654 two door hatchback. **5.** The full-size Catalina and Bonneville were dropped from the line. In their place, Pontiac offered the Bonneville G, a rebadged LeMans sedan and wagon. Front-end styling was also new. **6.** Grand Prix got a revised grille. A 3.8-liter V-6 was standard, with 4.1 V-6 and 5.7 diesel V-8 engines optional. **7.** Pontiac 6000 was based on the corporate A-body front-drive chassis. Two- and four-door models were available in base and LE trim. This 6000 LE sedan sat five and started at $9258 with a 2.5-liter four-cylinder engine.

4

5

6

7

1

2

3

4

5

6

7

8

9

1. The 1983 Buick Riviera started at $15,238 with the base 4.1-liter V-6. Coupe sales totaled 47,153. **2.** Buick sold 1750 Riviera convertibles this year, with prices starting at $24,960. **3.** A Riviera convertible was the Official Pace Car for the 1983 Indianapolis 500. **4.** This Electra Park Avenue proudly displays Buick's traditional "ventiports" as part of the bodyside moldings. **5.** This LeSabre Estate Wagon has the optional diesel V-8 engine. **6.** The subcompact Buick Skyhawk was offered in three body styles. This coupe was joined by a four-door sedan and a four-door wagon. **7.** Buick's compact Skylark was little changed this year. **8.** The front-drive intermediate Century was now available with sporty T Type trim. All were painted silver over charcoal and had unique body trim and aluminum wheels. A 110-horsepower 3.0-liter V-6 was standard on T Types. **9.** All Buick Regal models sported new grilles. Regal Limited coupes (shown) had standard cloth-trimmed interiors with a 55/45 split front seat. Buyers could opt for the optional leather and vinyl seat trim with cloth door panels.

1. This 1983 Cadillac Fleetwood Brougham coupe has the optional 5.7-liter diesel V-8 and locking wire wheels. **2.** Cadillac's Eldorado Touring Coupe returned for 1983. Sable Black and Sonora Saddle Firemist were the only available body colors. The standard HT4100 V-8 had 10 more horsepower, bringing the total to 135. **3.** Cimarron received a few changes, including a fuel-injected 2.0-liter four-cylinder engine and foglamps mounted under the front bumper. A 5-speed manual transmission was standard with a 3-speed automatic optional. Prices started at $12,215. **4-5.** Chevy was back into

1

2

3

4

stock-car racing thanks to Monte Carlo. To better compete with the dominant Buick Regal, Chevy created the aggressively styled Monte Carlo SS. The SS featured a track-friendly wind-cheating front-end design. The package also included a heavy-duty suspension and a 5.0-liter V-8 good for 175 horsepower. First-year SS production was sluggish, with just 4,714 built.

5

1. Celebrity was virtually unchanged, but there was a welcome increase in sales, up about 50 percent to 139,239. Two-door models started at $8059 and accounted for only 19,221 orders. The popular four-door sedans started at $8209. 2. Caprice coupe and Impala wagon were dropped. Even so, Chevrolet's full-size sales were up about 17 percent to 220,795. A Caprice Classic sedan is shown. 3. Chevrolet engineers were able to extract another 10 horsepower from the "Cross-Fire" injected 305 V-8, bringing the total to 175. 4. The X-11 package for the Citation hatchback now cost $998. The lower price was a result of making the high-output V-6 a separate option available on any Citation. 5. Citation sales continued to suffer because of bad publicity over brake problems, falling 44.3 percent to 92,184. 6. This year Chevy Chevette offered a new S (for Sport) package with black moldings and red stripes.

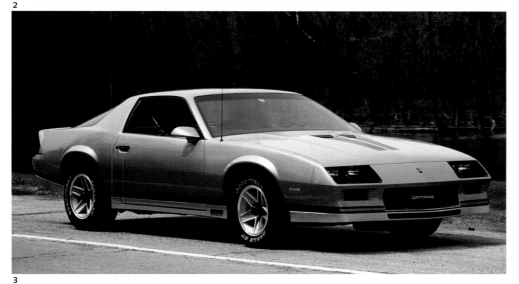

1. Oldsmobile's Toronado had few changes other than a new grille. The 4.1-liter V-6 remained standard, with 5.0 gas and 5.7 diesel V-8s optional. 2. Ninety-Eights, like this Regency Brougham, had the same engine choices as the Toronado. A 4-speed automatic was the only transmission. 3. The Delta 88 Royale coupe

started at $9202. 4. To celebrate the 15th anniversary of the first Hurst/Olds, the "executive hot rod" returned to showrooms for '83. 5. Cutlass Supreme coupes, like this Brougham, remained very popular. 6. This Omega Brougham sedan had new, more aerodynamic door mirrors. 7. Firenza now offered two station wagon models: Cruiser and, as shown here, LX Cruiser. 8. Olds dropped the base Cutlass Ciera models this year, leaving this LS the lowest priced sedan at $8892.

1. Pontiac's subcompact J-Car went from J2000 to just 2000. The 1.8-liter OHC four-cylinder engine was now standard. New this year was an LE convertible—only 626 were sold. **2.** Phoenix was offered in sporty SJ trim. A high-output 2.8-liter V-6 and aluminum wheels with Goodyear Eagle GT tires were standard on SJ. **3.** Pontiac's 1000 was a Chevy Chevette in disguise. Grille and trim changes were the main differences. **4.** The 6000 STE (Special Touring Edition) was an enthusiast-oriented four-door that represented Pontiac's challenge to sporty European sedans. The car was tastefully understated and generously equipped. STE served notice that Pontiac was once again building driver's cars. **5.** The Bonneville lost the "G" suffix used the year before. This Brougham sedan started at $9399. **6.** Pontiac Grand Prix was little changed this year, but a gasoline-powered V-8 option returned. The 305-cid engine put out 150 horsepower. **7.** Though the Firebird Trans Am looked little-changed on the outside, a new five-speed manual transmission was a welcome addition.

1. For 1984, Buick Riviera benefited from minor styling changes including new taillights. **2.** This convertible shows off Riviera's new grille. Convertible production was only 500 units, due in part to a $25,832 base price. **3.** Buick only offered one full-size wagon this year, the Electra Estate Wagon. The woodgrain trim on the sides was standard. **4.** Buick's fullsize LeSabre models, like this Custom sedan, had new grille and taillight styling this year. **5.** After a one-year hiatus, a Grand National package was once again available for the Regal T Type. Looking sinister with its all-black exterior, the "GN" was powered by a turbocharged 3.8-liter V-6, now good for 200 horsepower. **6.** Regal Coupes, like this Limited, had a new grille and headlight bezels. **7.** Buick dropped the Regal wagon, but sedans were still offered. This Limited started at $10,263.

1. Returning for '84 was the Century T Type in coupe and sedan body styles. 2. Century was now available as a station wagon, in Custom or Estate trim. Seating for six was standard, but an optional rear-facing third seat increased seating capacity to eight. 3. Buick's smallest wagon was the Skyhawk; this Limited had a base price of $8379. 4. Body-color side moldings were one of the few changes Cadillac made to this year's Coupe de Ville. 5. Fleetwood Brougham coupes got a restyled vinyl top and smaller rear quarter windows. 6. Eldorado went topless for the first time since 1976. This Biarritz convertible started at a lofty $31,286. 7. This Seville has the optional Full Cabriolet Roof. This simulated convertible roof was available in Black, Dark Blue, Dark Briar Brown, and White. Cadillac advertising claimed the roof brought "an added look of distinction."

1. The big news at Chevrolet was the first fully redesigned Corvette since 1968. It arrived during the spring of 1983. 2. The 5.7-liter V-8 with "Cross-Fire" fuel injection now had 205 horsepower. Base price was $23,360. 3. T-tops gave way to a single liftoff roof panel or an all-new tilt-up glass hatch. 4. Camaro Z28's "Cross-Fire" injection was gone, but available horsepower still climbed 25, to 190. 5. Monte Carlo SS could be had in any color a buyer wanted, as long as it was white or dark blue. 6. A 5.0-liter V-8 was standard in the Chevrolet Caprice Classic wagon. The V-8 was available in other Impalas and Caprices, which came standard with a 3.8-liter V-6.

1. Chevrolet's intermediate Celebrity was now available with a Eurosport package that included a firmer suspension and a high-output V-6. 2. The Cavalier convertible was only offered with sporty Type 10 trim. 3. Chevy renamed its compact the Citation II, even though little was new. 4. Tradition held true: Oldsmobile treated the Delta 88 to yet another new grille. 5. Cutlass Ciera was now available in handy wagon guise. 6. Oldsmobile's subcompact Firenza enjoyed new front-end styling. This sedan has the optional ES package that included copious black trim. 7. Save for a revised grille, Toronado was unchanged.

1

2

1. Pontiac Fiero was one of the most exciting cars of the year. Its proper name, Fiero 2M4, described it nicely: two seats, mid-engine, four cylinders. Fiero had a full independent suspension, four-wheel disc brakes, and a plastic body comprised of panels attached to a steel space frame. **2.** Performance from the standard 2.5-liter overhead-valve four didn't live up to Fiero's good looks, even with the standard four-speed manual transmission. Sales were strong, however, with buyers snapping up 136,840 of the little two-seaters. **3.** This Firebird Trans Am has the optional aero package. A five-speed manual transmission was now standard on the T/A. **4.** Consumer Guide®'s auto editors were able to test this Pontiac 6000 STE with the new electronic instrument panel and four-wheel disc brakes. They were modestly impressed. **5.** Pontiac changed the name of their subcompact again, now becoming 2000 Sunbird. The standard engine on this S/E hatchback was a turbocharged 1.8-liter four with 150 horsepower. Base price was $9489. **6.** Pontiac's full-size Parisienne returned for its second year with few changes. The sedan came in base and Brougham models. For those so inclined, a base wagon was also available.

3

4

5

6

1

2

3

1. 1985 brought a second wave of downsizing. Slimmed-down C-body cars included Buick's Electra. The new Electra featured front-wheel drive and was about two feet shorter and 600 pounds lighter than its rear-drive predecessor.
2. Base price for the Electra Park Avenue sedan was $16,240. 3. Electra coupes, like this Park Avenue, were not nearly as popular as the sedans. 4. LeSabre remained rear-drive. 5. Though the Electra sedan was downsized, the Electra Estate Wagon remained large and rear-drive.
6. Riviera convertible sales remained sluggish, with only 400 sold for 1985. 7. No more sedans. This year all Regals, like this Limited, were coupes.
8. Century T Type now had a standard 125-horse 3.8-liter V-6. 9. The Skyhawk Custom coupe started at $7365.
10. Buick's version of the new GM N-body was the Somerset Regal. The Oldsmobile Cutlass Calais and Pontiac Grand Am were mechanically similar.

4

5

6

7

8

9

10

1

2

3

1. Cadillac used GM's front-drive C-body for the new Fleetwood. Power came from a 4.1-liter V-8 mated to a four-speed automatic transmission. **2.** Consumer Guide® found the new Fleetwood to be pleasant to drive, manageable in city traffic, and sumptuously appointed. On the downside, passenger space was down substantially compared with larger, rear-drive Caddies. **3.** De Ville models also switched to front-drive. Sedan and coupe models were available. A Coupe de Ville like this one started at $17,990. **4.** Seville saw few changes for 1985, the last year for this body. **5.** Chevrolet added Tuned Port Injection to the Corvette's 5.7-liter V-8. The switch brought 25 horsepower, for a total of 230. Corvettes also benefited from revised damping for improved ride comfort. **6.** Camaro's new top dog was the IROC-Z, meaning a immediated demotion for Z28. An available Tuned Port 5.0-liter V-8 produced a healthy 215 horsepower. Lesser Camaros made do with as little as a 2.5-liter four-cylinder engine.

4

5

6

1

2

4

5

6

7

8

1. The Monte Carlo SS was now available in more colors: white, maroon, silver, and black. Chevy sweetened the pot a little more with better-quality upholstery and revised exterior graphics. **2.** All full-size Chevrolet sedans, like this Caprice Classic, had a new 4.3-liter V-6 standard. **3.** Wagons, like this Caprice Estate, came only with a 5.0-liter V-8. **4.** The Eurosport package improved the Celebrity's ride and handling. **5.** The Isuzu-built Chevy Spectrum subcompact came as either a two-door hatch or four-door sedan. It was initially available in only 16 eastern U.S. states. **6.** Chevy Sprint was built in Japan by Suzuki. The $4949 base price included a 1.0-liter 3-cylinder engine. Like the Spectrum, early sales were limited to a handful of "launch" states. **7.** The subcompact Nova was based on Toyota's Corolla. It was built at GM and Toyota's joint-venture NUMMI plant in California. **8.** Citation was in its last year. This is an X-11 hatch.

1

1. The Oldsmobile Ninety-Eight was now riding on the new front-drive C-body chassis. Curb weight was down about 900 pounds. The landau vinyl roof was standard on this Regency Brougham Coupe.
2. Regency Broughams, like this sedan, had a standard 3.8-liter V-6. A 3.0-liter V-6 was standard on Regencys. 3. This one-off convertible version of the new N-body Calais served as the Official Pace Car of the 1985 Indianapolis 500.
4. The popular Cutlass Supreme Coupe was little changed beyond the expected new grille. Base price was $9797. 5. The Firenza LX Sedan started at $8255.
6. This Toronado has the optional Caliente package, 7342 Toros came so equipped.
7. The $14,331 Delta 88 Royale Brougham LS (Luxury Sedan) was Oldsmobile's top-shelf rear-drive sedan. Delta 88s would switch to front-drive for 1986. 8. This $10,488 Delta 88 Royale coupe had different grilles and unique back-up lamps to visually separate them from the more expensive Broughams. 9. The Custom Cruiser station wagon used the same grille design as the Delta 88 Royale. Total production for 1985 was 22,889.

2

3

4

5

6

7

8

9

1

2

3

4

5

6

1. Pontiac revived the Grand Am name for its version of the GM N-body. Only two-door coupes were offered, in base and LE (front) trim. 2. This Bonneville Brougham sedan started at $10,280. A 110-horse 3.8-liter V-6 remained standard this year. A 5.0-liter V-8 with 165 horsepower was optional. 3. Parisienne sedans gained added styling distinction this year by reverting to the rear-end sheetmetal last seen on the 1980–81 Bonneville. A new 130-horse 4.3-liter V-6 replaced the 3.8 as the standard engine. 4. Pontiac's personal-luxury Grand Prix saw few changes this year beyond a revised grille and tweaked taillights. This LE coupe has the optional removable glass hatch roof. 5. Pontiac offered the 6000 wagon in base (shown) and LE versions. There was seating for up to eight with the available rear facing seat. Base price for the 6000 wagon was $9435. 6. The big news for Fiero was an available 140-horsepower 2.8-liter V-6 that was standard in the new GT (shown) and could be had on the Sport Coupe and SE. The V-6 used an intake system designed specifically for the Fiero, and was available with either a 4-speed manual or 3-speed automatic transmission. 7. Pontiac's Firebird Trans Am enjoyed more aerodynamic styling with a revised lower-body "aero" kit, a vented hood, and a larger rear spoiler.

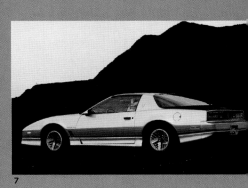

7

1

1. Buick introduced a down-sized Riviera for 1996. The new model shrank by 19 inches in length and lost 550 pounds. Styling, unfortunately, too closely resembled the much cheaper N-body Somerset. Buyers stayed away in droves, resulting in a 70 percent drop in sales. 2. LeSabre finally switched to front drive, losing 22 inches of length and more than 400 pounds in the process. The Limited coupe is shown here. 3. The Electra T Type tallied just 5,816 sales. 4. Skyhawk T Type was now available as a hatchback. All two-doors, save the Custom, had new front-end styling with concealed headlights. 5. With the X-body gone, Buick shifted the Skylark name to a four-door version of the Somerset. 6. An intercooler brought new muscle to the Regal T Type's turbocharged V-6. The engine was now good for 235 horsepower, a gain of 35. 7. Cadillac Coupe de Villes and Sedan de Villes (shown) added a new Touring package that included firmer suspension tuning, aluminum wheels, fog lights, a rear spoiler, and special trim. 8. The new year brought downsized Seville (shown) and Eldorado models. They lost their distinctive styling, and sales dropped sharply.

2

3

4

5

6

7

8

1. Chevrolet offered a Corvette convertible for the first time since 1975. Since a Corvette paced Indy this year, Chevy made every 'Vette ragtop a pace car replica. **2.** All Corvettes now had standard antilock brakes. **3.** The top engine option for the Camaro IROC-Z was a 215-horse 5.0-liter V-8. **4.** Chevy showed a Spectrum convertible at a press preview, but it never entered production. **5.** This Celebrity Classic displays the new front styling that came as part of a mild facelift. **6.** New RS models joined the Cavalier lineup, including this $12,530 convertible. **7.** Chevy dropped the Impala name, making all full-size models Caprices, like this plush Classic Brougham. **8.** Chevy built these "glass-back" Monte Carlo SS Aerocoupes so the slippery shape could be used for stock-car racing. Only 200 were made this year.

1. The Oldsmobile Delta 88 moved to the front-drive H-body shared with the Buick LeSabre. A 3.0-liter V-6 was standard with a 3.8 V-6 optional. Consumer Guide® liked the more manageable size and responsive road manners of the downsized cars, but they didn't care for the $1200-$1500 price increase. This Royale Brougham sedan started at $13,461. 2. This Delta 88 Royale Brougham shows off the coupe's sloped roofline. Like the comparable sedan, base price was $13,461. Delta 88 buyers wildly preferred the sedan, snapping up 200,000 of the four-doors, compared to just under 38,000 coupes. 3. Introduced in 1985, the Ninety-Eight Regency Brougham coupe was little-changed beyond the obligatory new grille pattern. 4. All Ninety-Eight models, including this Regency Brougham sedan,

1

2

3

4

now offered antilock brakes. 5. Cutlass Ciera shoppers found few changes beyond a new grille. This early two-door has the original notchback-style roof; midyear it was replaced with a new design that had a sloped rear window. Cutlass Ciera sales totaled 352,956. The most-popular single model was the LS sedan, with sales of 144,466.

5

1

2

3

4

5

6

7

8

1. The Oldsmobile Toronado marked its 20th birthday by being downsized for a second time. The new car was 18 inches shorter and 550 pounds lighter than the 1979–85 design. **2.** The only available engine for Toronado was a 3.8-liter V-6, but it had 10 more horsepower than the previous year's 5.0-liter V-8. Customers didn't embrace the new design, and sales fell to 15,924 from 42,185 in 1985. **3.** Calais could now be had in GT coupe guise that included composite headlights, a ground effects kit, and 14-inch Goodyear Eagle GT tires on aluminum wheels. **4.** A Calais four-door was new this year. **5.** The Oldsmobile Cutlass Salon coupe—and its high-performance 4-4-2 variant—faced the year with new aerodynamic composite headlights. **6-7.** Pontiac added a sporty new Sunbird GT model, available as a sedan, coupe, convertible (right) or hatchback (left). A turbocharged 1.8-liter four came standard. **8.** Firebird Trans Am was largely unchanged.

1

2

3

4

5

6

7

1. A Pontiac 6000 S/E wagon was added midyear. Production was only 1308. **2.** The 6000 STE received a new grille with aerodynamic composite headlights. **3.** Grand Am shoppers had a sporty new SE model to consider; it included a front air dam, extended lower body panels, and composite headlights. **4.** Like its N-body cousins from Buick and Oldsmobile, Grand Am was now available with four doors. **5.** The Pontiac 1000 was in its last year. Three-door and five-door hatchbacks were available. Base price of this five-door model: $5969. **6.** The big Parisienne was still available in sedan and station wagon guise. This Brougham sedan had a base price of $11,949. **7.** To better compete in stock car races with Chevy's slippery Monte Carlo SS, Pontiac built 200 Grand Prix 2+2 coupes. The wind-cheating fascia, sloping rear window, and rear spoiler were unique to this model. **8.** The Fiero GT returned midyear with restyled rear flanks and "flying buttress" roofline. The GT boasted a 140-horsepower V-6.

8

1. Buick Electra Park Avenue was freshened with flush-mounted composite headlights. Inside, a new analog gauge cluster could be ordered in lieu of the standard digital display. **2.** A new LeSabre T Type coupe included dual exhaust, a black-and-gray interior with a center console, blackout exterior trim, a front air dam, and a rear spoiler. **3.** The Riviera T Type was unchanged except for the price: $22,181. **4.** Buick sold 547 limited edition GNX models (built by contractor ASC), based on the Regal Grand National. The turbocharged and intercooled 3.8-liter V-6 produced 276 horsepower. Among other upgrades were flared fenders, front fender vents, and unique cast-aluminum wheels. Car magazines reported 0-60-mph times under six seconds and quarter-mile runs of about 14.5 seconds—Corvette territory. **5.** A small power bump brought the standard Grand National to 245 horsepower. Production reached 20,441. **6.** The Century Limited Estate Wagon started at $11,998. **7.** The Buick Skylark sedan and its two-door coupe companion, the Somerset, got an updated "Tech IV" base engine. **8.** Good-bye carburetor. The 2.0-liter engine in Skyhawks—including this Custom sedan—was now fuel injected.

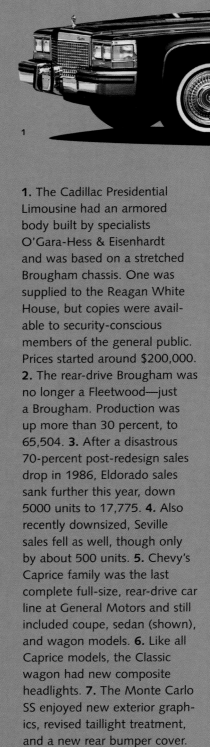

1

2

1. The Cadillac Presidential Limousine had an armored body built by specialists O'Gara-Hess & Eisenhardt and was based on a stretched Brougham chassis. One was supplied to the Reagan White House, but copies were available to security-conscious members of the general public. Prices started around $200,000. 2. The rear-drive Brougham was no longer a Fleetwood—just a Brougham. Production was up more than 30 percent, to 65,504. 3. After a disastrous 70-percent post-redesign sales drop in 1986, Eldorado sales sank further this year, down 5000 units to 17,775. 4. Also recently downsized, Seville sales fell as well, though only by about 500 units. 5. Chevy's Caprice family was the last complete full-size, rear-drive car line at General Motors and still included coupe, sedan (shown), and wagon models. 6. Like all Caprice models, the Classic wagon had new composite headlights. 7. The Monte Carlo SS enjoyed new exterior graphics, revised taillight treatment, and a new rear bumper cover. 8. In its second (and last) year, Monte Carlo SS Aerocoupe sales were up, now 6052. 9. Monte Carlo was now without a base model, sporting just SS and LS variants. A 3.8-liter V-6 was standard on LS models.

3

4

5

6

7

8

9

1. Corvettes found another ten horsepower thanks to roller-type valve lifters and a revised exhaust system. Coupe and convertible (shown) models remained available. **2.** Chevy teamed with converter ASC to offer a factory-approved convertible conversion of the Camaro. Offered in all trim levels, production was only 1007 units. **3.** Buyers in Southern California were offered the Camaro RS, in effect a V-6-powered Z28. **4.** Eurosport VR, a $3550 cosmetic package, was offered on Celebrity sedans (shown) and wagons. **5.** Cavalier wagons were still offered on the base, CS, or the sporty RS model shown here. **6.** Cavalier Z24 again offered V-6 power. **7.** This was the last full year for Chevy's half truck/half car El Camino. **8.** Chevy produced 8072 1987 Beretta models like this GT for rental fleets. Public sales started in early 1987, but the cars were marketed as 1988 models.

1. After a very disappointing 1986, Oldsmobile Toronado sales fell a little more this year, to 15,040. **2.** Calais got an optional GT package for coupes and sedans (shown). The GT package included "aero look" rocker panel extensions, two-tone paint, a special grille, and full analog instrumentation. **3.** The Cutlass Cruiser Brougham featured standard composite halogen headlights. **4.** Oldsmobile still offered a 4-4-2 package for the rear-drive Cutlass Supreme coupe. The option included 5.0-liter V-8 good for

170 horsepower and an Olds claimed 0-60-mph time of 9.5 seconds. **5.** This Ninety-Eight Regency Brougham coupe has the optional Grande interior package that featured leather seats with pigskin inserts, a custom storage console, and pigskin trimmed door panels. **6.** Pontiac's Grand Prix was largely unchanged for what would prove to be its last year with rear drive. This Brougham started at $12,519 and saw sales of only 1717 units. **7.** This Pontiac 6000 S/E had a standard "Generation II" 2.8 V-6 with 135 horsepower. **8.** Pontiac replaced last year's intermediate Bonneville and the full-size Parisienne with a new front-drive Bonneville based on GM's H-body platform. This LE started at $14,866.

1

2

3

4

1. Pontiac introduced a GTA package aimed at those seeking the "ultimate" Trans Am. A 210-horsepower 5.7-liter Tuned Port V-8, cross-lace aluminum wheels, and 4-wheel disc brakes were part of the package.
2. The Formula package added some kick to base Firebirds. A carbureted 5.0-liter V-8 was standard, and Tuned Port V-8s were available. 3. Pontiac treated base and Sport Coupe Fieros to new front and rear fascias.
4. Pontiac's Grand Am SE was treated to a new analog instrument cluster with tachometer. Plus, the steering wheel, shift knob, and parking brake lever were now leather-wrapped.
5. The Sunbird GT convertible started at $15,569.

5

1. New, and for 1988 only, the Buick LeSabre Olympic Edition sedan had special gold trim and badges. 2. Like all Electras, this T Type sedan had a new standard engine. The "3800" was a heavily revised 3.8-liter V-6 that GM said was smoother, quieter, and more power-

1

2

ful. Horsepower was up 15 to 165. 3. Regal was all-new this year, and the first version of GM's front-drive "W-body" to appear in showrooms. Initially only two-door coupes were offered. A 125-horse-power 2.8-liter V-6 mated to a four-speed automatic was standard. This Limited started at $12,782. 4. Riviera received the new "3800" engine as standard equipment. A special hood ornament and dash-board trim plate were added to help celebrate the Riv's 25th anniversary. 5. Brand new for 1988, Reatta was a two-seat coupe based on a shortened Riviera chassis. Buick sold 4708, with prices starting at $25,000. 6. At 221 inches, the Cadillac Brougham sedan was the longest production car sold in America. 7. This Coupe de Ville has the cabriolet roof. A new 4.5-liter V-8 was stan-dard. With 155 horsepower, the new V-8 trumped the out-going 4.1-liter engine by 25. 8. Caddy's popular Sedan de Ville now started at $23,404.

3

4

5

6

7

8

1

2

3

4

5

6

1. Looking for some show-room presence, the Eldorado received some dramatic styling updates: The rear fenders were stretched three inches and squared off, new vertical taillights and a revised bumper were added, and the rear roof pillars were reshaped. Up front, a new grille, a "power dome" hood, and edgier front fenders were implemented. 2. Seville was restyled too, though just up front. Like the Eldorado, Seville had a new 4.5-liter V-8 standard. 3. Cimarron was in its last year. Sales slid to 6454. 4. Chevy offered a 35th Anniversary package for Corvette coupes. Models so equipped were easy to spot, with their all-white lower bodies and black tops. 5. This Corvette has new-design standard 16-inch wheels. 6. Camaro lost its Z28 and LT models, leaving just the IROC-Z (left) and base Sport Coupe. Both models were available in coupe and convertible body styles.

1. A formal-look "landau" roof remained a hallmark of the top-line caprice Classic Brougham LS sedan. 2. The Isuzu-built Spectrum Turbo was available only as a four-door sedan. The turbocharged 1.5-liter four was good for 110 horsepower. 3. The popular compact Cavalier enjoyed its first major facelift this year. Besides a new fascia, the rounded front end included a new grille, bumper, fenders, hood, and composite headlights. In back, a different deck lid, end panel, bumper, and taillights completed the update. The convertible was now offered only in sporty Z24 trim. 4. The two-door Beretta (front) and four-door Corsica compacts were underskin twins. Both were built on General Motors' front-drive "L-body" platform, which borrowed heavily from the departed X-cars and GM's N-body compact platform that hosted the Pontiac Grand Am. The new cars went on sale to the public in March 1987 (they had seen rental fleet action earlier). In their extended debut season, 283,170 Berettas and 300,136 Corsicas found buyers. 5. Chevy offered a sporty GTU package, commemorating Beretta's IMSA Championship. The option package included lower-body skirts, a rear spoiler, and 16 inch wheels and tires.

1

1. The all-new front-drive W-body Cutlass Supreme coupe debuted in spring 1988. It was available in base, SL, or, as shown here, sporty International Series trim. The only engine was a 2.8-liter V-6. 2. Olds added an International Series to the Cutlass Ciera line-up; it was available in coupe or sedan guise. 3. Oldsmobile now called its N-body compact the Cutlass Calais. 4. Firenza

2

3

4

5

entered its last year with new front and rear styling and just one trim level. 5. A standard "3800" engine and revised front-end styling were among the few Toronado changes. 6. The Ninety-Eight line lost its two-door body. The surviving four-door is shown here in Regency trim. 7. Olds added "electronic spark control" to the Custom Cruiser wagon. 8. Pontiac now offered the Oldsmobile-developed 2.3-liter Quad 4 engine on all Grand Am models. 9. This Sunbird GT shows off the new coupe roofline it shares with Chevy's Cavalier. 10. Pontiac added a "little bit of Seoul" with the Opel-designed LeMans, built in South Korea by Daewoo.

6

7

8

9

10

1. Pontiac introduced its new front-drive "W-body" Grand Prix for 1988. Pontiac boasted that the GP's .299 drag coefficient made it one of the most aerodynamic production cars available. *Motor Trend* named it 1988 Car of the Year. The award is shown on the hood of this Grand Prix SE. 2. To the Bonneville line a sporty new SSE model was added; Pontiac billed it as having "European touring sedan flair." The SSE had a more aggressive look than lesser Bonnevilles thanks to aero ground-effects pieces, 16-inch body-color cast-aluminum wheels, a deck lid spoiler, and fog lights. It also had sport suspension, antilock brakes, electronic ride control, and new "3800" V-6. 3. The 6000 STE started at $18,699. Late in the model year, Pontiac added a 6000 STE AWD, with all-wheel drive, a 3.1-liter V-6, and independent rear suspension. 4. A new "notchback" body was exclusive to the Trans Am GTA. The notchbacks included a body-color hatch with a much smaller and nearly vertical rear window. The original glass hatch was still available for GTA. 5. A step below the GTA was the "regular" Trans Am. The standard T/A engine was a 170-horsepower 5.0-liter V-8. Optional were a 190-horse 5.0-liter and a 225-horse 5.7. Both V-8s boasted Tuned Port fuel injection. 6. Fiero was treated to a revised suspension this year. This new Formula model included a 2.8-liter V-6 and WS6 performance suspension. 7. The top-dog Fiero GT was also party to the suspension upgrades. Exclusive to GT were new monochromatic color schemes. Fiero was discontinued after this year.

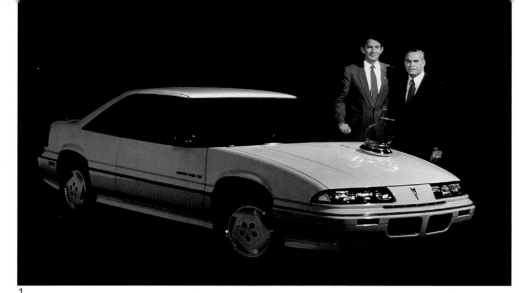

1

2

3

4

5

6

7

1. Buick still offered the sporty two-door LeSabre T Type for 1989. **2.** The Electra Park Avenue was little changed this year. A new remote keyless entry system was offered that used radio-frequency technology instead of the infrared signal used by many competitors. **3.** Several new options arrived for Regal this year, including antilock brakes, a power sunroof, and keyless entry. **4.** Buick attempted to rekindle interest in the slow-selling Riviera. By adding 11 inches to its overall length, Buick hoped to recapture the look of more classic predecessors. **5.** Reatta was largely unchanged for its second year. **6.** Skyhawk was in its final season. This coupe has the optional S/E package. **7.** Skylark was treated to a new Luxury Edition package that included a formal vinyl roof. **8.** Century models, like this Estate Wagon, had a new top engine: a 160-horsepower "3300" V-6. Also new was Buick's Dynaride suspension. **9.** Century models were restyled with new roof pillars, a rounded rear window, a new deck lid, and full-width taillights. Shown is a Custom coupe.

1. Cadillac substantially updated the Allanté this year, giving it a larger engine, variable-assist power steering, automatically adjusting shock absorbers, and larger tires. Base price: $57,183, including a $650 Gas Guzzler Tax. 2. This Allanté sports the standard removable hardtop. 3. New standard Eldorado features included 6-way power front seats, a stereo cassette player with graphic equalizer, and "pass-key" theft-deterrent system. 4. The big Brougham got a new grille and more standard features. 5. Cadillac brought back the Fleetwood Coupe after a two-year absence. A restyling added 5.8 inches to the overall length of De Ville and Fleetwood coupes. Rear fender skirts were standard on Fleetwoods. 6. Sedan de Ville (shown) and Fleetwood sedans enjoyed a 3-inch wheelbase stretch and a facelift that added 8.8 inches in overall length. 7. Standard maple wood trim was new for Seville.

1. Chevrolet made GM's "pass-key" theft-deterrent system standard on all Camaro models. IROC-Zs came with a 170-horse V-8. There were two optional Tuned Port V-8s: a 220-horse 5.0-liter and a 230-horse 5.7. An available performance exhaust system provided a 10-horsepower boost for either optional V-8. 2. All Caprice models now had standard V-8 engines and air conditioning. This top-of-the-line Caprice Classic Brougham LS started at $16,835. 3. Celebrity lost its slow-selling coupe and manual transmission. The optional Eurosport package for sedans (shown) and wagons was still available. 4. New to the Corsica line was a sporty LTZ model with a standard V-6, sport suspension, high-performance tires, and 15-inch aluminum wheels. 5. This Cavalier Z24 convertible now had standard gas-charged shocks. All Cavaliers adopted rear shoulder belts for 1989. 6. The Cutlass Supreme International Series now had standard air conditioning and was offered with optional anti-lock brakes. 7-8. New to show-rooms this year was a sporty Cutlass Calais International Series with new front and side ground-effects body trim, monochromatic paint, fog lights, and 16-inch tires. Late in the year, a 185-horse "HO Quad Four" became optional.

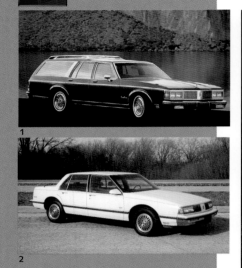

1

2

3

4

5

6

7

1. Oldsmobile added 3-point shoulder belts for the rear outboard seating positions; otherwise the Custom Crusier wagon was unchanged. **2.** The "Delta" name, used since 1965 on 88 models, was killed, reducing the moniker to "88 Royale" for the full-size, front-drive family car. Coupe and sedan (shown) body styles remained available. **3.** The Oldsmobile Toronado was now available with a Visual Information Center, a $1295 option that used a touch screen color cathode ray tube (similar to the one found on Buick Riviera) for some radio and climate control functions. **4.** Steering-wheel-mounted radio controls and antilock brakes were now optional on the Bonneville LE. **5.** All Pontiac Bonneville models, including this SE, now had a standard 165-horse 3.8 V-6. **6.** Pontiac offered a limited-edition Turbo Grand Prix, developed in conjunction with ASC/McLaren. It was powered by a 200-horsepower 3.1 V-6 and finished in monochrome red or black. Other features unique to the Turbo were a vented hood, fender flares, and specific lower-body panels. **7.** The Pontiac 6000 S/E looked more like an STE than ever before.

1

2

3

4

5

1. Pontiac Grand Ams, like this LE 2-door, had revamped front and rear styling and more powerful engines. The base 2.5-liter four gained 12 horsepower for a total of 110. **2.** Grand Am SE models had a 165-horse 2.0-liter turbo four standard. The 150-horse Quad 4 was a credit option. **3.** This Sunbird GT convertible had a standard 165-horse 2.0-liter turbo four. Base price was $16,899. **4.** Trans Am GTA buyers were still able to choose between the GTA-exclusive notchback (shown) or glass hatchback body styles. GM's "PASS-Key" theft-deterrent system was now standard on all Firebird models. **5.** Pontiac made 1555 20th Anniversary Trans Ams, basically a GTA powered by the turbocharged 3.8-liter V-6 from Buick's recently departed GNX. The result was the most-potent T/A in more than a decade, packing 250 horsepower. The anniversary T/A served duty as the Official Pace Car of the 1989 Indianapolis 500.

GM

CHAPTER TEN

1990-1999

"He that will not apply new remedies must expect new evils; for time is the greatest innovator."

—Francis Bacon

By the end of the Eighties, GM had lost more than 11 points of market share, now at about 35 percent. It might have been worse had the Japanese makers not agreed to voluntary export restrictions in 1981. By the early 1990s, though, the Japanese had found a convenient solution to those export restrictions and an answer to some Americans' distaste for foreign cars: build factories in the United States. And while the Asian makers were busy establishing themselves as American auto builders, GM, Ford, and Chrysler set to work exploiting a long neglected market opportunity: trucks.

GM faced internal problems as the 1990s began. In the early 1980s, GM had the lowest per-unit assembly costs of the Detroit Three. By the early '90s, it was the highest. Chairman Roger Smith's 1984 plan to divide the company into large car and small car factions had failed, creating confusion and raising costs, exactly the opposite of its goal. Compounding GM's financial struggle was a weakening U.S. economy.

Roger Smith did see two of his pet projects realized before his retirement in 1990. GM showed the Impact electric car at the 1990 Los Angeles Auto Show. The slippery two-seater drew such positive attention that GM announced plans to market the Impact as soon

as possible. The Impact's clean-air possibilities led California to mandate that a percentage of new-car sales in the state would have to be zero-emissions vehicles by 1998.

Smith's other pet project came to life on July 30, 1990, when the first Saturn car rolled off the assembly line at Spring Hill, Tennessee. Smith was at the wheel, and it was one of his final acts as GM Chairman. The cars went on sale in the fall as 1991 models.

Two days later, Smith was replaced as Chairman and CEO by Robert Stempel, a 57-year-old engineer and the former head of the Buick-Olds-Cadillac group. At the same time, Lloyd Reuss took over as president for Stempel. The new leadership had its plate full, as GM would go on to post a $2 billion dollar loss for the fiscal year.

On the product side, part of the problem was the drawn-out rollout of the GM10 front-drive midsize cars. The company finally added four-door sedan body styles to the Olds Cutlass Supreme and Pontiac Grand Prix lineups and introduced the first Chevrolet GM10 W-body, the Lumina. (Buick Regal would have to wait one more year for its family car.) Lumina sales were good, but it was outsold by the Ford Taurus, Honda Accord, and Toyota Camry.

Chevrolet unleashed its meanest performance monster to date in 1990 in the form of the Corvette ZR-1. The ZR-1 featured the Mercury Marine-built, dual-overhead-cam LT5 V-8. The 32-valve 5.7-liter engine made a whopping 375 horsepower that first year, and that figure jumped to 405 for 1993. Dealers were initially able to get substantially more than the $58,995 sticker price for the "King of the Hill" ZR-1, but demand faded and Chevy produced only 448 of them in each of its final three model years. Production ended in 1995 after a total of 6939 were built.

If things were bad in 1990, they got worse in 1991. Industry-wide sales were at their lowest since 1982, and GM posted a $4.5 billion loss. It was the worst loss in American corporate history, but that doesn't even tell the whole story. GM's North American operations lost $7 billion. There was even talk of bankruptcy. In the face of this dire situation, Stempel announced plans to close 21 U.S. and Canadian assembly and manufacturing facilities over the next four years, and to reduce the number of hourly and salaried employees by 74,000.

GM was hoping the new Saturn lineup could help pave the way for profitability. SC two-door coupes and SL four-door sedans were offered. Hoods, trunks, and roofs were steel, but the rest of the body panels were made of a thermoplastic polymer material. A new 1.9-liter four-cylinder engine was offered in two states of tune: an 85-horsepower single-overhead-cam unit and a dual-overhead-cam version with 123 horsepower. What really made Saturn different from its Japanese rivals was the dealership experience. Saturn adopted a no-haggle price policy and strived to deliver red-carpet service. Production capacity was limited to some 48,000 in 1991, but model year production climbed to more than 300,000 by 1997. The $3.5 billion Saturn project would turn a profit for GM in calendar 1993.

Buick got its first Roadmaster in 35 years in 1991, as GM redesigned its B-body large rear-drive cars, including the Chevy Caprice and Olds Custom Cruiser. The look was more rounded than the previous models, so much so that they were called "jelly bean" cars. Buick also redesigned its C-body flagship sedans, lengthening them eight inches and changing the name from Electra to Park Avenue.

Not happy with the pace at which management was leading a turnaround, the board of directors demoted president Lloyd Reuss in April and replaced him with John F. Smith, Jr., who had been the international boss. Board pressure also led Robert Stempel to retire November 1. He was replaced as chairman by John A. Smale, former CEO of Proctor & Gamble, and Smith was given the CEO role.

The new leadership immediately set to undoing the 1984 corporate restructuring that had divided the automotive operation into the Buick-Olds-Cadillac and Chevy-Pontiac-Canada groups. The reorganization established two new groups, North American Operations (NAO), based in Warren, Michigan, and General Motors International Operations (GMIO), based in Zurich, Switzerland. The move combined all of the passenger car divisions under NAO and reduced the number of executives at the central office. As part of the shake-up, the Midsize and Rear Drive Automotive Divisions were consolidated into the Midsize Car Division. Similarly, Cadillac Motor Car Company Engineering and Manufacturing and Flint Automotive Division were consolidated into Cadillac/Luxury Car Engineering and Manufacturing Division (CLCD).

On the product front, GM redesigned its Pontiac Grand Am, Olds Cutlass Calais, and Buick Skylark compacts for 1992, combining their N-body platform with Chevrolet's L-body (Beretta/Corsica) platform. With three cars called Cutlass, Olds realized it had watered down that name and changed the Calais to the Achieva. An Achieva SCX model replaced the Calais 442 as the line's top performer. While Grand Am thrived, Skylark continued to lose sales, and it was dropped after the 1997 model year, not to be replaced. Achieva sales were respectable in the first year at more than 80,000, but they fell off quickly and never approached Grand Am level before the car disappeared in 1999.

GM also redesigned its H-body Pontiac Bonneville, Olds 88, and Buick LeSabre for 1992, cutting the available coupe body style as Detroit aimed at more efficient interior space. Bonneville got an exciting SSEi model with the monochrome treatment and a 205-horsepower supercharged version of the 3.8-liter V-6. Buick's top-line Park Avenue was also offered with the supercharged 3.8 and was capable of an 8.0-second 0-60 sprint.

In the face of competition from the Europeans as well as new luxury makes from Japan (Acura, Infiniti, and Lexus), Cadillac released all-new versions of the Seville sedan and Eldorado coupe for 1992. The new, tauter design proved popular, and production nearly doubled from the previous year.

Camaro and Firebird, meanwhile, were redesigned for 1993. The cars still rode a 101.1-inch wheelbase, but the front suspension was redesigned, and front fenders were now plastic to reduce weight. Power for the performance models came from a 275-horsepower version of Corvette's LT1 5.7-liter V-8. The V-8 Camaro started under $17,000 and was immediately hailed as a performance bargain.

Also for 1993, the rear-drive Cadillllac Brougham gave way to a new Fleetwood based on the Chevy Caprice and Buick Roadmaster. The bigger news came under the hood of Cadillac's Allanté, Seville STS, and Eldorado ETC. The new 4.6-liter dual-overhead cam Northstar V-8 was a thoroughly modern engine that made as much as 295 horsepower.

GM's truck and SUV offerings paid off for the company in 1993.

Market-wide SUV sales rose 16.5 percent this year, leaving the Japanese makes out in the cold. An increase in the value of the yen also gave the Americans some price flexibility. Sales finally started looking up, and so did profits after several years of heavy losses. The corporation posted a profit of more than $2 billion, though North American Operations still lost money.

Profits were even bigger for 1994, a record $4.9 billion, with North American Operations having made money for the first time in five years. Then-current Chairman John Smale was also starting to implement his brand management-style marketing approach. Taken from his days at Proctor & Gamble, the brand management philosophy held that products in a given category are basically the same, so consumers choose a product based on its perceived brand image. The new system gave managers responsibility for developing product features and ad programs to match the images of their vehicles. Pontiac was the first division to adopt the approach. Brand management was just in its beginning stages at GM in 1994 but would become more important later in the decade.

Chevrolet added some spice for 1994 with the release of the Impala SS. The Caprice-based muscle car featured a 260-horsepower version of the Corvette's LT1 V-8. The car was a hit with the magazines and customers. Chevy sold 6000 that first year, despite a projection of just 4000. Sales rose to 42,000 by 1996, but that would be the end as GM killed its full-size rear-drive lineup for 1997.

At Cadillac, the De Ville was redesigned in 1994 on a larger version of the Seville's K-Special platform, and a Concours version was added as the top trim level. The cars looked like slightly smaller versions of the rear-drive Fleetwood.

GM sales outside North America exceeded three million units for the first time in 1995, as the company enjoyed another year of record profit, netting $6.9 billion. Lower incentives and lower materials costs aided the performance.

Most of the business news in 1995 came from outside the U.S. General Motors signed an agreement with Shanghai Automotive Industry Corporation (SAIC) for a joint vehicle venture and a joint venture technical development center in Shanghai, China. China was a sleeping giant at the time, but the deal would eventually pay off for GM. GM also announced plans to sell U.S.-made right-hand-drive Saturn cars in Japan through its own network of dealers starting in 1997. Due to a Japanese economic recession, however, GM gave up on the endeavor after four years and only 4324 sales.

At home, GM introduced two cars on an important new G-body platform for 1995, a reborn Buick Riviera coupe and the Oldsmobile Aurora four-door sedan. GM claimed the G-body architecture was the stiffest in its history. Aurora represented a new direction for Oldsmobile. Though the Olds had aimed for sportiness in the late 1980s, Aurora was meant to impart Oldsmobile with a European flair. Its lone engine was a 4.0-liter, 250-horsepower version of Cadillac's 4.6-liter Northstar V-8, and the car was capable of an 8.2-second 0-60 sprint. Olds built some 48,000 Auroras for that first model year, a promising number, but it quickly fell to about half that level. Riviera also sold well at first, topping 41,000 units for its extended 1995 model year. Sales declined after that, and the Riv was phased out after a small run of 1999 models.

After 13 model years, Cavalier and Sunbird were redesigned for 1995. Sunbird also changed its name to Sunfire. After five model years, Lumina received its first reskin. At this time, coupe versions were now badged with the resurrected Monte Carlo name. Though not significantly different than the last Lumina, the new model sold well at more than 240,000 units; Monte Carlo added some 93,000 sales.

GM stood mostly idle product-wise for 1996 but made a number of significant business moves. John Smith took over for John Smale as Chairman of the Board, in addition to his roles as CEO and president. The company launched a Web site this year, and merged the

Pontiac and GMC divisions to form Pontiac-GMC Division. It also purchased the Renaissance Center in Detroit to serve as its global headquarters. Profits continued, though they were down 17.2 percent to $4.96 billion for the year.

Aided by strong truck, SUV, and van sales (which now accounted for almost 50 percent of the market), GM made $6.5 billion in 1997, up 38 percent from 1996.

General Motors released the two-seat EV1 electric vehicle in December 1996. The first EV1 had a front-mounted AC induction motor that was powered by 1175 pounds of lead-acid batteries. It was capable of sprinting from 0-60 mph in about 8.0 seconds. The cars could be charged in three to four hours using 220-volt power and had a range of about 60 miles. About 650 were built for what would have been the 1997 model year. The EV1 was available only in Arizona and California and could only be leased.

GM would eventually fit the EV1 with more efficient nickel-metal-hydride batteries in 1999, which increased the driving range to about 100 miles. GM canceled the program in 2003 after California repealed its zero-emissions mandate. The majority of EV1s were eventually crushed, though a few were sent to museums and kept for internal purposes. Because the cars were leased, none were left in the hands of private owners.

After a light 1996 model year, GM unleashed a product assault for 1997. Chevrolet replaced the Corsica and Beretta with a more space-efficient Malibu sedan, and Olds got a Cutlass version as a replacement for the elderly Ciera. The Malibu was arguably a better package than the larger Lumina, and it sold more than 200,000 units most years after its short inaugural season.

Chevrolet also redesigned the Corvette for the first time since 1984. The wheelbase was 8.3 inches longer at 104.5, but overall length was only up 1.2 inches and weight was down 80 pounds. The 'Vette's LS1 5.7-liter V-8 was new, too, and output was up to 340 horsepower. The new Corvette was originally offered only as a hatchback, but a convertible arrived for '98 and a hardtop coupe was available for '99. The car was a hit with the media and customers alike. After a short introductory production year with only 9752 units built, Chevy's sports car sold comfortably more than 30,000 units a year for the remainder of the decade.

The General began redesigning its midsize cars in 1997. First up were the Buick Regal and Pontiac Grand Prix. Oldsmobile celebrated its 100th anniversary this year, but 1997 would be the final year for the W-body Cutlass Supreme. Olds also waved goodbye to the Achieva after its '97 run, and Buick redesigned the Park Avenue on the G-body platform first used for the Oldsmobile Aurora.

Cadillac responded to its dwindling market share in 1997 with a Euro-flavored entry-luxury car called Catera. An upscale version of the Opel Omega from GM's German subsidiary, the Catera was a modern-looking rear-wheel-drive sedan with a spunky 3.0-liter V-6. Sales topped 30,000 in 1998, but Catera's subtle lines were an odd fit in Cadillac dealerships and sales fell sharply until the car's demise after the 2001 model year. General Motors also introduced OnStar telematics service on Cadillacs for '97 (see sidebar on page 375).

A major strike in 1999 would give GM the impetus to make some significant changes. On June 5, UAW workers at two Flint, Michigan, plants walked off the job. The strike quickly spread, effectively shutting down GM North American vehicle production. The strikes were resolved on July 28, but not until they cost the company approximately $2.5 billion. Thanks to strong sales of full-size trucks, the company still made $3.0 billion.

The strikes paved the way for a shakeup at the top. John Smith remained Chairman and CEO, but G. Richard "Rick" Wagoner took over as president and Ron Zarrella became president of North American Operations. Zarrella was a big proponent of brand management, and in August he was a key figure in a restructuring of the North American sales and marketing operations. The move replaced marketing division-specific organizations with a single sales, service, and parts system divided into five regions in the U.S. The company also eliminated GM International Operations by combining all automotive operations worldwide into a single organization, GM Automotive Operations.

Product changes were less dramatic this year. Chevrolet's Geo line of import-flavored cars was gone for 1998. Remaining Geos, including Tracker, Prizm, and Metro, were now called Chevrolets.

GM completed its W-body redesign for '98 with the all-new Oldsmobile Intrigue. Intrigue replaced the Cutlass Supreme and was the only W-body car available with a V-6 version of Cadillac's Northstar V-8. The "Shortstar," as it was known, was a nod to technology-seeking import shoppers and a key part of the division's efforts to reinvent itself. Meanwhile, Cadillac redesigned the Seville on the G-body platform shared with Buick Park Avenue and Olds Aurora. In performance news, Camaro and Firebird adopted the Corvette's LS1 5.7-liter V-8 with an impressive 305 horsepower in base tune and 320 hp in models equipped with special option packages.

Profits were still high—at $5.7 billion in 1999—as the industry posted record sales of 16.9 million new cars and light trucks, smashing the 16,026,426 mark set in 1986. GM spun off a number of its subsidiary parts divisions into the independent Delphi Automotive Systems. In June, General Motors agreed to acquire exclusive rights to the Hummer automotive brand from AM General Corporation. Then, in December, General Motors spent $1.4 billion to acquire 20 percent equity in Fuji Heavy Industries, the manufacturer of Subaru brand vehicles. Also this year, GM and Honda Motor Company agreed that Honda would provide engines for a future North American GM vehicle, and GM's partner Isuzu would provide Honda with diesel engines for the European market. Isuzu would later provide GM with diesel engines for its light-duty pickups and medium-duty commercial vehicles.

In product news, Pontiac redesigned the Grand Am for 1999, extending the wheelbase 3.6 inches to 107. The new Grand Am still wore Pontiac's trademark lower-body cladding. Olds celebrated 50 years of the Eighty Eight with an anniversary edition in 1999, but then dropped it, much to the dismay of dealers who still wanted a full-size family car. With that, all of the traditional Olds nameplates were gone, each dying in the name of brand modernization. Olds dealers were now stocked with fresh, perhaps unfamiliar products with names like Alero, Aurora, Bravada, and Intrigue. The Alero, which was based heavily on the Grand Am, received positive reviews and sold well, but the brand continued to post losses, leading to speculation about Olds' future.

Saturn added a rear-hinged third door on the driver's side of coupes for 1999, but the cars had basically stayed the same since their release in 1991. With other struggling brands, General Motors didn't see fit to allocate resources to Saturn for product development. While the company had managed to make money mid-decade, sales started to creep downward late in the decade. It would take several more years before Saturn would receive significantly new product.

It would be unfair not to mention that Chrysler and Ford fared no better in the face of strong product from the likes of Honda, Nissan, and Toyota. Indeed, the Honda Accord and Toyota Camry had become sales juggernauts, luring customers with attractive prices and a growing reputation for long-term reliability. In retrospect, many analysts believe that the Big Three gave in too easily on the car front, distracted by the growing demand for high-profit SUVs and full-size trucks. Yet, as industry sales grew, GM's share of the pie shrank. Between 1990 and 1999, The General's market share fell from 35 percent to a little more than 30. Though trucks were making GM money, they weren't keeping customers in the fold.

—Kirk Bell

1. The Reatta convertible was the first ragtop offered by Buick since the 1982–85 Riviera. Like many other Buicks, this one was powered by GM's venerable 3.8-liter V-6, with 165 hp in this application. 2. The Regal coupe was due to get a four-door linemate for 1990, but it got delayed until '91. 3. Rivieras received an interior upgrade that included conventional switchgear instead of the previous touch-sensitive video screen. 4. Electras such as this T Type were largely unchanged for 1990, but the ritzier Park Avenue gained a new, top-end Ultra model. 5. The LeSabre benefited from a minor facelift with a new vertical-bar grille and composite headlights. 6. Skylark Custom was one step up from the "premium value" base model. Coupe (shown) and sedan versions were offered. 7. The top-line Skylark was the Luxury Edition sedan. 8. Cadillac's Brougham had standard antilock brakes for 1990. A 5.7-liter V-8 was newly optional in place of the standard 5.0.

1

2

3

4

5

6

7

8

1. This Cadillac Eldorado has the new Touring Coupe option package. Power from the standard 4.5-liter V-8 increased to 180 horsepower from 155 thanks to new multi-point fuel injection. **2.** Seville's STS option package became a full model. Like the Eldorado Touring Coupe, leather and wood interior trim was standard. **3-4.** Coupe and Sedan de Ville models profited from the same power increase to their 4.5-liter V-8s. A driver-side airbag and GM's Pass Key anti-theft system were standard. **5.** The Allanté, Cadillac's most expensive car at the time, became the first front-wheel-drive car to be equipped with traction control. Also added was a soft-top-only version that deleted the removable hardtop but came in at a lower price point. **6.** The long-awaited Chevrolet Corvette ZR-1 made its debut in 1990. This ultra-high-performance 'Vette featured a 375-horse 5.7-liter V-8 designed by Lotus (then a GM subsidiary) and built by Mercury Marine. ZR-1s were among the fastest cars in the world at the time, with 0-60 mph acceleration of about 4.5 seconds and a top speed of 180 mph. **7.** Of course, Chevy also offered "base" Corvettes with a 275-horse 5.7-liter V-8. All Corvettes had a revised interior for 1990 that had a new dashboard and a driver-side airbag. **8.** The Beretta coupe received a new sporty model, the GTZ. A 180-horsepower version of GM's Quad 4, 4-cylinder engine was standard.

1. In an attempt to attract shoppers of small import vehicles, GM established the Geo brand for 1989. Geos were sold at Chevrolet dealerships throughout North America. The entire 1990 product lineup is pictured. It included (front to back): Storm, Prizm, Metro, and Tracker. Storm was produced by Isuzu in Japan. Prizm was built at the GM/Toyota joint venture NUMMI plant in California. Metro and Tracker came from the GM/Suzuki joint venture CAMI factory in Ontario, Canada. **2.** Chevy phased out the Celebrity in favor of the new Lumina. This line was available as a two-door coupe (front), four-door sedan (center), or a minivan called the Lumina APV (rear). Coupes and sedans were offered with a 110-hp 2.5-liter four-cylinder engine or a 135-hp 3.1-liter V-6. APVs had a 120-hp version of the 3.1. The vans were unique in that they featured dent-resistant composite body panels. **3.** Every body panel except the hood was new on the 1990 Oldsmobile Toronado and Trofeo (pictured). Interior space didn't change, but the trunk grew an impressive 2.5 cubic feet. **4.** Coupe versions of the Cutlass Supreme (shown) were largely unchanged, but this midsize line gained a four-door sedan model. **5.** Cutlass Calais sedans, like the SL shown, didn't change much, but coupes received a new "4-4-2" option. Back in the 1960s, 4-4-2 designated a four-barrel carburetor, four-speed manual transmission, and dual exhaust. Calais's 4-4-2 tag meant Quad 4 (four-cylinder) engine, four valves per cylinder, and twin camshafts. **6.** Oldsmobile's Silhouette was similar to the Chevy Lumina APV.

1

2

3

4

5

6

1

2

3

4

5

6

7

1. Not one to be left out, Pontiac got its own version of GM's new-for-1990 minivans. Aside from trim and detail changes, the Trans Sport was basically identical to the Chevy Lumina APV and Olds Silhouette. **2.** The full-size, front-drive Bonneville got a few detail changes this year. All models, including the sport-themed SSE (pictured), had GM's proven 165-horse 3.8-liter V-6 engine. **3.** New to the midsize Grand Prix lineup was a four-door sedan body style, shown in STE trim. The STE had a slightly altered grille and taillights, and its standard features included high-performance tires, alloy wheels, sport suspension, anti-lock brakes, analog instrumentation, and upgraded interior. **4.** Oldsmobile's high-output, 180-horse Quad 4 engine also made an appearance in Pontiac's N-body Grand Am. It was standard equipment on the top-end SE model (pictured), and was available as a two-door coupe or four-door sedan. SE buyers could choose a 160-hp Quad 4 as a $140 credit option. **5.** The 6000 S/E became the only A-body GM vehicle to be available with all-wheel drive. This $3635 option split torque in a 60/40 front/rear distribution. **6.** Pontiac's Korean-built subcompact LeMans got a few detail changes. Aerocoupes like the one pictured started at $6599 and came with a 74-hp 1.6-liter four-cylinder engine. Transmission choices included a four- and five-speed manuals and 3-speed automatic. **7.** The Firebird benefited from some engine revisions. Base models received the 3.1-liter V-6. This Trans Am's 5.0-liter V-8 received port fuel injection, which added five or 10 horsepower depending on transmission choice.

1. Buick revived the Roadmaster name for 1991, applying it first to the Estate Wagon. Four-door sedans would follow later as early '92 models. The Estate Wagon had a 170-horse 5.0-liter V-8 engine and four-speed automatic overdrive transmission. It rode the same 115.9-inch wheelbase as the 1990 Estate Wagon but had fresh styling inside and out. **2.** The 1991 Park Avenue wore new sheetmetal on an updated front-drive chassis. At 205.2 inches, the new body was eight inches longer than the previous year's Electra/Park Avenue, despite the wheelbase remaining unchanged at 110.8 inches. This was one of the first cars with GM's new electronic automatic transmission. The transmission would shift according to signals from a computer that integrated controls for the transmission, engine, and cruise control. The only available engine was the 3.8-liter V-6. **3.** The most significant change for the 1991 Riviera was a revised 3.8-liter V-6 engine. It produced 170-hp this year, an increase of five. Antilock brakes moved to the standard features list from the options column. **4.** Reattas also benefited from the same power increase as the Riviera. The electronic automatic transmission was also updated. To facilitate quicker acceleration, all Reatta models received a shorter final-drive ratio for 1991. While it could move more quickly, Buick elected to smooth out the ride a bit by changing the tires from high-performance Goodyear Eagle GT + 4s to softer Goodyear Eagle GAs.

1

2

3

4

1

2

3

4

5

6

7

1-2. Cadillac's Seville (left) and Eldorado were slated for a 1992 redesign, but that didn't stop GM's luxury division from further updating these cars for '91. Their standard V-8 engine grew to 4.9 liters from 4.5, with horsepower increasing to 200 from 180. Standard on these models was Cadillac's Computer Command Ride (CCR) speed-dependent damping system. As vehicle speed increased, computers upped the firmness of the shock absorbers. 3. The De Ville and Fleetwood (shown) lineups also received the revised 4.9-liter V-8. The CCR damping system was standard on Fleetwoods and optional on De Villes. 4. Cadillac's Brougham received a new, Chevy-designed 5.0-liter V-8 with 170 horsepower. The optional 5.7-liter V-8 gained 10 horses to 185. 5. Chevrolet restyled the full-size, rear-drive Caprice for 1991. New "aero" styled four-door sedans and station wagons sat atop the same basic chassis used since 1977. Wheelbase remained unchanged at 115.9 inches, but the new body was longer and wider by about two inches. The sole engine was the 170-horse 5.0-liter V-8. A driver-side air-bag and antilock brakes were standard. The Caprice Classic LTZ sedan is shown. 6. Chevy's compact Cavalier was spiffed up with a subtle facelift including new front and rear fascias. Two-door coupe (pictured), four-door sedan, and four-door wagon body styles were offered. Most models had a 2.2-liter four-cylinder engine. 7. Corvettes received their first facelift since the C4 generation bowed in 1984. Base models now sported a convex tail panel and square taillights similar to the design previously reserved for the ZR-1.

1. With various state highway patrols running Ford Mustangs, Chevy countered with a Police Package Camaro, here fronting a Z28 coupe. Chevy resurrected the Z28 badge for the high-performance versions of the 1991 Camaro. **2.** The performance-oriented Lumina Z34 coupe (front) made its debut in 1991 and took its name from its dual-cam, 24-valve, 3.4-liter V-6 engine. Horsepower was 210 with the standard five-speed manual transmission and 200 with the optional four-speed automatic. A louvered hood, lower body addenda, and rear lip spoiler helped distinguish Z34s from other Luminas. **3.** Oldsmobile's Cutlass Supreme convertible was available in a single trim level, similar to the luxury SL trim on other Cutlass Supreme models. **4.** The Cutlass Supreme SL sedan could be equipped with the new 3.4-liter, dual-cam V-6. This engine was standard on the International Series and optional on all other models except the convertible. **5.** Oldsmobile's Eighty-Eight Royale Brougham was little changed, but intermittent wipers and a tilt steering wheel were now standard. **6.** Oldsmobile rolled out a redesigned Ninety-Eight, just in time to celebrate the model's 50th anniversary. The '91 edition rode the same front-drive chassis as the 1985–90 models but had new styling and was 9.5 inches longer overall. Power came from GM's revised 3.8-liter V-6 with 170-hp. This top-line Ninety-Eight Regency Elite was available with Cadillac's Computer Command Ride electronic suspension damping system. **7.** The Olds Custom Cruiser was reskinned for 1991, sharing much of the Chevy Caprice's new look.

1

2

3

4

1. More power and additional luxury touches marked 1991 for the Oldsmobile Toronado. Like many other GM vehicles, this luxury-oriented coupe received the revised 170-horsepower 3.8-liter V-6 engine. Steering wheel controls for the audio and climate systems that were not offered in 1990 (due to the addition of a driver-side airbag) once again became standard on the topline Trofeo and optional on the base Toronado (shown). **2.** Oldsmobile's desire to field a winner in stock-based road racing led to the creation of a W41 performance option for the 1991 Cutlass Calais Quad 4-4-2. Power was supplied by a Quad 4 engine reworked to 190 hp, teamed with a Getrag-built five-speed manual transmission. Only 200 W41 models were produced. **3.** Pontiac gave its ponycar a facelift in the spring of 1990 and labeled it a '91 model. The cosmetic changes were inspired by Pontiac's Banshee show car. All four models—base, Formula, Trans Am (pictured), and GTA—received new front and rear fascias and smaller headlamps. Trans Am and GTA also sported fresh taillamps and shared new bodyside skirting. The Trans Am's standard powerplant was a 230-hp 5.0-liter V-8, with the 240-hp 5.7-liter V-8 optional. During the year, a Firebird convertible joined the fleet. **4.** GM dropped the available turbocharged engine from the Grand Prix lineup, electing instead to use the company's twin-cam 3.4-liter V-6 in the new GTP performance model. Available only as a coupe, GTP retained the old Turbo model's fender flares, hood louvers, and crosslace alloy wheels. All coupes had new front-end styling with four mini headlamps.

SATURN: A NEW DIVISION IS BORN

General Motors' "Project Saturn" was conceived in 1982 by then-chairman Roger Smith as an all-out effort to stem the growing Japanese dominance of the U.S. small-car market. The first prototype was unveiled in November 1983, and Smith promised Saturn would be "a quantum leap ahead of the Japanese, including what they have coming in the future." Originally, Saturn vehicles were to be sold by Chevrolet, starting with a $5000-$7000 front-drive sedan that was smaller than a contemporary Chevy Cavalier. Introduction was vaguely described as in "the late '80s."

GM made it clear Saturns would be different. Body panels would be either plastic or metal and attached to a steel space-frame. A new four-cylinder engine would have an aluminum block and head cast using a precision "lost foam" technique. Fuel economy of 45 mpg city and 60 mpg highway was promised. Saturn was free to devise its own engineering and manufacturing methods and components didn't have to come from corporate bins. A major goal was closing the estimated $2000 per car cost gap with "Japan, Inc." Smith declared Saturn "the key to GM's long-term competitiveness, survival, and success."

By January 1985, Saturn was a wholly owned subsidiary of GM with its own plant, employees, UAW contract, and dealer network. GM funded a new $3.5 billion factory in Spring Hill, Tennessee. Saturn was to pioneer new ideas not only in product, but also in sales and service. Presumably, the most successful innovations would then spread throughout GM.

Saturn's mission was to "market vehicles developed and manufactured in the United States that are world leaders in quality, cost, and customer enthusiasm through the integration of people, technology, and business systems and to exchange knowledge, technology, and experience throughout General Motors." The job was monumental, and the ensuing months witnessed delays, cost overruns, and difficulty signing up dealers.

Smith envisioned Saturn as a marvel of automated manufacturing. Some robots were used, but the real innovation came in labor/management relations. Base pay was 80 percent of GM's national average, but there were bonuses for productivity and profit sharing. Saturn's labor agreement had few "shop rules" and employees had a say in how they did their jobs. Workers were organized into teams responsible for monitoring the quality of parts and their own work, including the ability to stop the

assembly line to fix problems on the spot. This was common practice in Japan, but unheard of in U.S. plants.

Production finally got under way in time for the 1991 model year. In one of his last public appearances as GM chairman, Roger Smith drove Job One off the line on the morning of July 30, 1990.

Saturn greeted the world with four-door sedans and two-door coupes sharing a basic front-drive platform. Each had its own styling, but they were criticized for looking similar to other GM products. While slightly shorter than a Cavalier, they were about seven inches longer than a Honda Civic. As promised, body panels were bolted to a spaceframe. Steel was used for horizontal panels, while plastic was used for vertical surfaces.

Saturn's 1.9-liter four-cylinder engine came in two forms: an 85-horsepower single-overhead-cam version and a 123-horse dual-overhead-cam unit. Both came standard with a five-speed manual transmis-

sion; a four-speed automatic was optional. Gas mileage was good but fell short of promises, as the best was the 27 mpg city and 37 mpg highway for the base engine/five-speed combo.

The Scrooge-special SL sedan started at $7995, a whopping $1495 less than a base Civic. Better-equipped SL1 and SL2 models were also offered. The coupe, dubbed SC, came only with the 123-horse engine. Early road tests were generally positive.

Project Saturn had its greatest impact in the retail arena. Carefully selected dealers agreed to build separate showrooms and service facilities and operate under strict customer treatment guidelines. Sales personnel did not engage in hard-sell tactics, and all cars were sold at sticker prices—no more, no less. The red-carpet treatment extended to the service department as well. In its first year, Saturn ranked third, behind Japanese luxury brands Lexus and Infiniti, in J.D. Power and Associates' new-car owner surveys.

1

2

3

4

5

6

7

1. Buick redesigned the 1992 LeSabre, picking up major styling cues from the plusher Park Avenue. At 200 inches overall, the LeSabre was more than three inches longer than the previous one. The slow-selling coupe was dropped, leaving only the four-door sedan in Custom or Limited (shown) trim. **2.** Park Avenues gained an available supercharged engine for the top-line Ultra model. The boosted 3.8-liter engine produced 205 horsepower, an increase of 35 over the non-supercharged engine. **3.** Roadmaster Estate Wagons lost their 5.0-liter V-8 engine for '92. In its stead came a 5.7-liter V-8. A new option for the wagon was a power-reclining front passenger seat. **4.** The four-door sedan was a new addition to the Roadmaster lineup. It, too, had the 5.7-liter V-8. **5.** The compact Skylark wore flashy new styling this year in an effort to lure younger buyers into Buick showrooms. The chassis also was updated. Two- and four-door models were available. This base version had a 120-hp 2.3-liter four-cylinder engine. Optional on base models and standard on the top-end Gran Sport was a 160-horse 3.3-liter V-6. Both engines teamed with a three-speed automatic transmission. **6-7.** Cadillac's Eldorado coupe (left) and Seville sedan (right) were both redesigned for '92. Eldorados had the same wheelbase as '91 models but grew 11 inches in overall length. Sevilles had a three-inch-longer wheelbase than their predecessors and were more than 12 inches longer overall. The 200-horse 4.9-liter V-8 was a carryover from '91. While Eldorado and Seville shared their chassis and powertrain, they did not share any body panels.

1. A new base engine and a traction-control system were among the changes for Chevy's sports car. Called the LT1, the new base V-8 still displaced 5.7 liters, but it produced 300 horsepower, a gain of 50 over the L98 V-8 it replaced. The ultra-high-performance ZR-1 (shown) returned with its Lotus-developed 375-horse twin-cam 5.7-liter V-8. A six-speed manual transmission was offered for the first time this year. The traction-control system was developed by Bosch and called ASR. It worked by curtailing engine power or applying the rear brakes to maximize traction. **2.** Chevy passed a major milestone in 1992 by building its 1,000,000th Corvette, a white convertible with the new LT1 V-8. Here, the historic millionth 'Vette poses with a 1953 original at the Corvette's assembly plant in Bowling Green, Kentucky. **3-4.** Chevy's rear-drive ponycar celebrated its 25th anniversary in 1992. Camaro was offered in hatchback or convertible form, both shown here in Z28 guise. A "Heritage Appearance Package" was offered that included striping, a body-color grille, and black headlamp pockets. **5.** 1992 Luminas were available with antilock brakes for the first time. Joining the performance-oriented Z34 two-door coupe (pictured) was a four-door sedan version. Each was powered by GM's twin-cam 3.4-liter V-6. **6.** The full-size Caprice carried forward with minor changes. Sedans were offered in base, Classic, or LTZ trim. All Caprices, including this Classic sedan, had a standard 170-horse 5.0-liter V-8. Wagon buyers could specify an optional 180-horse 5.7-liter V-8 with 300 lbs/ft of torque.

1

2

3

4

5

6

1. Oldsmobile retired the N-body Cutlass Calais in 1992, replacing it with the front-drive Achieva. It was offered in two- and four-door body styles. Four-cylinder and V-6 engines were available. The Achieva SL sedan shown here came standard with a 160-hp Quad 4 teamed with a three-speed automatic. Antilock brakes were standard on all Achievas. **2.** The Ninety-Eight sedan lineup started with a base-model Regency, followed by the Regency Elite (shown), and top-shelf Touring sedan. Traction control was optional on all three models, and the Touring Sedan was available with the supercharged 205-horsepower 3.8-liter V-6. **3.** Custom Cruiser wagons gained an optional 180-hp 5.7-liter V-8 engine for their last year on the market. **4.** The Toronado and Trofeo (shown) soldiered on virtually unchanged. **5.** The Eighty-Eight was redesigned and lost its two-door body style in the process. It continued to share its platform with the Buick LeSabre and Pontiac Bonneville. While the wheelbase remained the same, overall length and interior volume increased. The sole engine was the 170-horse 3.8-liter V-6. This Eighty-Eight LS started at $21,395. **6.** This year, Pontiac offered a Richard Petty Edition Grand Prix to honor the legendary NASCAR driver's final season of competition. Only 1000 were built—five for each of "The King's" 200 career wins. **7.** Grand Prix sedans were offered in LE, SE (shown), and STE trim. All sedans had a standard 140-hp 3.1-liter V-6, as Grand Prix was no longer offered with a four-cylinder engine. **8.** Firebird Trans Am convertibles were powered by a 205-horse 5.0-liter V-8. **9.** The ultimate Trans Am continued to be the GTA, only available as a hatchback.

1

2

3

4

1. The reworked 1992 Pontiac Grand Am had a new look and saw the return of V-6 power. Two- and four-door body styles were offered, both shown here in sporty GT trim. The optional 160-hp 3.3-liter V-6 was the first V-6 offered in Grand Am since 1987. **2.** Bonneville celebrated its 35th anniversary with a new skin and new interior that featured an available passenger-side airbag. Still a front-drive, four-door sedan, its wheelbase was unchanged at 110.8 inches. The SE (rear) and SSE models shared a 170-horse 3.8-liter V-6. The high-performance SSEi (front) had unique styling cues and the 205-horse supercharged 3.8-liter V-6. **3.** Antilock brakes were standard on all versions of the compact Sunbird. Unlike the similar Chevy Cavalier, Sunbird's base engine was a 111-hp 2.0-liter four-cylinder (Cavaliers had a 110-hp 2.2). The top-end GT (pictured) had the 140-hp 3.1-liter V-6. **4.** Production at GM's Saturn division ramped up to full speed. SL, SL1, and SL2 sedans, and the SC coupe shown here returned, this time with new engine and transmission mounts designed to reduce noise and vibration. The Saturn brand earned high marks for dollar value, fuel economy, and customer service.

1

2

3

4

5

6

1. Buick marked its 90th anniversary with this special LeSabre Custom model that included a cassette player, power driver seat, and other features that were normally optional. The 90th Anniversary model cost $18,999, nearly $1500 less than the regular Custom without those features. **2.** Roadmaster Estate Wagons were little changed. With the optional Trailer Towing Package, towing capacity was 5000 pounds. **3.** The Century lineup received a 110-hp 2.2-liter four-cylinder as the base engine. Buick added a base Custom model, shown here in coupe form, to the roster. **4.** After its 1992 redesign, Skylark shuffled its model lineup. A new entry-level Custom model was added, and the previous base model was renamed Limited (shown). Gran Sport remained the top model. **5.** Cadillac redesigned its rear-drive sedan. The Fleetwood name was pulled from the front-drive sedan and applied here. Brougham, which was the previous model, became a top-end option package. At 225 inches, Fleetwood was the longest vehicle sold in the United States. **6.** The pricey, slow-selling Allanté sang its swan song in 1993. For its last model year, the standard engine was Cadillac's "Northstar" twin-cam, 32-valve aluminum V-8 that produced 295 horsepower.

1. Upscale versions of the Cadillac De Ville became the Sixty Special, relinquishing the Fleetwood name to the large, rear-drive sedan. The Sedan de Ville's base price was $32,990. **2.** Eldorado Touring Coupe (shown) had a standard "Northstar" 4.6-liter V-8 rated at 295 horsepower. Eldorado Sport Coupe had a 270-horse Northstar, while the base Eldorado still used the 200-hp 4.9 V-8. **3.** Cadillac offered two versions of Seville. The base model shown here was powered by the 4.9-liter V-8. The 295-horse Northstar was standard on the top-line Seville STS. A new four-speed overdrive automatic transmission and traction control were other new features on the STS. **4.** Chevrolet celebrated the 40th birthday of its sports car with an option package (shown) that included embroidered seats, wheel hub emblems, and a chrome hood emblem. Even bigger news for Corvette concerned the ZR-1. Horsepower of its exotic, twin-cam V-8 increased from 375 to a whopping 405. However, the added muscle did little for sales, as demand dropped from 502 units in '92 to just 448 for '93. **5.** Camaro was redesigned for 1993. Though built on the same 101.1-inch wheelbase as the previous model, Camaros were now slightly longer, wider, taller, and heavier. A two-door hatchback coupe was the only body style offered. Base models had a 3.4-liter V-6 engine. The Z28 performance model returned with a 275-hp 5.7-liter V-8 derived from the Corvette's LT1 motor. A Camaro Z28 served as the Official Pace Car for the 1993 Indianapolis 500. Chevrolet offered 645 limited edition replicas for retail sale.

1

2

3

4

5

1

2

3

4

5

6

1. Camaro's styling was fresh and bore many cues from the 1990 California Camaro concept car. This view of the Z28 highlights the new design's pronounced wedge profile with sharply upswept beltline. 2. The Lumina Z34 lost its seldom-ordered manual transmission in the middle of the '93 model year. All subsequent models used a four-speed automatic. 3. The sporty front-drive Chevy Beretta saw few changes for '93. The GTZ (shown) was powered by a 175-hp 2.3-liter Quad 4 four-cylinder engine. GTZ buyers who wanted an automatic transmission had to settle for a 140-horse 3.1-liter V-6. 4. For its fourth model year, Oldsmobile's Silhouette was graced with revised front and rear fascias, parking and turn signal lamps, and alloy wheels. 5. The Cutlass Supreme convertible was now available with GM's twin-cam 3.4-liter V-6. This engine could only be paired with an automatic transmission; the manual was no longer offered. 6. Other news for the Cutlass Supreme line was the addition of one-price versions of the two-door coupe and four-door sedan. These models marked Olds' 95th anniversary. The $15,995 price included cruise control, cassette player, and 16-inch tires

and wheels. The sporty Cutlass Supreme International Series coupe (rear) and sedan (front) models shown here had the 3.4-liter V-6 standard.

1. The Olds Achieva added a one-price "Value Edition" model for 1993. It included air conditioning and an automatic transmission. The high-performance SCX (pictured) was retired after production of just 500 units. **2.** Though the Cutlass Supreme was supposed to be Oldsmobile's volume leader, the midsize Cutlass Ciera sedan and Cutlass Cruiser wagon (pictured) outsold it. Cutlass Ciera's value in particular was strengthened for '93 with the addition of "Value Edition" and "Special Edition" models. Value Editions came equipped with a 160-hp 3.3-liter V-6 engine, cruise control, and cassette player. Special Editions added a driver-side airbag and power windows. **3.** Many Grand Prix models, including this LE sedan, had a 140-hp 3.1-liter V-6 and three-speed automatic transmission standard. This year, Pontiac made a four-speed electronic automatic transmission available on models equipped with the 3.1-liter V-6. **4.** The Pontiac Trans Sport minivan lost the GT model, so now it was available only in SE trim. Antilock brakes and seats for five were standard. Seating for six or seven was optional. **5.** Antilock brakes were now standard on all Bonnevilles. The 205-horse 3.8-liter supercharged V-6 engine was standard on the range-topping SSEi (center) and optional on the mid-level SSE model. A new Sport Luxury Edition (SLE) package was available on the base SE model. The SLE package (front) included monotone exterior appearance, rear spoiler, and 16-inch aluminum wheels. The Bonneville SE (rear) started at $19,444, while the line-topping SSEi had a base sticker of $29,444.

1

2

3

4

5

1

2

3

1. Grand Am was Pontiac's best-selling car for 1993 and one of the top sellers for GM. Two-door coupes and four-door sedans were available in SE (right) or GT (left) trim. A 115-hp OHC 2.3-liter four cylinder was standard on SEs, while GTs were motivated by a spunky 175-horse Quad 4.

2. Pontiac's ponycar was redesigned for 1993, sporting fresh styling and more power. Base models had a 160-hp 3.4-liter V-6 engine. Formula and top-line Trans Am versions had a 275-hp 5.7-liter V-8. Trans Ams (pictured) had specific bucket seats, performance axle ratio, and Z-rated 16-inch tires.

3. With GM's Saturn division growing in popularity, it was natural for the product roster to expand. A lower-cost SC1 coupe (center) was added. It had the same 85-hp 1.9-liter four-cylinder engine as the SL and SL1 sedan. The 124-hp coupe became the SC2. A four-door wagon body style joined the SL sedan lineup. Wagons were offered in SW1 and SW2 flavors. The $10,895 SW1 came with the 85-horse-power engine. The fancier SW2 wagon (front) and SL2 sedan (rear) received the 124-horse engine. Saturn's production totaled 244,621 in its third model year.

1. There was a whole lot of Chevy Corvette under the hood of Buick's full-size, rear-drive Roadmaster sedan and Estate Wagon (shown) for 1994. All Roadmasters received a modified version of the Corvette's 5.7-liter LT1 V-8 engine. In the Buick, it produced 260 hp. The standard dual exhaust system was made of stainless steel and had separate mufflers and catalysts for each side. **2.** The supercharged Park Avenue Ultra (shown) received a 20-horsepower boost, now totaling 225. Base Park Avenues retained the naturally-aspirated 170-hp 3.8-liter V-6. **3.** Not much was new for the '94 LeSabre, but the front-drive sedan did gain a standard passenger-side airbag. Custom and Limited (shown) models remained available, both powered by the 3.8 V-6. **4.** Regal Custom was the base series, available in two-door coupe and four-door sedan body styles. The 3.1 V-6, now rated at 160 horsepower, and a four-speed automatic transmission were standard. In an effort to boost sales in California, Buick created special models for that market that included several options at a lower cost. The Custom 3800 had the 3.8-liter V-6, cruise control, and leather upholstery for less than $19,000. This Custom sedan was the most popular Regal model with sales of 46,543. Prices started at $18,299. **5.** Regal Gran Sports remained Buick's sportiest midsize offerings. The coupe (pictured) and sedan had a 170-horse 3.8 V-6 standard. Buick added a driver-side airbag, power windows, and automatic door locks as standard equipment on all Regal models.

1

2

3

4

5

1. Skylark Gran Sports had a new standard V-6. The 3.3-liter V-6 was replaced by a 155-hp 3.1-liter unit. 2. Buick Century wagons were now offered only in Special trim. 3. The largest car sold in the United States got a new standard engine, the 260-hp 5.7-liter V-8 derived from the Corvette's LT1. Cadillac said the '94 Fleetwood could accelerate from 0-60 mph in 8.5 seconds—not bad for a 225-inch, 4500-lb sedan. 4-5. Cadillac's best-selling model was redesigned for 1994, and it came in two distinct flavors. Base models were called Sedan de Ville (left), and the top-line version was called De Ville Concours (right). The former used a 200-hp 4.9-liter V-8 engine. Concours models used a 270-hp version of the 4.6-liter Northstar V-8. These sedans were built on the same platform as the Seville sedan but were nearly three inches longer in wheelbase. 6-7. The Northstar engine became standard equipment on '94 Eldorados and Sevilles. Base versions produced 270 hp. Eldorado Touring Coupes (top) and Seville STS sedans (bottom) had the 295-horse Northstar. Though base prices were up, the Seville still cost considerably less than comparable Japanese rivals like the Lexus LS 400 and Infiniti Q45.

1. In a nod to performance Chevrolets from the 1960s, GM's volume division resurrected the Impala SS moniker, applying it to a sporty version of the rear-drive Caprice. The Impala SS came standard with the 260-hp 5.7-liter LT1 V-8 that was optional on "regular" Impalas and augmented that with a sport suspension, 17-inch Z-rated performance tires on distinctive five-spoke alloy wheels, a unique "dogleg" rear roof-pillar design, monochromatic exterior trim, and front bucket seats. Black was the only available body color. The car was an immediate hit among enthusiasts. Chevy planned to sell 4000 '94 Impala SS models but ended up moving more than 6000. 2. Aside from a standard passenger-side airbag, not much was new for the '94 Corvette. 3. Chevy added a convertible to the Camaro roster for 1994. Like the coupe, the ragtops were available as the base V-6 or high-performance V-8 Z28 (pictured). 4. Chevy's minivan got a name change, a restyled nose, and an optional power-sliding side door, but retained its composite body panels. The Lumina Minivan was called just that, rather than the APV. 5. The sporty Beretta coupe shuffled its model lineup for '94. GT and GTZ model designations were dropped in favor of a single Z26 trim level. The Z26 came standard with a 170-hp 2.3-liter Quad 4. Optional was a 160-hp 3.1-liter V-6. 6. Oldsmobile redesigned the Eighty-Eight's dashboard for '94, giving this front-drive full-size sedan a standard passenger-side airbag in the process. Exterior changes included a body-color grille and new headlamps. An Eighty-Eight Royale is shown.

1

2

3

4

5

6

1. The International Series of the Cutlass Supreme was dropped for '94. A 160-hp 3.1-liter V-6 became the standard engine, and the 210-hp 3.4-liter V-6 was still available. A driver-side airbag became standard equipment. 2. The 3.1 V-6 was a newly available engine for the smaller Achieva. Olds' compact coupes and sedans also received a standard driver-side airbag. 3. The Cutlass Ciera Sedan and Cutlass Cruiser wagon (pictured) entered their 13th season with a standard driver-side airbag and antilock brakes. Two new engines also highlighted these midsize cars: a standard 120-hp 2.2-liter four-cylinder and an optional 160-hp 3.1-liter V-6. A $13,995 Special Edition sedan had the V-6 engine, power windows, and cruise control. These cars continued to outsell the Cutlass Supreme. 4. Though Oldsmobile promised it for 1993, it wasn't until '94 that the Silhouette minivan was the beneficiary of an available power-operated sliding side door. 5. While the performance-oriented Bonneville SSEi was no longer a separate model, its name and much of its content became an option package for the SSE. The supercharged 3.8-liter V-6 engine got a power boost to 225 hp from 205. 6. Pontiac simplified the Grand Prix model lineup for '94, and its interior got a redesign. All Grand Prixs were now SE models and had standard dual airbags. 7. This Grand Prix has the Special Edition Coupe package that also served as the basis for the available GTP Performance package. 8. The Pontiac Trans Sport minivan was freshened with a reworked front end for '94. All Trans Sports had SE trim.

1

1. To no one's surprise, Pontiac released a special trim package in 1994 to celebrate the Trans Am's 25th anniversary. These Firebirds all wore white paint with blue stripes—just like the originals a quarter-century before. **2.** Formula, Trans Am, and Trans Am GT models equipped with the 275-hp 5.7-liter V-8 engine and six-speed manual transmission benefited from a revised final drive ratio designed to sharpen throttle response. The Trans Am had a reduced level of standard equipment and adopted the Formula's smaller rear spoiler. Trans Am GT (shown) was the new top-line model and retained the flamboyant rear wing. **3.** Saturn's lineup stood pat for '94. Coupes returned in SC1 and SC2 (rear) guise. Sedans were offered as the SL, SL1, and SL2 (center), and station wagons came as the SW1 and SW2 (front). Traction control was now included on models equipped with antilock brakes and automatic transmission.

2

3

1

2

3

4

5

1. A redesigned Riviera went on sale as an early 1995 model. The new version of this two-door luxury coupe was nine inches longer than its predecessor. It was built on the same platform as Oldsmobile's new Aurora sedan. Power came from two versions of GM's reliable 3.8-liter V-6 engine. The "Series II 3800" produced 205 hp. A supercharged version made 225. With 0-60-mph acceleration times in the upper seven-second range, a supercharged Riv could hold its own against V-8-powered luxury coupes like Cadillac's Eldorado. **2.** Roadmaster, here in Limited trim, saw no major changes but gained several new features including automatic transmission fluid that didn't need to be changed for 100,000 miles under normal conditions. Larger, foldaway outside mirrors were also added. **3.** Regal's interior got a makeover for '95. A new dashboard sported larger analog gauges and dual airbags. Seats were also new, and all door panels now had map pockets. **4.** Buick's compact Skylark got more standard power and a revised rear suspension for 1994. A 150-hp version of GM's dual-overhard-cam Quad 4 2.3-liter four-cylinder replaced the 115-hp single-cam "Quad OHC" in Custom and Limited models. The Gran Sport shown here had a standard 185-horse 3.1-liter V-6. **5.** Cadillac's Eldorado got a small power boost for 1995. Both versions of its Northstar V-8 added five horsepower, to 275 in standard models and 300 in the top-line Touring Coupe (shown). Eldorado featured a standard Road-Sensing Suspension that adjusted suspension firmness based on road conditions.

1. Cadillac's Sedan de Ville and De Ville Concours (pictured) got some new features for 1995. Traction control became standard instead of optional on the Sedan de Ville. Also, both models received new transmission fluid that didn't need changing for 100,000 miles. **2.** The Northstar V-8-powered Seville sedan got the same five-hp boost as its Eldorado siblings. Seville SLS (shown) models now had 275 hp, and the image-leader STS produced 300. **3.** Chevrolet Caprice sedans adopted the SS model's "dog-leg" rear roof pillars for 1995. Also, they now came standard with a 200-hp 4.3-liter V-8 base engine, which was essentially a 5.7-liter LT1 cut down to the small-block Chevy's original 1955 displacement. Wagons, like this Caprice Classic, had the 5.7-liter engine standard. **4-5.** The high-performance Impala SS had few changes for its second season. Dark Green Gray Metallic (top) and Dark Cherry Metallic (bottom) were new color choices. The Impala SS was still available in basic black as well. Base price was $22,910. **6-7.** Chevy redesigned its midsize two- and four-door cars for '95. The two-door took on the Monte Carlo moniker while the four-door remained the Lumina. Standard power for both models came from the 160-hp 3.1-liter V-6. Standard on the Monte Carlo Z34 and optional on the Lumina LS was the 210-hp twin-cam 3.4-liter V-6. Inside, the new dashboard sported a clean, contemporary layout with standard dual airbags. Its midsize proportions afforded ample room for four adults in the Monte Carlo. The Monte Carlo LS (top) started at $16,670, while the base Lumina (bottom) had a $15,460 starting price.

1

2

3

4

5

6

7

1

2

3

4

5

1-2. For the first time in 13 years, Chevrolet redesigned its best-selling car. The 2005 Cavalier had a longer wheelbase, fresh styling, and a new interior with standard dual airbags. Two-door coupe, convertible, and four-door sedans were offered. All had a 104.1-inch wheelbase, 2.8 inches longer than previous models. The lineup included base versions of the coupe and sedan, an LS sedan, a sporty Z24 coupe (top), and an LS convertible. Base and LS models used a 120-hp 2.2-liter four-cylinder engine. Standard on the Z24 and optional on the LS sedan was GM's Quad 4 150-hp four-cylinder. Cavalier started at $10,065 for a base coupe and $10,265 for a base sedan (bottom). **3.** Oldsmobile introduced the Aurora sedan as an early 1995 model. This luxury four-door targeted Japanese brands such as Acura and Lexus. Aurora was built on a completely new chassis. Power came from a 250-hp 4.0-liter V-8 engine that was derived from Cadillac's 4.6-liter Northstar unit. This sedan represented a huge step in a new and better direction for Oldsmobile. It was highly competitive against established Japanese rivals, but at a starting price of $31,370, Aurora cost thousands less. **4.** Olds cut the Ninety-Eight lineup, leaving only the Recency Elite in Series I and II trim. GM's revised "Series II" 205-hp 3.8-liter V-6 was standard, and the 225-horse supercharged 3.8 V-6 was optional. **5.** A redesigned dashboard with dual airbags and a simpler model lineup highlighted '95 for the Cutlass Supreme. Coupe and sedan (shown) models were now only available in a single SL trim in Series I and II equipment levels.

1. Base Firebird models gained a second V-6 engine. While the standard powerplant continued to be the 160-hp 3.4-liter V-6, a 200-hp 3.8-liter V-6 was now an option. The Trans Am (pictured) still had the 275-horse 5.7-liter V-8. 2. The 225-hp supercharged 3.8-liter V-6 was an option for both the Bonneville SE model with the SLE package and the top-end SSE. When equipped with the blown engine, the SSE became an SSEi (shown). 3. Variable-effort power steering was a new option on the '95 Grand Prix. A GTP option package on coupes (pictured) included GM's twin-cam, 210-hp 3.4-liter V-6 engine. 4. Like its Buick Skylark and Olds Achieva cousins, the Pontiac Grand Am received the 150-hp Quad 4 2.3-liter four-cylinder engine as standard equipment. Value pricing of $12,904 for a base SE coupe and $14,854 for a GT coupe (shown) helped Grand Am remain Pontiac's best-selling car. 5. Pontiac shelved the Sunbird after 13 years, replacing it with the Sunfire, a compact that shared its chassis with the Chevy Cavalier. Coupe, sedan, and convertible body styles were available in SE trim. A GT coupe was also offered. This SE coupe was the most popular Sunfire model, with sales of 42,313 units. 6. Saturn's base engine got a power boost in '95. The single-overhead-cam 1.9-liter unit produced 100 hp, a gain of 15 over the previous year. The DOHC unit was unchanged. Inside, all Saturns received a new dashboard with dual airbags. The top-line SC2 coupe (front) received a slight exterior freshening. The sedan, here in SL1 trim (center), and the wagon, shown in SL2 guise (rear), were little changed.

1. Despite the fact that Buick's Roadmaster only had minor changes for 1996, the car was still the subject of big news. GM announced 1996 would be the last model year for Roadmaster, as well as the structurally similar Cadillac Fleetwood and Chevrolet Caprice/Impala SS. This 1996 Roadmaster sedan is pictured with Buick's original Roadmaster model, the 1936. **2.** The Roadmaster Estate Wagon was also in its final year. **3.** GM's "Series II" 3.8-liter V-6 engine made its way into the LeSabre as standard equipment. Custom and Limited (pictured) models were offered. **4.** GM added a supercharger to the Series II 3.8-liter V-6 on the '95 Riviera. That engine produced 240 hp, 15 more than the previous year's supercharged engine. **5.** Buick extensively revised the '96 Skylark, giving it a redesigned dashboard with dual airbags, a larger standard engine, and fresh styling. The new engine was a revised Quad 4 that displaced 2.4 liters versus 2.3 in previous models. Horsepower was unchanged, however, at 150. The Gran Sport coupe (shown) started at $17,701. **6.** Regals in '96 became the only midsize GM cars available with the Series II 3.8-liter V-6 engine. It was standard in the Gran Sport coupe (shown). **7-8.** Cadillac's front-drive, midsize Eldorado coupe (left) and Seville sedan (right) received a new dashboard design for '96. Available for the first time on both cars was an eight-way power driver seat. The topline Eldorado ETC and Seville STS were available with a new feature called Rainsense, which would automatically activate the windshield wipers when needed.

1. Cadillac's 1996 lineup included (from left to right) the De Ville Concours, the Sedan de Ville, the Seville STS, and the Eldorado ETC.
2. The Fleetwood entered its final model year of production with only minor changes.
3. Sedan De Ville versions of Cadillac's large, front-drive sedan dropped their 4.9-liter overhead-valve V-8 engine in favor of the 275-horse dual-overhead-cam Northstar V-8. The De Ville Concours (shown) was powered by a 300-horse version of the Northstar V-8. Other Concours features included Magnasteer variable-assist steering, dual exhaust, leather seats, and real Zebrano wood trim.
4. With more money to be made building big SUVs, the Chevy Caprice and Impala SS would be dropped after the '96 model year. Enthusiasts were sad to see the hot-rod Impala disappear. Impala SS improvements included a floor-mounted shifter for the four-speed automatic transmission, an analog speedometer, and a tachometer. With word out that this would be its final year, sales of the SS nearly doubled to almost 42,000, far outpacing the Caprice on which it was based.
5. The twin-cam 3.4-liter V-6 offered in the Monte Carlo and Lumina received a boost from 210-hp to 215 for 1996. It was again standard on the Monte Carlo Z34 and optional on the Lumina LS. The Lumina sedan and Monte Carlo LS (shown) were still powered by the 160-horse 3.1-liter V-6.

1

2

3

4

5

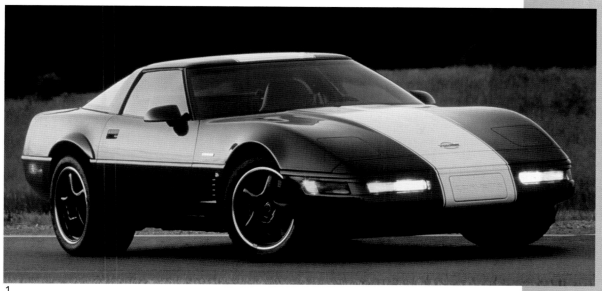

1

2

3

4

5

6

1-2. Chevy's sports car marked the final year of the C4 generation with a pair of special models. With the high-performance ZR-1 out of production, the Grand Sport became Corvette's flagship. It had a 330-hp 5.7-liter V-8 engine dubbed LT4. Production of the Grand Sport was limited to just 1000 copies between coupes (top) and convertibles (bottom). The other special model was the Collector Edition, with the 300-hp 5.7-liter LT1 V-8, silver paint, and special trim. **3.** The Beretta and Corsica entered their final model year. This Beretta Z26 started at $16,690. **4.** Corsica was only offered in LT trim. **5.** Cavalier's big news for '96 was the addition of a revised dual-camshaft four-cylinder engine. Dubbed "Twin Cam," the 150-hp 2.4-liter four was the new standard engine in the sporty Z24 coupe (shown). It was optional on the mainstream LS sedan. Twin Cam replaced the previous year's 2.3-liter Quad 4. Traction control was a new safety feature added to Cavaliers equipped with the Twin Cam engine and automatic transmission. **6.** The '96 Oldsmobile Aurora came equipped with daytime running lights. It retained its 250-hp 4.0-liter V-8 engine and four-speed automatic transmission. New options included chrome-plated aluminum wheels and gold trim for the hood ornament and rear badging. The base price increased $1295 to $34,360, but Aurora was still priced lower than comparable import luxury sedans.

1. Ninety-Eight, a name Oldsmobile first used in 1941 and one of the oldest in the auto industry, would be retired after the 1996 model year. Only Regency Elite trim was offered with Series I and II equipment. 2. Oldsmobile's slow-selling Cutlass Supreme convertible went away in '96, but the division expanded the lineup to include four price levels rather than two. The division opted for a strategy of encouraging dealers to sell well-equipped cars with few available options. In a Saturn-like move, Olds wanted vehicles sold at suggested retail pricing to eliminate the traditional haggling that turned off shoppers. 3. Pontiac showed the 300 GPX concept that featured many of the styling cues that would eventually make their way into the new 1997 Grand Prix. What didn't make it into production was the GPX's engine: a 300-hp version of the supercharged 3.8-liter V-6. 4. 1996 Grand Prixs, like this SE coupe, were basically unchanged. 5. Key changes to the '96 Bonneville were slightly revised front and rear styling, as well as more power for the available supercharged engine. The supercharger was attached to the Series II 3.8-liter V-6 and put out 240 hp. This Bonneville SLE also received new-design alloy wheels. 6. V-8 versions of the Firebird gained 10 hp (for a total of 285) for '96. Formula (shown) and Trans Am models were also available with a "WS6 Ram Air Performance and Handling" package that included stiffer springs, 17-inch tires, and a ram-air induction system that boosted engine output to a whopping 305 hp. The ram-air system required a new hood with dual scoops (pictured).

1

2

3

4

5

6

7

1. Pontiac continued to offer the Firebird convertible in base, Formula, and Trans Am (shown) versions. Not wanting to neglect base Firebirds, Pontiac made standard the previously optional 200-hp 3.8-liter V-6. **2-3.** A new base engine, revised styling, and a standard passenger-side airbag made 1996 news for Pontiac's Grand Am. The new base engine was the "Twin Cam" 2.4-liter 150-hp four-cylinder. The passenger side airbag was housed in a revised dashboard. Coupe and sedan body styles were offered in sporty GT (left) and base SE (right) trims. **4-5.** The compact Pontiac Sunfire received a few updates. Newly available was the 150-horsepower Twin Cam four-cylinder engine, and models equipped with it and the four-speed automatic gained traction control. GT trim (left) was still limited to the coupe, while SE trim was available on the coupe, convertible, and sedan (right). **6.** For its final season, Pontiac's plastic-body minivan got a new standard engine. The new powerplant was a 180-hp 3.4-liter V-6 that replaced both the 3.1- and 3.8-liter V-6s used previously. Trans Sport was only offered in SE trim. **7.** Saturn sedans and wagons received an extensive exterior makeover, but coupes retained their 1990 styling for one more model year. All cars continued to be built with dent-resistant polymer panels. Powertrains were unchanged, with SL and SL1/SW1/SC1 models retaining their 100-hp 1.9-liter four-cylinder engine. SL2 (rear), SC2 (center), and SW2 (front) had Saturn's twin-cam 124-hp 1.9-liter four. The automatic transmission had a new adaptive shift program that adjusted shifts based on how the car was driven.

1. A restyled LeSabre was introduced as an early 1997 model. In its freshening, it retained the basic shape of the 1992–96 models, but there were numerous appearance changes. Among the styling tweaks was a new grille; new front and rear fascias; front air dam; and body side moldings. Interior changes included new imitation-walnut wood trim for the dashboard and doors. The lone powertrain remained a 205-horsepower 3.8-liter V-6 engine. **2.** Buick also redesigned its top-line luxury sedan, though it maintained strong visual ties to its predecessor. The Park Avenue was now based on the G-body platform shared with the Buick Riviera and Oldsmobile Aurora. Powertrains were unchanged, with base models using the 205-hp 3.8-liter V-6. Park Avenue Ultras (shown) were supercharged and had 240 hp. A redesigned interior had an optional head-up display that projected the speedometer and other gauge readings onto the windshield. Standard on both models was Buick's Personal Choice package. It included a remote entry transmitter that could automatically adjust the driver seat, outside mirrors, automatic door locks, lighting, and other accessories to one of two settings. **3.** The midsize Century received its first complete makeover since the front-drive version was introduced for 1982. Century was no longer built on the A-body platform; it was now a W-body like the Regal. The revised Century came only as a four-door sedan in Custom or Limited (shown) trim. **4.** Skylark entered 1997 with minor changes. This Skylark Custom sedan is equipped with the optional Limited package.

1

2

3

4

ONSTAR: GM'S GOT YOUR BACK

In February 1996, Rick Wagoner, GM's president of North American Operations, officially launched OnStar at the Chicago Auto Show. A collaboration of GM, Electronic Data Systems (EDS), and Hughes Electronics Corp., OnStar was to serve as an all-in-one vehicle communications, monitoring, and tracking service.

GM provided the design, vehicle integration, and distribution for the system. EDS brought much of the information management and customer service tools. Hughes provided the communications and satellite technologies, as well as the vehicle electronics.

The first OnStar system appeared in the fall of 1996 in the 1997 Cadillac De Ville, Seville, and Eldorado. When customers purchased a new vehicle equipped with OnStar, they received the first year of standard service at no cost. After that, the service could be renewed on a monthly or yearly basis.

The OnStar system communicates through mobile phone networks. These networks provide location information using Global Positioning System (GPS) technology. If a car equipped with OnStar runs out of gas, the driver can push a button on the rearview mirror and connect with a live representative who can call for assistance or direct the user to the nearest gas station. If the user locks his or her keys in the car, he or she can call OnStar, and in many cases the agent can send a signal to the vehicle and unlock the doors.

OnStar also is touted for its usefulness in emergency situations. Its GPS capability can assist law enforcement in tracking stolen vehicles. In March 2004, OnStar assisted Tennessee police in locating a stolen Hummer H2 SUV. The vehicle was tracked to Ohio, and the individual arrested was also wanted by the FBI in connection with federal bank robbery charges. Ironically, the individual was featured on the crimestopping TV show *America's Most Wanted* the day before his arrest. The use of OnStar was featured in a follow-up segment.

In the event of a traffic accident, OnStar agents can call to check if the occupants are OK and contact emergency personnel if needed.

Other OnStar services include hands-free calling, where the system operates like a voice-activated cellular phone. Owners can receive diagnostic e-mails, notifying them of potentially dangerous mechanical problems. "Turn-by-turn" navigation allows drivers to tell an OnStar agent where they would like to go, and the agent will then send directions to the vehicle where a voice prompt will guide drivers to the destination.

While initially available as an option on a select few GM vehicles, OnStar has expanded to include 95 percent of the company's products for model-year 2008.

1. Catera was a new model for Cadillac. This midsize sedan was built in Germany by GM subsidiary Opel. Intended to compete against near-luxury cars such as the BMW 328i and Mercedes-Benz C280, the rear-drive Catera rode a 107.4-inch wheelbase. It was powered by a 200-hp 3.0-liter V-6 engine and four-speed automatic transmission. Pricing started at $29,995 and included many standard features such as traction control, power front seats, and automatic climate control. **2.** The Cadillac De Ville was treated to a mild facelift. Also new was a De Ville d'Elegance model, which slotted between the Sedan De Ville and top-end Concours (shown). **3-4.** The biggest news for the Eldorado coupe and Seville sedan were lower base prices. Seville SLS (left) started at $39,995, and Eldorado's (right) base price was $37,995. OnStar was optional for all Seville and Eldorado models.

1-2. For Camaro's 30th anniversary, Chevy gave its ponycar a new dashboard. Base and RS Camaros had a 200-hp 3.8-liter V-6 engine. Z28s used a 285-hp 5.7-liter V-8. A $3999 SS option package (top) for the Z28 increased horsepower to 305. The 30th Anniversary option package for the Z28 (bottom) mimicked colors available on the 1969 Indy pace car and included white exterior paint with broad orange stripes, white wheels, and white seats. **3.** The '97 Corvette was new from the ground up. C5 'Vettes were longer by 1.2 inches overall but grew 8.3 inches in wheelbase. The sole engine was the new, aluminum-block LS1 V-8. It displaced 5.7 liters and produced 345 hp. The new 'Vette could do 0-60 mph in less than 5 seconds and reach a top speed of 172 mph. **4.** Malibu replaced the Corsica as Chevy's sedan that slotted between the Cavalier and Lumina. Standard on the base Malibu (pictured) was GM's 150-hp 2.4-liter Twin Cam four-cylinder engine. Optional on the base model and standard on the top-end LS was a 155-hp 3.1-liter V-6. **5.** GM's minivans were redesigned for '97. Chevy changed the name of its vans to Venture from Lumina. The previous models' plastic body panels were replaced by steel ones. Regular- (left) and extended-wheelbase (right) models were offered. The extended-wheelbase version offered optional power-sliding passenger side and manual sliding driver side doors.

4

1

2

3

5

1 2 3 4 5 6

7

1. Though the brand was not much longer for this world, Oldsmobile celebrated its 100th birthday in 1997 (see Intrigue sidebar, page 382). The departed Ninety-Eight was replaced with a new top-end Eighty-Eight Regency (shown), with standard traction control and dual-zone climate control. **2.** Cutlass Supreme was down to one trim level in coupe and sedan (shown) models. The 160-hp 3.1 V-6 was the sole engine. **3.** The 1997 Cutlass replaced the aged Cutlass Ciera as Oldsmobile's mainstream sedan. It shared its design with the Chevy Malibu. Cutlasses were available only with the 160-hp 3.1-liter V-6 engine. At $17,325 to start, the Cutlass offered a lot of value for the money. **4.** Oldsmobile's Silhouette minivan was redesigned for '97. These steel-bodied vans were available in two lengths: one with a 112-inch wheelbase, the other on a 120-inch span. The sole engine was a 180-hp 3.4-liter V-6. All Silhouettes seated seven passengers, but consumers could choose the middle seats: a 60/40 split bench or a pair of captain's chairs. **5.** Air conditioning was now standard on all Pontiac Grand Am models, including this SE sedan. **6.** The Sunfire SE coupe was Pontiac's most popular compact. Prices started at $12,059. **7.** Pontiac's biggest news was the redesign of its Grand Prix. Available as a coupe or sedan, these cars had a wider stance that Pontiac touted as a revival of the "Wide Track" look of the '60s. Power came from a trio of V-6s: a 160-hp 3.1-liter; a 195-hp 3.8; or a 240-hp supercharged 3.8. The high-performance GTP package (shown) included the blown V-6.

1. Bonneville, Pontiac's largest car, was largely unchanged for 1997. The hot SSEi (shown) still used the 240-horse super-charged V-6. **2.** Formula was the least expensive V-8-pow-ered Firebird. Prices started at $20,654. **3.** This base Firebird coupe has the optional Sport Appearance Package. Air con-

ditioning was now standard equipment on all versions of the Firebird. **4.** Pontiac's Trans Sport was redesigned and offered in both 112- and 120-inch-wheelbase versions. Standard seating was for seven, but three-place bucket seats for the 2nd row were optional and increased capacity to eight. Trans Sport offered the Montana Package (shown), which included two-tone paint, charcoal lower accents, a lug-gage rack, firmer suspension, automatic level control, alloy wheels, traction control, and self-sealing all-season tires. **5.** Hot on the heels of the sedan's 1996 redesign, Saturn launched a revamped coupe for '97. Wheelbase length increased to 102.4 inches from 99.2, matching the sedans and wagons. SC1 and SC2 (shown) designations returned with the same 1.9-liter engines as used previously. The retracting head-lights used on previous coupes were replaced with exposed lamps.

1

2

3

4

5

1. Changes for the 1998 Buick Park Avenue were limited to revised safety and convenience features. The Park Avenue Ultra (pictured) had the 240-hp supercharged 3.8-liter V-6 standard. **2.** A redesigned Regal entered its first full year of production in '98. Buick introduced the reskinned Regal during the 1997 model year. Only a four-door sedan was available. This Regal LS is equipped with the 25th Anniversary Edition package. **3.** Buick shelved the Riviera's previous base engine, opting to go with the 240-hp supercharged 3.8-liter V-6 as standard. Since this big coupe wasn't for everyone, Buick pitched it as an impractical, indulgent reward for upscale achievers. **4.** LeSabre earned the distinction of being the best-selling full-size sedan in the United States for its fifth straight year in '98. Not wanting to mess with success, this year's versions were little changed. LeSabre's sole powerplant was the 205-hp 3.8-liter V-6—which seemed perfectly fine to LeSabre's buyers. Custom and Limited trim levels were available. This LeSabre Custom tipped the price scales at $22,465. **5.** The Cadillac Catera entered its second model year with few changes. This was Cadillac's only rear-drive car and was still built in Germany by GM's Opel subsidiary. OnStar assistance was a new dealer-installed option. Catera's extra-cost Bose-brand audio system gained radio data system (RDS) capability. RDS enabled the radio to display such broadcast information as station call letters and song titles, as well as to break into programming with emergency broadcast alerts. The feature became more common on vehicles through the end of the decade and into the 2000s.

1. A new option on base models of Cadillac's De Ville was GM's StabiliTrak antiskid system, which could activate individual brakes to enhance control in emergency maneuvers. This feature was standard on the top-end Concours model shown here. **2.** Though its future was in doubt, the Eldorado soldiered on into 1998 with minimal changes. The Eldorado Touring Coupe is shown. **3-4.** A reworked Seville was the big news for Cadillac in '98. Though it retained the Northstar V-8 power of its predecessor, Seville was now based on the G-body platform shared by Oldsmobile's Aurora and Buick's Park Avenue and Riviera. SLS and STS (pictured) models continued. Its stiffer body structure, revised steering, and new rear suspension gave these new models much improved ride and handling. **5.** Monte Carlo, the coupe companion to Chevy's midsize Lumina sedan, got a new top-of-the-line V-6 engine: the 200-hp 3.8-liter unit. This engine was standard on the sporty Z34. This Monte Carlo LS still used the 160-hp 3.1 V-6. **6.** The Geo brand went belly up for the 1998 model year, and its existing products, like this Metro, were now sold wearing Chevy's bow-tie badge. **7.** Camaros wore a restyled nose for '98. This Z28 received even more V-8 power. Though still a Corvette-derived 5.7-liter V-8, the new LS1 engine's aluminum construction allowed the motor to pump out 305 hp, an increase of 20 over the old cast-iron V-8. **8.** Lumina LTZ models became available with the 3.8-liter V-6 engine as a new option, though the 160-hp 3.1-liter V-6 remained the standard powerplant in all Luminas, including this LS.

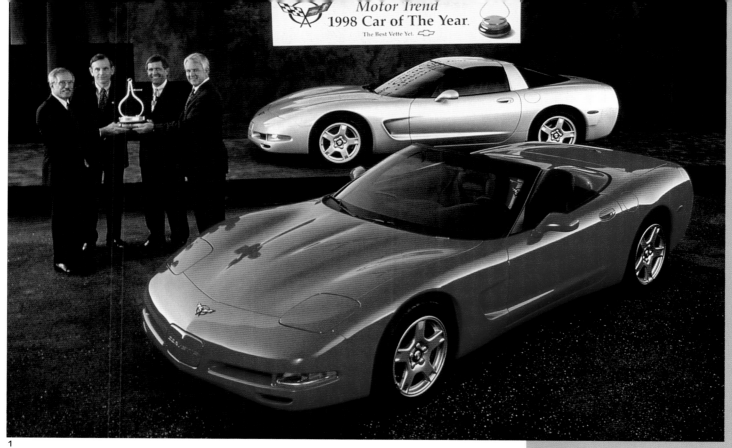

1. When Chevrolet designers set about creating the fifth-generation Corvette, they engineered it to accommodate a convertible body with no added structural bracing. That planning came to fruition for 1998 as a convertible joined the coupe version of GM's flagship sports car, and the dynamic duo won the coveted *Motor Trend* "Car of the Year" award. The convertible was the first 'Vette with a traditional trunk since the 1962 model. The top in the '98 version had to be folded manually. 2. A Corvette was chosen to pace the Indy 500 for the fourth time in 1998. The inevitable replicas were convertibles decorated with unique paint and flamboyant exterior and interior trim (foreground). The $5039 Pace Car Replica option package was ordered by 1163 buyers. 3. Changes to the Corvette for '98 included optional magnesium wheels and a provision that allowed the automatic transmission to start in second gear for cleaner slippery-surface getaways.

THE OLDS INTRIGUE: GO DOWN SWINGING

Economic, social, and other conditions were creating a perfect storm in and around the floundering Oldsmobile division during the mid-1990s. GM's market share had dwindled to less than 34 percent by 1995, prompting massive cost cutting. Around the same time, the start of the dot-com boom and cheap gasoline had the "nouveau riche" in dealerships purchasing GM's highly profitable large SUVs.

So while the company as a whole was making money, corporate bean counters were particularly dismayed by the continuous slide in Olds sales, which were then barely a third of record 1985's nearly 1.2 million units.

Enter the 1995 Olds Antares concept, with styling that would offer inspiration for the May 1997 launch of the '98 Intrigue. Alongside Aurora, Intrigue was part of the "Centennial Plan" that envisioned "more-international" Oldsmobiles designed to appeal to younger, more affluent customers who typically bought imports.

Intrigue, though related to the Buick Regal and Pontiac Grand Prix, was arguably Detroit's strongest challenger to the all-conquering Honda Accord and Toyota Camry. Intrigue rode a 109-inch wheelbase, the same as Regal's, but shorter than Grand Prix's. Styling was clean and understated, with more than a hint of Aurora. The interior, also tastefully restrained, featured clear, well-placed gauges and controls, plus comfortable space for four adults, or five in a pinch.

The only engine at first was GM's decidedly un-European 3.8-liter pushrod V-6. For 1999, Oldsmobile phased in a new 3.5-liter twin-cam V-6, derived from the all-aluminum Cadillac Northstar V-8.

All Intrigues came with premium features such as antilock four-wheel disc brakes, traction control, and 16-inch wheels at low- to mid-$20,000 prices.

Praise from the press was near-unanimous, hailing Intrigue as sophisticated and nimble, with a thoughtful blend of features and performance.

Despite a quality product and healthy initial sales of 108,000 for the extra-long '98 model year, "units moved" dropped by more than 20 percent for 2000.

GM announced the termination of the Oldsmobile brand in late 2000. Production of the Intrigue was unceremoniously halted in June 2002.

Nothing, it seemed, was sacred in Detroit at the turn of the millennium, not even America's oldest surviving automotive nameplate.

1. In addition to the Intrigue, the 1998 Oldsmobile car lineup included the little-changed Aurora (pictured), Eighty-Eight/LSS/Regency, and Cutlass. A few thousand 1998-model Achievas were built but were sold only to rental companies. This year would also prove to be the last for the Cutlass. When the car went away, that hallowed moniker was retired. The Bravada sport utility vehicle received a modest facelift. The Silhouette minivan added standard front side-impact airbags and available eight-passenger seating.

1

1

2

1. The Oldsmobile Eighty-Eight continued with two distinct front end appearances. Base, LS, and LSS (shown) models continued with the look introduced for 1996. The Regency was aimed at a more traditional buyer and maintained its own front end appearance adopted for 1997. 2. After its 1997 redesign, the midsize Grand Prix entered '98 with few changes. The new design was a hit, with sales running more than 35 percent ahead of its predecessor. This Grand Prix GT sedan has the GTP Performance Package. 3. This year, Bonneville SE sales totaled 48,778 units. 4. The SSEi Supercharger Package added $1170 to a Bonneville SSE's $29,390 base price. 5. The compact Sunfire, here in SE coupe form, had few changes since being introduced for

3

4

5

1995. Of special note in the Sunfire lineup was the sporty GT coupe, with styling that was radically different from the mechanically similar Chevy Cavalier Z24. Its attractive $15,495 base price bought a 150-hp engine, five-speed manual transmission, and 16-inch tires with alloy wheels. Power windows and a leather-wrapped steering wheel with radio controls were optional.

1-2. Like its Camaro sibling, the Pontiac Firebird got a new V-8 engine for 1998. Used in the Formula (top) and Trans Am (bottom), the V-8 was based on the Chevy Corvette's aluminum engine. It continued with a displacement of 5.7 liters but produced 305 horsepower, an increase of 20. Firebird's front end styling featured new fenders, hood, and fascia. At the rear there was a revised taillight panel. **3-4.** Seven years into its life, the Saturn division had won a devoted following by selling reliable cars with a one-price strategy. Saturn's biggest sellers were its sedans and wagons. Though prices had steadily increased over the years, they remained relatively reasonable. Just $10,595 could get shoppers into the base SL, with its 100-hp 1.9-liter four-cylinder engine and five-speed manual transmission. Those wanting more power could get into the 124-hp SL2 for $12,755. For added luxury, the SL2 sedan (top) and SW2 wagon (lower left) could be had with leather trim. **5.** Saturn's two-door coupes were heavily revised for 1997, so they carried into '98 with few changes. Engine choices for the SC1 and SC2 (shown) were identical to their sedan and wagon counterparts. Coupe prices ranged from just $12,595 to $15,715.

1

2

3

4

5

SILVER ARROW

1

2

3

4

5

1. Slow sales prompted Buick to stop production of the Riviera after about 2000 of the 1999 models were built. About 200 were Silver Arrow versions with distinctive silver exterior paint and special logos. The example pictured here stands with the 1963 Silver Arrow concept car that was based on the original Riviera. Also ending in 1999 was Buick production in Flint, Michigan. "Buick City," which began building front-drive vehicles in 1985, closed its doors in June. The division's administration had moved to GM's new headquarters at the Renaissance Center in downtown Detroit the previous year. **2.** Buick's LeSabre celebrated its 40th anniversary in 1999 and continued as Buick's best-selling model. This Limited sedan started at $25,790. **3.** Buick's flagship sedan was available in Park Avenue (shown) and Park Avenue Ultra versions. **4.** Buick's supercharged 240-horsepower Regal GS (shown) was fast, clocking 0-60 mph in just 6.9 seconds. Regal LS models used a 200-horsepower 3.8-liter V-6 engine. **5.** Cadillac's sporty import-fighter gained a few additional luxury touches for '99. GM set its sights on the Lexus LS 400 and BMW 5-Series with the Seville. An option on both Seville SLS and STS (shown) was Cadillac's "adaptive" heated front seats with internal air bladders that continuously adjusted to the passenger's contours. Another new feature was the addition of an optional massage feature for the front seats. Special rolling lumbar bolsters would massage passengers' lower backs in 10-minute cycles.

1. Though rumors abounded about a rear-drive replacement, Cadillac's front-drive luxury coupe went into 1999 unchanged from previous years. Eldorado was the best-selling car in the luxury-coupe segment, but declining sales in a shrinking market continued to cloud its future. 2. While the Seville was positioned to challenge midsize import rivals, Catera continued in its quest to win over shoppers of the near-luxury BMW 3-Series and Mercedes-Benz C-Class. It entered 1999 with no major changes. 3. Cadillac's largest car also gained massaging front seats as a new option. This feature was available on the mid-level De Ville d'Elegance and top-end Concours (shown). 4. Chevy Lumina received more standard equipment including cruise control, power windows, and automatic headlights. Base and LS (pictured) models had a front bench seat for six-passenger capacity. The sporty LTZ received as standard the 200-hp 3.8-liter V-6 engine, suspension upgrades, and 16-inch alloy wheels. 5. Chevy continued to offer the subcompact Metro as a vehicle for those who wanted a new, fuel-efficient car with a full warranty but didn't have a lot of money. Indeed, a spartanly equipped Metro hatchback could still be had for less than $10,000. Its 55-hp three-cylinder engine was rated at a thrifty 44 mpg city and 49 mpg highway, according to EPA fuel economy estimates. 6. Chevy's Venture minivan became available with eight-passenger seating. The Venture LS Extended Wheelbase model is shown. 7. Chevy further refined the '99 Malibu by offering a thicker windshield designed to cut down on road noise.

1

2

3

4

5

6

7

1

2

3

1. While 1999 brought few changes for the carryover coupe (rear) and convertible (center), it brought big news in the form of a new model. Dubbed "hardtop" by Chevy marketing, the new 'Vette (front) featured a solid, one-piece roof instead of the removable-panel top found on the coupe. The simpler construction afforded greater structural rigidity (though Corvette was already earning praise for its stout construction) and a modest 92-pound weight reduction. The hardtop was now the lowest-price Corvette, coming in at $38,777, a few hundred dollars less than the coupe. Intended to be a serious sports car, the hardtop came standard with the six-speed manual transmission and extra-firm Z51 performance suspension. These options would have totaled $1195 on the coupe or convertible. The hard-nosed hardtop attracted a small following its first year, accounting for just 4000 of the 33,270 'Vettes sold. New for the coupe and convertible was a head-up instrument panel display system that projected speed and engine rpm onto the windshield. **2.** Factory-backed Corvettes would return to international racing in 2000. This pair of specially equipped C5 hardtop pace cars were used in the 1999 running of the 24 Hours of LeMans in France. **3.** Chevrolet's Camaro clinged to life despite slow sales. Camaro came as a hatchback coupe or convertible in base V-6 and V-8 Z28 form. Convertibles had a power top with a glass rear window. The Z28-based SS package (shown) included a 320-horse V-8, functional hood scoop, larger tires, rear spoiler, and upgraded suspension.

1. The hallowed Eighty-Eight moniker celebrated its 50th, and final, year in 1999. The special Eighty-Eight 50th Anniversary Edition sedan shown here came with standard traction control, dual-zone climate control, load-leveling suspension, and 16-inch alloy wheels. **2.** Also ending production in 1999 was the first-generation Aurora. Its replacement would have the same name and basic platform, but the new model would actually replace the Eighty-Eight. **3.** The big news for the 1999 Intrigue was the addition of a new engine. Instead of the venerable 3.8-liter overhead-valve V-6, buyers could opt for a sophisticated twin-cam 3.5-liter V-6. Derived from Cadillac's Northstar V-8, the "Shortstar" produced 215 horsepower, 20 more than the 3.8. At first, the engine was standard only in the Intrigue GLS shown here. Eventually, it would power all Intrigues. **4-5.** Oldsmobile launched the Alero as the replacement for the slow-selling Achieva. Based on the Pontiac Grand Am, Alero was offered in four-door sedan (left) and two-door coupe (right) body styles, each with a choice of two engines. Standard on the base GX (left) and mid-level GL models was a 2.4-liter four-cylinder. Available on GL sedans and standard on GLS coupes (right) and sedans was a 3.4-liter V-6 engine borrowed from the Silhouette minivan. **6.** Pontiac's special edition 30th Anniversary Trans Am is shown here resplendent in its unique white and blue color combination. This color scheme was inspired by the only colors available on the original 1969 Trans Am parked in the background.

1

2

3

4

5

1. In anticipation of a redesigned model for the year 2000, Bonneville essentially stood pat for '99. GM did make the OnStar assistance system available on all trim levels of the Bonnie, including this SE. 2. Grand Prix benefited from a number of detail changes. GT models, like this coupe, now had a standard rear spoiler. 3. Grand Am got a much-needed redesign for '99. These versions had a 3.6-inch-longer wheelbase and were two inches wider than their predecessors. Overall length was unchanged, however. Two-door coupes and four-door sedans remained available. SE, SE1 (shown), and SE2 trim levels were joined by sportier GT and GT1 versions. No manual transmission was offered. An interesting feature of the Grand Am's interior was its speedometer; it had one hash mark for every mile per hour—120 in all. 4. Sunfire convertibles went from SE to GT trim for 1999. That change included an engine swap from a 115-hp 2.2-liter four-cylinder to the 150-hp 2.4-liter engine. 5. This 1999 Saturn family photo groups an SC2 (front), SW1 (center), and SL2 (rear). 6. Saturn's biggest news was the addition of a back-hinged rear access door on the driver side of its SC coupes. It didn't open independently of the front door, but it allowed for much easier access to the rear seating area. This was a unique feature among small coupes.

6

CHAPTER ELEVEN

2000-2008

"Adversity is a stimulus."

—James Broughton

GM watched its market share steadily decline in the 1990s, from 35.6 percent in 1990 to 29.4 percent in 1999. A boom economy for most of the decade kept the profits coming, despite increasing competition from Japanese automakers. For the year 2000, its market share dropped another 1.1 points to 28.3 percent, the lowest for a full year since 1926. But the company still made $4.5 billion as the industry enjoyed record sales of 17.4 million cars and light trucks. Profits would have been higher if not for an industry-wide average of $2800 in incentives per vehicle.

General Motors reached out once again to foreign automakers to expand globally. In February 2000, GM increased its equity in Swedish automaker Saab to 100 percent, making it a full-fledged GM division. In March, General Motors spent $2.4 billion to create an alliance with Italian automaker Fiat to share powertrains and other components. With the deal, GM held 20 percent equity in Fiat. Fiat would go on to struggle mightily, and in February 2005, GM paid $2 billion to free itself from the partnership. GM did benefit from the short-lived partnership, gaining diesel technology, but industry analysts felt it came at too high a cost. Then, in September, GM spent $600 million to increase its share in Suzuki to 20 percent. The move was made to help GM boost sales in Asia.

Rick Wagoner, who had been elected president in 1998, was named CEO June 1, 2000, with Jack Smith remaining as Chairman of the Board. Under pressure to maximize profits and cut costs, management made the difficult decision in December to phase out Oldsmobile over the next few years. Olds was losing an estimated $120 million a year, making it a prime candidate for the chopping block. Though the product portfolio had changed for the better, there simply weren't enough buyers. The phase-

out of the brand was protracted until the 2004 model year as GM worked out an estimated $1 billion worth of settlements with dealers.

On the product side, Saturn added a second model line for the 2000 model year. The new midsize sedans and wagons were called L-Series. The carryover compacts took on the S-Series name. Loosely related to the Opel Vectra from GM's German arm, L-Series cars had Saturn's trademark plastic body panels. "The next big thing from Saturn," as they were advertised, didn't turn out to be that big after all. Saturn spent $1.2 billion to develop the cars and projected as many as 300,000 sales per year. Sales topped out at about 100,000 units in 2002. The line was unceremoniously dropped after the 2005 model year.

Pontiac Bonneville, Buick LeSabre, and Cadillac DeVille were redesigned for 2000 on the G platform used for the Buick Park Avenue and Olds Aurora. DeVille was loaded with technology and was a better car than the previous model, but sales never broke 100,000.

Chevy replaced the Lumina this year with its first-ever front-drive Impala, which used a revised version of the W-body platform. Traditionalists and police agencies had hoped for a rear-drive configuration, but the car sold well regardless. More than 200,000 were sold that first year, with sales climbing to more than 300,000 for 2004. The two-door Monte Carlo coupe was revised on the Impala's platform for 2000, too.

GM had more management news for 2001. Rick Wagoner hired industry veteran Bob Lutz as vice chairman for product development in September, and Lutz added the title of chairman of GM North America in November when Ron Zarrella returned to Bausch & Lomb to become its CEO. Lutz, a noted car guy and the former Chrysler Corp. president, was hired to shake up the status quo and energize the product portfolio.

About a week after the September 11 terrorist attacks, GM launched its "Keep America Rolling" zero-percent financing retail-marketing program. The program was meant to inspire consumer confidence, and that it did. GM vehicle sales increased 31 percent in the first month of the program, but it was criticized for hurting profits and pulling vehicle sales forward instead of bringing new buyers to the market. Despite the low margins, GM still made a profit of $601 million in 2001.

Product news was light for 2001. The Olds Aurora was redesigned on the G-body platform and, for the first time, offered a V-6 engine in addition to a V-8. Corvette added a new performance model for 2001 called Z06. Under the hood was the LS6, a revised version of the LS1 5.7-liter V-8 that made 385 hp that first year and 405 the next. Exterior and suspension changes were also made in the name of performance, and perform it did, blasting from 0-60 mph in 4.3 seconds.

Heavy incentives continued for 2002, forcing GM to raise prices three times. But industry wide sales remained strong at 16.6 million units, and GM turned a $1.7 billion profit. Strong SUV sales were the biggest help, but product czar Bob Lutz was pushing car development, too. GM announced that its entire North American midsize car portfolio would be revamped over the next three years.

After more than a year of negotiations, GM paid $400 million to buy parts of bankrupt Korean automaker Daewoo Motor Company this year. The agreement created a new company called GM Daewoo Auto & Technology, with GM owning 42 percent. It was yet another example of GM reaching out to a foreign manufacturer to help build small cars for the domestic market.

Chevy's Camaro and Pontiac's Firebird were now in the midst of a steep sales slide. Looking to cut costs, GM killed its ponycars after 2002, even while celebrating the Camaro's 35th anniversary with a special red and silver anniversary option package.

GM was once again at the forefront of heavy incentives in 2003 despite complaints from other automakers that were forced to follow suit. CEO Rick Wagoner even told his rivals that it was "time to stop whining" as GM kept on the pressure. Once again, strong truck sales helped bolster profits, and GM made $3.8 billion in 2003, despite the fact that its market share was down 0.3 percent to 28.0 percent after two years of modest gains. In addition to his CEO responsibilities, Wagoner was elected Chairman effective May 1, 2003, following the retirement of Jack Smith.

The company then split off the remaining components of its Hughes Electronics subsidiary and sold its economic interest in Hughes to Rupert Murdoch's News Corp. GM also completed the sale of its GM Defense unit to General Dynamics Corporation.

In product news, Saturn replaced the S-Series in 2003 with a new car called Ion. Offered as a four-door sedan or four-door coupe (with two rear-hinged back doors), the Ion used GM's new Delta platform. About the only S-Series feature to carry over to Ion was the use of plastic body panels. Sales never reached Saturn's projected 160,000 annual figure. Ions became more fun in 2004, when Saturn released a "Red Line" variant with performance chassis tuning and a 205-hp supercharged version of GM's Ecotec 4-cylinder engine.

Corvette celebrated its 50th anniversary in 2003 with a $5000 option package that included red paint and champagne-colored wheels. Pontiac added the latest product to emerge from its joint venture with Toyota, the compact Vibe four-door wagon. Based on the Toyota Corolla, the Vibe was the twin to the Toyota Matrix, and it posted more than 84,000 sales in its extended inaugural model year.

Cadillac began a renaissance for its car lineup this year with the release of the midsize CTS. Introduced as an early 2003 model and based on the new, rear-drive "Sigma" architecture, CTS replaced the Catera. With CTS, GM made an all-out effort to build a world-class, entry luxury sport sedan, tuning the suspension on Germany's Nurburgring race circuit. Styling was polarizing, using Cadillac's new hard-edged "Art & Science" design. Though it wasn't the most powerful entry in the class, CTS moved more than 75,000 units during an extended debut model year.

Thanks to the continued heavy use of incentives, the 2004 calendar year was the fifth in a row for the industry over 16 million units. GM made $2.8 billion, including $1.2 billion from automotive operations.

Chevrolet had three new cars for 2004. Slotting beneath the Cavalier was the new, subcompact Aveo, a product of GM's acquisition of Korean automaker Daewoo. Chevy also redid Malibu, placing it on the front-drive "Epsilon" platform used by the near-luxury Saab 9-3. Four-door sedans were offered, as was a four-door wagon/hatchback called Malibu Maxx. Maxx models had a six-inch-longer wheelbase than sedans.

At Pontiac, the Bonneville was treated to a 275-hp version of the Northstar V-8, the first Bonneville V-8 in almost two decades. More importantly, the Grand Prix four-door sedan was heavily revised on the circa 1988 W-body platform. Pontiac's trademark lower-body cladding was gone, and the roof was given a coupelike rake. A performance Comp G package came with a 260-hp supercharged 3.8 V-6, pushing the GP to 60 mph in 6.6 seconds. The bigger engine news came in the middle of the 2005 model year, when the Grand Prix GXP debuted with a 303-hp 5.3-liter V-8.

Pontiac's biggest news for 2004, though, was the return of a hallowed name: GTO. Based on the rear-drive Monaro coupe from GM's Australian division Holden, the GTO had a 350-hp 5.7-liter V-8, derived from the Corvette. The new Goat could blast from 0 to 60 mph in 5.3 seconds, and, unlike its storied predecessors of the 1960s and early '70s, it could slice through corners, too. Pontiac tweaked the car with bold hood scoops and a switch to Corvette's 6.0-liter LS6 V-8 with 400 bhp for 2005, but weak sales prompted Pontiac to drop the GTO after the 2006 model year.

Cadillac made several important product moves for the 2004 model year. The CTS got more power from two new engine choices. Optional on base models was GM's new "high-feature" 3.6-liter V-6. The dual-overhead-cam engine produced a healthy 255 hp. Also available was the new, high horsepower CTS-V. Outfitted with the Corvette Z06's LS6 V-8, the CTS-V made 400 hp and could sprint from 0 to 60 mph in less than five seconds. GM even took the CTS-V racing in the SCCA's Speed World Challenge series.

For the first time since the ill-fated Allanté, Cadillac got a two-seat convertible in 2004, the XLR. Developed by the team working on the next Corvette, the XLR used the same type of architecture—a spaceframe with a central spine—but it also had a convertible hardtop. Power came from the Northstar V-8, and the base price was $75,385. Cadillac sold just 4387 XLRs that first year, but it was meant as a halo car, not a high-volume money-maker. For all its efforts (including the release of the SRX cross-over), Cadillac's U.S. sales rose 8.4 percent, the division's best performance since 1990.

The wheels came off in 2005, as numerous factors conspired to cause GM to lose a total of $10.4 billion. In February, GM paid $2 billion to extract itself from Fiat. Increasing fuel costs caused customers to turn away from highly profitable trucks and SUVs. The company introduced its "GM Employee Discount for Everyone" marketing program in June to increase sales, and it worked. However, the aftermath of Hurricane Katrina, combined with Middle East unrest, helped push the price of gas to more than $3.00 a gallon. This further hurt truck sales, which finished the year down almost 10 percent. Heavy legacy obligations were also a growing burden for GM, as healthcare costs and pension liabilities accounted for anywhere from $1500 to $2000 for every vehicle GM sold. Some relief arrived in October when the UAW agreed to healthcare and pension concessions, but it was clear more would need to be done. Also in October, Delphi, the parts supplier GM had spun off in 1999, filed Chapter 11. Delphi's financial crisis was especially troubling for GM management, as a protracted shutdown of its largest vendor could have crippled operations. For the year, GM incurred $3.6 billion in restructuring and benefit guarantee costs in relation to the Delphi bankruptcy.

Given all the negative news, GM announced plans to slash 30,000 jobs and close 12 manufacturing facilities by 2010. With the painful cutbacks, leadership hoped to reduce operating costs by $6 billion in 2006. Adding to GM's woes, market share was down to 26.2 percent—off 1.3 points from 2004.

Despite the struggles, GM continued to spend money on product development and CEO Rick Wagoner said that would continue. The biggest 2005 model-year news at Chevrolet was the next generation Corvette, or C6. Though not a clean-sheet redesign like the C5 before it, the C6 was 85 percent new by weight, according to chief engineer Dave Hill. The standard V-8, bored to 6.0 liters, was now called LS2, and it made 400 hp. Hatchback and convertible body styles were offered. Chevy replaced the aged Cavalier in 2005 with Cobalt, a compact based on the Delta platform used by the Saturn Ion.

Pontiac replaced its Grand Am with the G6 in mid-2004 as an early 2005 model. Pontiac introduced the car to the public by giving away 276 of them in September 2003 on the *Oprah Winfrey Show*. The car was built on the same Epsilon platform as the Chevy Malibu Maxx and was initially only available as a four-door sedan with a single V-6 engine. Model-year 2006 saw the G6 lineup expand to include an available 4-cylinder engine, two-door coupe, and two-door convertible models. The convertible used a power-retractable hardtop instead of a traditional soft top.

The Buick LaCrosse replaced Regal for 2005. It was built on 110.5-inch-wheelbase W-body platform shared with Grand Prix. Sporty CXS models benefited from a 240-bhp version of GM's 3.6-liter V-6. At Cadillac, the Seville was redesigned as the STS for 2005, using a longer version of the CTS's Sigma platform. Power came from the 3.6-liter V-6 or the 4.6-liter Northstar V-8, and all-wheel drive was offered.

GM's turnaround plan started to show signs of progress in 2006. Approximately 35,000 U.S. hourly employees agreed to buyouts, and the company lowered operating costs by $6.8 billion, exceeding its goal by $800 million. To raise cash, GM sold off 51 percent of its highly profitable GMAC financing arm to a consortium of investors led by Cerberus Capital Management, LP. Cerberus would go on to buy Chrysler from Daimler-Benz in 2007. Amidst rumors of his ouster, Chairman Rick Wagoner demanded a vote of confidence from the board of directors and got it in April. That helped him fend off an assault by billionaire investor Kirk Kerkorian in October. Kerkorian had accumulated a 9.9 percent stake in GM and put his advisor Jerry York on the board of directors. Together York and Kerkorian urged GM to enter into a strategic alliance with Renault, which had been led to profitability by Carlos Ghosn. Instead, Wagoner got his way—GM passed on the proposal, and York left the board soon thereafter.

In addition to the GMAC sale, GM reduced its equity stake in Suzuki Motor Corp. from 20.4 percent to 3.0 percent and sold off its 7.9 percent equity stake in Isuzu Motors Ltd. As part of both deals, GM continued business alliances with the companies.

When all was said and done, GM sold 9.1 million vehicles worldwide in 2006. U.S. market share dropped another 1.7 points to 24.5 percent, and the company lost $2 billion. Though still a considerable sum of money, the total loss was better than many analysts expected.

Chevrolet added the compact HHR for 2006. Based on the Cobalt, the retro styling of the HHR (for Heritage High Roof) recalled the 1950 Chevy Suburban, but in a much smaller package. Chevy also reskinned the Impala and Monte Carlo this year. The W-body platform was retained, but the big news was the availability of GM's 5.3-liter V-8 in SS models. Like the Pontiac Grand Prix GXP, the V-8 pumped 303 hp through the front wheels, making these cars downright quick.

Corvette added its most monstrous performance model yet for 2006, with a new Z06. Using lessons learned in its C5-R racing program, the Z06 had a fixed-roof coupe body, a stiffer structure, and body-integrated cooling ducts. Most importantly, it featured a 7.0-liter version of the LS2 V-8 called LS7, which made a whopping 505 hp. Capable of a 3.6-second 0-60 blast and starting at under $65,000, the Z06 was a performance bargain compared with its exotic competitors.

In 2006, Pontiac released its first-ever two-seat sports car, the Solstice. A pet project of product chief Bob Lutz, the Solstice concept car was completed in just 18 weeks and shown at the 2002 Detroit Auto Show. GM announced in 2004 that Solstice would make it to production, and it hit the streets just 27 months thereafter. With a starting price just shy of $20,000, Solstice was a

smash hit with buyers. GM booked more orders than it could build that first year and sold almost 20,000 for calendar year 2006.

Buick and Cadillac had new models based on the G-body front-drive architecture. Lucerne replaced both LeSabre and Park Avenue, while the Cadillac DTS replaced the DeVille. Lucerne offered V-6 or Northstar V-8 power, and the DTS came only with the V-8. Cadillac also released racy "V" variants of the STS and XLR for 2006, giving them performance suspensions and a supercharged 4.4-liter version the Northstar V-8 that made up to 469 hp. Each was capable of 0-60 mph in about five seconds.

GM's turnaround plan started to bear real fruit in 2007, as the company began to turn a profit, all while continuing a product offensive.

Saturn became the poster child for a revitalized General Motors, a company that would make greater use of its assets outside North America. In 2006, GM product chief Bob Lutz had announced that most of Saturn's products would now be essentially rebadged versions of Opel cars designed by GM's German subsidiary. Small cars would no longer be the main focus. The division's new midsize sedan, called Aura, used the Epsilon platform shared with Pontiac G6 and Chevy Malibu. It was a far cry from the L-Series of old. Plastic body panels were gone, and Aura offered two V-6 engines, as well as a gas/electric hybrid variant, a first for a GM car (the division's Vue crossover SUV introduced the hybrid powertrain earlier in the 2007 model year).

Saturn also got a two-seat roadster for model year 2007 based on the Pontiac Solstice's architecture, but the Sky was more angular than the rounded Solstice. Base Skys were powered by the same 2.4-liter 4-cylinder as the Solstice, but a new engine was offered this year for both cars. GM developed a new 2.0-liter turbocharged 4-cylinder with 260 hp and installed it in performance-oriented Sky Red Line and Solstice GXP.

GM's product lineup for 2008 and beyond is even more promising. Cadillac's renaissance is complete, and the company is moving forward with fine products, including an outstanding redesign of the CTS for 2008. Saturn's move upmarket has gotten off to a good start with popular cars such as Sky and Aura. GM also plans to transform Pontiac into an affordable performance brand with a lineup of rear-wheel-drive cars. The first step in the process is the 2008 G8, which replaces the Grand Prix. Other performance cars, such as the reborn Chevy Camaro and the possible 700-hp, $100,000 Corvette SS, should spark the imagination of enthusiasts and bring people into the showrooms.

While enthusiasts should have plenty to cheer about, GM is also working toward achieving better fuel economy. The company rolled out its "Two Mode" hybrid technology in 2008. Introduced on the Chevrolet Tahoe and GMC Yukon full-size SUVs, the fuel-saving system should eventually be available on other traditionally thirsty vehicles including GM's full-size pickups and the Cadillac Escalade.

The Chevrolet Volt concept vehicle shown at the 2007 Detroit Auto Show could make a plug-in hybrid a reality within a few years, if development of battery technology is swift. GM is also at work on efficient diesel engines for both cars and trucks and has been developing a viable hydrogen fuel cell vehicle. The company plans to offer a pilot program where 100 Chevrolet Equinox fuel-cell SUVs will be driven by the general public and government officials.

The last few years leading to General Motors' 100th anniversary have been fraught with adversity. Though many things may have conspired against it, General Motors remains resolute in its desire to be on the forefront of automotive manufacturing, design, and technology. Current products bear this out, and if things move ahead as planned, the future for this very American institution looks promising indeed.

—*Kirk Bell*

1. Front side impact airbags became standard on Buick's flagship Park Avenue sedan for 2000. **2.** Regals gained a split folding rear seatback. A GS is shown here. **3.** Cadillac's DeVille sedan was redesigned for 2000, with new styling and a host of high-tech features. The most notable addition was an infrared night vision system. Night vision would detect heat-generating objects beyond headlight range and project a black-and-white image onto the windshield just above hood level. Power for the DeVille came from a choice of two Northstar V-8s. **4.** The DeVille DTS boasted 300 horsepower. Lesser DeVilles made do with a 275-horse version of the Northstar V-8. **5.** Freshened styling, a revised interior, and suspension revisions highlighted changes to the entry-level Catera. Cadillac hoped its newly firmed-up chassis would bring the sedan more in step with the dynamic abilities of most European-brand rivals. An available Sport Package (shown here) included unique wheels, an even firmer suspension, and articulating sport seats with adjustable thigh bolsters. **6.** Cadillac fielded an entry in the 2000 24 Hours of LeMans endurance race. **7.** This dressed-up Seville helped pace the LeMans race.

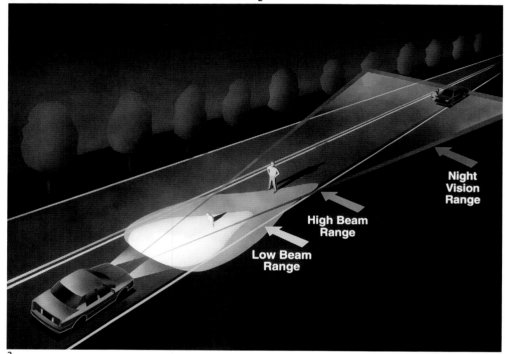

Night Vision Range

High Beam Range

Low Beam Range

1

2

3

4

5

1. Chevrolet revived the Impala moniker in 2000. Instead of a large, rear-drive car, this latest iteration was a midsize, front-drive sedan. No V-8 engines here, just a pair of V-6s: a 180-hp 3.4-liter unit for base models and the 200-hp 3.8 for the uplevel LS shown here. About the only thing this Impala shared with the V-8-powered SS of the mid-1990s was a roomy interior. **2.** Chevy also used 2000 to debut a redesigned Monte Carlo coupe. This SS came standard with aluminum wheels. **3.** Camaro headed into 2000 with few changes. A base coupe is shown here. Camaro sales had been shrinking rapidly for last several model years. Production in 1994 was nearly 120,000 units. For 2000, that number was less than 50,000. **4.** GM's best-selling car, the Chevy Cavalier, entered 2000 with subtle styling changes inside and out. Chevy added more value to this car by moving air conditioning to the standard equipment. The sporty Z24 received a revised 5-speed manual transmission. Designed by Getrag, it offered slicker shifts than previous versions. A base coupe is shown here. **5.** Changes to the '00 Corvette were minor. Enthusiasts were waiting with bated breath for a new high-performance hardtop model that was slated to appear next year. It would have the potential to trump the late, lamented ZR-1. At $2000, the Sport Magnesium wheels on this convertible were the most expensive option available. As such, they weren't especially popular—of the approximately 33,000 'Vettes sold in 2000, less than 2700 came equipped with the lightweight rims.

1

1. Two weeks before Christmas 2000, GM announced plans to phase out the Oldsmobile brand over the next several years. All future-model development was halted. Shown here from left to right is the brand's final lineup: Silhouette, Bravada, Aurora, Intrigue, and Alero. 2. The biggest news at Pontiac in 2000 was a redesigned Bonneville. Outside, the look was edgy. Inside, a redone interior was made more conventional with easier-to-use controls. This SSEi had a supercharged version of the 3.8-liter V-6 good for 240 horsepower. 3-4. Like its Chevy Cavalier sibling, the Pontiac Sunfire received a subtle exterior facelift along with standard air conditioning. A GT convertible and coupe are shown here. 5. There were Trans Ams, and there were *Trans Ams.* This king of the hill Firebird Trans Am boasts the optional WS6 performance package. The most important part of the WS6 upgrade was a horsepower boost from 310 to 325. Contributing to the extra muscle was a freer-flowing intake courtesy of the Ram Air hood shown here. The WS6 package was available on the midline Formula model as well.

2

3

4

5

1. After nearly a decade of exclusively marketing small cars, Saturn introduced the midsize L-Series for 2000. Available as a sedan or wagon, these cars featured Saturn's trademark plastic body panels and the choice of a 137-hp 4-cylinder or 182-hp V-6 engine. The L-Series was based on the German Opel Vectra but built in the U.S.
2. All S-Series models received a revamped interior. Sedans and coupes got exterior styling revisions as well. Powertrains were unchanged, but sedans and wagons were 1.2 inches longer.

1. Buick Park Avenues received optional ultrasonic rear parking assist for 2001. The system used a series of lights visible in the inside mirror to warn of obstacles when the car was put in reverse. A self-leveling rear suspension was standard. An optional Gran Touring Package included firmer suspension tuning and more aggressive tires. Leather upholstery became standard on all Park Avenue models this year, not just the top-end Ultra (shown here). The base model also gained the Ultra's interior memory system, which allowed a choice of two driver-programmed presets for climate controls, front seats, and outside mirrors. **2.** LeSabres remained the best selling full-size car in the U.S. Not wanting to mess with the formula, 2001 editions were largely unchanged. Aluminum wheels were standard on the Limited shown here. **3.** Olympic-themed editions were new to the '01 Buick Regal. The Olympic editions came in LS and GS trims. They added special gold, silver, or graphite paint with a lighter lower body color, plus taupe leather interior, USA Olympic insignia, and the firmer Gran Touring suspension. The Olympic cars' look was done by clothing designer Joseph Abboud. Later in the model year, Buick introduced Regals with special Abboud trim packages. **4.** The 2001 Cadillac DeVille, including this DTS model, continued to offer luxury car buyers lots high-tech gadgetry. The available navigation system included a touch-screen display. Standard DTS features included 17-inch chrome wheels and Cadillac's Stabilitrak antiskid system. Night vision remained optional.

1

2

3

4

1

2

3

4

1. Cadillac's Eldorado rolled into 2001 largely unchanged. 2. The Seville STS got an optional "Infotainment" system that could display e-mail messages on a color dashboard screen. 3. Cadillac's German-built Catera replaced its solid rear-disc brakes with higher-performance vented units. 4. Buyers of 2001 Chevrolet Monte Carlos could purchase their cars with some newly optional appearance packages. The High Sport Appearance Package on the SS (pictured) includes lower-body cladding, unique wheels, and bright exhaust tips. 5. Impala LS models like this one received standard OnStar assistance for 2001. This feature became optional for base models. 6. The 2001 Malibu received some minor upgrades, one of which involved the remote entry system. Each keyfob could be programmed to remember the driver's pre-set radio stations. This Malibu is shod with the extra-cost aluminum wheels.

5

6

1

2

3

4

1. Corvette enthusiasts rejoiced in 2001 with the introduction of the ultra-high-performance Z06 model (foreground). This hardtop coupe came with a new, 385-hp 5.7-liter "LS6" engine. LS6 was named after an early 1970s high-performance Chevrolet V-8. It came with a 6-speed manual transmission, and Chevy claimed it could go from 0 to 60 mph in 4 seconds flat. **2-3.** Though the division was headed for extinction, Olds brought out a redesigned Aurora in early 2000 as an '01. The 250-hp 4.0-liter V-8 engine was still available, but Aurora could now be had as a less-expensive V-6 model. To make room for the Aurora's broader price range, Oldsmobile killed the same-size Eighty Eight. **4.** Though a 2001 model, the new Aurora was introduced early enough to pace the 2000 Indy 500.

1

2

3

4

1. With the redesigned Aurora making news for Oldsmobile in 2001, the rest of the lineup shuffled some features. The 170-hp 3.4-liter V-6 engine became available on more Alero models this year. Also, Intrigues gained traction control as standard equipment on all models. **2.** After a one-year hiatus, OnStar assistance was once again available on Pontiac Bonnevilles like this SE. **3.** Part car, part SUV, part minivan, and altogether polarizing, Pontiac's Aztek "crossover" launched as an '01 model. Loosely based on the Montana minivan, Aztek had four conventional doors and hatchback styling. Though it had the versatility of an SUV, Aztek wasn't designed to venture very far off the beaten path. It debuted with front-wheel drive, and all-wheel drive was added later in the model year. Power was derived from the Montana's 185-hp 3.4-liter V-6 engine and 4-speed automatic transmission. The press panned Aztek's unusual look, and the public responded accordingly. Pontiac planned to sell 60,000 annually, but 18 months after launch, just over 38,000 had been sold. A GT is shown. **4.** Like all Grand Prix models, this GTP saw little change for 2001.

1. Both base- and WS6 Trans Am V-8s got a five-horsepower boost for 2001, to 310 and 325, respectively. 2. The WS6 Ram Air option shown here was no longer available on the Formula; it could only be ordered on the Trans Am. 3. Saturn's large cars got revised model names for '01 and also received optional side curtain airbags. Instead of LS, LS1, and LS2 designations, sedans became the L100, L200, and L300, respectively. Wagons, formerly the LW1 and LW2, became the LW200 and LW300. 4. Saturn's 2001 S-Series coupes arrived in the spring of 2000 with freshened styling. They retained their unique, driver-side rear-hinged back door. 5-6. SL2 sedans and SW2 wagons (pictured here) were largely unchanged this year. The price-leader SL added some new standard features including power steering and body-color bumpers.

BOB LUTZ: GM'S RENAISSANCE MAN

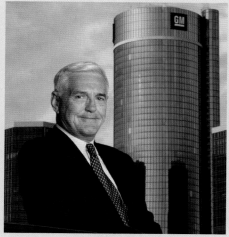

Robert "Bob" A. Lutz was born February 12, 1932, in Zurich, Switzerland. Lutz has had a long and storied career in the automotive industry, having worked for all three Detroit-based manufacturers at some point.

Lutz served in the United States Marine Corps from 1954–1965 as a jet-attack aviator, where he attained the rank of captain. During his service, he received a bachelor's degree in production management from the University of California–Berkeley, where he earned distinction as a Phi Beta Kappa. He received a master's degree in business administration, with highest honors, from the same university in 1962. He also received an honorary doctorate of law from Boston University in 1985 and an honorary degree of doctor of management from Kettering University on June 21, 2003. The Society of Automotive Engineers Foundation named him the recipient of its 2006 Manufacturing Leadership Award, which recognizes individuals who have made meaningful contributions to the development of the automotive industry.

Interestingly enough, Lutz began his automotive career at General Motors in 1963, where he held a variety of senior positions in Europe until December 1971. For the following three years, he served as executive vice president of sales at BMW in Munich and as a member of that company's board of management.

Until he rejoined GM in 2001 as chairman of GM North America, Lutz was probably best known for his time with the former Chrysler Corporation. He began his service with Chrysler in 1986 as executive vice president and was shortly thereafter elected to the company's board. Lutz spent 12 years at Chrysler, and during that time he helped oversee the development of such vehicles as the Dodge Viper and Plymouth Prowler sports cars. Lutz left Chrysler and later joined Exide Technologies as chairman and chief executive officer.

Lutz came back to GM in September 2001, where he was named vice chairman of product development. He also served as president of GM Europe on an interim basis from March to June 2004. He then became GM's Vice Chairman of Global Product Development.

In his role as vice chairman, Lutz was one of GM's biggest champions of leveraging the corporation's worldwide holdings to bring products to North America. He was largely responsible for bringing the Holden Monaro to the United States as the reborn Pontiac GTO.

Perhaps his most significant pet project was the Pontiac Solstice, a project that went from concept to production in less than four years. He had to break many of GM's internal rules to get it done, but the swoopy Solstice was a fine example of what GM could achieve, given the opportunity.

And Lutz hasn't showed signs of slowing down either, helping GM realize new vehicles that are proving critical to the company's turnaround efforts. Those models include the Buick Enclave crossover SUV, next-generation Cadillac CTS, and compact Saturn Astra.

1. Shoppers weren't interested in big luxury coupes like they used to be. By 2002, volume of the Cadillac Eldorado was only about a third of what it was a decade before: less than 10,500 units when Cadillac pulled the plug. About 1600 were Eldorado Collector Series cars, which had the usual "Collector Edition" badges plus a exhaust system tuned to mimic the original 1953 Eldorado. With its passing went the iconic and long-running Eldorado nameplate, as the division decided that most of its future models would have three-letter monickers. 2. The Cadillac DTS received a new navigation system for 2002. It incorporated DVD mapping and voice recognition. Video DVDs could be played on the dashboard screen when the car was in Park.

1-2. Chevy added standard dual-zone climate control to all Impala models, including this base car, for the 2002 season. **3.** The Cavalier Z24 model was dropped. It was replaced by the LS Sport (pictured). Instead of a 2.4-liter twin-cam 4-cylinder engine, the LS Sport offered GM's new "Ecotec" 2.2-liter 4-cylinder engine. It also had dual-overhead cams but produced 140 hp. The pushrod 2.2-liter 4-cylinder engine remained available on base and LS Cavaliers. **4.** The last remnants of the ill-fated Geo brand went away after the 2002 model year, when the Prizm (branded as a Chevrolet) was discontinued. Though it was mechanically identical to the Toyota Corolla, the Prizm was outsold by the Japanese-branded car 4-to-1. **5.** The '02 Monte Carlo carried forward without any major changes this year. **6-7.** Just one year after its introduction, the high-end Corvette Z06 got a 20-hp boost for '02, giving it a total of 405. Despite a $2650 increase in price (to $50,150), sales of the Z06 reached 8300, 2500 more than a year ago. **8.** Camaros could be outfitted as police cars. These sporty law-enforcement vehicles were a far cry from those that used to be built on the old Caprice platform. **9.** GM basically ended the ponycar wars by discontinuing the Chevy Camaro and Pontiac Firebird after 2002. For Camaro's final year, a 35th Anniversary Package (pictured) with special trim was available.

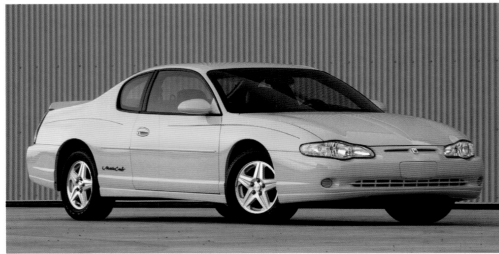

1

2

3

4

5

1-2. Former Oldsmobile public relations director Gus Buenz put the plight of the division in very succinct terms. He said, "We've got good products, but not enough people know about [them]." GM originally planned to build Oldsmobiles until the end of their product lifecycles, or as long as the division remained economically viable. That plan changed rather quickly, when it was announced that production was indeed unprofitable and that 2004 would be the division's final model year. This particular news stunned (and angered) dealers, as well as those working at Oldsmobile itself. Some designers, engineers, and marketers were also caught completely off guard. With the news that Olds was to officially become history, GM acted quickly when making the initial round of product reductions. Having survived just three model years, Intrigue production stopped in June 2002. Shown here are a regular-production 2002 Intrigue and a one-off OSV (Oldsmobile Specialty Vehicle) show car that sported custom wheels, an aero body kit, and an Aurora V-8 (top). **3.** V-8-powered Auroras hung around after 2002. But production of the base model with the Intrigue's V-6 engine was halted in June '02 as well. Though recent years saw Oldsmobile receive one of its strongest product lineups, GM decided it was time to take the division off life support. **4.** Pontiac added some value to its Montana minivans by making them available with all-wheel drive for 2002. The Versatrak system allowed for improved grip in wet or snowy conditions. **5.** Newly available on the Montana was a rear DVD entertainment system.

1

2

3

4

5

6

1. Pontiac's Grand Prix celebrated its 40th anniversary in 2002 by offering a special option package and increased equipment levels. The base SE model gained standard cruise control and dual-zone climate control. Midline GT models like this sedan came standard with alloy wheels and a 200-hp 3.8 V-6. **2.** Grand Am swapped base engines for '02. The previously standard 150-hp 2.4-liter 4-cylinder was replaced with the Ecotec 140-hp 2.2-liter unit. **3.** The 2002 model year was the end of the road for the little-changed Firebird/Trans Am. **4.** The SUV market was beginning to see a shift in consumer preference from large and midsize body-on-frame vehicles to smaller, more efficient unibody crossovers. Vue (pronounced "view") introduced the "Theta" platform destined for similar crossovers at other GM divisions, but maintained Saturn tradition by wearing plastic body panels. Vue borrowed its 4-cylinder and V-6 engines from the L-Series. The V-6 came with a new 5-speed automatic transmission. Front- and all-wheel-drive models were offered with both engines. **5.** With the Vue available as Saturn's utility vehicle, the wagon body style for the compact S-Series was discontinued for the 2002 model year. **6.** The midsize L-Series sedan (pictured) and wagon were largely unchanged.

1

2

3

4

5

1. Retro portholes returned from Buick's past to mark the 2003 version of the super-charged Park Avenue Ultra. Buick added three chrome-plated "VentiPorts" on each front fender. **2.** The 2003 LeSabre was offered with a "Celebration Edition" package to mark Buick's 100th anniversary. **3.** A package named for fashion designer Joseph Abboud added special paint and trim to the '03 Regal. **4.** With the launch of the new entry-level CTS, Cadillac said goodbye to the Catera. This US-built sedan marked the beginning of a renaissance for GM's top brand. CTS used an all-new, rear-wheel-drive architecture dubbed "Sigma." The platform was also designed to accept all-wheel-drive powertrains and would underpin other vital new near-term models. Power came from a 220-hp 3.2-liter version of the Catera's V-6. It teamed with a 5-speed manual or 5-speed automatic transmission. Staking its claim as a true sports sedan, CTS was the first Cadillac in more than 50 years to offer a manual transmission. Engineers spent much time tuning the chassis on Germany's demanding Nurburgring race circuit. The sharp-edged styling was unlike anything from anyone else, but took a while to catch on with the public. The first of Cadillac's new guard was a fine effort right out of the box. CTS sales got off to a strong start, helped by attractive base prices in the $30,000 range. Cadillac built nearly 75,700 for the extra-long debut model year. This was a good showing in light of the brash styling and an increasingly difficult market. **5.** All versions of Cadillac's DeVille and DTS (pictured) received a standard tire-pressure monitor for 2003.

1

1-3. Corvette's 50th-birthday year brought some developments worth celebrating. In addition to commemorative insignias on all models, the convertible and hatchback offered an optional 50th Anniversary Package with special red paint, champagne-colored wheels, and unique trim. The package also included a new suspension trick called Magnetic Selective Ride Control. MSRC used special shock absorbers filled with a fluid containing tiny metal particles. When acted on by an electric current, the fluid could change viscosity, and thus, damping firmness. Almost 12,000 2003 'Vettes were ordered with the anniversary package, which was about a third of total production. MSRC was also available on 'Vettes that didn't have the special package. **4.** It was only fitting that Corvette be selected to pace the Indy 500.

2

3

4

1

2

3

4

5

1-2. Further downsizing marked 2003 for Oldsmobile. The only vehicles to survive for Olds' final year in 2004 were the pictured Alero (left) and Silhouette (right), as well as the Bravada SUV. **3.** Pontiac Bonneville SEs came standard with a 205-hp 3.8 V-6 for $26,115. **4.** The topline Bonneville SSEi started at $33,565 and sported a unique front fascia, along with a supercharged 3.8 with 240 horsepower. **5.** Sunfire survived into 2003, but Pontiac dropped the sedan body style, as well as the sporty GT coupe. The sole model was an SE coupe, but it inherited the GT's 140-hp 2.2-liter Ecotec 4-cylinder engine. The overhead-valve 2.2-liter engine also was discontinued. **6.** Though the Toyota-sourced Chevy/Geo Prizm was history, GM retained its joint venture relationship with the Japanese automaker. The latest product was the 2003 Pontiac Vibe. This small wagon would have the same basic design and powertrain as the also-new Toyota Matrix. Vibe was built alongside the Toyota Corolla at the GM/Toyota New United Motor Manufacturing, Inc. (NUMMI) plant in California. All Vibes offered 1.8-liter 4-cylinder engines. Front- and all-wheel-drive base models had 130 and 123 hp, respectively. Base models offered a 5-speed manual or 4-speed automatic transmission. The sporty Vibe GT pictured here had 180 hp and a mandatory 6-speed manual. These wagons enjoyed a spacious and practical interior design. Sales topped 84,000 for Vibe's long debut season.

6

1-3. The 2003 Ion was Saturn's belated successor to the compact S-Series. Its "Delta" platform was conceived largely by Opel, one of GM's European holdings. Ion styling was Saturn's own, and dent-resistant plastic was once again used for the front fenders and outer door skins. A 4-door sedan and a "Quad

1

2

3

Coupe" model were offered. The coupe had a pair of rear-hinged access doors, versus the S-Series coupe's single rear door. The Ecotec 145-hp 2.2-liter 4-cylinder engine was used for Ion's debut. A bold (and controversial) departure was a central dashtop gauge cluster, which was canted toward the driver. Ions ascended in price and standard equipment through 1, 2, and 3 trim levels, with the base Ion 1 models available as sedans only. **4.** L-Series models got a mild facelift for '03. Revisions to the suspension and steering systems improved road feel and ride. **5.** GM expanded the 2003 Saturn Vue's model roster. The available V-6 engine could be had with front-wheel drive. Previously, only all-wheel drive was offered on the V-6.

4

5

1

2

3

4

1. 2004 marked the swan-song year of Buick's midsize Regal (pictured) and Century. As such, both cars entered the model year with few changes. **2.** The Rendezvous crossover received a new top-line model with a new V-6 engine. Rendezvous Ultra models (pictured) were among the first GM vehicles to use the company's new dual-overhead-cam 3.6-liter V-6. It produced 245 hp, a whopping 60 more than the pushrod 3.4-liter V-6 found in lesser Rendezvous models. **3-4.** For 2004, Cadillac unwrapped a new two-seat convertible, a car that made everyone forget the hapless Allanté ever existed. Called XLR, in line with the brand's adopted three-letter naming scheme, it was basically a C6 Corvette engineered to Cadillac standards of quality and refinement. Though the XLR was easy to dismiss as a Corvette in Caddy clothing, there were many key differences. The public got a preview of the XLR's styling in Cadillac's 1999 Evoq concept car. XLR came only as a hardtop convertible, with a power-retractable solid roof that pirouetted into the trunk like that of the rival Mercedes SL. Other distinctions included specific suspension tuning, slightly slower steering, and slimmer 18-inch tires. And then there was the all-Cadillac powertrain. A heavily revised "Gen II" version of the 4.6-liter Northstar V-8 boasted several internal improvements over previous versions. Output was an impressive 320 hp when teamed with its 5-speed automatic trasmission. XLR was arguably the most exciting new Cadillac since the 1967 Eldorado.

1. The first in a planned "V" series of high-performance Cadillac models debuted in 2004 with the launch of the CTS-V. While this factory-tuned performance car had plenty of chassis, suspension, and other underskin upgrades, the biggest news came under the hood. GM engineers shoehorned the 5.7-liter V-8 engine from the C5-genera-tion Corvette under the CTS-V's hood. Rated output was a beefy 400 hp. Paired with a 6-speed manual transmis-sion, this luxury hot rod could scoot from 0 to 60 mph in 4.8 seconds. 2-3. Cadillac used the CTS's Sigma platform to develop the midsize SRX luxury crossover SUV. SRX was avail-able with rear-wheel drive or all-wheel drive and could seat up to seven. Power came from a 260-hp 3.6-liter V-6 or the 320-hp 4.6-liter Northstar V-8. Available features included GM's Magnetic Ride Control suspension; power folding for the optional 3rd-row seat; and Cadillac's UltraView sunroof that had a 5.6-foot glass pane.

1

2

3

4

5

1. A redesigned Malibu debuted in 2004. It shared a new "Epsilon" front-drive platform with the near-luxury 9-3 from GM-owned Saab. Base sedan versions used a 145-hp 2.2-liter 4-cylinder. A 200-hp 3.5-liter V-6 was standard on the LS and LT (pictured). Standard antilock brakes, traction control, and curtain side airbags for all but base models were laudable safety features. **2-4.** Bread-and-butter Malibu sedans were joined by extended-body Maxx hatchbacks, which rode a 6-inch-longer wheelbase. Chevy was trying to woo more-active buyers to the brand, equipping the Malibu Maxx LS and LT (pictured) with a fore/aft sliding back seat for apportioning cargo space and rear leg room as needed. Reclining rear seatbacks were also standard, as was a fixed "skylight" above. Another exclusive was an optional DVD entertainment system, a boon to families who wanted to keep their children occupied during long car rides. **5.** In 2001, GM purchased most of the assets of bankrupt Korean automaker Daewoo. GM turned the company around, and in 2004, GM Daewoo Automotive Technologies (GMDAT) started producing the subcompact Chevy Aveo for sale in the U.S. Aveo was offered as a 4-door hatchback (pictured) or a 4-door sedan, powered by a 103-hp 1.6-liter 4-cylinder engine. Aveo was part of a new wave of subcompact cars from rival Asian automakers such as Hyundai, Kia, and Toyota's new Scion division. Aveo's sub-$10,000 starting price and the security of a full new-car warranty made it attractive for shoppers who needed basic transportation.

1-3. For 2004, Olds sold only Aleros (top), Silhouettes (lower left), and Bravadas (lower right). As a farewell gesture, the last 500 units of each model rolled out with special "Collector Edition" wheels, badges, and interior trim. The very last Oldsmobile, a black Alero, came off the line on Thursday, April 29, 2004. It was immediately sent to the R.E. Olds Transportation Museum in Lansing, Michigan, the city where the story had begun 106 years before. The protracted phaseout gave GM plenty of time to settle with Olds dealers, many of whom suddenly found themselves without a business. By some estimates, GM spent more than $1 billion in buyouts and other dealer compensation between 2001 and 2006—proving, perhaps, that one must sometimes spend money to save money. **4-5.** Fresh styling and more available power marked a major revamp to the 2004 Pontiac Grand Prix. Overall exterior and interior dimensions didn't change much, but the styling was fresh and new. The engine for GT models (shown) remained the 200-hp 3.8-liter V-6. **6.** Buyers who chose the top-line GTP trim (pictured) were treated to the super-charged 3.8, this time with 260 hp. A special GTP "Comp G" option package included Pontiac's new "TAPshift" controls—steering-wheel-mounted paddles that allowed manual control of the standard 4-speed automatic transmission. **7.** Bonneville, whose sales were stuck in reverse, had a final fling with the GXP. The big front-driver used a 275-hp version of the Cadillac Northstar V-8. It was the first V-8 Bonneville in nearly two decades.

1

2

3

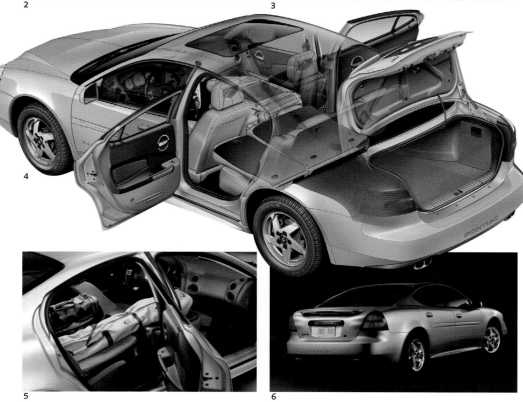

4

5

6

7

1

2

3

4

5

1-2. Overshadowing Grand Prix's renewal in 2004 was the surprising return of the fabled GTO. Aside from rear-wheel drive and thumping V-8 power, it shared nothing with the legendary "Goats" of yore, being an Americanized version of the four-seat Holden Monaro coupe from GM's Australian branch. A split-grille Pontiac face and badging were the only real external differences between the Monaro and GTO. **3.** The $32,000 list price included leather upholstery, power seats, and a premium Blaupunkt audio system. **4.** Under the hood was the 5.7-liter LS1 V-8 engine that packed a healthy 350 hp. A 4-speed automatic transmission was standard. $695 bought a 6-speed manual and was the GTO's only option for its debut model year. **5.** Saturn added visceral appeal to its Vue SUV (pictured rear) and Ion compact car (front) by adding sporty Red Line models. Vues received a sport suspension, 18-inch tires, and aero body addenda. Also making news for the '04 Vue was a new V-6 engine sourced from an unlikely place: Honda. The 3.5-liter V-6 used in Honda's Odyssey minivan produced a healthy 250 hp in the Vue, an increase of 69 over the SUV's old 3.0 V-6. Ion Red Line's upgrades were similarly dramatic. These coupes came with a supercharged 2.0-liter Ecotec 4-cylinder engine that produced 205 hp. The reasonable $21,000 list price also included a mandatory 5-speed manual transmission, taut suspension tuning, 17-inch tires, more supportive seats, and unique trim bits. After so many years of sensible shoes, the Red Lines were a refreshing dash of exuberance.

1

1-2. Buick consolidated the midsize Century and Regal for 2005, creating a single car called LaCrosse. Based on a slightly larger version of the Century/Regal platform, LaCrosse came in CX, CXL, and CXS (pictured) trims. The former two models had the standby 200-hp 3.8-liter V-6. CXS was the sport-themed version, and it came with a 240-hp 3.6-liter dual-cam V-6, sportier suspension tuning, and 17-inch tires versus the others' 16s. All used a 4-speed automatic transmission. Styling was cleaner than the Century and Regal and showed the new direction of Buick design. LaCrosse was a significant improvement over the two models it replaced. All versions were comfortable and critics said the CXS offered good handling. **3.** The 2005 Buick Terraza was a GM minivan with an SUV-style nose added to create what the company called a "crossover sport van." It shared its basic design with similar vans from Chevrolet, Pontiac, and Saturn. Like its siblings, power came from a 200-hp 3.5-liter V-6 engine. Terraza, however, was the costliest and most luxurious of the quartet.

2

3

1

2

3

1-2. Cadillac replaced the front-drive Seville with rear-drive 2005 STS. Also leveraging the CTS/SRX Sigma platform, STS was almost 5 inches shorter than the Seville but an inch taller and about 4 inches longer in wheelbase. Power came from a choice of two engines. Standard on V-6 models was the 255-hp 3.6-liter V-6 that was made standard on CTS in 2004. V-8 STS models used the same 320-hp Northstar V-8 as in the SRX. V-8 versions could be equipped with all-wheel drive at an extra cost, though it required a pricey option package be ordered first. The sole transmission was a 5-speed automatic. STS was another milestone in Cadillac's product renaissance. **3.** The STS interior was unique from that of the CTS or SRX, with a simpler, yet still contemporary look. The design was praised by critics for its uncomplicated controls and lack of buttons compared with many midsize luxury rivals.

1. Chevrolet received its own unibody crossover SUV in 2005. Dubbed Equinox, it debuted on a slightly stretched version of the Theta platform that underpinned the 2003 Saturn Vue. Equinox came in LS or LT (shown) models with front-wheel drive or all-wheel drive. Instead of a 4-cylinder engine or the Saturn's 250-hp Honda-sourced V-6, Equinox had to make do with an older 185-hp 3.4-liter overhead-valve V-6 engine. **2.** Cobalt entered the Chevy stable as a replacement for the Cavalier. It was built on the same Delta platform as the Saturn Ion, but the Chevy had more conventional styling and a different interior design. Power for most models came from the Ion's 140-hp 2.2-liter Ecotec 4-cylinder engine. The top-line LT (pictured) was available with heated leather seats and had chrome-plated trim accents to dress up the exterior. **3.** Chevy's answer to the popular high-performance compact car segment was the Cobalt SS Supercharged. It packed the same 205-hp 2.0-liter blown Ecotec engine and 5-speed manual transmission as the Saturn Ion Red Line. **4.** The crown jewel among Chevy's new cars for 2005 was the 6th-generation Corvette. Engineers beefed up the 'Vette's engine to 6.0 liters from 5.7, resulting in a 50-hp increase to an even 400. Slippery new styling, additional chassis refinements, and a reworked interior promised (and delivered) the high-performance driving experience enthusiasts expected but at still-reasonable prices. Base hatchbacks started at $43,445. Z06 was gone in '05 but not forgotten, as GM was preparing the baddest 'Vette yet for a model-year '06 introduction.

1

2

3

4

1

2

4

1-2. Pontiac replaced its best-selling Grand Am for 2005 with a new midsize that rode the same front-drive Epsilon platform as the Chevy Malibu Maxx. Instead of keeping the Grand Am name, this new sedan was called G6. Only a 4-door sedan with a V-6 engine was offered during this car's inaugural year, and it came in base and GT (pictured) trims. It was the same 200-hp 3.5-liter unit found in the Malibu. To build buzz for the car, Pontiac arranged for Oprah Winfrey to give away 276 G6s on her top-rated TV

3

talk show, one for each person in the audience. Pontiac said the publicity was worth $20 million, at least four times the total retail value of the cars. 3. One of G6's unique features was this optional "panoramic" sunroof with a tilt-up front section and three rear-sliding panels that opened to about the full length of the passenger compartment. 4. This Grand Prix GXP was the first V-8 Grand Prix in two decades. It packed a 5.3-liter pushrod engine. The engine was enhanced with GM's new "Active Fuel Management" system that would shut off four cylinders under light throttle conditions in order to save fuel. To help mitigate the inevitable torque steer that would come from running 303 hp through the front wheels, Pontiac retuned the suspension and gave the GXP larger tires up front than in the rear.

1. Pontiac retired one of its longest-running nameplates in 2005, when the last Bonnevilles were built. GXP models came standard with a 275-hp 4.6 V-8. **2.** Pontiac hoped to drum up more interest in the GTO for 2005 by giving it the same 400-hp 6.0-liter V-8 engine as the C6 Corvette. Also added were twin hood scoops, though customers could substitute a smooth hood at no additional cost. **3.** Pontiac's version of the new GM "crossover sport vans" was called Montana SV6. Like the Buick Terraza, Chevy Uplander, and Saturn Relay with which it shared its basic underpinnings, Montana SV6 used the 1997–2004 GM minivan chassis. All these vans were available with GM's Versatrak all-wheel drive and came standard with a 200-hp 3.5-liter V-6 engine. **4.** Though it received styling updates to give it a somewhat more conventional look, the unpopular Aztek was dropped after the 2005 model year. It might have been an innovative vehicle for the time, but customers just couldn't get past the looks. Pontiac wanted to move 60,000 Azteks annually; calendar-year 2005 sales were a paltry 5020. **5.** Ion sedans received a facelift for 2005, including a new grille design. Coupes and sedans got a slightly revised interior with upgraded materials and a new steering wheel with a design similar to that of the Chevy Cobalt. The cars retained their center-mounted instrument pod. Ion "3" trim levels (pictured) could be outfitted with a new 2.4-liter Ecotec 4-cylinder engine that produced 170 hp, an increase of 30 over the base 2.2-liter engine. **6.** Relay was Saturn's version of GM's quartet of crossover sport vans.

1

2

3

4

5

6

1

2

3

4

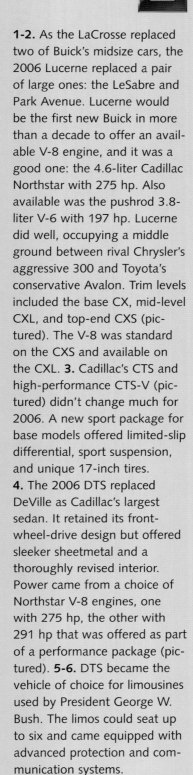

5   6

1-2. As the LaCrosse replaced two of Buick's midsize cars, the 2006 Lucerne replaced a pair of large ones: the LeSabre and Park Avenue. Lucerne would be the first new Buick in more than a decade to offer an available V-8 engine, and it was a good one: the 4.6-liter Cadillac Northstar with 275 hp. Also available was the pushrod 3.8-liter V-6 with 197 hp. Lucerne did well, occupying a middle ground between rival Chrysler's aggressive 300 and Toyota's conservative Avalon. Trim levels included the base CX, mid-level CXL, and top-end CXS (pictured). The V-8 was standard on the CXS and available on the CXL. **3.** Cadillac's CTS and high-performance CTS-V (pictured) didn't change much for 2006. A new sport package for base models offered limited-slip differential, sport suspension, and unique 17-inch tires. **4.** The 2006 DTS replaced DeVille as Cadillac's largest sedan. It retained its front-wheel-drive design but offered sleeker sheetmetal and a thoroughly revised interior. Power came from a choice of Northstar V-8 engines, one with 275 hp, the other with 291 hp that was offered as part of a performance package (pictured). **5-6.** DTS became the vehicle of choice for limousines used by President George W. Bush. The limos could seat up to six and came equipped with advanced protection and communication systems.

2006

1. Cadillac expanded its V-Series lineup in 2006 by creating the XLR-V. This potent convertible used a supercharged, 4.4-liter Northstar V-8 engine that produced a healthy 443 hp. Other performance enhancements included run-flat tires, sport suspension, and uprated brakes. This was also the most expensive production Cadillac ever, with a starting

1

2

price of $97,485. **2.** Standard XLRs were largely unchanged for '06. **3.** Also joining the V-Series lineup was the STS-V, the most powerful production Cadillac to date. Like the XLR-V, this tuned midsize sedan used a supercharged 4.4-liter Northstar V-8. In this guise, however, the engine produced 469 hp. GM said STS-V's powertrain was good for a 0-60-mph acceleration time of 4.8 seconds. In addition to expected tire, suspension, and brake upgrades, STS-V also had a unique mesh grille. Its base price was $74,270.

3

1. Impala got a reskin for 2006 that included revised sheet-metal and powertrains. Engine choices included a 211-hp 3.5-liter V-6 for LS (shown) and LT models, or a 242-hp 3.9-liter V-6 for the LTZ. The high-performance SS had the 303-hp 5.3-liter V-8 borrowed from the Pontiac Grand Prix GXP. **2.** The smaller Malibu got a minor facelift as well. Sedan and Maxx hatchback (shown) models also added sporty SS trim that included a 240-hp version of the Impala's 3.9-liter V-6. **3-4.** Enthusiasts hailed the return of the Corvette Z06 to Chevy's stable. This 'Vette promised even higher performance than the C5 generation, and it didn't disappoint. The Z06 was the beneficiary of lessons learned from Chevy's highly successful racing program. Use of lightweight materials such as aluminum, carbon fiber, and magnesium kept the Z06's weight in check. But what really set it apart was the Z06's mighty LS7 V-8 engine. Though it used small-block architecture, it displaced a big-block-like 7.0 liters. A massive 505 hp was on tap in this brute. When run through the mandatory 6-speed manual transmission, 0-60-mph acceleration clocked in at less than 4 seconds, making the Corvette Z06 one of the fastest cars in the world. The price? Just $64,890. **5.** Making its debut for 2006, the Chevy HHR was a five-seat compact wagon that used the Delta platform found on the Cobalt. HHR stood for "Heritage High Roof," and the styling recalled early 1950s Chevy Suburbans. Power came from the Cobalt's 4-cylinder engines: a 143-hp 2.2 liter or a 172-hp 2.4. GM wanted to have HHR start at less than $16,000 and made it so. HHR started at $15,325.

1. Pontiac expanded the mid-size G6 line. Sedans could be had with a 167-hp 4-cylinder engine instead of just a V-6. New body styles also were part of the extended lineup. Two-door coupes were available with the 201-hp 3.5-liter V-6 that sedans offered. The GTP coupe (shown) had the 240-hp 3.9-liter V-6, which was shared with the Chevy Impala and Malibu. **2.** Hoping to steal sales from Chrysler's popular Sebring was a G6 convertible model. Pontiac teamed with German firm Karmann to engineer a power-retractable hardtop, rather than a conventional soft top. GT (shown) and GTP convertibles were offered. A group of sensors and electric motors worked together to fold the top into the trunk for top-down motoring. **3.** Optional 18-inch wheels were the only change to the 2006 GTO. Lackluster sales caused Pontiac to pull the plug on its high-performance machine after this model year. **4.** With crossover SUVs continuing to tear up sales charts across the industry, Pontiac entered the game with the Torrent, a version of Chevy's popular Equinox. Aside from a twin-port Pontiac grille and some trim bits, there wasn't much to tell these corporate cousins apart. They even had the same powertrain that used the 185-hp 3.4-liter V-6 and 5-speed automatic transmission. Not offered was the Honda-sourced 250-hp 3.5-liter V-6 used in the Saturn's Vue crossover. Saturn had exclusive rights to use that engine. **5.** In similarly disappointing performance news, 2006 was the last year Pontiac would sell the high-revving Vibe GT wagon. Like GTO, low demand caused this model to be discontinued.

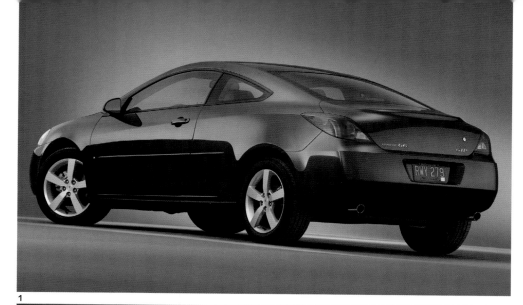

1

2

3

4

5

1

2

3

4

5

1-2. While Pontiac discontinued one sports car in 2006, it created another that year. The two-seat Solstice convertible hit the streets less than four years after rabid public response to a we-might-build-it concept. Solstice, under the direction of Bob Lutz, was a demonstration that GM could get out fresh, exciting cars as fast as anyone in the world. GM developed a whole new rear-drive platform called Kappa to create this convertible. Exterior styling was fresh and hip. Under the hood and inside the cabin was a clever blend of fresh design and part-sharing with other GM products. The 177-hp 2.4-liter 4-cylinder engine was similar to what was offered in the Chevy Cobalt and Saturn Ion. The 5-speed manual transmission was from Chevy's Colorado compact pickup truck. Climate control switchgear was straight out of the also-new-for-2006 Hummer H3 SUV. All this helped Solstice hit the marketplace with a base price just $5 shy of $20,000. Solstice's natural rival was the established Mazda MX-5. The Pontiac had one big advantage over the Mazda: It was all-American, a big emotional tug for many folks at a time when GM seemed fast headed for ruin. Dealers booked some 13,000 orders. The refurbished factory in Wilmington, Delaware, could only manage about half that volume, but people seemed happy to wait. Solstice was worth waiting for. **3.** Saturn Vues, this Red Line version included, got a mild facelift and an interior freshening. **4-5.** Ion largely stood pat, with Red Line versions (below) getting an available "Competition Package" that included a limited-slip differential and lights to guide shifting.

1-2. As Buick's LaCrosse (left) and Lucerne (right) were relative newcomers to the marketplace, they entered 2007 with only minor changes. Buick was basically in a holding pattern, as some new high-performance products were waiting in the wings for model-year 2008. **3-4.** The body-on-frame Rainier (left) SUV and Rendezvous crossover (right) based on Chevy's minivan platform went away after a brief '07 production run. The launch of the Saturn Outlook midsize crossover would serve as the foundation for a new Buick people-mover, which was on tap for an early model-year 2008 introduction. **5.** V-8 versions of Cadillac's SRX crossover adopted the 6-speed automatic transmission that was introduced in the high-performance XLR-V convertible. **6.** But the biggest news for Cadillac's crossover could be found inside. The interior received a complete makeover with substantially revised controls. Interior materials also took a gigantic leap forward, with genuine wood trim and visible stitching to impart a look that wouldn't be out of place in a much more expensive luxury vehicle. The SRX started at $37,110 in V-6 form, $43,315 with a V-8. **7.** The big, front-drive DTS, which was revamped in '06, didn't change much for 2007, aside from the usual shuffling of trims. **8.** CTS, Cadillac's strongest threat in the near-luxury market at its time of introduction four years earlier, also was little changed. It was for a good reason, though, as GM was preparing a new CTS designed to once again rattle the cages of established European and Japanese rivals. The CTS-V is pictured.

1

2

3

4

5

1. Ever-increasing fuel prices kept consumer interest in small cars high. Chevy responded by facelifting its popular Aveo sedan for 2007. The top-line Aveo LT is shown here. **2.** Corvette was once again tapped to pace the Indianapolis 500 race. The 'Vette has always been the U.S.-made sports car that, though not inexpensive, could be had with enough hard work, determination, and desire. Corvette has unfailingly been the dream car one could point to and reasonably say, "Maybe someday." **3.** Chevy added some more flair to the HHR wagon lineup by offering a special "Panel" model for '07. This two-seater made for an ideal delivery vehicle. **4.** Mainstream Equinox crossovers received some suspension and interior upgrades for '07. In bigger news, GM wanted to make a splash in environmental automotive technologies. The company built a concept Equinox powered by a fuel cell. Fuel cells work by taking hydrogen and combining it with oxygen to produce water. In the conversion, electricity is generated, which is what powers the vehicle. The water produced by the system comes out the tailpipe as vapor. There are no carbon dioxide emissions, such as what are produced by a gasoline-powered internal combustion engine. Chevy planned to produce 100 Equinox fuel cell vehicles and give them to the public and government officials for evaluation. Fuel cell models were about 500 pounds heavier than gasoline Equinoxes, though GM mitigated the gain by using a carbon fiber hood and aluminum door panels. **5.** This would be the final year for the Monte Carlo. The 303-hp SS model is shown here.

1. Though once reserved for GM's top-end brands, the company's "high feature" dual-overhead-cam 3.6-liter V-6 engine made its way into the mainstream by appearing on the Pontiac G6. Top-line GTP models (shown) used it, where the engine made 252 hp when teamed with a 6-speed automatic transmission. **2.** Grand Prix was largely unchanged for '07. The GT (pictured) was one of the last GM cars to offer the supercharged 3.8-liter V-6 engine that was popular on several GM vehicles just a few model years earlier. **3.** The Solstice lineup got some spice for '07 by adding a high-performance GXP variant (pictured). These convertibles used a new turbocharged 2.0-liter Ecotec 4-cylinder engine. In addition to the boost, these motors also featured high-pressure direct injection designed to further increase performance while also enhancing fuel economy. GM pegged GXP 0-60-mph acceleration at 5.5 seconds. **4.** Non-turbo Solstices carried over with few changes. **5.** Compared to the doomed Aztek, the Torrent Crossover was a rousing success. As such, it went into 2007 with few changes. **6.** The Toyota-derived Vibe was pared down to a single model for '07; a front-drive model was all that was left. **7.** Since it didn't have a mainstream compact car, Pontiac was given a derivative of the Chevy Cobalt for '07. Called G5, it was offered only as a 2-door coupe. Cobalt's 2.2- and 2.4-liter 4-cylinder engines were available. The 2.4 was offered on the G5 GT shown here. The G5 actually had been on sale in Canada (where it was called the Pursuit) since the Cobalt launched in 2005.

1

2

3

4

5

6

7

1. Saturn dramatically increased its product portfolio for 2007. The division added three new models, including this midsize sedan called Aura. It shared the same front-drive Epsilon platform as the Pontiac G6 but was tuned for a more European-flavored driving experience, particularly the sporty XR model shown here. It was nothing like Saturn's previous midsize L-Series cars, and critics responded by naming it the 2007 North American Car of the Year. **2.** Midyear saw the launch of the Saturn Outlook crossover. Outlook, and the similar GMC Acadia, were based on GM's new "Lambda" platform. Power came from a 270-hp version of GM's now-ubiquitous 3.6-liter V-6 and a 6-speed automatic transmission. What distinguished these crossovers was their size. Many midsize crossovers offered five-passenger seating. Outlook provided accommodations for seven. **3-4.** Following the launch of the Pontiac Solstice convertible was Saturn's variant: the Sky. It offered the same normally aspirated and turbocharged engines as the Pontiac but with unique sheetmetal and interior trim. The turbocharged Sky Red Line is pictured here. **5.** The Vue crossover received a gas/electric "Green Line" hybrid model. The "single mode" hybrid system allowed for a fuel economy boost without adding a lot of extra cost. While many rival hybrids cost thousands more than conventional gasoline cars or crossovers, Vue Green Line actually cost less than a front-drive Vue with the V-6 engine. **6.** Ion called it quits after the '07 model year as GM prepared a new small Saturn for 2008.

1. 2008 would be a "Super" year for Buick in more ways than one. That particular moniker would find its way back to the Buick lineup after an extended absence and apply to tuned versions of the Lucerne and LaCrosse. Lucernes would become Supers by adding the 292-hp 4.6-liter Northstar V-8 engine found in the Cadillac DTS Performance model. Lucerne Supers would look different from their "regular" counterparts via a new grille, fascias, rocker panels, and exhaust tips. Lucerne was also a launch vehicle for GM's new "Lane Departure Warning" and "Side Blind Zone Alert" systems. A camera, mounted inside the rearview mirror, could identify traffic lanes and warn drivers of inadvertent lane changes. The Blind Zone Alert used radar sensors on both sides of the vehicle to "look" for other cars. Vehicles entering one of seven zones identified by the system would illuminate an LED light in the outside rearview mirror. **2.** LaCrosse Supers were enhanced through the addition of the 300-hp 5.3-liter V-8 engine found in the Pontiac Grand Prix GXP. They also received appearance changes, including a new grille inspired by the Velite concept car. The interior also received a freshening with unique gauges. **3-4.** Replacing the departed Rainier, Rendezvous, and Terraza as Buick's people-mover was the Enclave SUV. Buick's new crossover used the same Lambda platform and 3.6-liter V-6 engine as the Saturn Outlook and GMC Acadia but was a significantly more-upscale vehicle. Enclave features included premium interior materials, a "library-quiet" ride, and voluptuous (for an SUV) bodywork.

1

2

3

4

1

2

3

4

1. Cadillac unveiled a completely redesigned CTS for 2008. This new-generation model brought high-pressure direct injection to GM's established 3.6-liter V-6, giving it a total of 304 hp. This engine was optional, as buyers could elect to go with a 3.6 V-6 without direct injection for 263 hp. While most buyers would likely opt for the 6-speed automatic transmission, enthusiasts could choose a 6-speed manual. Another new CTS feature was available all-wheel drive. While GM could have lifted CTS's interior from the already excellent SRX crossover, the company elected to go with a completely original design, including optional genuine Sapele wood trim. Audiophiles would rejoice with the availability of a 40-gigabyte hard drive that could be used to store digital music files. **2.** The direct injection 3.6-liter V-6 became standard equipment on a freshened 2008 STS sedan. Like the CTS, STS's grille featured styling cues inspired by Cadillac's Sixteen concept car. **3-4.** Chevy's biggest launch for 2008 was the redesigned Malibu. Gone was the Maxx hatchback, leaving only a 4-door sedan that rode on the same Epsilon platform as the Pontiac G6 and Saturn Aura. Malibu was to become a statement of the company's commitment to getting Chevy back on track as not only a leader in truck sales, but also for cars. Chevy kept it simple for Malibu, offering just two engines: a 169-hp 2.4-liter 4-cylinder or 252-hp 3.6-liter V-6. Both engines were available on the Malibu LT and LTZ (pictured), along with a 6-speed automatic, the first time this transmission was offered on a 4-cylinder GM vehicle.

1

1-2. While Corvettes continued to excel on the racetrack, Chevy gave its street cars more performance. The 6.0-liter V-8 engine got a displacement boost to 6.2 liters. Power of this new "LS3" V-8 increased accordingly to 430 hp, up 30 over '07. Improved steering feel and a revised manual-transmission shift linkage helped make an already smooth sports car even more easy to live with as a daily driver, despite the nearly 10-percent increase in horsepower. **3.** In an effort to add more spice to the Equinox crossover, Chevy made the high-performance 3.6-liter V-6 engine available on a new model called Sport (shown). When teamed with a 6-speed automatic transmission, Sports offered 264 hp, quite a leap from the 185 offered in other Equinoxes. **4.** Announced at the 2007 Woodward Dream Cruise was the '08 HHR SS. This potent wagon would offer the 260-hp 2.0-liter turbocharged 4-cylinder engine found in the Pontiac Solstice GXP and Saturn Sky Red Line. **5.** Like the Equinox Sport, Pontiac's Torrent crossover got treatment designed to make it more sporty. Dubbed GXP, this SUV also received the 3.6-liter V-6 engine and the same suspension tuning as the Chevy.

2

3

4

5

1

2

3

4

1-2. Introduced at the 2007 Chicago Auto Show was the Pontiac G8, a large, rear-wheel-drive sedan that promised serious performance. G8 was the North American debut of GM's new, global rear-drive platform, developed largely by the Holden subsidiary in Australia. Base G8 models would come with a 261-hp verison of GM's 3.6-liter V-6. Performance-minded folks would want to pony up for the G8 GT (show car shown), which featured a 362-hp 6.0-liter small-block V-8. G8 would represent the new face of Pontiac performance. **3.** 2008 would mark the complete turnaround of Saturn's North American product offerings. When Saturn introduced the compact Astra as Ion's replacement, the Sky officially became Saturn's oldest product sold in the United States—at the ripe old age of 1. GM tapped European subsidiary Opel for the Astra. As a radical departure from the old S-Series and Ion, Astra would launch as a hatchback in XE or XR (shown) trim. Gone were Saturn's trademark plastic body panels. Astra was launched with a 140-hp 1.8-liter 4-cylinder engine. **4.** Also coming from Opel was the redesigned Saturn Vue compact crossover. The new Vue offered the choice of a 4-cylinder or a pair of V-6s. The Vue Green Line (shown) was carried over to the new platform, offering the same 4-cylinder gas/electric hybrid engine as the previous-generation Vue. The swift and thorough revamp of the entire Saturn product line was evidence of a new philosophy at GM—an increased focus on utilizing the corporation's global resources to efficiently bring fresh vehicles to the marketplace.

![GM]

CHAPTER TWELVE

TRUCKS

"The wheel is come full circle."

—William Shakespeare

The word "truck" comes from the Latin noun "trochus," which, literally translated, means "wheel." And like the origin of the wheel, the genesis of what we call a truck is nebulous.

Discussions of this topic usually assign creation of the first gasoline-powered truck to Gottlieb Daimler or Armand Peugeot. Depending on whom you believe, one of these same two men also invented the modern automobile. And this makes perfect sense, as the first trucks were little more than cars with flatbeds instead of passenger accommodations.

In 1902, Max and Morris Grabowsky built what can be safely considered the first General Motors truck. In 1908, knowing a promising enterprise when he saw one, GM founder William Durant began buying up stock in the Grabowskys' Rapid Motor Vehicle Co., adding it to his company's expanding portfolio and renaming it GMC.

Despite some rough spots, America has been in a near perpetual growth mode since GM's inception, and the auto giant has always been happy to produce the work vehicles to fuel that expansion. Concurrent with GMC's success, Chevrolet branched out into trucks, progressing from light delivery vehicles to a full family of workhorses.

In recent decades, trucks have been promoted from the work lot to the driveway. The rise of the sport utility vehicle saw Americans embrace a new kind of transportation. A fresh breed of SUVs and pickup trucks offered power, passenger-car luxury, and off-road prowess both real and imagined. So complete was this revolution that even Cadillac began offering SUVs.

By the year 2000, more than half the vehicles sold in America were trucks, and the auto business had come full circle. One hundred years ago, trucks were little more than cars with space for freight. Today General Motors sells more trucks to families than cars.

1. The history of General Motors trucks actually predates GM itself. The story starts in 1900 when brothers Max and Morris Grabowsky began designing vehicles in their

Detroit mechanical repair shop. In 1902, the brothers sold their first truck (pictured) to the American Garment Cleaning Co. in Detroit. The truck wasn't much more than a frame with a one-cylinder engine driving two chains to provide propulsion.
2. Oldsmobile came early to the manufacture of trucks. A "pie wagon" panel truck based on its famous Curved-Dash car was made in 1904 and '05. In August 1918, word came that Olds would start building a commercial truck for the 1919 model year. Called the Economy Truck, it was built on a 128-inch wheelbase and was 178 inches long with a standard body. Similar to the truck pictured, it rolled on pneumatic cord tires and was powered by a 224-cubic-inch four-cylinder engine rated at 40 horsepower. **3.** This ½-ton 1919 Chevrolet Model 490 Commercial light delivery was a Model 490 passenger car chassis with heavier springs and only the forward sheetmetal in place. The factory did not yet supply truck bodies, so buyers had to source them on their own. Power came from a 37-hp four-cylinder engine.

1

2

3

4

5

6

1. Chevrolet introduced a new one-ton truck chassis for 1923. The Series D replaced the ¾-ton Model G and one-ton Model T. With the demise of the Series FB passenger cars, production of the 224-cid engine also used for trucks ceased, leaving only Chevy's 171-cid "Superior" engine for use in the truck line. **2.** This 1925 Chevrolet Series K Light Delivery has been fitted with a "C-cab" panel body, a style that was losing popularity by the mid-Twenties. **3.** Outside firms made wood station wagon bodies that mounted on light-duty truck frames like this 1928 Chevy National AB. **4.** This restored 1928 Chevrolet National AB wears a wooden body styled after those manufactured by the York-Hoover Body Company. The pickup body features a one-piece cab and bed, much like the Chevy El Camino would some 40 years later. The National AB rode a longish, 107-inch wheelbase. Mechanical four-wheel brakes were standard. The basic National chassis retailed for $495, and several body styles other than the pickup were listed. **5.** For 1929, Chevrolet introduced the soon-to-be-famous "Stovebolt" six-cylinder engine. This DeLuxe Panel Delivery was built on the 1½-ton Series LQ truck chassis. **6.** The 1929 GM Yellow Coach Model U was the product of the Yellow Truck and Coach Mfg. Co. of Pontiac, Michigan. The 21-passenger bus rode a wheelbase of 185 inches, measured 24 feet long and 7½ feet wide, and weighed 10,000 pounds empty. This was the first Yellow Coach with a raised—or "monitor"—roof to make moving around inside easier. Power was supplied by a Buick six-cylinder engine.

1

2

3

4

1. This 1930 Chevrolet Series AD roadster delivery pickup featured a body that, for the first time, was distinct from the passenger-car body. Pickup beds were supplied by outside companies. 2. This 1931 Chevy 1½-ton tanker truck was originally a long-wheelbase stake bed. 3. For 1935, Chevrolet introduced the Suburban Carryall. The steel-bodied station wagon was created from the basic panel truck body. 4. This 1936 Chevrolet Series FB panel delivery is a "first series" model built at the beginning of the year. 5. Chevrolet's 1936 "second series" trucks arrived midyear with a new round-corner all-steel cab that reduced overall height by two inches. 6. This 1936 GMC T-16 stake truck is a late production model. Early models had a visor above the windshield. 7. GMC went Deco for '37. This fire truck sports the new line-wide front-end design. 8. The 1937 GMC T-14 panel delivery had a standard 230-cid six. 9. This heavy-duty 1937 GMC has the two-piece windshield introduced in mid-1936. 10. For 1937, Chevy added an urban-friendly "forward control" chassis with the engine moved to the driver's right. This Metropolitan Body van was a typical application of the new platform.

5

6

7

8

9

10

1

2

3

4

5

6

7

8

9

1. Chevrolet introduced a cab-over truck for 1938. The 1½-ton truck was available with three different wheelbases and was popular for city use. **2.** This 1938 GMC T-14B ½-ton pickup was powered by a 230-cid six-cylinder good for 86 horsepower. **3.** A 1938 Chevrolet truck is shown loaded up with factory-fresh 1939 Chevy passenger cars. **4.** These two school buses are built on 1940 GMC chassis. Note the new sealed-beam headlights and front-fender-mounted parking lights. **5.** In 1940, the largest trucks offered by Chevy were 1½-ton models like this stake bed. Larger models were sold under the GMC banner. **6.** GMC light-duty trucks boasted revised styling for 1941. This model CC-102 pickup is a long-bed ½-ton model, built on a 125-inch wheelbase. Chevy trucks looked similar but had vertical grille bars. **7.** In terms of styling, 1941 GMCs were virtually unchanged from the '40 models. **8.** One of Chevrolet's contributions to the war effort was the 1½-ton four-wheel-drive G-7100 series truck. Shown here is a 1942 G-7117 cargo version in Navy livery. **9.** GMC's 1946 CC series flatbed trucks were powered by a 270-cubic-inch six-cylinder engine mated to a four-speed manual transmission.

1. Chevrolet resumed civilian truck production on August 20, 1945, shortly before the war ended. Meeting pent-up demand was a priority, so there were few changes to the pre-war designs. Shown here is a 1946 Suburban Carryall. **2.** Redesigned for 1948, Chevy's new-look trucks—and their GMC siblings—were the first GM vehicles designed entirely postwar. The mainstay ½-ton pickup rode a 116-inch wheelbase and was two inches wider than previous models for extra cargo and cab space. This 1949 Chevy 3100-series pickup still wears the new-for-'48 styling. **3.** Chevy also built truck chassis for special applications, like this 4400 series with Holmes wrecker body. This rig originally handled towing chores for a Pennsylvania Chevy dealer. **4.** This 1951 GMC tractor is powered by a "Million-Miler" diesel engine. Developed by GMC and Detroit Diesel (a subsidiary of GM), the Million Mile engines were two-strokes offered in three-, four-, and six-cylinder versions. They earned their name because of their reputation for long life expectancy. **5.** These 1951 GMC Model 650 diesel trucks, powered by 150-hp "Million-Miler" engines, are on their way to Fort Eustis, Virginia, to undergo U.S. Army testing. **6.** This 1953 GMC 100 DeLuxe cab ½-ton pickup was powered by a 228-cid straight six. **7.** Chevrolet's 1955 "first series" trucks were still based on the 1948 redesign. Shown is a 3100 series panel truck. **8.** Chevy's all-new "Task Force" 1955 truck fleet included this flashy Cameo Carrier that sported a unique fiberglass-skinned flush-side bed. Carlike features, such as Chevy's new V-8, added to the appeal.

1. GMC dubbed its new 1955 "Second Series" trucks "Blue Chip" models. GMCs were offered as more-powerful, better-appointed—and cost-lier—alternatives to Chevy trucks. This 1956 GMC has the optional Pontiac-built 317-cubic-inch V-8, which was good for 180 horsepower. **2.** A Chevy truck staple since 1935, the roomy Suburban Carryall looked good in 1957 trim. Loading up the back was easy through the buyer's choice of either a liftgate/tailgate or dual center-opening cargo doors. **3.** For 1958, Chevy trucks enjoyed new front fas-cias with quad headlamps. This example has the traditional "Stepside" bed, but a new flush-fender Fleetside with a wider bed was also offered. **4.** For 1960, Chevy offered new forward-control tilt-cab trucks in 20 models with pay-load ratings ranging from 1½ to 2½ tons. **5.** Chevrolet and GMC pickups were restyled for 1960. An independent front suspension and trailing-arm rear suspension were also new. This Chevy Apache 10 wears a prototype body intended for Southwestern Bell Telephone. **6.** For 1961, Chevrolet intro-duced three "Corvair 95" trucks based on the rear-engined Corvair compact car. This Rampside pickup is a 1963 model. A Corvan panel van and Greenbrier passenger van were also offered. **7.** Chevy's workhorse C-10 pickup was little changed for 1966. **8.** Chevy pickups received a complete restyle for 1967. This basic design would soldier on through 1972 with only minor facelifts. A 1968 model is shown here.

1. From 1967 through 1972, GMC pickup styling went largely unchanged. A 1970 model is shown. 2. Chevy's first compact pickup, the LUV (Light Utility Vehicle), was built in Japan by Isuzu. This 1979 model has newly optional four-wheel drive. Chevy sold LUV trucks from 1972 through 1982. 3. This 1979 GMC Sierra Classic was powered by Oldsmobile's 350-cubic-inch diesel V-8 engine. The same engine was optional in Chevy and GMC ½-ton two-wheel-drive pickups from 1978 through 1981. 4. American-made GM compact pickups arrived for 1982. Chevy's version was called S-10, and GMC's S-15. This S-15 is in Gypsy Magic guise with the optional sport fairing and bed rails. The "magic" was in the unique striping: It looked black in daylight, but at night turned red when struck by light. 5. By 1982, Chevy's popular Suburban could be outfitted like a luxury car but was still prepared to work like a truck. It came with rear- or four-wheel drive (shown) in ½-ton C-10 and ¾-ton C-20 models. 6. A logical spinoff of the S-series compact pickup trucks were "baby" sport utilities. Chevy's S-10 Blazer and GMC's S-15 Jimmy debuted for 1983. Two- and four-wheel-drive versions were offered. This 1986 S-10 Blazer is outfitted with that year's new "High Country" trim package. 7. In 1985, GM responded to the 1984 Plymouth Voyager and Dodge Caravan minivans with a larger, rear-drive minivan of its own. The Chevy Astro and GMC Safari were based on the S-series pickup-truck platform. This 1986 Astro is decked out in fancy CL trim.

1

2

3

4

5

6

7

1. Chevrolet introduced an all-new full-size truck platform for 1988, but some truck-based models, including this Blazer, continued on the old platform. **2.** The last year for heavy-duty GMC-branded trucks was 1988. A joint venture with Volvo resulted in heavy-duty models being sold under the WHITEGMC name until 1995. A 1988 GMC General is shown. The General was introduced for 1977. Chevrolet's version was called Bison. **3.** The last year for GMC's heavy-duty cab-over Astro also was 1988. Astro had an aluminum cab and was new for 1969. The Titan was Chevy's version. **4.** If you're macho enough to drive a 4x4 pickup, why be shy? In 1989, buyers could choose this larger-than-life body-side graphic as an option for Chevy's Silverado. **5.** Syclone was a high-performance version of the compact GMC Sonoma pickup introduced for 1991. This short-bed, regular-cab truck had a turbocharged 4.3-liter V-6 good for 280 horses, permanently engaged 4WD, and antilock brakes. A 1992 model is shown. **6.** The Chevy 454 SS was a blast from the past. The short-box C-10 truck had special trim, a sport suspension, and a 230-horse-power "big-block" 454-cubic-inch (7.4-liter) V-8. Shown is a 1992 model.

1. For 1995, the compact GMC Jimmy (shown) sport-utility and its corporate cousin Chevy Blazer were redesigned. Two-door models like this one rode a 100.5-inch wheelbase; four-doors rode a 6.5-inch longer span. **2.** As the police-friendly Caprice sedan—along with its popular 9C1 police package—was about to be discontinued, Chevy put together a concept police package for the Tahoe SUV in 1996. It entered production in 1997, but never saw the sales volume of the police-package Caprice. **3.** Chevy offered the 1997 S-10 Electric Pickup to fleet customers. Power came courtesy of a GM Electric Propulsion System driving the front wheels. **4.** During 1999, GM entered into an agreement with AM General to take over marketing and distribution of the Hummer to retail and commercial buyers. **5.** For 2001, Chevy's ¾- and one-ton pickups adopted the styling that ½-ton trucks introduced for 1999. **6.** For 2001, GMC introduced the HT (Hot Truck) based on the regular cab, Stepside ½-ton Sierra. **7.** The new 2002 Chevy Avalanche was part Suburban, part pickup, and loaded with clever features—including a rear bench seat that folded flat to extend the cargo-bed load floor. **8.** First shown as a concept in 2000, Chevy rolled out the retro-styled SSR roadster pickup as a 2003 model. The racey bodywork was inspired by the 1948 Chevy pickup.

1

2

3

4

5

6

1. Cadillac's popular Escalade full-size SUV was joined in 2002 by the Chevy Avalanche-based Escalade EXT. 2. Monroe Truck Equipment and GM teamed up to develop the "ultimate pickup truck." Introduced in 2005, these medium-duty trucks were perfect for towing fifth-wheel campers, horse trailers, and big boats. Chevrolet Kodiak (shown) and GMC TopKick versions were available. 3. Chevrolet replaced the long-running S-10 with the all-new Colorado compact pickup for 2004. This 2005 model sports the Xtreme package, which included a sport suspension, 18-inch wheels, bodyside cladding, unique front and rear styling, and special exterior graphics. 4. Cadillac introduced its third-generation Escalade for 2007. A regular-length model is shown. Extended-length ESV and pickup EXT models completed the lineup. 5. A Hybrid version of the Chevrolet Tahoe (shown) and the closely related GMC Yukon arrived for 2008. GM claimed its Two-Mode full-hybrid propulsion system boosted fuel economy by more than 25 percent. The Two-Mode system mated a 6.0-liter V-8 with a pair of 60-kilowatt electric motors. The Hybrid could operate on either or both power sources, depending on driving demand. 6. Hummer introduced its smallest model, the midsize H3, for 2006. This top-line H3 Alpha model was new for 2008 and included a 295-horsepower 5.3-liter V-8. Lesser H3 models made do with a 242-hp five-cylinder engine. Slow sales led Hummer to drop the gigantic, military-bred H1 from the lineup at the end of 2006.

THE FUTURE

Looking Ahead:
Recovery or Bust

The unthinkable has become expected in American business, especially the American auto business. Who, for example, could have predicted that Germany's Daimler-Benz would take over Chrysler Corporation, only to unload it nine years later? Who could have imagined that Ford Motor Company would be forced to mortgage all manner of assets, even the iconic blue-oval logo, just to have cash to keep going? And who would have believed that Toyota would outsell perennial "USA-1" Chevrolet for two straight months? Yet all this was making news as this book was prepared in the summer of 2007. No wonder trade weekly *Automotive News* now refers to General Motors, Ford, and Chrysler as simply the "Detroit 3." The Big Three just aren't what they used to be.

But the world isn't the same either, and that's one reason why Detroit's road to the future looks very bumpy. Some of the bumps are landmines. The big one is the enormous "legacy" costs of covering health care and pension benefits for current and retired union workers. Reflecting lush contracts negotiated in palmier days, these obligations put U.S. automakers at a per-vehicle price disadvantage variously estimated at $1000-$5000 versus import brands. With that kind of handicap, it's hard to make a buck.

Detroit also still struggles to come up with cars and trucks that Americans will buy without rebates, discounts, cheap financing, and other sweeteners that eat up company earnings. Import brands use incentives too, but don't need them nearly as much. That's because those brands have grown very popular—so much so that in July 2007 they outsold the Detroit producers for the first time ever, taking 51.9 percent of U.S. light-vehicle sales. While this may prove a one-month fluke, a number of industry-watchers don't think so. One reason: GM, Ford, and Chrysler have been ceding market share since at least the mid-1990s and seem powerless to stem the slide. GM, for example, was down to just 21.7 percent in June 2007, a far cry from its perennial 50-60 percent in the 1950s and '60s market. Back then, Federal antitrust regulators thought that GM was too powerful and should be broken up to foster competition. Today the concern is whether GM (Ford, too) will have to file for Chapter 11 as "victims" of import-brand competition. (Chrysler found at least temporary shelter on being sold in August 2007 to private-equity firm Cerberus Capital Management.)

Some analysts say a GM bankruptcy is inevitable. Consider this bleak assessment from investment maven Porter Stansberry,

written as if CEO Rick Wagoner were addressing GM shareholders:

"The truth of the matter is, we've been operating at a capital loss for a long, long time [and] we've racked up a stupendous amount of debt...more debt than we can afford to service. You can probably do the math in your head: $83 billion of long-term obligations multiplied by steadily rising interest rates, thanks to our deteriorating credit ratings...In the last two years [2005–2006], we've gone from being one of the best credit risks in the world to being a junk-bond debtor....Unless something radical happens to free us from our employee obligations, there is no way I can honestly tell you that GM will not go bankrupt."

Talk about unthinkable! And Stansberry wrote this shortly before the subprime mortage business began to unravel, touching off a crisis of confidence among banks and investors that squeezed available credit and accelerated a downturn in the housing industry.

Needless to say, bankruptcy has never been an option for Mr. Wagoner or anyone else at General Motors, no matter how bad things may seem. And as if to defy doomsayers, GM posted a net profit for the second quarter of 2007. The amount was a modest $891 million, but it sure beat the $3.4 billion loss of the prior-year period. Here, surely, was proof that GM's belt-tightening turnaround plan was working. *Automotive News* found it "striking" that "despite eroding market share and rising fuel prices, GM virtually broke even in North America."

The more important point was that strong business everywhere else accounted for that surprise profit. Which was really no surprise. According to company figures cited by *AN*, the percentage of GM's automotive revenue earned outside North America has increased from 17.8 percent in 2001 to a projected 34 percent in '07. "For years, Wagoner has talked about a balanced international portfolio," *Automotive News* reported. "But suddenly, GM's globalization-speak was more than rhetoric. Wagoner...credited the [second-quarter] results to 'our heavy commitment to key growth markets around the world.'" Markets like booming China, where Buick, which still languishes in the U.S., is now the top-seller among some 100 nameplates.

Lest we forget, GM has been "international" ever since buying Britain's Vauxhall in 1925 and Germany's Opel four years later. What's different now is that GM is acting as a truly global enterprise, rather than as an American company that happens to have overseas subsidiaries. Significantly, as several critics note, this same approach helped grow Toyota to the point that it will soon surpass GM as the world's largest, most profitable automaker. For analyst John Casesa, GM's new global vision is a very good thing and somewhat overdue. "In moving to a business model that allows it to be profitable at a smaller size, [GM] will have much better revenue diversification," he told *Automotive News*. "It will be less dependent than it's historically been on this one [North American] market."

GM has made progress on other fronts. As *The Economist* reported in August 2007, "GM reckons it is about 18 months ahead of its rivals in trying to address its problems [in North America]. It has slashed factory capacity and jobs, cut back on dealer incentives and dramatically curbed cut-price sales to rental firms....In this year's Harbour Report, an influential study of North American automotive productivity, GM boasted four of the ten most efficient assembly plants. It now takes an average of 32.36 man-hours to build a vehicle, just 2.4 more than Toyota.... Product quality is improving, too. In recent industry studies, GM either matched or exceeded the quality levels of Toyota's American 'transplant' factories."

Despite this good news, several factors cloud GM's near-term prospects. "Right-sizing" at home and building up overseas business do not by themselves guarantee survival, let alone prosper ity. All markets have their ups and downs. Second, Congress will soon enact higher fuel-economy standards—the first CAFE change in 25 years—to combat global warming and American dependence on foreign oil. Detroit worries that lawmakers will set the bar too high, throwing their budgets and product plans for a loop. Crucial contract talks with the United Auto Workers union are underway as we write. The UAW isn't what it used to be either but could still hamper necessary cost-cutting by refusing to make meaningful concessions on wages and benefits. Prices for energy and raw materials keep rising, a result of fast-growing demand from China, India, and other emerging auto markets, which only increases pressure on Detroit to trim down even more. And all this assumes gotta-have cars and trucks that sell on merit more than price.

Fortunately for this story—and after too many years of letdowns—GM is delivering some very impressive new models, with more on the way. Its redesigned 2007 full-size pickups and SUVs are a big advance on their popular predecessors, and 2007's new Lambda-platform crossover SUVs—Buick Enclave, GMC Acadia, and Saturn Outlook—are off to a strong sales start. A Chevrolet version, likely named Traverse, is slated to expand the family for 2009.

On the car side, 2008 brings a redesigned Cadillac CTS and Pontiac's new G8, both genuine sports sedans offering all-American performance with European design flair. The G8 is notable for using a new rear-wheel-drive platform developed at Holden in Australia. It's one example of how GM is marshalling its worldwide resources as never before. Other examples include Saturn's new midsize Aura sedan, a close cousin of the Opel/Vauxhall Vectra, and the upcoming Saturn Astra compact based on the European Astra design. Another new global architecture, Epsilon 2, premieres with Chevrolet's redesigned 2008 Malibu, which looks a far more competitive midsize family sedan versus the class-leading Toyota Camry and Honda Accord. GM says Buick's success in China will influence the brand's future U.S. models. Hinting at things to come is the striking Riviera concept, created at GM's China-based Pan-Asian Technical Center for the 2007 Shanghai Auto Show.

Back in the U.S. of A., enthusiasts are all abuzz about the all-new 2009 Camaro. Also built on the global rear-drive platform and modeled closely on a show-stopping concept,

Chevy's reborn ponycar revives the long-famous rivalry with the Ford Mustang and a resurrected Dodge Challenger—"yesterday once more" for sure. Coming, too, for '09 is an even higher-performance Chevy Corvette. Variously referred to as Stingray, SS, and Z07, it should be wicked-fast, with an alleged 650 horsepower and enough high-tech engineering to take on every other supercar extant.

But exciting though all this is, no automaker can ignore the pressing worldwide problems of global warming, diminishing fossil-fuel reserves, and environmental stewardship. That's why GM is accelerating its work to market more economical "green" vehicles—and sooner than some people think. Already its full-size pickups offer a "mild hybrid" gasoline/electric powertrain. For 2008, this option spreads to the Chevrolet Malibu, Saturn Aura, and Saturn Vue compact SUV. By 2010, GM is expected to offer hybrid vehicles with a more advanced "dual mode" system, developed with DaimlerChrysler and BMW, that allows driving on one or both power sources.

GM is also well along with development of plug-in hybrids, reflecting its belief that future vehicles must run on electricity instead of petroleum, given today's energy and climate conditions. To that end, GM unveiled the Chevrolet Volt prototype in 2007 with an innovative new "E-Flex" architecture that's designed to accommodate a plug-in hybrid drive or, eventually, a hydrogen fuel cell. Unlike conventional "full" hybrids that use a battery-driven motor to supplement a gasoline engine, GM's plug-in system uses a very small engine to recharge the batteries, not for propulsion. The vehicle thus operates as a clean, quiet pure-electric, yet can travel as far as a normal gasoline-fueled vehicle—the best of both worlds. At this writing, GM and batterymaker A123 Systems are close to finalizing a safe, cost-effective lithium-ion battery pack that could put a Volt-like plug-in hybrid on America's roads as early as 2010. If GM manages that—and if buyers respond—the company's future is secure.

No automaker has done more to shape the automotive landscape than General Motors, and that's still true, current difficulties notwithstanding. Of course, GM is no stranger to adversity. And if past is prologue, as it often is, we have little doubt that General Motors will remain a dominant player on the world stage, as it has been for 100 years.

Chevrolet Volt Concept